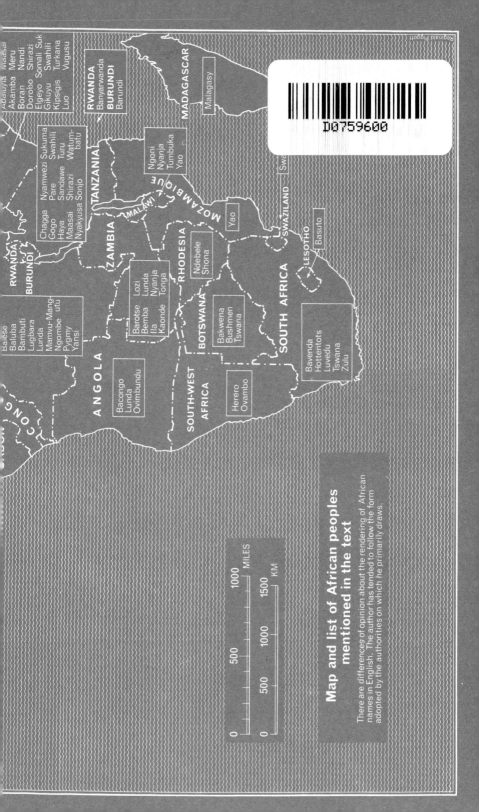

Map and list of African peoples mentioned in the text

There are differences of opinion about the rendering of African names in English. The author has tended to follow the form adopted by the authorities on which he primarily draws.

Reginald Piggott

MADAGASCAR
Malagasy

RWANDA
Banyarwanda
BURUNDI
Barundi

Abaluyia Meru
Akamba Nandi
Boran Shirazi
Dorobo Somali Suk
Elgeyo Swahili
Gikuyu Turkana
Kipsigis Vugusu
Luo

Sukuma
Nyamwezi Swahili
Pare Turu
Sandawe Watum-
Shirazi batu
Sonjo

Chagga
Gogo
Haya
Lunda
Nyakyusa

TANZANIA

Ngoni
Nyanja
Tumbuka
Yao

MOZAMBIQUE

ZAMBIA

MALAWI

Yao

RHODESIA

Ndebele
Shona

SWAZILAND

Swa

LESOTHO

Basuto

Balese
Baluba
Bambuti
Lugbara
Lunda
Mamvu-Mangbutu
Ngombe
Pygmy
Yansi

CONGO

Barotse
Lozi
Bemba
Lunda
Ila
Nyanja
Kaonde
Tonga

Bakwena
Bushmen
Tswana

BOTSWANA

Bacongo
Lunda
Ovimbundu

ANGOLA

SOUTH-WEST
AFRICA

Herero
Ovambo

Bavenda
Hottentots
Luvedu
Tswana
Zulu

SOUTH AFRICA

| | | MILES |
|0|500|1000|

| | | KM |
|0|500|1000|1500|

291.042   Mbiti
M478a   African religions and
          philosophy

CHRISTIAN HERITAGE COLLEGE
2100 Greenfield Dr.
El Cajon, CA 92021

291.042
M478a

AFRICAN RELIGIONS & PHILOSOPHY

CHRISTIAN HERITAGE COLLEGE

CHRISTIAN
HERITAGE
COLLEGE
LIBRARY

PRESENTED BY

The CRowell Foundation

AFRICAN RELIGIONS & PHILOSOPHY

JOHN S. MBITI

c/ wB

PRAEGER PUBLISHERS

New York · Washington

70-76092

200.'96

wB

BOOKS THAT MATTER

Published in the United States of America in 1969
by Praeger Publishers, Inc.
111 Fourth Avenue, New York, N.Y. 10003

Second printing 1970
Third printing 1971

© 1969, by J. S. Mbiti

All rights reserved

Library of Congress Catalog Card Number: 70–76092

Printed in Great Britain

In grateful and loving memory of my uncle, Joel Mutia wa Ngaangi died 1 January 1967

43496

49498

CONTENTS

PREFACE

This book is an expansion of lectures to my students at Makerere University College, Uganda, and Hamburg University, Germany. Not only did the students in both universities show continued interest in the lectures, but many requested that they be available in book form to meet a need for a textbook on the subject of African traditional religions and philosophy. I hope that this book will be a contribution in the study of the subject which is increasingly coming into the curricula of universities, seminaries, colleges and senior secondary schools not only in Africa but overseas as well. The book is intended therefore for use in such institutions of higher learning and by readers who may have reached that standard of education. It is primarily an introduction to the subject, and for that reason I have kept to a minimum analytical interpretation. For the same reason I provide fairly substantial references and bibliography, so that readers wishing to pursue certain lines of interest might have a reading list with which to start. As journals are not easily accessible except in large libraries, I have not included them in the footnote references, except occasionally, but a number are listed in the select bibliography.

African Religions and Philosophy deals almost exclusively with traditional concepts and practices in those societies which have not been either Christian or Muslim in any deep way, before the colonial period in Africa. In my description I have generally used the present tense, as if these ideas are still held and the practices being carried out. Everyone is aware that rapid changes are taking place in Africa, so that traditional ideas are being abandoned, modified or coloured by the changing situation. At the same time it would be wrong to imagine that everything traditional has been changed or forgotten so much that no traces of it are to be found. If anything, the changes are generally on the surface, affecting the material side of life, and only beginning to reach the deeper levels of thinking pattern, language content, mental images, emotions, beliefs and response in situations of need. Traditional concepts still form the essential background of many African peoples, though obviously this differs from individual to individual and from place to place. I believe, therefore, that even if the educated Africans do not subscribe to all the religious and philosophical practices and ideas described here, the majority of our people with little or no formal education still hold on to their traditional corpus of beliefs and practices. Anyone familiar with village gossip cannot question this fact; and those who have eyes will also notice evidence of it in the towns and cities.

In this study I have emphasized the unity of African religions and philosophy in order to give an overall picture of their situation. This approach does not give room for the treatment in depth of individual religious and philosophical systems of different African peoples. There is an increasing number of monographs coming out through which this aspect of study is being met, and I do not feel it necessary to duplicate the work when so many other fields remain scarcely harvested. I have therefore chosen to highlight both similarities and differences considering the African picture as a whole. For this reason, I have drawn examples from all over Africa, both making general observations and giving detailed illustrations.

Since modern change cannot be ignored, I have devoted one chapter to it towards the end of the book, emphasizing particularly the human aspects of this change and how these affect individuals and families. In another chapter I discuss the present situation of Christianity, Islam and other religions in Africa, all of which are very relevant to any study of traditional religions. Both Christianity and Islam are 'traditional' and 'African' in a historical sense, and it is a pity that they tend to be regarded as 'foreign' or 'European' and 'Arab'. It is, however, in their contact or relationship with traditional religions that I have discussed these other religions. The final chapter is an attempt to assess the place and role of religion in modern Africa which has inherited these different religious systems and is subjected to a world-wide and radical change.

I want to express my deep gratitude to my students at Makerere (since 1964) and Hamburg (1966–7), for reacting with such encouraging and stimulating response to the original lectures. Many who heard these lectures enriched some of the points with illustrations and comments from their own reflection and experiences. I valued these comments very much, and have incorporated some of them into the book, for which I am equally grateful. In innumerable ways my dear wife has been a constant source of help while I was working on the lectures and the book, especially in Hamburg, and to her I am duly indebted. The publishers have given me unending encouragement and co-operation from the time I contacted them about the manuscript. For this and for the quick production of the book, I am very thankful.

As much as possible I have acknowledged in the footnotes the sources of my information and quotations. Where a particular work is mentioned half a dozen or more times, only the author and pages of his book are given in the footnotes and full details of the work concerned will be found in the select bibliography. I apologize for any omissions in acknowledging the sources, for misinterpreting or misrepresenting anyone's ideas, and for errors in quoting other people's writings, where this may have happened without my knowledge.

John Mbiti

Makerere University College
Kampala, Uganda

ACKNOWLEDGEMENTS

Grateful acknowledgement is made for permission granted by either the authors or publishers to make quotations from the following works: J. B. Danquah, *The Akan Doctrine of God*, Lutterworth (an Edinburgh House Press book) 1944; E. E. Evans-Pritchard, *Witchcraft, Oracles and Magic among the Azande*, Clarendon Press, 1937; and *Nuer Religion*, Clarendon Press, 1956; M. J. Field, *Religion and Medicine of the Ga People*, Oxford University Press, 1937; D. Forde, ed., *African Worlds*, Oxford University Press, 1954; G. W. B. Huntingford, *The Nandi of Kenya*, Routledge, and Kegan Paul, 1953; E. B. Idowu, *Olodumare: God in Yoruba Belief*, Longmans, Green & Co., 1962; J. Jahn, *Muntu*, Faber and Faber, ET 1961; I. M. Lewis, ed., *Islam in Tropical Africa*, Oxford University Press, 1966; G. Lienhardt, *Divinity and Experience, the Religion of the Dinka*, Clarendon Press, 1961; R. A. Lystad, *The Ashanti: a Proud People*, Rutgers University Press, 1958; J. H. Nketia, *Funeral Dirges of the Akan People*, Accra 1955; A. Oded, 'A Congregation of African Jews in the heart of Uganda', in *Dini na Mila: Revealed Religion and Traditional Customs*, Vol. 3 No. 1, 1968; J. Okot p'Bitek, 'The Concept of Jok among the Acholi and Lango', in *The Uganda Journal*, Vol. XXVII No. 1, 1963; E. G. Parrinder, *West African Religion*, Society for Promoting Christian Knowledge (S.P.C.K.) 1961; P. Schebesta, *My Pygmy and Negro Hosts*, Hutchinson & Co., ET 1936; *Revisiting my Pygmy Hosts*, Hutchinson & Co., ET 1936; E. W. Smith and A. M. Dale, *The Ila-Speaking Peoples of Northern Rhodesia*, Macmillan, Vol. 1, 1920; E. W. Smith, ed. (later E. G. Parrinder), *African Ideas of God*, Lutterworth (an Edinburgh House Press book) 1950; T. C. Young, *Contemporary Ancestors*, Lutterworth (an Edinburgh House Press book) n.d.

1

INTRODUCTION

Africans are notoriously religious, and each people has its own religious system with a set of beliefs and practices. Religion permeates into all the departments of life so fully that it is not easy or possible always to isolate it. A study of these religious systems is, therefore, ultimately a study of the peoples themselves in all the complexities of both traditional and modern life. Our written knowledge of traditional religions is comparatively little, though increasing, and comes chiefly from anthropologists and sociologists. Practically nothing has been produced by theologians, describing or interpreting these religions theologically.

We speak of African traditional religions in the plural because there are about one thousand African peoples (tribes), and each has its own religious system. These religions are a reality which calls for academic scrutiny and which must be reckoned with in modern fields of life like economics, politics, education, and Christian or Muslim work. To ignore these traditional beliefs, attitudes and practices can only lead to a lack of understanding African behaviour and problems. Religion is the strongest element in traditional background, and exerts probably the greatest influence upon the thinking and living of the people concerned.

While religion can be discerned in terms of beliefs, ceremonies, rituals and religious officiants, philosophy is not so easily distinguishable. We shall consider different religions in terms of their similarities and differences, to give us a picture of the overall situation in Africa. But, since there are no parallel philosophical systems which can be observed in similarly concrete terms, we shall use the singular, 'philosophy', to refer to the philosophical understanding of African peoples concerning different issues of life. Philosophy of one kind or another is behind the thinking and acting of every people, and a study of traditional religions brings us into those areas of African life where, through word and action, we may be able to discern the philosophy behind. This involves interpretation of the information before us, and interpretation cannot be completely free of subjective judgment. What, therefore, is 'African Philosophy', may not amount to more

I

than simply my own process of philosophizing the items under consideration: but this cannot be helped, and in any case I am by birth an African. Philosophical systems of different African peoples have not yet been formulated, but some of the areas where they may be found are in the religion, proverbs, oral traditions, ethics and morals of the society concerned. I have incorporated some of these areas into this study, but proverbs in particular deserve a separate treatment since their philosophical content is mainly situational. We do not however have many comprehensive collec' tions of African proverbs out of which an overall analysis of this type of philosophy could be undertaken. 'African philosophy' here refers to the understanding, attitude of mind, logic and perception behind the manner in which African peoples think, act or speak in different situations of life.

Because traditional religions permeate all the departments of life, there is no formal distinction between the sacred and the secular, between the religious and non-religious, between the spiritual and the material areas of life. Wherever the African is, there is his religion: he carries it to the fields where he is sowing seeds or harvesting a new crop; he takes it with him to the beer party or to attend a funeral ceremony; and if he is educated, he takes religion with him to the examination room at school or in the university; if he is a politician he takes it to the house of parliament. Although many African languages do not have a word for religion as such, it nevertheless accompanies the individual from long before his birth to long after his physical death. Through modern change these traditional religions cannot remain intact, but they are by no means extinct. In times of crisis they often come to the surface, or people revert to them in secret.

Traditional religions are not primarily for the individual, but for his community of which he is part. Chapters of African religions are written everywhere in the life of the community, and in traditional society there are no irreligious people. To be human is to belong to the whole community, and to do so involves participating in the beliefs, ceremonies, rituals and festivals of that community. A person cannot detach himself from the religion of his group, for to do so is to be severed from his roots, his founda' tion, his context of security, his kinships and the entire group of those who make him aware of his own existence. To be without one of these corporate elements of life is to be out of the whole picture. Therefore, to be without religion amounts to a self-excommunication from the entire life of society, and African peoples do not know how to exist without religion.

One of the sources of severe strain for Africans exposed to modern change is the increasing process (through education, urbanization and industrialization) by which individuals become detached from their traditional environment. This leaves them in a vacuum devoid of a solid religious foundation. They are torn between the life of their forefathers which, whatever else might be said about it, has historical roots and firm traditions, and the life of our technological age which, as yet, for many Africans has no concrete form or depth. In these circumstances, Christianity and Islam do not seem to remove the sense of frustration and uprootedness. It is not enough to learn and embrace a faith which is active once a week, either on Sunday or Friday, while the rest of the week is virtually empty. It is not enough to embrace a faith which is confined to a church building or mosque, which is locked up six days and opened only once or twice a week. Unless Christianity and Islam fully occupy the whole person as much as, if not more than, traditional religions do, most converts to these faiths will continue to revert to their old beliefs and practices for perhaps six days a week, and certainly in times of emergency and crisis. The whole environment and the whole time must be occupied by religious meaning, so that at any moment and in any place, a person feels secure enough to act in a meaningful and religious consciousness. Since traditional religions occupy the whole person and the whole of his life, conversion to new religions like Christianity and Islam must embrace his language, thought patterns, fears, social relationships, attitudes and philosophical disposition, if that conversion is to make a lasting impact upon the individual and his community.

A great number of beliefs and practices are to be found in any African society. These are not, however, formulated into a systematic set of dogmas which a person is expected to accept. People simply assimilate whatever religious ideas and practices are held or observed by their families and communities. These traditions have been handed down from forefathers, and each generation takes them up with modifications suitable to its own historical situation and needs. Individuals hold differences of opinion on various subjects; and the myths, rituals and ceremonies may differ in detail from area to area. But such ideas or views are not considered as either contrary or conforming to any orthodox opinion. Therefore, when we say in this book that such and such a society 'believes', or 'narrates', or 'performs' such and such, we do not by any means imply that everybody in that society subscribes to that belief or performs that ritual. These are corporate beliefs and acts, and there can be no unanimity in such beliefs, ideas and practices. In traditional religions there are no creeds to be recited; instead, the creeds are written in the heart of the individual, and each one is himself a living creed of his own religion. Where the individual is, there is his religion, for he is a religious being. It is this that makes Africans so religious: religion is in their whole system of being.

One of the difficulties in studying African religions and philosophy is that there are no sacred scriptures. Religion in African societies is written not on paper but in people's hearts, minds, oral history, rituals and religious personages like the priests, rainmakers, officiating elders and even kings. Everybody is a religious carrier. Therefore we have to study not only the beliefs concerning God and the spirits, but also the religious journey of the individual from before birth to after physical death; and to study also the persons responsible for formal rituals and ceremonies. What people do is motivated by what they believe, and what they believe springs from what they do and experience. So then, belief and action in African traditional society cannot be separated: they belong to a single whole.

Traditional religions are not universal: they are tribal or national. Each religion is bound and limited to the people among whom it has evolved. One traditional religion cannot be propagated in another tribal group. This does not rule out the fact that religious ideas may spread from one people to another. But such ideas spread spontaneously, especially through migrations, intermarriage, conquest, or expert knowledge being sought by individuals of one tribal group from another. Traditional religions have no missionaries to propagate them; and one individual does not preach his religion to another.

Similarly, there is no conversion from one traditional religion to another. Each society has its own religious system, and the propagation of such a complete system would involve propagating the entire life of the people concerned. Therefore a person has to be born in a particular society in order to assimilate the religious system of the society to which he belongs. An outsider cannot enter or appreciate fully the religion of another society. Those few Europeans who claim to have been 'converted' to African religions—and I know some who make such fantastic claims!—do not know what they are saying. To pour out libation or observe a few rituals like Africans, does not constitute conversion to traditional religions.

African religions have neither founders nor reformers. They may, however, incorporate national heroes, leaders, rulers and other famous men and women into their body of beliefs and mythology. Some of these figures are elevated to high national positions and may even be regarded as divinities responsible for natural objects or phenomena. These heroes and heroines form an integral part of the religious milieu of their society, whether or not they played a specifically religious role in their time.

Belief in the continuation of life after death is found in all African societies, as far as I have been able to discover. But this belief does not constitute a hope for a future and better life. To live here and now is the most important concern of African religious activities and beliefs. There is little, if any, concern with the distinctly spiritual welfare of man apart from his physical life. No line is drawn between the spiritual and the physical. Even life in the hereafter is conceived in materialistic and physical terms. There is neither paradise to be hoped for nor hell to be feared in the hereafter. The soul of man does not long for spiritual redemption, or for closer contact with God in the next world. This is an important element in traditional religions, and one which will help us to understand the concentration of African religiosity on earthly matters, with man at the centre of this religiosity. It is here also that the question of African concept of time is so important. Traditional religions and philosophy are concerned with man in past and present time. God comes into the picture as an explanation of man's contact with time. There is no messianic hope or apocalyptic vision with God stepping in at some future moment to bring about a radical reversal of man's normal life. God is not pictured in an ethical-spiritual relationship with man. Man's acts of worship and turning to God are pragmatic and utilitarian rather than spiritual or mystical.

With our incomplete knowledge of African religions, it is impossible to describe their history. On the whole, however, they seem to have remained fairly stable, quietly assimilating new ideas and practices from one another. National crises like warfare, famines, epidemics, locust invasions and major changes in the weather cause a revival of religious activities or innovation of new ones. Since people are so intimately bound up with their religious life and outlook, their history constitutes the history of their religion. This is an area of study which calls for interdisciplinary co-operation between historians, anthropologists and theologians. I have made no attempt in this book to deal with the historical aspects of African religions, and I am not aware of any study having been done along those lines. My approach here is chiefly descriptive and interpretive, bringing together in a comparative way those elements which are representative of traditional religions from all over Africa. In such a general survey, there is no room to treat in depth the unique and complex religious system of each people; but it is hoped that the detailed illustrations used here and drawn from many parts of Africa will not only indicate this complexity of African religions, but also remedy in part what otherwise could not be covered in depth.

2
THE STUDY OF AFRICAN RELIGIONS & PHILOSOPHY

The world is just beginning to take African traditional religions and philosophy seriously. It is only around the middle of the twentieth century that these subjects have begun to be studied properly and respectfully as an academic discipline in their own right. During the preceding one hundred years African religions were described by European and American missionaries and by students of anthropology, sociology and comparative religion. It is from these writers that we have most of our information, although some of them had never been to Africa and only a few had done serious field study of these religions. In the early part of that period, the academic atmosphere was filled with the theory of evolution which was applied in many fields of study. It is this theory which colours many of the earlier descriptions, interpretations and explanations of African religions. We shall consider briefly some of the early approaches before coming to the present situation.[1]

[a] *The early approaches and attitudes*
One of the dominating attitudes in this early period was the assumption that African beliefs, cultural characteristics and even foods, were all borrowed from the outside world. German scholars pushed this assumption to the extreme, and have not all abandoned it completely to this day. All kinds of theories and explanations were put forward on how the different religious traits had reached African societies from the Middle East or Europe. It is true that Africa has always had contact with the outside world, but religious and cultural influence from this contact cannot have flowed only one way: there was always a giveandtake process. Furthermore, African soil is not so infertile that it cannot produce its own new ideas. This game of hunting for outside sources is dying out, and there are writers who now argue that in fact it was Africa which exported ideas, cultures and civilization to the

---

[1] For further study of the earlier theories see E. E. EvansPritchard *Theories of primitive religion* (Oxford 1965).

outside world.[1] But surely a balance between these two extremes is more reasonable.

These earlier descriptions and studies of African religions left us with terms which are inadequate, derogatory and prejudicial. They clearly betray the kind of attitude and interpretation dominant in the mind of those who invented or propagated the different theories about traditional religions. *Animism* is a word derived from the Latin *anima* which means breath, breath of life, and hence carries with it the idea of the soul or spirit. This term has become the most popular designation for African religions and is found in many writings even this day. It was invented by the English anthropologist, E. B. Tylor, who used it first in an article in 1866 and later in his book, *Primitive Culture* (1871). For Tylor the basic definition of religion was the 'belief in spirit beings'. He saw the anima as a shadowy vaporous image animating the object it occupied. He thought that the so-called 'primitive people' imagined the anima to be capable of leaving the body and entering other men, animals or things; and continuing to live after death. Pursuing the theory further, Tylor went on to say that such 'primitive' men considered every object to have its own soul, thus giving rise to countless spirits in the universe.

Tylor's ideas were popularized by his disciples. Since then, the term *animism* has come to be widely used in describing traditional religions of Africa and other parts of the world. In an atmosphere filled with the theory of evolution, the notion of countless spirits opened the way for the idea of religious evolution. This led on to the theory that single spirits existed over each major department of nature. For example, all the spirits of the rivers would have one major spirit in charge of them, and the same for trees rocks, lakes and so on. Accordingly, this gave man the idea of many gods, (*polytheism*), which in turn evolved further to the stage of one supreme God over all the other departmental spirits. We might illustrate this point with a diagram (see page 8).

This type of argument and interpretation places African religions at the bottom of the supposed line of religious evolution. It tells us that Judaism, Christianity and Islam are at the top, since they are monotheistic. The theory fails to take into account the fact that another theory equally argues that man's religious development began with a monotheism and moved towards polytheism and animism. We need not concern ourselves unduly here with either theory. We can only comment that African peoples are aware of all these elements of religion: God, spirits and divinities are part

[1] For example: J. Jahn *Muntu* (E. T. London 1961); B. Davidson *Black Mother* (London 1961), and *The growth of African civilization* (London 1965); C. A. Diop *Antériorité des civilisations nègres: Mythe ou vérité historique?* (Paris 1963).

Monotheism — *Supposed line of religious evolution* — One Supreme God

Polytheism — Major spirits (gods)

Animism — Countless spirits

of the traditional body of beliefs. Christianity and Islam acknowledge the same type of spiritual beings. The theory of religious evolution, in whichever direction, does not satisfactorily explain or interpret African religions. Animism is not an adequate description of these religions and it is better for that term to be abandoned once and for all.

In classifying the religions of the world, we hear that 'redemptive religions' like Christianity, Judaism and Islam incorporate into their teaching the doctrine of the soul's redemption in the next world. 'Morality religions' like Shintoism and the teachings of Confucius lay a great emphasis on moral considerations. Finally, 'primitive religions' are those whose followers are described by some writers as 'savage', 'primitive' and lacking in either imagination or emotion.[1] Of course the word primitive in its Latin root *primus* has no bad connotations as such, but the way it is applied to African religions shows a lack of respect and betrays derogatory undertones. It is extraordinary that even in our day, fellow man should continue to be described as 'savage' and lacking in emotion or imagination. This approach to the study of African religions will not go very far, neither can it qualify as being scientifically or theologically adequate. Some traditional religions are extremely complex and contain elements which shed a lot of light on the study of other religious traditions of the world.

In his book, *Principles of Sociology* (1885), the anthropologist Herbert Spencer used the phrase *ancestor worship* to describe his speculation that 'savage' peoples associated the spirits of the dead with certain objects, and in order to keep on good terms with the spirits of their ancestors, people made sacrifices to them. Other writers have borrowed this term and applied it almost to anything that Africans do in the way of religious ceremonies. Many books speak of 'ancestor worship' to describe African religions. Certainly it cannot be denied that the departed occupy an important place in African religiosity; but it is wrong to interpet traditional religions simply in terms of 'worshipping the ancestors'. As we shall see later in this book,

[1] See for example J. N. D. Anderson, ed., *The World's Religions* (third edition London 1960), p. 9 f.

the departed, whether parents, brothers, sisters or children, form part of the family, and must therefore be kept in touch with their surviving relatives. Libation and the giving of food to the departed are tokens of fellowship, hospitality and respect; the drink and food so given are symbols of family continuity and contact. 'Worship' is the wrong word to apply in this situation; and Africans themselves know very well that they are not 'worshipping' the departed members of their family. It is almost blasphemous, therefore, to describe these acts of family relationships as 'worship'. Further-more, African religions do not end at the level of family rites of libation and food offerings. They are deeper and more comprehensive than that. To see them only in terms of 'ancestor worship' is to isolate a single element, which in some societies is of little significance, and to be blind to many other aspects of religion.

Other writers have tried to study or refer to African religions in terms of magic. Some consider magic to have evolved before religion, as man's attempt to manipulate the unseen world. When man failed to control natural objects and phenomena by means of magic, he then resigned himself to forces beyond him, which in turn led to a belief in God as the Source of all power. As such, magic is considered to be the mother of religion.[1] Since every African society has both magic and religion, it was inevitable to conclude that Africans had not evolved beyond the stage of detaching religion from magic. Some writers even tell us that Africans have no religion at all and only magic. We shall devote a whole chapter to this subject of magic, and there is an increasing amount of good literature on it. We need here only comment briefly. A careful examination of the situation in African societies shows that magic is part of the religious background, and it is not easy to separate the two. Some of the ceremonies, for example in rainmaking and preventing of epidemics, incorporate both religion and magic. So long as magical acts are beneficial to the community involved, they are acceptable and people may even pay a great deal of their wealth in order to secure such help. This gives no contradiction to their beliefs. Magic belongs to the religious mentality of African peoples. But religion is not magic, and magic cannot explain religion. Religion is greater than

[1] See earlier writers like: E. Durkheim *The elementary forms of the religious life* (E.T. London 1915); J. Frazer *Totemica* (London 1937); B. Malinowski *A scientific theory of culture and other essays* (London 1944); E. O. James *The origin of religion* (London 1937); P. Radin *Primitive religion* (London 1938); R. Allier *The mind of the savage* (London 1929). See also, for further general discussion, E. G. Parrinder *African Traditional Religion* (London 1954); A. C. Boquet *Comparative Religion* (London 1942); W. Schmidt *Der Ursprung der Gottesidee* (Vol. IV deals specifically with Africa, under the title of: 'Die Religionen der Urvölker Afrikas', Münster 1933).

magic, and only an ignorant outsider could imagine that African religions are nothing more than magic.

Other terms employed to describe African religions include *Dynamism, Totemism, Fetishism* and *Naturism*. We need not go into them here. These and the previous terms show clearly how little the outside world has under-stood African religions. Some of the terms are being abandoned as more knowledge comes to light. But the fact remains that African religions and philosophy have been subjected to a great deal of misinterpretation, mis-representation and misunderstanding. They have been despised, mocked and dismissed as primitive and underdeveloped. One needs only to look at the earlier titles and accounts to see the derogatory language used, prejudiced descriptions given and false judgments passed upon these religions. In missionary circles they have been condemned as superstition, satanic, devilish and hellish. In spite of all these attacks, traditional religions have survived, they dominate the background of African peoples, and must be reckoned with even in the middle of modern changes.

[b] *Modern and current studies*

In recent years a change of approach and attitude has begun to take place. We mention here some of the books and new methods, without elaborating on them. The first of these new approaches is represented by writers like Tempels, Jahn and Taylor. In his book, *Bantu Philosophy* (French edition 1945, English 1959), P. Tempels presents his understanding of Baluba religion and philosophy, starting from the attitude that 'primitive peoples have a concrete conception of being and of the universe'. He goes on to say that 'this "ontology" of theirs will give a special character and a local colour to their beliefs and religious practices, to their language, to their institutions and customs, to their psychological reactions and, more generally, to their whole behaviour'. For Tempels the key concept to African religions and philosophy is what he calls 'the vital force'. He isolates this as the essence of being: 'force is being, and being is force'. His philosophy of forces explains for him everything about African thinking and action.

Whatever else is said about Tempels' book, it opens the way for a sympathetic study of African religions and philosophy. His motive and that of the fellow colonialists whom he addresses, is 'to civilize, educate and raise the Bantu'. The book is primarily Tempels' personal interpretation of the Baluba, and it is ambitious to call it 'Bantu philosophy' since it only deals with one people among whom he had worked for many years as a missionary. It is open to a great deal of criticism, and the theory of 'vital force' cannot be applied to other African peoples with whose life and ideas I am familiar. The main contribution of Tempels is more in terms of sympathy and change of attitude than perhaps in the actual contents and theory of his book.

In the same group is J. Jahn's book, *Muntu* (German edition 1958, English 1961), which deals primarily with what he calls 'neo-African culture'. He devotes one section to African philosophy, while others are on art, dance, history and literature. It covers a great part of Africa, the basic material being collected through wide reading. In the religious-philosophical section Jahn adopts the categories of A. Kagame (from Rwanda), and squeezes everything into one of four categories:

> *Muntu* is the philosophical category which includes God, spirits, the departed, human beings and certain trees. These constitute a 'force' endowed with intelligence.
>
> *Kintu* includes all the 'forces' which do not act on their own but only under the command of *Muntu*, such as plants, animals, minerals and the like.
>
> *Hantu* is the category of time and space.
>
> *Kuntu* is what he calls 'modality', and covers items like beauty, laughter, etc.

According to Jahn's interpretation, 'all being, all essence, in whatever form it is conceived, can be subsumed under one of these categories. Nothing can be conceived outside them'. He sticks to Tempels' concept of 'force', and tells us that 'man is a force, all things are forces, place and time are forces and the "modalities" are forces'. These items are supposed to be related in the purely linguistic stem - NTU which occurs in all the four words on which the categories are based. Jahn supposes this - NTU to be 'the universal force . . . which, however, never occurs apart from its manifestations: Muntu, Kintu, Hantu and Kuntu. NTU is Being itself, and cosmic universal force . . . NTU is that force in which Being and beings coalesce . . . NTU expresses, not the effect of these forces, but their being. But the forces act continually, and are constantly effective' (pp. 99 ff.). Accordingly, this mythical or imaginary NTU would be revealed only if the whole universe came to a standstill.

The main contribution of Jahn's book is in pointing out the fact that Africa has something of philosophical value which deserves to be taken seriously and studied accordingly. In his enthusiasm about Africa, Jahn may have overstated his case (he says, for instance, that Europe has nothing to compare with African philosophy). But he has argued his ideas with conviction and has put them across persuasively, whether one accepts or rejects them.

In the English world this sympathetic approach to African religions and philosophy is best represented by J. V. Taylor in his book, *The primal vision* (1963). This is a contribution to studies in the series 'Christian Presence', and the book is clearly directed towards that end. With one foot in Christian theology and the other in contemporary Africa with its traditional and modern life, Taylor managed to penetrate considerably African thought, in describing mainly for European readers, what he calls 'the primal world'. In this attempt he is carried away by that world, becoming too sympathetic and insufficiently critical. He presents everything as if it were so sacred, holy, pure and clean that it is being polluted by Christianity, westernism, urbanization and the ways of technological life. The book has a disturbingly sharp distinction between the 'we' (Europeans) and the 'they' (Africans), seen against the background of what 'we' can learn from 'them'. From the point of view of the Christian contact with African traditional world, this is, however, the best study so far. It is stimulating and challenging; and its material, which is drawn from many parts of Africa both through reading and personal experience, makes a representative survey of the whole continent.

These three books have in common the attitude that African religions and philosophy are a reality which colours the whole life of African peoples. As such, they deserve to be taken seriously and studied sympathetically.

The second modern approach is represented by writers from England, France and West Germany. This approach attempts to treat African religions systematically, putting together information from various peoples. Representative authors include Parrinder, Deschamps and Dammann. The pioneer work is E. G. Parrinder's *African Traditional Religion* (1954), which has been re-issued several times. This relatively short book gives an excellent and accurate presentation of the main items in African religions. The writer is both sympathetic and critical, and handles his material from many parts of Africa in a simple but scholarly way. Having lived and worked in western Africa, Parrinder has made field study of African religions (both traditional and Christian), and writes with confidence. This book is to be recommended as a basic introduction to the study of our subject, and in some ways complements what I attempt to cover here. Our interpretations are different, however, and his presentation puts less emphasis on the philosophical content of African religions.

Les religions de l'Afrique noire (1960) by H. Deschamps represents this approach in the French world. It is of less value than Parrinder's book, and draws its material almost entirely from western Africa and the French-speaking countries. The writer is an anthropologist, and his treatment of the subject is anthropological and sociological.

From West Germany comes E. Dammann's book, *Die Religionen*

Afrikas (1963), which is a sizeable and well documented volume. It draws the material from English, French and German sources. It leans towards the search for outside influence and the use of some of the earlier phraseology and theories. But it is a comprehensive work, and valuable particularly in its descriptive parts. It also treats, but too briefly, other religions like Judaism, Christianity and Islam in Africa, and the impact of modern change upon religion.

The third approach in the modern trend is represented best of all by two books by anthropologists. E. E. Evans-Pritchard's *Nuer Religion* (1956) is the fruit of a long study of the Nuer people. The writer went and lived with them, learnt their language and participated as much as possible in all their activities. So he describes Nuer religion from within, using the scientific tools of an anthropologist but looking at it through the eyes of the Nuer themselves. He demonstrates how profoundly religious the Nuer are, with deep conception of God as Spirit. G. Lienhardt in *Divinity and Experience: the religion of the Dinka* (1961) follows exactly the same method. He brings out the importance of the personal encounter between God and men, which the Dinka recognize in every aspect of their life. They see the world of the spirit beings and of men converging in human experience; and this constitutes the essence of Dinka religion.

There are other books on the same lines, but these two are the classical representatives.[1] The main contribution here is in concentrating on the religion of individual peoples and treating it both in depth and in relation to the total situation of the people concerned. If such studies could be made for most African peoples, they would be of infinite value as a bank of information on African traditional religions. Such studies place African religions in the context of their sociological and cultural environment. It is to be hoped that more attention will be given to modern trends of these traditional religions.

Another way of studying African religions and philosophy is represented by African scholars who take up single subjects and study them in depth within the situation of their people. This also has great value in that it concentrates on a given topic, describing it and interpreting it through African experience and understanding. One of the main advantages here is that the scholars themselves have a knowledge of the language and their people, from within and not without. Representative examples include: J. B. Danquah, *The Akan doctrine of God* (1944), J. H. Nketia, *Funeral dirges of the Akan people* (1955), A. Kagame, *La philosophie bantu-rwandaise de l'Être* (1956), and E. B. Idowu, *Olodumare: God in Yoruba belief* (1962).

[1] See the select bibliography under the names of Middleton, Nadel, Pauw, Sangree, Tanner and Wilson.

There are, in addition, articles and essays contributed by African scholars. There is great potential in African scholars studying African religions and philosophy, with the aid of scientific tools and methodology and with the advantages of being part of the peoples of Africa, having almost unlimited access to information and speaking the languages which are the key to serious research and understanding of traditional religions and philosophy.

My approach in this book is to treat religion as an ontological pheno-menon, with the concept of time as the key to reaching some understanding of African religions and philosophy. I do not pretend that the notion of time explains everything, but I am convinced that it adds to our under-standing of the subject, and if that much is achieved, these efforts will have been more than adequately rewarded.

3

THE CONCEPT
OF TIME

Religion is a difficult word to define, and it becomes even more difficult in the context of African traditional life. I do not attempt to define it, except to say that for Africans it is an ontological phenomenon; it pertains to the question of existence or being. We have already pointed out that within traditional life, the individual is immersed in a religious participation which starts before birth and continues after his death. For him therefore, and for the larger community of which he is part, to live is to be caught up in a religious drama. This is fundamental, for it means that man lives in a religious universe. Both that world and practically all his activities in it, are seen and experienced through a religious understanding and meaning. Names of people have religious meanings in them; rocks and boulders are not just empty objects, but religious objects; the sound of the drum speaks a religious language; the eclipse of the sun or moon is not simply a silent phenomenon of nature, but one which speaks to the community that observes it, often warning of an impending catastrophe. There are countless examples of this kind. The point here is that for Africans, the whole of existence is a religious phenomenon; man is a deeply religious being living in a religious universe. Failure to realize and appreciate this starting point, has led missionaries, anthropologists, colonial administrators and other foreign writers on African religions to misunderstand not only the religions as such but the peoples of Africa. This, among other things, has resulted in the tragedy of establishing since the missionary expansion of the nineteenth century only a very superficial type of Christianity on African soil. Although Islam has generally accommodated itself culturally more readily than western Christianity, it also is professed only superficially in areas where it has recently won converts. Neither faith has yet penetrated deeply into the religious world of traditional African life; and while this is so, 'conversion' to Christianity or Islam must be taken only in a relative sense.

Africans have their own ontology, but it is a religious ontology, and to understand their religions we must penetrate that ontology. I propose to divide it up into five categories, but it is an extremely anthropocentric ontology in the sense that everything is seen in terms of its relation to man. These categories are:

1. *God* as the ultimate explanation of the genesis and sustenance of both man and all things
2. *Spirits* being made up of superhuman beings and the spirits of men who died a long time ago
3. *Man* including human beings who are alive and those about to be born
4. *Animals and plants,* or the remainder of biological life
5. *Phenomena and objects without biological life*

Expressed anthropocentrically, God is the Originator and Sustainer of man; the Spirits explain the destiny of man; Man is the centre of this ontology; the Animals, Plants and natural phenomena and objects constitute the environment in which man lives, provide a means of existence and, if need be, man establishes a mystical relationship with them.

This anthropocentric ontology is a complete unity or solidarity which nothing can break up or destroy. To destroy or remove one of these categories is to destroy the whole existence including the destruction of the Creator, which is impossible. One mode of existence presupposes all the others, and a balance must be maintained so that these modes neither drift too far apart from one another nor get too close to one another. In addition to the five categories, there seems to be a force, power or energy permeating the whole universe. God is the Source and ultimate controller of this force; but the spirits have access to some of it. A few human beings have the knowledge and ability to tap, manipulate and use it, such as the medicine-men, witches, priests and rainmakers, some for the good and others for the ill of their communities.[1]

To see how this ontology fits into the religious system, I propose to discuss the African concept of time as the key to our understanding of the basic religious and philosophical concepts. The concept of time may help to explain beliefs, attitudes, practices and general way of life of African peoples not only in the traditional set up but also in the modern situation (whether of political, economic, educational or Church life). On this subject there is, unfortunately, no literature, and this is no more than a pioneer attempt which calls for further research and discussion.

[a] *Potential time and actual time*
The question of time is of little or no academic concern to African peoples

---

[1] This is approximately what the anthropologists call *mana* but it has nothing to do with Tempels' 'vital force'.

in their traditional life. For them, time is simply a composition of events which have occurred, those which are taking place now and those which are immediately to occur. What has not taken place or what has no likelihood of an immediate occurrence falls in the category of 'No-time'. What is certain to occur, or what falls within the rhythm of natural phenomena, is in the category of inevitable or *potential time*.

The most significant consequence of this is that, according to traditional concepts, time is a two-dimensional phenomenon, with a long *past*, a *present* and virtually *no future*. The linear concept of time in western thought, with an indefinite past, present and infinite future, is practically foreign to African thinking. The future is virtually absent because events which lie in it have not taken place, they have not been realized and cannot, therefore, constitute time. If, however, future events are certain to occur, or if they fall within the inevitable rhythm of nature, they at best constitute only *potential time*, not *actual time*. What is taking place now no doubt unfolds the future, but once an event has taken place, it is no longer in the future but in the present and the past. *Actual time* is therefore what is present and what is past. It moves 'backward' rather than 'forward'; and people set their minds not on future things, but chiefly on what has taken place.

This time orientation, governed as it is by the two main dimensions of the present and the past, dominates African understanding of the individual, the community and the universe which constitutes the five ontological categories mentioned above. Time has to be experienced in order to make sense or to become real. A person experiences time partly in his own individual life, and partly through the society which goes back many generations before his own birth. Since what is in the future has not been experienced, it does not make sense; it cannot, therefore, constitute part of time, and people do not know how to think about it—unless, of course, it is something which falls within the rhythm of natural phenomena.

In the east African languages in which I have carried out research and tested my findings, there are no concrete words or expressions to convey the idea of a distant future. We shall illustrate this point by considering the main verb tenses in the Kikamba and Gikuyu languages. (See table on page 18.)

The three verb tenses which refer to the future (numbers 1–3), cover the period of about six months, or not beyond two years at most. Coming events have to fall within the range of these verb tenses, otherwise such events lie beyond the horizon of what constitutes actual time. At most we can say that this short future is only an extension of the present. People have little or no active interest in events that lie in the future beyond, at

Analysis of African Concept of Time, as illustrated by a consideration of Verb tenses among the Akamba and Gikuyu of Kenya

	Tense	Kikamba	Gikuyu	English	Approximate Time
	1. Far Future or Remote Future	Ningauka	Ningoka	I will come	About 2 to 6 months from now
	2. Immediate or Near Future	Ninguka	Ninguka	I will come	Within the next short while
	3. Indefinite Future or Indefinite Near Future	Ngooka (ngauka)	Ningoka	I will come	Within a foreseeable while, after such and such an event
	4. Present or Present Progressive	Ninukite	Nindiroka	I am coming	In the process of action, now
Sasa	5. Immediate Past or Immediate Perfect	Ninauka (ninooka)	Nindoka	I came (I have just come)	In the last hour or so
	6. Today's Past	Ninukie	Ninjukire	I came	From the time of rising up to about two hours ago
	7. Recent Past or Yesterday's Past	Nininaukie (nininookie)	Nindirokire	I came	Yesterday
	8. Far Past or Remote Past	Ninookie (ninaukie)	Nindokire	I came	Any day before yesterday
Zamani	9. Unspecified Tene (Zamani)	Tene ninookie (Nookie tene)	Nindookire tene	I came	No specific time in the 'past'

most, two years from now; and the languages concerned lack words by which such events can be conceived or expressed.

[b] *Time reckoning and chronology*

When Africans reckon time, it is for a concrete and specific purpose, in connection with events but not just for the sake of mathematics. Since time is a composition of events, people cannot and do not reckon it in vacuum. Numerical calendars, with one or two possible exceptions, do not exist in African traditional societies as far as I know. If such calendars exist, they are likely to be of a short duration, stretching back perhaps a few decades, but certainly not into the realm of centuries.

Instead of numerical calendars there are what one would call *phenomenon calendars*, in which the events or phenomena which constitute time are reckoned or considered in their relation with one another and as they take place, i.e. as they constitute time. For example, an expectant mother counts the lunar months of her pregnancy; a traveller counts the number of days it takes him to walk (in former years) from one part of the country to another. The day, the month, the year, one's life time or human history, are all divided up or reckoned according to their specific events, for it is these that make them meaningful.

For example, the rising of the sun is an event which is recognized by the whole community. It does not matter, therefore, whether the sun rises at 5 a.m. or 7 a.m., so long as it rises. When a person says that he will meet another at sunrise, it does not matter whether the meeting place takes at 5 a.m. or 7 a.m., so long as it is during the general period of sunrise. Likewise, it does not matter whether people go to bed at 9 p.m. or at 12 midnight: the important thing is the event of going to bed, and it is immaterial whether in one night this takes place at 10 p.m. while in another it is at midnight. For the people concerned, time is meaningful at the point of the event and not at the mathematical moment.

In western or technological society, time is a commodity which must be utilized, sold and bought; but in traditional African life, time has to be created or produced. Man is not a slave of time; instead, he 'makes' as much time as he wants. When foreigners, especially from Europe and America, come to Africa and see people sitting down somewhere without, evidently, doing anything, they often remark, 'These Africans waste their time by just sitting down idle!' Another common cry is, 'Oh, Africans are always late!' It is easy to jump to such judgments, but they are judgments based on ignorance of what time means to African peoples. Those who are seen sitting down, are actually *not wasting* time, but either waiting for time or in the process of 'producing' time. One does not want to belabour this small point, but certainly the basic concept of time underlies and influences the life and attitudes of African peoples in the villages, and to a great extent those who work or live in the cities as well. Among other things, the economic life of the people is deeply bound to their concept of time; and as we shall attempt to indicate, many of their religious concepts and practices are intimately connected with this fundamental concept of time.

The day in traditional life, is reckoned according to its significant events. For example, among the Ankore of Uganda, cattle are at the heart of the people. Therefore the day is reckoned in reference to events pertaining to cattle. Thus approximately:

6 a.m. is milking time (*akasheshe*).

12 noon is time for cattle and people to take rest (*bari omubirago*), since, after milking the cattle, the herdsmen drive them out to the pasture grounds and by noon when the sun is hot, both herdsmen and cattle need some rest.

1 p.m. is the time to draw water (*baaza ahamaziba*), from the wells or the rivers, before cattle are driven there to drink (when they would pollute it, or would be a hindrance to those drawing and carrying the water).

2 p.m. is the time for cattle to drink (*amasyo niganywa*), and the herdsmen drive them to the watering places.

3 p.m. is the time when cattle leave their watering places and start grazing again (*amasyo nigakuka*).

5 p.m. is the time when the cattle return home (*ente niitaha*), being driven by the herdsmen.

6 p.m. is the time when the cattle enter their kraals or sleeping places (*ente zaataha*).

7 p.m. is milking time again, before the cattle sleep; and this really closes the day.[1]

The month. Lunar rather than numerical months are recognized, because of the event of the moon's changes. In the life of the people, certain events are associated with particular months, so that the months are named according to either the most important events or the prevailing weather conditions. For example, there is the 'hot' month, the month of the first rains, the weeding month, the beans harvest month, the hunting month, etc. It does not matter whether the 'hunting month' lasts 25 or 35 days: the event of hunting is what matters much more than the mathematical length of the month. We shall take an example from the Latuka people, to show how the events govern the approximate reckoning of months:

[1] Cf. J. Roscoe *The Northern Bantu* (1915), p. 139 f., which is not completely accurate. My version is an improvement on Roscoe's.

October is called 'The Sun', because the sun is very hot at that time.

December is called 'Give your uncle water', because water is very scarce and people become thirsty readily.

February is called 'Let them dig!', because it is at this time that people begin to prepare their fields for planting, since the rains are about to return.

May is known as 'Grain in the ear', for at that time grain begins to bear.

June is called 'Dirty mouth', because children can now begin to eat the new grain, and in so doing get their mouths dirty.

July is known as 'Drying grass', because the rains stop, the ground becomes dry and the grass begins to wither.

August is 'Sweet grain', when people eat and harvest 'sweet grain'.

September is known as 'Sausage Tree', because at this time the sausage tree (*kigalia africana*) begins to bear fruit.[1] (The fruit looks like a huge sausage, hence the name.)

And so the cycle is complete, the natural phenomena begin to repeat themselves once more and the year is over.

The year is likewise composed of events, but of a wider scale than those which compose either the day or the month. Where the community is agricultural, it is the seasonal activities that compose an agricultural year. Near the equator, for example, people would recognize two rain seasons and two dry seasons. When the number of season-periods is completed, then the year is also completed, since it is these four major seasons that make up an entire year. The actual number of days is irrelevant, since a year is not reckoned in terms of mathematical days but in terms of events. Therefore one year might have 350 days while another year has 390 days. The years may, and often do, differ in their length according to days, but not in their seasons and other regular events.

Since the years differ in mathematical length, numerical calendars are both impossible and meaningless in traditional life. Outside the reckoning of the year, African time concept is silent and indifferent. People expect the years to come and go, in an endless rhythm like that of day and night, and like the waning and waxing of the moon. They expect the events of the rain season, planting, harvesting, dry season, rain reason again, planting again, and so on to continue for ever. Each year comes and goes, adding to the time dimension of the past. Endlessness or 'eternity' for them is something that lies only in the region of the past, i.e. something in tense number 9 of our chart multiplied endless times. (When Christians speak of eternity

[1] Cf. L. F. Nalder, ed., *A tribal survey of Mongalla Province* (1937), p. 11 f., from which this has been adapted.

in Kikamba or Gikuyu, they say 'tene na tene', i.e. 'tene and tene', or the period or state of tense number 9 multiplied by itself. This means that what is 'eternal' lies beyond the horizon of events making up human experience or history.)

[c] *The concept of past, present and future*
We must discuss further time dimensions and their relationship with African ontology. Beyond a few months from now, as we have seen, African concept of time is silent and indifferent. This means that the future is virtually non-existent as *actual* time, apart from the relatively short projection of the present up to two years hence. To avoid the thought associations of the English words past, present and future, I propose to use two Swahili words, 'Sasa' and 'Zamani'.

In our chart of the verb tenses, Sasa covers the 'now-period' of tenses 1 to 7. Sasa has the sense of immediacy, nearness, and 'now-ness'; and is the period of immediate concern for the people, since that is 'where' or 'when' they exist. What would be 'future' is extremely brief. This has to be so because any meaningful event in the future must be so immediate and certain that people have almost experienced it. Therefore, if the event is remote, say beyond two years from now (tense number 4), then it cannot be conceived, it cannot be spoken of and the languages themselves have no verb tenses to cover that distant 'future' dimension of time. When an event is far in the future, its reality is completely beyond or outside the horizon of the Sasa period. Therefore, in African thought, the Sasa 'swallows' up what in western or linear concept of time would be considered as the future. Events (which compose time) in the Sasa dimension must be either about to occur, or in the process of realization, or recently experienced. Sasa is the most meaningful period for the individual, because he has a personal recollection of the events or phenomena of this period, or he is about to experience them. Sasa is really an experiential extension of the Now-moment (tense number 4) stretched into the short future and into the unlimited past (or Zamani). Sasa is not mathematically or numerically constant. The older a person is, the longer is his Sasa period. The community also has its own Sasa, which is greater than that of the individual. But for both the community and the individual, the most vivid moment is the NOW point, the event of tense number 4. Sasa is the time region in which people are conscious of their existence, and within which they project themselves both into the short future and mainly into the past (Zamani). Sasa is in itself a complete or full time dimension, with its own short future, a dynamic present, and an experienced past. We might call it the *Micro-Time* (Little-Time). The Micro-Time is meaningful to the individual or the community only through their participating in it or experiencing it.

Zamani is not limited to what in English is called the past. It also has its own 'past', 'present' and 'future', but on a wider scale. We might call it the *Macro-Time* (Big Time). Zamani overlaps with Sasa and the two are not separable. Sasa feeds or disappears into Zamani. But before events become incorporated into the Zamani, they have to become realized or actualized within the Sasa dimension. When this has taken place, then the events 'move' backwards from the Sasa into the Zamani. So Zamani becomes the period beyond which nothing can go. Zamani is the graveyard of time, the period of termination, the dimension in which everything finds its halting point. It is the final storehouse for all phenomena and events, the ocean of time in which everything becomes absorbed into a reality that is neither after nor before.

Both Sasa and Zamani have quality and quantity. People speak of them as big, small, little, short, long, etc., in relation to a particular event or phenomenon. Sasa generally binds individuals and their immediate environment together. It is the period of conscious living. On the other hand, Zamani is the period of the myth, giving a sense of foundation or 'security' to the Sasa period; and binding together all created things, so that all things are embraced within the Macro-Time.

[d] *The concept of history and pre-history*

Each African people has its own history. This history moves 'backward' from the Sasa period to the Zamani, from the moment of intense experience to the period beyond which nothing can go. In traditional African thought, there is no concept of history moving 'forward' towards a future climax, or towards an end of the world. Since the future does not exist beyond a few months, the future cannot be expected to usher in a golden age, or a radically different state of affairs from what is in the Sasa and the Zamani. The notion of a messianic hope, or a final destruction of the world, has no place in traditional concept of history. So African peoples have no 'belief in progress', the idea that the development of human activities and achieve-ments move from a low to a higher degree. The people neither plan for the distant future nor 'build castles in the air'. The centre of gravity for human thought and activities is the Zamani period, towards which the Sasa moves. People set their eyes on the Zamani, since for them there is no 'World to Come', such as is found in Judaism and Christianity.

Both history and pre-history are dominated by the myth. There are innumerable myths all over the continent of Africa explaining items like the creation of the universe, the first man, the apparent withdrawal of God from the world of mankind, the origin of the tribe and its arrival in its present country, and so on. People constantly look towards the Zamani, for Zamani had foundations on which the Sasa rests and by which it is explainable or should be understood. Zamani is not extinct, but a period full of activities and happenings. It is by looking towards the Zamani that people give or find an explanation about the creation of the world, the com/ing of death, the evolution of their language and customs, the emergence of their wisdom, and so on. The 'golden age' lies in the Zamani, and not in the otherwise very short or non/existent future.

Such history and pre/history tend to be telescoped into a very compact, oral tradition and handed down from generation to generation. If we attempt to fit such traditions into a mathematical time/scale, they would appear to cover only a few centuries whereas in reality they stretch much further back; and some of them, being in the form of myths, defy any attempt to describe them on a mathematical time/scale. In any case, oral history has no dates to be remembered. Man looks back from whence he came, and man is certain that nothing will bring this world to a conclusion. According to this interpretation of African view of history, there are innumerable myths about Zamani, but no myths about any end of the world, since time has no end.[1] African peoples expect human history to continue forever, in the rhythm of moving from the Sasa to the Zamani and there is nothing to suggest that this rhythm shall ever come to an end: the days, months, seasons and years have no end, just as there is no end to the rhythm of birth, marriage, procreation and death.

[e] *The concept of human life in relation to time*
Human life has another rhythm of nature which nothing can destroy. On the level of the individual, this rhythm includes birth, puberty, initiation, marriage, procreation, old age, death, entry into the community of the departed and finally entry into the company of the spirits. It is an ontological rhythm, and these are the key moments in the life of the individual. On the community or national level, there is the cycle of the seasons with their different activities like sowing, cultivating, harvesting and hunting. The

[1] The only possible exception to this statement comes from the Sonjo of Tanzania who think that the world will one day shrink to an end. This is not, however, something that dominates their life, and they go on living as though the idea did not exist. It could be that at one point in their history, their volcanic mountain (known in Maasai as Oldonyo Lengai: Mountain of God) erupted and caused an 'end of the world' in their small country. This event may have been retained in the form of a myth which has been transferred to the unknown future, as a warning about possible future eruptions. See R. F. Gray *The Sonjo of Tanganyika* (1963) who, however, does not offer an explanation of this myth.

key events or moments are given more attention than others, and may often be marked by religious rites and ceremonies. Unusual events or others which do not fit into this rhythm, such as an eclipse, drought, the birth of twins and the like, are generally thought to be bad omens, or to be events requiring special attention from the community, and this may take the form of a religious activity. The abnormal or unusual is an invasion of the ontological harmony.

[f] *Death and immortality*
As the individual gets older, he is in effect moving gradually from the Sasa to the Zamani. His birth is a slow process which is finalized long after the person has been physically born. In many societies, a person is not considered a full human being until he has gone through the whole process of physical birth, naming ceremonies, puberty and initiation rites, and finally marriage (or even procreation). Then he is fully 'born', he is a complete person.

Similarly, death is a process which removes a person gradually from the Sasa period to the Zamani. After the physical death, the individual continues to exist in the Sasa period and does not immediately disappear from it. He is *remembered* by relatives and friends who knew him in this life and who have survived him. They recall him by name, though not necessarily mentioning it, they remember his personality, his character, his words and incidents of his life. If he 'appears' (as people believe), he is recognized *by name*. The departed appear mainly to the older members of their surviving families, and rarely or never to children. They appear to people whose Sasa period is the longest.

This recognition by name is extremely important. The appearance of the departed, and his being recognized by name, may continue for up to four or five generations, so long as someone is alive who once knew the departed personally and by name. When, however, the last person who knew the departed also dies, then the former passes out of the horizon of the Sasa period; and in effect he now becomes completely *dead* as far as family ties are concerned. He has sunk into the Zamani period. But while the departed person is remembered by name, he is not really dead: he is alive, and such a person I would call the *living-dead*. The living-dead is a person who is physically dead but alive in the memory of those who knew him in his life as well as being alive in the world of the spirits. So long as the living-dead is thus remembered, he is in the state of *personal immortality*. This personal immortality is externalized in the physical continuation of the individual through procreation, so that the children bear the traits of their parents or progenitors. From the point of view of the survivors, personal immortality is expressed or externalized in acts like respecting the departed, giving bits of food to them, pouring out libation and carrying out instruc' tions given by them either while they lived or when they appear.

This concept of personal immortality should help us to understand the religious significance of marriage in African societies. Unless a person has close relatives to remember him when he has physically died, then he is nobody and simply vanishes out of human existence like a flame when it is extinguished. Therefore it is a duty, religious and ontological, for everyone to get married; and if a man has no children or only daughters, he finds another wife so that through her, children (or sons) may be born who would survive him and keep him (with the other living'dead of the family) in personal immortality. Procreation is the absolute way of insuring that a person is not cut off from personal immortality.

The acts of pouring out libation (of beer, milk or water), or giving portions of food to the living'dead, are symbols of communion, fellowship and remembrance. They are the mystical ties that bind the living'dead to their surviving relatives. Therefore these acts are performed within the family. The oldest member of the family is the one who has the longest Sasa period, and therefore the one who has the longest memory of the departed. He it is who performs or supervises these acts of remembrance on behalf of the entire family, addressing (when the occasion demands it) the symbolic meal to all the departed (living'dead) of the family, even if only one or two of the departed may be mentioned by name or position (e.g. father, grandfather). There is nothing here about the so'called 'ancestor worship', even if these acts may so seem to the outsiders who do not understand the situation.

With the passing of time, the living'dead sink beyond the horizon of the *Sasa* period. This point is reached when there is no longer anyone alive who remembers them personally by name. Then the process of dying is completed. But the living'dead do not vanish out of existence: they now enter into the state of *collective immortality*. This is the state of the spirits who are no longer formal members of the human families. People lose personal contact with them. The departed in this state become members of the family or community of the spirits, and if they appear to human beings they are not recognized by name and may cause dread and fear. Their names may still be mentioned by human beings, especially in genealogies, but they are *empty names* which are more or less without a personality or at best with only a mythological personality built around fact and fiction. Such spirits have no personal communication with human families; in some societies, however, they might speak through a medium, or become guardians of the clan or nation, and may be mentioned or appealed to in religious rites of local or national significance. In other societies such spirits are incorporated into the body of intermediaries between God and man, and human beings approach God through them or seek other help from them. In reality, these spirits of the departed, together with other spirits which may or may not have been once human beings, occupy the ontological state between God and men. Beyond the state of the spirits, men cannot go or develop. This then is the destiny of man, as far as African ontology is concerned. African religious activities are chiefly focused upon the relationship between human beings and the departed; which really means that man tries to penetrate or project himself into the world of what remains of him after this physical life. If the living-dead are suddenly forgotten, this means that they are cast out of the Sasa period, and are in effect excommunicated, their personal immortality is destroyed and they are turned into a state of non-existence. And this is the worst possible punishment for anyone. The departed resent it, and the living do all they can to avoid it because it is feared that it would bring illness and misfortunes to those who forget their departed relatives. Paradoxically, death lies 'in front' of the individual, it is still a 'future' event; but when one dies, one enters the state of personal immortality which lies not in the future but in the Zamani.

[g] Space and time

Space and time are closely linked, and often the same word is used for both. As with time, it is the content which defines space. What matters most to the people is what is geographically near, just as Sasa embraces the life that people experience. For this reason, Africans are particularly tied to the land, because it is the concrete expression of both their Zamani and their Sasa. The land provides them with the roots of existence, as well as binding them mystically to their departed. People walk on the graves of their forefathers, and it is feared that anything separating them from these ties will bring disaster to family and community life. To remove Africans by force from their land is an act of such great injustice that no foreigner can fathom it. Even when people voluntarily leave their homes in the countryside and go to live or work in the cities, there is a fundamental severing of ties which cannot be repaired and which often creates psychological problems with which urban life cannot as yet cope.

[h] Discovering or extending the future dimension of time

Partly because of Christian missionary teaching, partly because of western-type education, together with the invasion of modern technology with all it involves, African peoples are discovering the future dimension of time. On the secular level this leads to national planning for economic growth, political independence, extension of educational facilities and so on. But the change from the structure built around the traditional concept of time, to one which should accommodate this new discovery of the future dimension, is not a smooth one and may well be at the root of, among other things, the political instability of our nations. In Church life this discovery seems to create a strong expectation of the millennium. This makes many Christians escape from facing the challenges of this life into the state of merely hoping and waiting for the life of paradise. This strong millennial expectation often leads to the creation of many small independent churches centred around individuals who symbolize, and more or less fulfil, this messianic expectation.

The discovery and extension of the future dimension of time possess great potentialities and promises for the shaping of the entire life of African peoples. If these are harnessed and channelled into creative and productive use, they will no doubt become beneficial; but they can get out of control and precipitate both tragedy and disillusionment.

The traditional concept of time is intimately bound up with the entire life of the people, and our understanding of it may help to pave the way for understanding the thinking, attitude and actions of the people. It is against this background that I shall attempt to introduce and examine their religious systems and philosophy.

4

THE NATURE OF GOD

Expressed ontologically, God is the origin and sustenance of all things. He is 'older' than the Zamani period; He is outside and beyond His creation. On the other hand, He is personally involved in His creation, so that it is not outside of Him or His reach. God is thus simultaneously transcendent and immanent; and a balanced understanding of these two extremes is necessary in our discussion of African conceptions of God.[1]

In my larger work, *Concepts of God in Africa* (1969), I have collected all the information available to me concerning the traditional concepts of God. The study covers nearly 300 peoples from all over Africa outside the traditionally Christian and Muslim communities. In all these societies, without a single exception, people have a notion of God as the Supreme Being. This is the most minimal and fundamental idea about God, found in all African societies. Obviously there are many who have much more to say about God than this; but apart from a few comprehensive studies, our written information about the concepts of God held by individual peoples is incomplete.

African knowledge of God is expressed in proverbs, short statements, songs, prayers, names, myths, stories and religious ceremonies. All these are easy to remember and pass on to other people, since there are no sacred writings in traditional societies. One should not, therefore, expect long dissertations about God. But God is no stranger to African peoples, and in traditional life there are no atheists. This is summarized in an Ashanti proverb that 'No one shows a child the Supreme Being'. That means that everybody knows of God's existence almost by instinct, and even children know Him.

African concepts of God are strongly coloured and influenced by the

---

[1] Those wishing to get a more detailed and comprehensive account are referred to: J. S. Mbiti *Concepts of God in Africa* (S.P.C.K. London 1969 and Praeger, New York 1969), available in hard and paperback covers. This and the next two chapters draw considerably from that work, for which I am grateful to the publishers, the Society for Promoting Christian Knowledge (S.P.C.K.).

historical, geographical, social and cultural background or environment of each people. This explains the similarities and differences which we find when we consider the beliefs about God from all over the continent. It is this which partly accounts also for the beliefs parallel to those held by peoples of other continents and lands, where the background may be similar to that of African peoples. This does not rule out the fact that through contact with the outside world, some influence of ideas and culture has reached our continent. But such influence is minimal and must have operated in both directions. There are cardinal teachings, doctrines and beliefs of Christianity, Judaism and Islam which cannot be traced in traditional religions. These major religious traditions, therefore, cannot have been responsible for disseminating those concepts of God in traditional religions which resemble some biblical and semitic ideas about God, while at the same time omitting their infinitely more important aspects of belief and practice. I maintain that African soil is rich enough to have germinated its own original religious perception. It is remarkable that in spite of great distances separating the peoples of one region from those of another, there are sufficient elements of belief which make it possible for us to discuss African concepts of God as a unity and on a continental scale. But obviously the situation is more complex than the impression which that unity might give here. This is a task I have attempted to accomplish elsewhere; there are also other writers who deal with individual people's concepts of God; but we need not trace here ground which has been covered elsewhere.

[a] *The eternal and intrinsic attributes of God*
These attributes are difficult to grasp and express, since they pertain more to the realm of the abstract than concrete thought forms. Broadly speaking, African thought forms are more concrete than abstract. We find, however, considerable examples of how African peoples conceive of the eternal nature of God.

A number of societies consider God to be omniscient, that is, to know all things, to be simultaneously everywhere (i.e. omnipresent), and to be almighty (omnipotent). These are essential aspects of His being, they are part of His unique nature and no other being can be described in the same terms. It is these and other eternal attributes discussed below, which distinguish God from His creation and which make Him not only the genesis but also the sustainer of all things.

When African peoples consider God to be omniscient, they are at the same time conferring upon Him the highest possible position of honour and respect, for wisdom commands great respect in African societies. In so doing, people admit that man's wisdom, however great, is limited, incomplete and acquired. On the other hand, God's omniscience is absolute, unlimited and intrinsically part of His eternal nature and being. To the Zulu and Banyarwanda, God is known as 'the Wise One', and to the Akan as 'He Who knows or sees all'. It is a common saying among the Yoruba that 'Only God is wise' and they believe that God is 'the Discerner of hearts' Who 'sees both the inside and outside of man'.[1]

The metaphor of seeing and hearing explains the concept of God as omniscient in a concrete way which is easy to grasp. So we find examples from many areas of Africa, in which God is said to be able to see or hear everything. One name for Him among the Barundi is 'the Watcher of everything'; while the Ila say that His 'ears are long'.[1] Other peoples visualize God as 'the Great Eye' (like the Baganda), or 'the Sun' which beams its light everywhere. Whether or not people literally think of God as having one or more eyes, or long ears, is immaterial: the point is that they regard Him as the omniscient from Whom nothing is hidden, since nothing can escape His vision, hearing or knowledge. He knows everything, observes everything and hears everything, without limitation and without exception.

When the Ila say that 'God has nowhere or nowhen, that He comes to an end', they are speaking about His nature of omnipresence. The Bamum express the same concept in their name for God (*Njinyi* or *Nnui*) which means: 'He Who is everywhere'. This idea comes out among other peoples who say that God is met everywhere (e.g. Barundi and Kono); that the presence of God protects people (e.g. Akamba); that wrong-doers cannot escape the judgment of God (e.g. Yoruba, Kono); or that God is like the wind or air (e.g. Shilluk, Langi). These are attempts to describe another intrinsic and eternal attribute of God, His omnipresence.

That God is almighty is a concept easier to grasp than the attributes discussed above. Consequently we find many concrete examples from all over Africa, in which people speak of God as omnipotent. Among some peoples, like the Yoruba, Ngombe, Akan and Ashanti, one of the names for God describes Him as 'the All-powerful' or 'the Almighty'. His power is seen in practical terms. The Yoruba might say of duties or challenges, that they are 'easy to do as that which God performs; difficult to do as that which God enables not'.[2] The Zulu conceive of God's power in political terms, which for such a powerful nation is full of meaning. They describe Him as 'He Who bends down . . . even majesties', and 'He Who roars so that all nations be struck with terror'.[3] The Ngombe who live in the

[1] Danquah, p. 55 (Akan); Idowu, p. 41 (Yoruba); Guillebaud in Smith, p. 187 (Barundi); Smith and Dale, p. 208 (Ila).
[2] Idowu, p. 40 f.
[3] Smith, p. 109.

extremely thick forest in the Congo see God's omnipotence in relation to the forest, and praise Him as 'the One Who clears the forest'.[1] For these people, the forest is the symbol of power, and no doubt they struggle constantly to keep it under some form of control. Yet this is no problem with God: He can clear the forest without difficulties, therefore He is omnipotent.

Among many peoples, God's omnipotence is seen in His exercise of power over nature. A few examples will illustrate this. In two proverbs the Banyarwanda say that 'the plant protected by God is never hurt by the wind', and that 'God has very long arms'.[2] The Kiga refer to God as 'the One Who makes the sun set'; and when the Gikuyu make sacrifices and prayers for rain, they address God as the One Who makes mountains quake and rivers overflow. The wind, the sun and the rain are beyond human power of control, but not beyond God's power Who works through them and other natural phenomena or objects. There are those peoples, like the Akamba, Gikuyu, Teso, Vugusu and others, who see God's omnipotence in terms of His being able to deal with, or control the spirits—these being more powerful than men.

So in this context, power is viewed hierarchically in which God is at the top as the omnipotent; beneath Him are the spirits and natural phenomena; and lower still are men who have comparatively little or no power at all.

The attribute of God's transcendence must be balanced with that of His immanence, since these two are paradoxically complementary. This means that He is so 'far' (transcendental) that men cannot reach Him; yet, He is so 'near' (immanent) that He comes close to men. Many foreign writers have gone astray here, in emphasizing God's remoteness to the exclusion of His nearness.

In terms of time, God 'stretches' over and beyond the whole period of *Zamani*, so that not even human imagination can get at Him. He not only fills up the *Zamani* period, He also transcends it. This is what the Akan are attempting to express when they praise Him as 'He Who is there now as from ancient times';[3] and when the Tonga refer to Him simply as 'the Ancient of Days'. The Ngombe compare this essential nature of God to the forest, for which reason they speak of Him as 'the everlasting One of the forest'.[4] As far back as they can imagine, the forest has always been in existence; but God ante-dates it since He made it.

[1] Davidson in Smith, p. 167.
[2] Maquet in Forde, p. 169.
[3] Danquah, p. 55.
[4] Davidson in Smith, p. 166.

It is, however, in spatial terms that people more readily conceive of God's transcendence. God is thought of as dwelling far away in the sky, or 'above', beyond the reach of men. Obviously the sky in its great immensity invites people to gaze in it, both with their eyes and imagination. Practically all African peoples associate God with the sky, in one way or another. Some have myths telling of how men came from the sky; or of how God separated from men and withdrew Himself into the sky, whence nobody could directly reach Him.

The concept of God's transcendence is summarized well in a Bacongo saying, that 'He is made by no other; no one beyond Him is'.[1] There cannot be, and there is no 'beyond' God: He is the most abundant reality of being, lacking no completeness. He transcends all boundaries; He is omnipresent everywhere and at all times. He even defies human conception and description; He is simply 'the Unexplainable' as the Ngombe like to call Him. Ontologically He is transcendent in that all things were made by Him, whereas He is self-existent. In status He is 'beyond' spiritual beings, the spirits, men and natural objects and phenomena. In power and knowledge, He is supreme.

Yet, in spite of all this transcendence of God, He is immanent so that men can and do in fact establish contact with Him. One of the best known praise names of God among the Ngombe, describes Him as 'the One Who fills everything'. It is, however, in the many acts of worship that men acknowledge God to be near and approachable. Such acts include sacrifices, offerings, prayers and invocations. Men also associate God with many natural objects and phenomena, indicating their belief that God is involved in His creation: there is no space where, or time when, He cannot be found since He is contemporaneous with all things. This is not pantheism, and there is no evidence that people consider God to be everything and everything to be God.

For most of their life, African peoples place God in the transcendental plane, making it seem as if He is remote from their daily affairs. But they know that He is immanent, being manifested in natural objects and phenomena, and they can turn to Him in acts of worship, at any place and any time. The distinction between these related attributes could be stated that, in theory God is transcendental but in practice He is immanent.

A number of African peoples think of God as self-existent and pre-eminent. From the Zulu we get a clear expression of this concept. They give one name to God which means: 'He Who is of Himself' or 'He Who came of Himself into being'.[2] The Bambuti think that God 'was the First,

---

[1] Claridge, p. 269.
[2] Smith, p. 109.

Who had always been in existence, and would never die'.[1] These are theological and philosophical expressions; but there are others of a biological nature. Thus, the Gikuyu believe that God has

> *No father nor mother, nor wife nor children;*
> *He is all alone.*
> *He is neither a child nor an old man;*
> *He is the same today as He was yesterday.*

They go on to point out that He does not eat, and has no messengers.[2] In almost identical words, the Herero say that God has no father and is not a man. These statements indicate that God is self-sufficient, self-supporting and self-containing, just as He is self-originating. In human terms, it is clearly emphasized that God is uncreated, without parents, without family, without any of the things that compose or sustain human life. He is truly self-dependent, absolutely unchangeable and unchanging.

From this it follows that God is pre-eminently great and supreme. Many societies like the Akan, Baluba, Ngoni, Tonga and others, speak of Him as 'the Great One', or 'Great God', or 'the Great King', or 'the surpassingly great Spirit'. The main Zulu name for God, *Unkulunkulu*, carries with it the sense of 'the Great-great-One' and the same name is used by neighbouring peoples, such as the Ndebele for whom it means 'the Greatest of the great'.[3] The attributes of transcendence and self-existence also point in this same direction of the supremacy and pre-eminence of God.

It is commonly believed that God is Spirit, even if in thinking or talking about Him African peoples may often use anthropomorphic images. As far as it is known, there are no images or physical representations of God by African peoples: this being one clear indication that they consider Him to be a Spiritual Being. The fact that He is invisible also leads many to visualize Him as spiritual rather than physical. To grasp this aspect of God, some societies like the Ga, Langi and Shilluk compare Him with the wind or air. There is no information available to indicate that anyone has ever seen God; though there are a few vague accounts of theophanies, i.e. physical manifestations of God, but it is possible that these are hallucinations rather than external experiences.

One of the most explicit descriptions of God as Spirit occurs in a traditional Pygmy hymn which says:

> *In the beginning was God,*
> *Today is God,*

[1] Schebesta, II, p. 171 f.
[2] Routledge, p. 225 f.; Kenyatta, p. 233.
[3] Smith, p. 103; and Hughes & Velsen, p. 103.

> *Tomorrow will be God.*
> *Who can make an image of God?*
> *He has no body.*
> *He is as a word which comes out of your mouth.*
> *That word! It is no more,*
> *It is past, and still it lives!*
> *So is God.*[1]

In a Shona traditional hymn, God is addressed as 'the Great Spirit' Who piles up rocks to make mountains, causes branches to grow and gives rain to mankind.[2] Thus, God is pictured as an active and creative Spirit.

It is particularly as Spirit that God is incomprehensible. So the Ashanti rightly refer to Him as 'the fathomless Spirit', since no human mind can measure Him, no intellect can comprehend or grasp Him. To the Bacongo, He is 'the Marvel of marvels', and anything which seems beyond their understanding is attributed to Him as 'a thing of God'. Many people readily admit that they do not know what God is like, and that they do not possess the words of God—since words are vehicles of someone's thoughts and to a certain degree they give a portrait of the speaker. Some even say that God's proper name is unknown; or give Him a name like that of the Lunda, which means or signifies 'the God of the unknown', or that of the Ngombe which means 'the Unexplainable', or of the Maasai which means 'the Unknown'.[3] A person's name in African societies generally has a meaning descriptive of his personality and being. In the case of God, people might know some of His activities and manifestations, but of His essential nature they know nothing. It is a paradox that they 'know' Him, and yet they do not 'know' Him; He is not a Stranger to them, and yet they are estranged to Him; He knows them, but they do not know Him. So God confronts men as the mysterious and incomprehensible, as indescribable and beyond human vocabulary. This is part of the essential nature of God.

Ideas of God's eternal nature are expressed variously by different peoples. The Ngombe for whom the forest symbolizes agelessness, regard God and praise Him as 'the everlasting One of the forest'. The Ila, Baluba and others liken God's eternal nature to the apparent endurance of the sun, calling Him 'He of the suns', or 'He of many suns'. God's eternity is here compared

---

[1] Young, p. 146, without specifying which group of Pygmies.
[2] Smith, p. 127.
[3] Lunda name is *Njambi-Kalunga* (Campbell, p. 245); Ngombe name is *Endalandala* (Davidson in Smith, p. 167); Maasai name is *Ngai* (Hinde, p. 99; cf. other writers claim that it means 'rain and sky').

to the sun of many suns: He endures forever, and His eternal nature makes Him impervious to change and limitation. The Baganda and Ashanti address Him as 'the Eternal One'. The Yoruba on the other hand, consider God to be 'the Mighty, Immovable Rock that never dies'.[1] This metaphor of immortality is used also by the Tonga in their saying that 'Heaven never dies, only men do!',[2] (where 'Heaven' stands for God). The same idea is emphasized by the Yoruba in a popular song that 'one never hears of the death of God!'[1] God is eternal, beyond the effect or influence of change; He endures for ever and ever, as He was He continues to be, so that He cannot be other than being God.

Every African people recognizes God as One. According to some cosmologies, however, there are, besides Him, other divinities and spiritual beings some of whom are closely associated with Him. These beings are generally the personification of God's activities, natural phenomena and objects, or deified national heroes, or spiritual beings created by God as such. In a few cases, such as among the Bari, Lugbara and Turu, dual aspects of the One God are recognized, as an explanation of the transcendence and immanence of God, and of the problem of good and evil. A form of trinitarian concept of God is reported among the Ndebele and Shona peoples, according to which He is described as 'Father, Mother and Son'.[3] This is probably a logical convenience, rather than a theological reflection, to fit God into the African conception of the family.

[b] *The moral attributes of God*
Of the moral attributes of God we have little information. Many peoples, such as the Akamba, Banyarwanda, Ila, Herero and others, consider God to be merciful, showing kindness and taking pity over mankind. For that reason He is referred to as 'the God of pity', 'God is kind', or 'God is merciful'. The mercy or kindness of God is felt in situations of danger, difficulty, illness and anxiety, when deliverance or protection is attributed to Him, or He is called upon to help. Even when sorrows have struck, God may be called upon to comfort the people, as is done, for example, by the Nuer; and some societies like the Akamba and Akan, speak of Him as 'the God of comfort'.

The majority of African peoples regard God as essentially good, and there are many situations in which He is credited with doing good to His people. Some, like the Akamba, Bacongo, Herero, Igbo, Ila and others, say catergorically that God does them only what is good, so they have no

---

[1] Idowu, pp. 36, 43.
[2] Junod, p. 135.
[3] Hughes & Velsen, p. 104 f.; and Merwe, p. 11 f.

reason to complain. The Ewe firmly hold that 'He is good, for He has never withdrawn from us the good things which He gave us'.[1]

For some, the goodness of God is seen in His averting calamities, supplying rain, providing fertility to people, cattle and fields. Thus, the Langi consider rich harvests to come from God; the Vugusu believe that material prosperity comes from God; and the Nandi invoke God daily to grant fertility to their women, cattle and fields. Believing that God is essentially good, the Barundi do not wish to thank Him since it is His right to do good things to them.

There are, however, situations when calamities, misfortunes and suffering come upon families or individuals, for which there is no clear explanation. Some societies would then consider these to be brought about by God, generally through agents like spirits or magic workers, or as punishment for contravening certain customs or traditions. By so doing, they do not consider God to be intrinsically 'evil' as such: that is simply a rational explanation of what may otherwise be hard to explain. This dilemma comes out in a saying of some Katanga peoples, that God is 'the Father Creator Who creates and uncreates'.[2] The Ila show similar difficulties when they consider God to be responsible for giving and causing to rot. Some peoples hold that God is capable of showing anger; and death, drought, floods, locusts and other national calamities are interpreted to be manifestations of His anger. A few, like the Tonga and Tiv, look upon thunder and lightning as resulting from God's anger; while the Barundi fear that adultery will arouse His anger and cause Him to punish them with misfortune.

A number of peoples consider God to have a will which governs the universe and the fortunes of mankind. When the Bambuti Pygmies fail to kill game in their expeditions, they take this to be God's will against which they can do nothing. On the other hand, the Banyarwanda believe that only through God's will does one find a wife (or husband), wealth, job or is restored to good health. When planning to do something, the Akamba add the words 'if God wills'; and some like the Mende end their prayers with the phrase 'God willing'. Misfortunes, especially death, are accepted by some, such as the Gikuyu, Lugbara and Nuer, to be God's will, whatever other explanations may be advanced.

God has a personality, and in this personality there is a will which governs the universe and the life of mankind. It is an immutable will, and man generally has to invoke it or accept it in situations that seem beyond human power. This will of God is exercised, however, in a just way, and

---

[1] D. Westermann *The African Today and Tomorrow* (London 1939), p. 197.
[2] Campbell, p. 245.

African peoples consider Him to be just. No matter what befalls them, the Nuer believe that God is always right. They hold that 'God evens things out', rewarding good to those who follow good conduct, and evil to those who follow evil conduct, and overlooking breaches done accidentally or in error.[1] The justice of God is felt or invoked often in judicial situations, taking oaths, and pronouncing formal curses, all of which are taken seriously by African peoples. He is the ultimate Judge, and He executes judgment with justice and without partiality.

Concerning the holiness of God, little is said directly by African peoples as far as our records show. The Ila hold that God cannot be charged with an offence, since He is above the level of 'fault', 'failure', 'wrong' and 'unrighteousness'. In the eyes of the Yoruba, God is 'the pure King . . . Who is without blemish'.[2] The concept of God's holiness is also indicated from the fact that many African peoples have strict rules in performing rituals directed to God. Sacrificial animals, for instance, have to be of one sacred colour, and priests or officiating elders must refrain from sexual intercourse and certain foods or activities before and after the ritual. These ritual formalities clearly show that people regard God as holy.

As for the love of God, there are practically no direct sayings that God loves. This is something reflected also in the daily lives of African peoples, in which it is rare to hear people talking about love. A person shows his love for another more through action than through words. So, in the same way, people experience the love of God in concrete acts and blessings; and they assume that He loves them, otherwise He would not have created them. Whereas manifestations of evil, such as sickness, barrenness, death, failure in undertakings and the like, are attributed to malicious human (and occasionally, spiritual) agents, the manifestations of good, such as health, begetting many children, fertility, wealth, plenty and the like, are attributed to God: they are the tokens of His love to mankind. People experience the love of God, even though they do not speak of it as though it were detached from His activities.

The Nature of God escapes human comprehension. We have here presented only a few glimpses of it as seen in different parts of Africa. It is, however, in the realm of God's activities that we find the greatest number of examples of what people think and say about God. These activities are an essential dimension of God and reflect, ultimately, the nature of God— or, more accurately, what people imagine Him to be and to do. To these activities we shall now proceed.

[1] Evans-Pritchard, II, pp. 12, 19.
[2] Idowu, p. 47.

5

THE WORKS OF GOD

[a] *Creation*

Over the whole of Africa creation is the most widely acknowledged work of God. This concept is expressed through saying that God created all things, through giving Him the name of Creator (or Moulder, or Maker), and through addressing Him in prayer and invocations as the Creator. We have abundant examples of what African peoples say concerning the creative activity of God, and a few of these will suffice here.

The Akan title, *Borebore,* given to God means 'Excavator, Hewer, Carver, Creator, Originator, Inventor, Architect';[1] and the people hold firmly that it was God alone Who created the world. The universe is described as having its architectural origin and form from God, Who is here pictured as its Artist-in-Chief. Of the four most known Akamba names for God, two mean 'Creator' or 'Maker' and 'Cleaver'.[2] The second of these (*Mwatuangi*), is taken from human act of slicing meat with a knife or splitting wood with an axe. So God first creates, originates, moulds and makes; then He gives shape, supplies details and adds distinctiveness and character. These two names are complementary.

The metaphor of the potter is commonly used to describe God's creative activity, and of this we find many examples. Believing that God shapes children in the mother's womb, Banyarwanda women of a child-bearing age are careful to leave water ready, before they go to bed, so that God may use it to create children for them. It is known as 'God's water'; and He is known as 'the Giver of children'. The people hold that 'there was nothing before God created the world'.[3] This means that God created out of nothing, in the original act of creation, though now He may use existing materials to continue His creative activities. This concept of creation *ex nihilo* is also reported among the Nuer, Banyarwanda and Shona, and undoubtedly a careful search for it elsewhere is likely to show that there are other peoples who incorporate it into their cosmologies.

[1] Danquah, pp. 28, 30.
[2] Akamba names are *Mumbi* and *Mwatuangi*, respectively.
[3] Maquet in Forde, p. 166.

The Ila have three names for God by means of which they describe His creative work. They speak of Him as Creator, Moulder and Constructor. The Tiv who are famed for their woodwork think of God as the Carpenter Who 'carves' the world giving it different forms and shapes. When the Lunda speak of God as 'the Father Creator', they place Him on a parental level: He fathered all things, and exercises His fatherly care over them.

There is no general agreement as to the order in which creation was accomplished. The Vugusu, for example, tell that God created first the heavenly universe with the sun, moon, stars and clouds; then He created the earth, followed by the creation of man (both husband and wife); and finally plants, animals and other earthly creatures. The Akan think that creation took place in the order of the sky, then the earth, rivers, waters, plants, man and animals. A number of peoples, like the Lozi, Mende, Nandi and others hold that God ended His work with the creation of man. Generally it is explained that the creation of heaven preceded that of the earth; but we do not find any special order in the creation of 'minor' things.

Many peoples say that God not only created the material universe, but also established laws of nature and human customs. The Ashanti believe that God 'God created things in an ordered fashion', and made an orderly and harmonious world where everyone could perform his own duties.[1] The Yoruba think of God as the 'Author of day and night', and regard each day as His offspring.[2] The Zulu consider their marriage institution and circumcision custom to have been ordered by God. The Nuer, Ila, Lugbara, Nuba and many others, believe that God established their customs, laws and regulations, in addition to creating the world.

It is also held that God continues with His creative work throughout the universe. The Twi say, for example, that 'God never ceases to create things'.[3] Human procreation is particularly attributed to God. Some peoples like the Azande, Bambuti, Nyakyusa and others, believe that God causes conception to take place. Others simply say that God creates more people. According to the Bari, God keeps mankind alive by creating one hundred men every month; and the Indem hold that He sends the spirit into babies.

God not only continues to create physically, but He also ordains the destiny of His creatures, especially that of men. The Yoruba tell that before a person comes to this world, he stands before God to choose, receive or have his destiny affixed to him by God. They hold also, that when God

---

[1] Lystad, p. 164.
[2] Idowu, p. 39.
[3] D. Westermann *The African Today and Tomorrow* (London 1939), p. 197.

creates a person, He fixes how long that individual will live.[1] The Mende believe the same thing, expressing it in a proverb that: 'If God dishes your rice in a basket, do not wish to eat soup!' This is interpreted to mean that a person should not desire to change the state or condition in which God places him.[2] The Nuer say categorically that everything is as it is 'because God made or willed it so'.[3] Similar notions of predestination are found among peoples like the Ila, Tswana, Bacongo, Barundi, Yao and others.

[b] *Providence and sustenance*

The Ovimbundu name for God means 'He Who supplies the needs of His creatures'.[4] This is one of the most fundamental beliefs about God, and examples of it come from all over Africa. In various ways God provides for the things He has made, so that their existence can be maintained and continued. He provides life, fertility, rain, health and other necessities needed for sustaining creation. His providence functions entirely independently of man, though man may and does at times solicit God's help.

Sunshine is one of the expressions of God's providence, as held by some peoples like the Akan, Ankore, Igbira, Kpelle and Ila. The sun appears every day, providing light, warmth, change of seasons and the growth of crops. This is very vital. So the Akan call God 'the Shining One', to signify that He is involved in the light of the celestial bodies whose shining symbolizes His presence in the universe. One of the Ankore names for God means 'Sun', and the people believe that God makes the sun to shine by day and the moon by night. For the Igbira, the sun symbolizes God's benevolence, an expression of His providence.

Rain is, however, the most widely acknowledged token of God's providence. To African peoples rain is always a blessing, and its supply is one of the most important activities of God. Examples of this are found everywhere. For that reason, God is known as 'the Rain Giver' or 'Water Giver', among peoples like the Akan, Ila, Ngoni, Mende, Tswana, Akamba, Tiv and many others. Some of these even say that rain is God's spittle, this, in African societies, being the vehicle of blessing, so that formal pronouncing of a blessing is often accompanied by gentle spitting. The spittle symbolizes prosperity, health, happiness and good welfare.

It is also widely believed that God shows His providence through fertility and health of humans, cattle and fields, as well as through the plentifulness of children, cattle, food and other goods. Many societies

[1] P. A. Talbot *Tribes of the Niger Delta* (London 1932), p. 24.
[2] Little in Forde, p. 113.
[3] Evans-Pritchard, II, p. 6 f.
[4] Campbell, p. 245, with reference to the name *Suku*.

therefore pray for these items. Thus, the Nuba perform a ceremony at which they pray for the increase of cattle, saying:

> *God, we are hungry,*
> *Give us cattle, give us sheep!*

When making their sacrifices, the officiating elder prays:

> *God, increase cattle,*
> *Increase sheep, increase men!*.[1]

The Zulu teach their children that the Source of being is above, and that it is God Who gives men life and prosperity. When a Bambuti woman realizes that she is expecting a child, she prepares food and takes a portion of it to the forest where she offers it to God saying,

> *(God) from Whom I have received this child,*
> *Take Thou and eat!*[2]

Other societies, like the Ankore, Azande and Banyarwanda, incorporate God's name into their children's names, thereby recognizing that children come from Him.

In various ways, different peoples acknowledge the sustaining work of God. Some like the Abaluyia, Akan and Zulu say that God sustains human life, so that without Him mankind would vanish. Others see God's sustenance as functioning on a cosmic scale, upholding the whole universe. Thus, the Bambuti say that 'if God should die, the world would also collapse'.[3] A number of peoples, like the Barundi, Ashanti, Tonga, Nandi and others, consider God to be their Keeper, Guardian, Protector and Preserver. For example, the Barundi call Him 'the Protector of the poor, the Keeper of the poor' and 'Saviour',[4] and the Nyanja look upon Him as 'the Great Caretaker of life'.[5] Many pray that God would guard them, especially in special circumstances like pregnancy and sickness. The Nuer are very conscious of God's continual care over them, and speak of Him as 'God Who walks with you', or that 'God is present'.[6] Among the Shilluk, God is invoked to 'Protect us, we are in your hand, and protect us, save me . . .'.[7] The omnipresence of God is experienced as protective,

[1] Seligman, p. 394 f.
[2] Schebesta, I, p. 235.
[3] Schebesta, II, p. 171.
[4] Essays by my students J. Kamenge and D. Soboke (1965).
[5] Merwe, p. 13.
[6] Evans-Pritchard, II, p. 7 f.
[7] Lienhardt in Forde, p. 158; and Seligman, p. 75.

sustaining, upholding, saving and healing. One of the Baganda names for God (*Ddunda*), means 'Pastor', which obviously carries with it the idea of God shepherding His people. The Kiga describe God as *Biheko*, a name which means 'He Who carried everyone on His back'.[1] This comes from the widespread African custom of women or girls carrying babies on their back. The name vividly describes God as nursing and cherishing people with the tenderness and care of mothers.

Many societies believe that God heals the sick. For this reason, prayers, sacrifices and offerings are made to God, on behalf of the sick, the barren and those in distress. Examples of this practice are reported from among the Ila, Chagga, Indem, Shilluk and others. When healing comes, it is often attributed to God, even if medical agents may play a part in the healing process. God is thanked, or His help is otherwise acknowledged. For example, after recovery from a serious illness, Akamba say, 'Ah, if it were not for God's help, I (he) would be dead by now!' The same ideas are expressed concerning God's saving work. People take it to be the result of God's help when they are rescued from danger or illness. The Ila, for example, describe Him as 'the Deliverer of those in trouble'; and the Abaluyia name (*Wele*) for God carries, among other things, the idea of 'One Who saves, helps or steers' (guides). The Barundi have a name (*Haragakiza*) for God which means 'There is a Saviour'.

Thus, God is involved in the affairs of mankind, and people experience this involvement in terms of His continuing to create, sustain, provide, pastor, nurse, heal and save. Most of this functions on the physical and concrete level of being, and with special reference to the life of man.

[c] God and afflictions

While, as we have seen, God is actively sustaining His creation and providing for it, there are afflictions in human life which puzzle many societies. In a large number of peoples, explanation for these afflictions involves God in one way or another. This becomes clear as we consider some concrete examples. When the Tonga are in trouble, a person exclaims that 'Heaven (God) has forsaken me!' These people trace events of a sudden or unexpected nature to the influence of *Tilo*, this being a word which describes God and, or, heaven. For them the birth of twins is a great misfortune, and when it happens it is considered a manifestation of Tilo's power.[2]

The Lugbara believe that God brings upon people afflictions in form of mental disturbances and virulent diseases. When endless troubles continue

---

[1] Edel, p. 160.
[2] Junod, p. 134.

in a given family, people say that they come from, or are approved by, God.

Whereas magic, sorcery and witchcraft are universally regarded as the main causes of individual diseases, it is not uncommon, in addition, to consider God as responsible for diseases, especially epidemics. Mental disturbances tend to be blamed on the spirits, even if human agents may also be considered responsible. The Turkana believe that whereas God removes diseases, He may strike people who commit incest or contravene important rituals. Calamities and cattle diseases are interpreted by the Suk to be God's punishment for man's misdoings.

Some societies hold that God may use spiritual beings to bring afflictions to men. Thus, the Chagga say that He sends a spirit to cause smallpox and other sickness, though a person would only die when God permits it. The Basoga have a divinity of plague; the Gisu have one of smallpox and another of plague; and the Yoruba believe that the divinity of small-pox prowls about when the sun is hot.

It is also held by some societies that God has different aspects, one of which is responsible for misfortunes among men. We have already mentioned the Lugbara belief that the immanent aspect of God is con-sidered 'bad', and is associated with misfortunes. While holding that God is good to all men, the Ila nevertheless attribute much of the evils and sorrows of life to Him. The Gikuyu say that God has three aspects, one of which is responsible for various misfortunes though these are accepted as 'God's will'. In some areas, the cause of misfortunes is personified into an evil spiritual being, and examples of this belief are reported among the Vugusu, Sukuma, Nyamwezi, Darasa, Balese and others.

National calamities such as drought, epidemics, locust invasions, wars and floods are beyond individual human cause or control. They are generally attributed to God's activity, or to a spiritual being. If God is thought to be responsible, it is often taken that He is punishing people for their mischief. The Bavenda, for example, believe that when God is angry with their chief, He punishes the country with locusts and floods. The Langi, on the other hand, consider these calamities to be God's manifesta-tion, presumably of a judicial manner. The Ngoni, Suk, Nyanja and others, believe that calamities are sent by God; and some like the Nuer, accept these calamities as God's will about which they can do nothing.

Death is perhaps the most mysterious and puzzling of all misfortunes. For many peoples, God is paradoxically the Giver of life as well as the One Who takes it away (even if other agents may be and are generally blamed for the immediate cause). This paradox is expressed variously by African peoples. The Akan speak of God as 'the Ever-ready Shooter' (in His aspect of giving life to all things), and 'the Killer Mother'.[1] The Bacongo are convinced that God never wrongs anyone, yet, He may allow death occasionally to occur, at which time they say of the dead person, 'He died by God'. The Barundi consider God to be both 'the Giver of children' and 'He Who hates children' (because they think He kills them). At the Ovimbundu dances, the women wail that 'God has cheated us of a life',[2] to signify that He has robbed them of one member of their community. The Yoruba hold that God created death for the purpose of recalling the person whose time on earth is fulfilled. Those who, in one way or another associate death with God include the Ankore, Azande, Bachwa, Gikuyu, Luo, Meru, Nandi, Vugusu, Zulu and others. Some regard death as God's punishment; others as His manifestation, others as being for the good of the person concerned since God wants them to live with Him, and others think that death comes when people invoke a curse upon an offender. The sacrifices, offerings and prayers made to God during serious illness, are another indication that people associate death with God. In so doing, they may think that He is the ultimate cause; and at least they believe that He can avert or delay death. There are societies, like the Baganda, Basoga, Edo and Vugusu who hold that there is a divinity of death—this being either a personification of death itself, or an independent being.

On the whole, God is not blamed for calamities, misfortunes and sorrows which strike man. He is brought into the picture primarily as an attempt to explain what is otherwise difficult for the human mind; an explanation which also serves to comfort those struck by the particular form of suffering.

[d] *The governing work of God*

In this capacity, God is regarded as King, Ruler, Lord, Master and Judge. It is generally in societies which traditionally have or have had kings, chiefs or other central rulers, that we find the most explicit concept of God as King and Ruler. This obviously reflects the political structure of the peoples concerned, though the idea of God's governing work is not confined only to peoples of this political background. The image and work of the human rulers tend to be readily projected on to the image of God. Of this we have clear examples from many parts of Africa.

The Banyarwanda and Barundi regard God as their supreme Ruler and Governor. When the Barotse and Baluba pray, they address God as 'the Great King', Who rules or reigns over all things. The Akan say that God is the Ruler of the sky, earth and underworld. Among the Indem it is believed that God rules over all the tribes of the earth, including their own.

[1] Meyerowitz, pp. 24, 145.
[2] Hambly, p. 344.

When the Ila go hunting, they pray addressing God as Chief and pleading with Him to let them kill the game which they are going to hunt. This indicates that the people consider Him to rule not only in human affairs but also over nature. The Zulu consider Him to be King of kings, or Chief of chiefs, an attribute which conveys supreme authority and absolute power. There are many other peoples who speak of God in these terms of reigning or ruling over the universe. The portrait of Him as King is very much coloured by that of human rulers. He is pictured as supreme, absolute, rich, and the ultimate owner of all things.

As King, God is also Lord and Master. He is given these titles in many societies, indicating that all respect and honour are due to Him, and man's attitude to Him is one of humbleness and submissiveness. To the Banyar-wanda God is 'the Master of all'; to the Bambuti He is 'the Lord of magic power'; to the Yoruba He is 'the Lord of heaven'; and when lightning strikes cattle, the Zulu say that the Lord has taken His own food. As Lord and Master, He is omnipotent: He can do all things—help people when in distress, accomplish what man cannot, bring about justice and many other things. For this reason, He is referred to by various names by different peoples. For example, the Barundi call Him 'the One Who does all'; the Baluba look to Him as 'the Bearer of burdens' the Shilluk often appeal to Him as the final source of Help in trouble; and many others regard Him as the Giver (of life, of rain, of light, of all things). Thus, God is pictured as the benevolent Lord and Master, and not only as an absolute Ruler of the universe. As Ruler He is 'detached or removed' from creation; but as Lord and Master, He is involved in His creation. Some societies consider their human rulers to be in a sense sacral representatives of God ruling over men.

In His capacity as Ruler and Master, God is also thought to be Judge. This concept includes associations of justice, punishment and retribution. The notion of God as Judge also strengthens traditional ethical sanctions, which in turn uphold community solidarity. In praying during a crisis, the Azande declare to God that they have not stolen or coveted other people's goods, and they address Him as the One Who 'settles the difference between us who are men'.[1] For the Elgeyo, lightning is God's weapon by means of which He destroys people who secretly wrong their neighbours. The Nuba believe that God punishes those who contravene national traditions since He is thought to be the Guardian of the traditions. It is a firm belief among the Nuer that God punishes what is wrong and rewards what is right. For the Ovambo, rudeness to elderly people, murder and stealing are punishable by God. In all these concrete examples and others

[1] Seligman, p. 519 f.

that could be quoted, it is shown that African peoples conceive of God as the supreme Judge Who acts with impartiality.

[e] *God and human history*

African peoples have their different histories. In our discussion of time we pointed out that the dominant concept of history is an emphasis on the Zamani, so that history is viewed as moving from the Sasa to the Zamani period and not as movement towards the future. The anchor lies in the Zamani. This concept comes out in a number of ways. Thus, the Chagga tell that although God may take only little part in daily human affairs, twice He intervened in the past and destroyed people on account of their wickedness, saving only a few persons. The Meru believe that God led them long ago, out of their land of bondage through the agent of a religious leader (*Mugwe*). God equipped this man with the courage and strength for the task, and the people were delivered and brought to their present land. The Shilluk hold firmly that their king is mystically linked with God Whom he represents among men, and that it was God Who originally established their kingship.

Another aspect of God's participation in human history is the belief that God intervenes in the affairs of men. The Bavenda hold that from time to time, God reveals Himself to them especially by communicating with their chief by means of thunder. The Gisu believe that God comes to be with them at their circumcision rites; and the Lugbara say that He intervenes to bring about changes in their society. It is commonly said among the Gikuyu, that although God lives in the sky, He comes to earth from time to time to inspect it, bestow blessings and mete out punishment. When He comes He rests on Mt. Kenya and four other sacred mountains. Some of the Galla narrate that once God came to earth and talked with mankind, otherwise He now only looks on the world through the sun which they believe to be His eye.

It is to be remembered that for many African peoples, God's active part in human history is seen in terms of His supplying them with rain, good harvest, health, cattle and children; in healing, delivering and helping them; and in terms of making His presence felt through natural phenomena and objects. The people constantly turn to God in various acts of worship which in effect constitute man's response to God's interest and active part in human affairs. They do not sever man from his total environment, so that in effect human history is cosmic history seen anthropocentrically or microcosmically. God is not divorced from this concept of history: it is His universe, He is active in it and apparent silence may be a feature of His divine activity.

6

GOD & NATURE

According to African peoples, man lives in a religious universe, so that natural phenomena and objects are intimately associated with God.[1] They not only originate from Him but also bear witness to Him. Man's understanding of God is strongly coloured by the universe of which man is himself a part. Man sees in the universe not only the imprint but the reflection of God; and whether that image is marred or clearly focused and defined, it is nevertheless an image of God, the only image known in traditional African societies.

[a] *Anthropomorphic attributes of God*
Man, in some ways, considers himself to be the centre of the universe, and this egocentricism makes him interpret that universe both anthropocentrically and anthropomorphically. We have already mentioned that African ontology is firmly anthropocentric; and this makes man look at God and nature from the point of his relationship with them. We find, therefore, many expressions which attribute human nature to God. We shall refer to these as anthropomorphisms. How much African peoples take these anthropomorphisms literally is hard to tell; but at least they are an aid to people's conceptualization of God Whom they have not seen and about Whom they confess to know little or nothing.

Many visualize God as Father, both in terms of His position as the universal Creator and Provider, and in the sense of His personal availability to them in time of need. The Akamba consider the heavens and the earth to be the Father's 'equal-sized bowls': they are His property both by creation and the rights of ownership; and they contain His belongings. The Lunda, Bemba and others in the same region, speak of God as 'the universal Father' and mankind as His children. The Suk and Baganda hold that God is Father not only to men but also to the divinities and other spiritual beings. This idea of God being the Father of creation in general is

[1] For a detailed study, see my larger work, *Concepts of God in Africa* (1969), chapters 8–13.

reported among other African peoples, some of whose only or major personal name for God simply means 'Father'.

The fatherhood of God also comes out in prayers, indicating that people consider Him to be their personal Father with Whom they can communi-cate. So, in prayers and invocations, He is addressed as 'Father', 'our Father', 'my Father', 'Great Father', 'Father God' or 'Father of our/my fathers', by peoples like the Bambuti, Azande, Nuer, Gikuyu and others. The sense of God's fatherhood is needed and experienced most in times of need, such as danger, despair, sickness, sorrow, drought or calamity.

Some of the matriarchal societies, like the Ovambo and southern Nuba, conceive or speak of God as 'Mother', which conveys the same attributes as those who consider Him as 'Father'. The image of Mother also carries with it the idea of cherishing and nursing, and it is used even in patriarchal societies. We cannot draw conclusions, therefore, that the image of God as Father is confined to patriarchal societies, and that His image as Mother is confined only to matriarchal societies. In both cases, these images are used figuratively, to convey the idea of God originating all things, and caring for all things (particularly mankind). For that reason, many peoples like the Bachwa, Bemba, Lugbara, Nuer and others, refer to human beings (or a special group of them) as 'the children of God', or 'sons of God', or 'people of God'.

Bodily parts and activities are attributed to God by a few societies, while the rest emphasize that they do not know what God looks like. Some, like the Akan, Galla, Nandi and Ovambo, say that God has eyes, which are thought to be the sun, moon or firmament. Many think that God hears their prayers and what goes on; but only in one case, that of the Ila, is God actually said to have ears as such. The Bambuti and Jumjum picture God as having a long beard. Apart from these few examples, African peoples do not attribute a body to God.

Of bodily activities, however, we have more examples. In a liturgical context, sacrifices and offerings to God are meant for Him to 'eat' or 'drink', but people understand this in a metaphorical sense. We have already seen that God is thought to 'see' and 'hear' everything, this being a vivid way of expressing God's omniscience. As the Bambuti burn incense to God, they obviously believe that He 'smells' it, at least metaphorically. When there is thunder the Zulu take it to mean that God is playing merrily; and the Gikuyu think that it is the cracking of His joints as He goes by. Earthquakes are interpreted by peoples like the Bambuti and Shona to mean that God is taking a walk. Some, like the Shona, say that He sleeps among the clouds. A few believe that God gets angry and punishes people; and the apparent separation of God from men is generally attributed to His being grieved by human deeds.

Some of these anthropomorphisms may be literal but most of them seem metaphorical, poetical and liturgical. When people use them, they may not always draw these distinctions. It is to be noted also that ultimately every⁄ thing we say about God is in one way or another anthropomorphic, since it is expressed in human terms and human thought forms. Man does not know the language by which God describes Himself. Whatever mental picture we make of God, it is at best a human image.

[b] *God, Animals and Plants*

Animals and plants constitute human food, and their importance is obviously great. African peoples have many religious associations with them, some of which are linked with concepts of God. There are myths which tell how domestic animals originated at the same time or in the same way as man himself. Thus, the Zulu narrate that both men and cattle sprang from the same spot, and God instructed men saying, 'Let them be your food; eat their flesh and their milk!' If lightning strikes cattle, people say that God has slaughtered for Himself from among His own food, and this is taken to be a blessing upon the village where it occurs.[1] The Akamba hold that cattle, sheep and goats accompanied the first human beings whom God lowered from the sky. The Maasai firmly believe that since God gave them cattle from the very beginning, nobody else has the right to own cattle. As such, it is their duty to raid cattle from neighbouring peoples, without feeling that they are committing theft or robbery. In one myth, the Nuer narrate that once God offered men a choice between cattle and rifles. The Europeans and Arabs chose rifles, but the Nuer and Dinka chose cattle.

Cattle, sheep and goats are used for sacrificial and other religious purposes, and examples of this are found all over the continent. Many peoples have a sacred attitude towards their animals. For example, the Herero regard all cattle as sacred, and as having originated from their mythical 'tree of life', from where human and other life comes. They eat them only when sacrificed in religious ceremonies. For the Dinka, every bull or ox is ultimately destined for sacrifice. They believe that cattle and children belong to God, and that He gives them to men only as gifts from Him. Every day the Nandi pray to God for the safety and prosperity of their cattle.

Although we still have many wild animals in Africa, there is little information about their religious significance. Fierce animals, like the buffalo and lion, are associated with God, by the Langi and Turu, who consider them to be God's manifestation in His immanent aspect. A number

[1] Callaway, pp. 41, 53, 57, 60, 90.

of peoples (like the Fajulu, Nuer and Madi) along the Nile valley, blame the hyaena for having cut off the cow-skin rope which once joined the earth to heaven, thus causing a separation between the two worlds. The rock hyrax is used by the Akamba and Bakwena in praying for rain.

Creeping animals feature in religious concepts more than do other wild animals. The snake is thought by some peoples, like the Vugusu and Sidamo, to be immortal. Others have sacred snakes, especially pythons, which may not be killed by people. A considerable number of societies associate snakes with the living-dead or other human spirits, and such snakes are given food and drink when they visit people's homes. In many myths, the lizard is featured as the messenger who brought news from God that men should die. The chameleon, on the other hand, is featured as the messenger who should have brought news of immortality or resurrection, but either lingered on the way, or altered the message slightly or stammered in delivering it. Meanwhile the lizard (or other animal) arrived on the scene and delivered the tragic news.

Of the birds, chickens are used in most societies for religious purposes, chiefly as sacrifices, either to God or lower spiritual beings and the living-dead. The spider, though a small creature, appears in many myths and stories. Among the Akan and Ashanti, the spider symbolizes 'wisdom'; and for that reason, God is given the title of *Ananse Kokroko* which means 'the Great Spider, that is, the Wise One'.[1]

Mythical trees feature in a number of stories. For example, the Herero speak of their 'tree of life' said to be located in the netherworld and believed to be the source from which all life emanates. Some, like the Nuer and Sandawe, hold that men originated from a tree. Others narrate about 'the forbidden tree' whose fruit God forbade the early men to eat. When men broke that law and ate the forbidden fruit, death came into the world and God withdrew Himself from men. This myth, in one form or another, is told among the Bambuti, Chagga and Meru. The (wild) fig-tree is considered sacred by many societies all over Africa, and people make offerings, sacrifices and prayers around or under it. There are sacred groves and other trees, including the sycamore and the baobab, used for religious purposes or associated with God and other spiritual beings. Some societies, like the Maasai, Meru and Mao, use grass in performing rituals, saying prayers and making offerings to God.

[c] *God, natural objects and phenomena*

Many concepts are reported which associate God with natural objects and phenomena. We have already mentioned that African peoples regard this

---

[1] Busia in Forde, p. 192.

as a religious universe, and this attitude is fully illustrated by the way they 'read' God into various objects and phenomena. We shall consider first the heavenly group and then the earthly set.

It is generally assumed that God created the heaven as He created the earth. Heaven is the counterpart of the earth, and it is considered by African peoples to be the dwelling place of God. There are stories told all over Africa, of how originally heaven and earth were either close together or joined by a rope or bridge, and how God was close to men. These myths go on to explain how the separation came about; but we shall return to a discussion of some of them in chapter nine below.

As far as written sources available are concerned, all African peoples associate God with the sky or heaven, in one way or another. There are those who say that He reigns there; the majority think that He lives there; and some even identify Him with the sky, or consider it to be His chief manifestation. We have many peoples whose names for God mean sky, heaven, or the above. For example the Bari and Fajulu term for God is *Ngun lo ki* which means 'God in the sky (above)'; the Shona name *Nyadenga* means 'the Great One of the sky', and *Wokumusoro* means 'the One above'; the Tiv name, *Aondo,* means 'Heavens, sky'; and the Turkana word for God, *Akuj* , means '(of) Up, above'. Thus, God cannot be separated from heaven, and heaven cannot be separated from God; the object points to its Creator, and thoughts about the Creator point towards the heavens and the sky.

The sun, moon and stars feature in myths and beliefs of many peoples. The Zulu narrate that when God had created men, He gave them the sun and moon to be their light, so that they could see. The Balese regard the sun to be God's right eye, and the moon His left eye. Among the Kiga, God is the One Who causes the sun to set. For the Ila, the sun signifies God's eternity, and they describe Him as 'He of the suns (or days)'.

Among many societies, the sun is considered to be a manifestation of God Himself, and the same word, or its cognate, is used for both. Examples of this may be cited from among the Chagga (*Ruwa* for both God and sun), peoples of the Ashanti hinterland (*We* for both), Luo (*Chieng* for both), Nandi (*Asis* for God, *asista* for sun) and Ankore (*Kazooba* for both). Among others, like the Azande, Haya, Igbo and Meban, the sun is personified as a divinity or spirit, and thought by some to be one of God's sons. There is no concrete indication that the sun is considered to be God, or God considered to be the sun, however closely these may be associated. At best the sun symbolizes aspects of God, such as His omniscience, His power, His everlasting endurance, and even His nature.

Similar concepts exist concerning the moon, though on the whole there are fewer associations with God than is the case of the sun. I have no evidence of names for God being the same as for the moon. Among peoples like the Akan, Bambuti, Dorobo, Luo and Sandawe, the moon is personi-fied as a female divinity, or a companion of God, or the mother (or sister) of the sun, or simply as a spirit. The Zulu think that it has two wives—the morning and evening 'stars' (Venus at different positions). The 'morning star' feeds it (him) well, so that it grows bigger; but the 'evening star' feeds it poorly so that it grows thinner. To the Balese, the moon is God's left eye; and the Nuer believe that God shines through or in the moon. A number of societies, like the Banyoro, Bushmen, Katab and Kagoro, hold religious ceremonies monthly, especially when a new moon appears.

About stars, comets and meteors there is little available information. A few societies personify them as spirits; some, like the Azande, Bambuti and Chagga consider them to be God's children; and others, like the Bavenda, Gikuyu and Shona take them as God's manifestations. The position of the Pleiades is interpreted by the Akamba as an indication of when and how much the rains will come in a given season.

Rain is regarded by African peoples to be one of the greatest blessings of God. For that reason, He is commonly referred to as 'the Rain Giver'. Some peoples, like the Elgeyo, Igbo, Suk, Tonga and others personify rain as a divinity, a supernatural being, or a son of God. Others associate God with rain so closely that the same word (or its cognate) is used for both. For example, the Didinga name for God is *Tamukujen* and for rain *tamu*; the Idoma use *Owo* for both; the Maasai word *En-kai* is used for both God and rain (or sky); and some of the Suk have *Ilat* for both. The Ila and Nuer speak of God as 'falling in the rain', yet clearly distinguishing between Him and the rain. Others like the Akamba and Tiv, consider rain to be the saliva of God, this being a symbol of great blessing. Many societies make sacrifices, offerings and prayers to God in connection with rain, especially during periods of drought. Rainmakers are reported in all parts of the continent, their duties being to solicit God's help in providing rain, or in halting it if too much falls.

Thunder is taken by many, such as the Bambuti, Bavenda, Ewe and Ila, to be God's voice. Others like the Gikuyu and Zulu interpret it to be the movement of God; and some, like the Yoruba and Tiv, regard thunder as an indication of God's anger. Thunder is personified as a divinity, rooster, bird or other creature, by some including the Abaluyia, Banyoro, Basoga, Tonga and Yoruba. Concepts about lightning are similar to those held about thunder, since these two phenomena are closely associated. The Gikuyu take lightning to be God's weapon by means of which He clears the way when moving from one sacred place to another; the Nuer and

Shona believe that God is revealed or manifested in lightning. A good number of peoples, like the Bachwa, Bambuti, Ila, Langi, Zulu and others, look upon lightning as God's instrument by means of which He punishes wrong doers or accomplishes His intentions. There are those who, including the Bambuti, Banyarwanda, Igbo and Yoruba, personify lightning as a divinity or other living creature.

In a few cases the wind is associated with God. Some peoples describe Him metaphorically as being like the wind or air, or moving like the wind; and others think that the wind is one of the vehicles by which God travels in great power through the sky. Storms are considered by the Shona, Tonga and Zulu to be God's manifestations; and by the Watumbatu to be indications of His anger. The Bambuti who fear storms very much, think that they are used by God to punish wicked talk and actions. So also the Tswana interpret hail as God's punishment for departure from established usage.

Like the heavens, the earth has many natural objects and phenomena, and various concepts associate them with God or give them other religious meaning. The heaven and the earth are depicted as the first things that God created. Among several societies it is held that long ago, the earth and heaven were united by a rope or bridge which, however, got broken and the two parts of the universe separated. Some peoples, like the Haya, Igbo, Itsekiri and others, are reported to have a divinity or spirit of the earth, which is probably a personification.

Earthquakes occur fairly frequently in and around the region of the Great Rift Valley in eastern-central Africa. The Shona think that earthquakes are caused by God walking in them; the Basoga, Kiga and Ankore believe that there are earthquake divinities responsible for causing the earth to tremble.

Myths occur in different parts of the continent, like the Niger, Zambezi and Congo drainage basins, telling of great floods in the primeval days, which caused destruction of mankind and animals. No doubt the annual flooding of these great rivers has in the past caused much damage to human life and property, as well as to animals of the forest. Such damage has been incorporated into the mythology of the peoples concerned, and has survived through the centuries. In some areas, people personify rivers and streams, or attribute divinities or major spirits to them. This is reported among the Acholi, Baganda, Langi and Yoruba. Oceans, seas, lakes and permanent ponds are often thought to be inhabited by spirits or divinities who generally have to be propitiated when people are using the water in one way or another. Examples of this are reported in all parts of Africa, and we take only a few to illustrate the point. The Banyoro make offerings to the spirit of Lake

Albert, when a person wants to cross it in a canoe. The Baganda have *Mukasa* as the divinity of the seas and lakes, and he holds a high position in the hierarchy of the national divinities. The Haya recognize a spirit of Lake Victoria; and the Yoruba have a divinity of the sea (known as *Olokun*).

Some peoples, like the Lugbara and Langi, hold that rocks are a manifestation of God. The Luvedu claim that God left His footprints on certain rocks which are still soft and can be seen; and in one version of the creation of man, the Akamba tell that the first men were brought by God out of a rock which can still be seen today. A number of peoples like the Banyarwanda, Bari, Bavenda, Ingassana, Madi and Sonjo, are reported to have sacred stones and rocks, which are used for religious rites and observances. Sacred stones are often employed in rainmaking ceremonies. Many consider rocks and boulders to be the dwelling places of the spirits, the departed or the livingdead. Clay is said by the Bambuti, Shilluk, Barundi, Banyarwanda and Yoruba, to be or to have been used by God to form human beings.

Outstanding mountains and hills are generally regarded as sacred, and are given religious meaning. Information about this comes from many parts of the continent, and it will suffice to illustrate it by a few examples. The Bavenda and Shona consider the Matoba (or Matopo) mountains to be the place of God's special manifestation. Five high mountains, including Mount Kenya, visible from Gikuyu country, are believed to be sacred and to be the dwelling places of God when He visits the earth. The Gikuyu make prayers facing Mount Kenya, the chief of their sacred mountains. The Langi connect God with all hills, and these must be avoided; but Mount Agoro is the one used for pilgrimage. The Sonjo have Mogongo jo Mugwe, the Mountain of God, where their national founder and religious leader partly dwells.

Mountains, hills and other high standing earth formations, are in no way thought to be God: they simply give a concrete manifestation of His being and His presence. Furthermore, they are physically 'closer' to the sky than ordinary ground, and in that sense it is easy to associate them with God. They are on earth what the sun and, to a less extent, the moon and stars are in heaven. They are points of contact, drawing together, not only people in a given region, but also men, spiritual beings and God. Among many societies, mountains and hills are associated with spirits or divinities. Thus, for example, the Akamba say that they see fires of the spirits at night on the sides of some hills; the Alur believe that spirits are seen on mountains; and the Ga and Tumbuka have divinities of the hills.

Certain caves and holes are given religious meaning. In many societies, like the Akamba, Basuto, Ewe, Yao and others, it is told that God brought the first men out of a hole or cave. The Shona have their famous sacred caves from which God is supposed to speak. One Gisu legend tells that once God lived in a deep hole on Mount Elgon which is volcanic

A number of peoples keep or use a 'holy' fire for religious purposes. The Herero have sacred fires on the village altars, with which the whole welfare of the people is intimately connected. They mention God as being responsible for this fire, which symbolizes national life, prosperity and contact with the unseen world. The Gikuyu perform a ceremony of purifying the crops when they begin to bear. Part of this ceremony involves lighting the holy fire and carrying it to all the regions. People look upon it as a 'purifying flame', and eagerly wait to catch it with twigs, in order to take it to their homes where the old fires have been put out. The new fire is not allowed to die out until the next season when the cremony is repeated. This fire symbolizes the process of death and resurrection, and the conquest of renewal over destruction and degeneration. Probably the observance of this deeply meaningful ceremony has virtually died out today. The Nandi harvest ceremony also involves lighting a sacred fire and offering prayers to God for the welfare of both people and cattle.

Different religious meanings and uses are given to various colours. A number of peoples regard *black* as their sacred colour. Among the Bavenda, Luo, Nandi, Ndebele and Shona, black animals are sacrificed to God or used in religious ceremonies. On the other hand, the Abaluyia, Baganda, Watumbatu and Gofa use only *white* animals or birds for their religious rites, this being their sacred colour. We have little information on other colours.

Numbers, like colours, have religious meanings attributed to them. Our information on this aspect of African concepts is very little, and only a few concrete examples can be cited. The number 'four' seems to be sacred or special among the Nandi; number 'six' is sacred to the Shona and Jie who sacrifice six cattle or oxen to God. Both the Akamba and Vugusu have taboos attached to number 'seven', which the Akamba refer to as 'the seven of dogs'. The number 'nine' is sacred to the Baganda, and all their gifts, offerings, sacrifices and sacred vessels must number 'nine' (or its multiples). Counting people and livestock is forbidden in many African societies, partly for fear that misfortune would befall those who are numbered, and partly, perhaps, because people are not individuals but corporate members of society which cannot be defined numerically.

It emerges clearly that for African peoples, this is a religious universe. Nature in the broadest sense of the word is not an empty impersonal object or phenomenon: it is filled with religious significance. Man gives life even where natural objects and phenomena have no biological life. God is seen in and behind these objects and phenomena: they are His creation, they manifest Him, they symbolize His being and presence. The invisible world is symbolized or manifested by these visible and concrete phenomena and objects of nature. The invisible world presses hard upon the visible: one speaks of the other, and African peoples 'see' that invisible universe when they look at, hear or feel the visible and tangible world. This is one of the most fundamental religious heritages of African peoples. It is unfortunate that foreign writers, through great ignorance, have failed to understand this deep religious insight of our peoples; and have often either ridiculed it, or naively presented it as 'nature worship' or 'animism'. Traditional African societies have been neither deaf nor blind to the spiritual dimension of existence, which is so deep, so rich and so beautiful.

The physical and spiritual are but two dimensions of one and the same universe. These dimensions dovetail into each other to the extent that at times and in places one is apparently more real than, but not exclusive of, the other. To African peoples this religious universe is not an academic proposition: it is an empirical experience, which reaches its height in acts of worship. And to these we shall now proceed.

7

THE WORSHIP
OF GOD

In many and various ways, African peoples respond to their spiritual
world of which they are sharply aware. This response generally takes on the
form of worship which is eternalized in different acts and sayings. These
acts may be formal or informal, regular or extempore, communal or
individual, ritual or unceremonial, through word or deed. They vary from
one society to another, and from one area to another. It is reported, for
example, that peoples like the Dinka and Nuer spend nearly all their
waking time in acts of worship; while, at the other extreme, there are
societies reported to have only a few and occasional acts of worship. The
majority of Africans fall within these two positions, their worship being
regulated by both immediate needs and inherited practice. Worship is
'uttered' rather than meditational, in the sense that it is expressed in external
forms, the body 'speaking' both for itself and the spirit. What, when, how
and where are these acts of worshipping God? This chapter is concerned
with answering these questions.[1]

[a] *Sacrifices and offerings*
Sacrifices and offerings constitute one of the commonest acts of worship
among African peoples; and examples of them are overwhelmingly many.
Since these two terms are often used loosely, I shall try to draw a distinction
in this book. 'Sacrifices' refer to cases where animal life is destroyed in order
to present the animal, in part or in whole, to God, supernatural beings,
spirits or the living-dead. 'Offerings' refer to the remaining cases which do
not involve the killing of an animal, being chiefly the presentation of
foodstuffs and other items. In some cases, sacrifices and offerings are
directed to one or more of the following: God, spirits and living-dead.
Recipients in the second and third categories are regarded as intermediaries
between God and men, so that God is the ultimate Recipient whether or
not the worshippers are aware of that.

[1] A fuller account is to be found in my book *Concepts of God in Africa* (1969),
chapters 16–20.

Four main theories have been advanced to explain the function and meaning of sacrifices and offerings. They are the gift theory, the propitiation theory, the communion theory and the thank-offering theory. It is not our concern to debate these theories here, except to add that some of the ideas are probably present in the mind of African peoples when making sacrifices, but none of the theories would explain away these acts of worship. One may add that an ontological balance must be maintained between God and man, the spirits and man, the departed and the living. When this balance is upset, people experience misfortunes and sufferings, or fear that these will strike them. The making of sacrifices and offerings on the other hand, is also a psychological device to restore this ontological balance. It is also an act and occasion of making and renewing contact between God and man, the spirits and man, i.e. the spiritual and the physical worlds. When these acts are directed towards the living-dead, they are a symbol of fellowship, a recognition that the departed are still members of their human families, and tokens of respect and remembrance for the living-dead. Households and family groups, on the whole, direct their sacrifices and offerings to the living-dead; but larger communities direct theirs to God alone or through national or regional spirits (or divinities). Yet, the practice of making sacrifices and offerings varies so widely that we must be cautious and not push generalizations too far.

Concrete examples from different parts of Africa will illustrate these points more clearly. The Abaluyia believe that God is 'the One to Whom sacred rites and sacrifices are made or paid'. They have formal occasions when they make sacrifices to Him, including the time of birth, naming and circumcising a person, as well as at weddings, funerals and harvest time. They pray to God when making sacrifices; and at funerals, the prayers are intended to secure peace for the living-dead; while at harvest time they express joy and gratitude to God. The Akamba and Gikuyu also make sacrifices on great occasions, such as at the rites of passage, planting time, before crops ripen, at the harvest of the first fruits, at the ceremony of purifying a village after an epidemic, and most of all when the rains fail or delay. The Gikuyu generally use sheep of a particular colour; but the Akamba use oxen, sheep or goats of one colour, and in case of a severe drought they formerly sacrificed a child which they buried alive in a shrine.

The Akan and Ashanti have altars in their homesteads at which they make offerings of food, especially eggs, and wine. These are made to God, with prayers for the wellbeing of the people. The Bachwa and Bambuti Pygmies who depend on fruit gathering and hunting for their sustenance, are very careful to give portions of their animal meat, fruit and honey to God, believing that if they fail to do so, a person will fall sick or never kill any more animals. On becoming pregnant, a Bachwa woman cooks food and takes portions of it to the forest where she offers them to God, saying: 'God, from Whom I have received this child, take Thou and eat!'

The Barotse make daily offerings to God by placing a wooden plate full of water in the cattle shed every morning. This is carried out by the oldest member of the household, who kneels down facing east and then makes a salutation invocation. The Chagga, on the other hand, are reported to sacrifice to God only in times of great distress and at rare intervals. They make many sacrifices, however, to spirits and the living-dead. Similarly the Barundi make sacrifices to their hero spirit (*Kiranga*) who acts as the inter-mediary between them and God. If *Kiranga* fails, then they turn directly to God. The Ankore think that God does not expect any sacrifices, so they do not make them to Him. Instead, they give offerings to the spirits and the living-dead. The Baganda also direct their sacrifices and offerings to the divinities, spirits and living-dead.

The Ila have several occasions when they make sacrifices and offerings to God. Hunters do so when they have no success in hunting, as well as when they have killed an animal. Travellers do so when they come to a river, by taking some of the water, squirting on the ground and offering the water to God with a prayer that He would lead, shepherd and prosper them. When a man is smoking his pipe in the morning he offers some of the smoke to God by blowing it and thanking Him for raising him in health that day, and asking Him to give him a prosperous day. During a serious illness, the head of the family offers food and water which he places on the right threshold of the house, praying God to heal the sick.

It is reported that the Yoruba make many types of sacrifices and offerings, which constitute 'the essence of Yoruba religion'.[1] Almost all types of foods and drinks and living things are used for this purpose. As the Yoruba excel in the number of divinities which they recognize, it is these divinities who are the recipients, though in practice the worshippers are the ones who eat what has been given. In order to invoke special blessings, human beings were formerly sacrificed, and this may not even have died out altogether. Meal and drink offerings are made daily at the shrines; gift offerings are made to the divinities in appreciation for success, health and children; and propitiation offerings and sacrifices are made during drought, famine or serious illness. The people also make 'substitutionary' sacrifices and offerings when it is required to alter an agreement; while others are made to ward off attacks, evil or misfortunes or to appease the spirit of the earth. Every fortnight Yoruba blacksmiths sacrifice dogs to *Ogun* the divinity of iron and war.

[1] Idowu, 118-25, for a fuller account.

The Dinka regard every event or occasion as suitable for sacrifices; and for them 'every bull or ox is destined ultimately for sacrifice. . . . Animal sacrifice is the central religious act of the Dinka, whose cattle are in their eyes perfect victims'. As they give personal names to the cattle, before one is killed they announce to it 'the important and necessary purpose for which it is victimized', and compensate it for its death 'by naming the next child after it', thus 'preserving its memory'.[1] Since cattle are as valuable as human beings, sacrificing them to God is as serious and purposeful as sacrificing a person. To the Dinka sacrifices are the perpetual link between the plane of men and the plane of God.

The Nuer are also reported to have many occasions when they sacrifice to God. Cattle are the usual animals for this purpose, and on important occasions the people make long invocations. When a person is on a journey he knots grasses together at the side of the path and prays to God.

These are sufficient examples to illustrate how African peoples respond to the spiritual world through sacrifices and offerings. The items for sacrifices include cattle, sheep, goats, chickens, dogs and even human beings. Items used for offerings include foodstuffs like fruits, maize, millet, nuts, cassava, vegetables, leaves, honey and eggs; beverages like porridge, milk, beer, wine and water; and other things of a miscellaneous nature like the dung of the hyrax, cloth, money, chalk, incense, agricultural implements, ornaments, tobacco and cowrie-shells. Blood is also offered by a number of societies. Thus, almost everything that man can get hold of and use is sacrificed or offered to God and other spiritual beings, by one people or another. As a rule, there are no sacrifices without prayers: sacrifices and offerings are the silent responses, prayers are the verbal responses, and to the latter we shall now proceed.

[b] *Prayers, invocations, blessings and salutations*
Praying may or may not always be accompanied by sacrifices and offerings. It is the commonest act of worship, and most African prayers are short, extempore and to the point, though there are also examples of long and formal prayers. The majority of prayers and invocations are addressed to God, and some to the living-dead or other spiritual beings many of whom serve as intermediaries. Praying is reported among practically all African peoples though the actual prayers have not often been recorded in our written sources. We shall take a few examples from different parts of the continent, to illustrate the concepts and contents of African prayers.

When Abaluyia old men rise up in the morning, they kneel facing east and pray to God, spitting and asking Him to let the day dawn well, to

[1] Lienhardt, pp. 10, 21 f.

pour upon the people His medicine of health, and to drive away the evil divinity. Another common prayer used by old men runs (in part) as follows:

> *Oh God, give me mercy upon our children who are suffering;*
> *Bring riches today as the sun rises;*
> *Bring all fortunes to me today!*[1]

The Bachwa Pygmies pray when there is sickness, and before undertaking a journey or going to hunt, asking God to heal the sick, prosper the traveller and give game to the hunter. The Bambuti Pygmies also pray in difficulties, especially when there is a thunderstorm of which they are terrified. Prayer in the event of a thunderstorm goes like this:

> *Grandfather, Great Father, let matters go well with me, for I am going into the forest;*

or, if they are already in the forest when it arises:

> *Father, Thy children are afraid; and behold, we shall die!*[2]

They burn incense at the same time, and believe that God hears their prayer, stretches out His hand and the storm flees away. They also pray before going to gather food and to hunt, so that God may help them find fruit or game; and barren women pray to Him to bless them with children.

It is reported that the Galla make frequent prayers and invocations to God. They pray in the morning and evening every day, asking Him to protect them, their cattle, their crops and their families. One such prayer says:

> *O God, Thou hast given me a good day,*
> *Give me a good night;*
> *Thou hast given me a good night,*
> *Give me a good day!*[3]

It is also customary among the Barotse to pray every day, which old men do, rising up early in the morning and making an offering of water to God. They address God as the great King to Whom no man can be compared, and Who shows compassion and innumerable favours to His servants.

The Ila are said to pray in special need, soliciting God's help. When there is a drought, they come together and join in singing and invoking God saying,

> *Come to us with a continued rain, O God, fall!*

---

[1] S. Yokoo *Death among the Abaluyia*, dissertation (Kampala 1966), p. 66.
[2] Schebesta, II, p. 235.
[3] Huntingford, p. 74 f.

If men are on a hunting expedition and do not kill anything, they sit down round the oldest man in the group who leads them in this prayer:

> *O Mutalabala, Eternal One . . . We pray Thee,*
> *Let us kill today before sunset.*

The rest, falling on the ground respond,

> *O Chief, today let us kill!*

And when they succeed in killing an animal, they cut up pieces of the meat which the oldest man offers to God saying,

> *I thank Thee for the meat which Thou givest me.*
> *Today Thou hast stood by me.*

The others clap their hands, and when the ceremony is over, they divide up the meat among themselves and return home.[1]

Before they start sowing their fields the Lozi assemble at sunrise, under the leadership of their local headman who erects an altar of sticks and clay. A dish is placed on this altar into which every household puts some seeds, hoes and axes. The headman kneels before the altar and, facing east, puts his hands together, bows down, looks up and stretches out his hands. He turns right, then left, and repeatedly stands up and kneels down. The people repeat the same movements. Finally the headman prays on behalf of the community, asking God to bless the people and the agricultural implements, as well as the seeds, so that by His power the people may use them beneficially. The people bow many times and clap their hands. This over, planting may now start. The Lozi also pray before going hunting, after dreaming and in sickness. A sick person observes a whole day of rest from work which he spends praying to God until sunset.

Although the Mende may pray directly to God, they often address their prayers through the intermediaries of the spirits and the living-dead, ending them with the words: 'God willing!' This reflects the structure of their social and political life, in which intermediaries play an important role. The following prayer clearly illustrates this point:

> *O God, let it reach to (through?) Kenei Momo,*
> *Let it reach to (through?) Nduawo,*
> *Let it reach all our forefathers who are in Thy hands.*

Names of the forefathers and living-dead are invoked, the people believing

[1] Smith & Dale, p. 208 f.

that such intermediaries will convey their prayers to God. They pray for blessings, deliverance from trouble and even God's retribution where injustice has been committed.[1]

Every adult Nandi is supposed to recite a common prayer twice a day, and old men are particular in observing it. They sit down with their arms crossed, every morning, and pray:

> *God guard for me the children and the cattle,*
> *God guard for us the cattle,*
> *God give us health!*

During a war, mothers whose sons are fighting, pray for them every morning; and an elder accompanying the soldiers also prays for their safe return home. If the raid is successful, they thank God; but if not, they hold a ceremony of repentance, asking God to forgive them. When there is a drought in the country, they pray for rain and the protection of their pregnant women and cattle.[2]

The Nuer pray often addressing God as 'Grandfather', 'Father', or 'Our Father', and raising their eyes and hands towards heaven. Some of their prayers are said to be quite long, and the person who is praying may walk up and down his cattle kraal brandishing his spear; or may remain sitting or squatting with eyes towards the heavens, and only moving his hands up and down with the palms facing upwards. The prayers are chiefly for deliverance from evil, and request that the people may live in peace. The Nuer hold the attitude that they may pray at any time because 'they like to speak to God when they are happy' and when they go about their daily work. Here is a typical prayer:

> *Our Father, it is Thy universe, it is Thy will, let us be at peace, let the souls of Thy people be cool; Thou art our Father, remove all evil from our path.*[3]

It is said that prayers, like the making of sacrifices and offerings, are at the heart of Yoruba religious life. For that reason, people pray at any time and at any place, even when they are on the way to the shrines. Some of them go to the shrines to pray every morning before they speak to anyone else. The prayers are for material blessings and protection against sickness and death, or for victory over enemies and longevity of life.[4]

From these and similar examples, it is evident that African peoples communicate with God through prayer, pouring out their hearts before

[1] Harris in Smith, p. 281 f.; Little, p. 218.
[2] Hollis, A. C., *The Nandi* (1909), p. 41 f.; Huntingford, I, pp. 135, 144 f., 153.
[3] Evans-Pritchard, II, p. 7, 9, 22 f.
[4] Idowu, 111–18 for a fuller account.

Him, at any time and in any place. The prayers are chiefly requests for material welfare, such as health, protection from danger, prosperity and even riches. Some prayers express gratitude to God; and in a few cases the people dedicate their belongings or activities to Him. Although most prayers are addressed directly to God, there are societies which offer prayers through the intermediary of the spirits, forefathers and living-dead. On the whole, individuals may pray to God, but it is often the head of the household, or the priest where the need is on a regional or national scale, who prays on behalf of the household or the people. When praying, people assume different positions. Some societies kneel, others stand; some fall down before God, others sit; some cross their arms and others clap their hands. In some societies, people spit—the spittle being a symbol of blessing; in others they raise hands and eyes towards heaven; and in a few cases they face a particular mountain or direction, such as the east.

Invocations are shortened and common versions of prayers. They are reported everywhere, and show a spontaneous response to God, asking Him to intervene for a particular purpose. For example they may be in the form of: 'God, give us rain!'; 'God give you fruit!'; 'Help me O God!'; 'God, pity me!'; or 'Oh, Great God!' Invocations are usually what the individual prays spontaneously and unceremoniously, on the spur of the moment. They show that people consider God to be ever close to them, ready to respond to their need, and not subject to religious formalities.

The pronouncing and requesting of formal blessings play an important role in the social and religious life of African peoples. Formal blessings are another aspect of prayer; but as a rule, the person who pronounces the blessing is older or of a higher status than the one who receives it. It is normally understood that God confers the articulated blessing. The rite is generally simple, but in some societies it may be accompanied with spitting or sprinkling water (or other substance) upon those who are being blessed.

Words used in blessings are very much alike throughout Africa. For example: 'May God go with you!', 'God preserve you and keep you until you see your children's children!', 'May God help you!', 'May God bless you!', 'God give you fruit!' (to a childless woman or couple), 'May God make your feet light!' (i.e. protect and speed you along your journey), 'May God give you a clean face!' (i.e. may you have good fortune) or 'May God make your forehead big!'

There are, in some societies, communal blessings. For example, we have mentioned the case of the Lozi who bring their farm implements and seeds to a ceremony led by their headmen so that these may be blessed before the planting season begins. A number of societies hold harvest ceremonies to ask God's blessings upon the new crop. At the Gisu initiation rite, the priest pronounces God's blessing upon the initiates. The Maasai hold periodic ceremonies for blessing childless women. Personal blessings are requested or given when people are parting from one another, and when parents are about to die; but communal blessings are solicited formally and in times of need.

Salutations, greetings and farewells take on the form of prayer in a number of societies. For example, among the Banyarwanda and Barundi, when two people are parting, one says, 'Go with God!', to which the other responds, 'Stay with God!' If they are sleeping in the same house or compound, one says, 'Pass the night with God!', or 'May you meet with the Kindly-disposed One!', to which the answer is the same. The Banyarwanda have many congratulations for different occasions, and these congratulations incorporate the name of God or His blessings. Thus, if a woman who has been barren for a long time gets a child, people congratulate the couple, saying, 'God has taken you from between the teeth of scorners', or 'God has removed your shame!' On escaping from danger, a person is congratulated: 'God shielded you', or 'He still stands upon you' (meaning that God still keeps the person alive).[1] When two Mende people meet and one asks the other how he is, the reply is: 'No fault with the Chief (God)', meaning that all is well. In bidding farewell to one another they say, 'May God walk you well', or 'God take care of you'.[2] In their greetings the Shilluk say, 'May God guard you!'

[c] *Miscellaneous other acts and expressions of worship*
Among some African peoples it is customary to incorporate God's name into children's names. This is an expression of worship, signifying in some cases that the child has been born in answer to prayer and therefore the parents want to thank God for the child; in other cases it signifies a particular attribute of God which may be suggested by the circumstances surrounding the child's birth; or it may indicate the parents' wish to praise God through the name of their child. These names become life-long testimonies of particular concepts of God which people want to express; and when so used, the concepts are immortalized, made concrete and externalized. This practice is reported among the Azande, Banyarwanda, Barundi and Nuer, and we can illustrate it with examples.

In expressing God's wisdom and power, the Banyarwanda and Barundi name their children *Ntawuyankira* which means 'No one can refuse Him His way', or *Bizimana* which means 'God knows everything'. If it is to

[1] Guillebaud in Smith, p. 189 f.
[2] Harris in Smith, p. 280.

express gratitude they name them *Ndihokubgayo* which means 'I am alive because of Him', or *Ntirandekura* which means 'He has not let me drop yet'. In order to show the parents' trust in God, children may be named *Niyibizi* which means 'He knows all about it', or *Ndayiziga* ('I depend on Him').[1] Such names are additional examples that people are religious beings living in a religious universe.

Proverbs are common ways of expressing religious ideas and feelings. Unfortunately little study of proverbs has been made, and our information on the subject is scanty. It is in proverbs that we find the remains of the oldest forms of African religious and philosophical wisdom. For example, the Barundi warn a proud person, saying, 'The creature is not greater than its Creator'; and as a safeguard against worrying, they say, 'God knows the things of tomorrow'. When a person is in distress, the Banyarwanda comfort him with the words: 'The enemy prepares a grave, but God prepares you a way of escape (little door)'.[2]

God is often worshipped through songs, and African peoples are very fond of singing. Many of the religious gatherings and ceremonies are accompanied by singing which not only helps to pass on religious knowledge from one person or group to another, but helps create and strengthen corporate feeling and solidarity. Some of the songs are used in hushing or pacifying babies, others at ceremonies marking the birth, initiation, marriage or death of a person; hunters like the Ngombe use religious songs acknowledging their dependence upon God or attributing their success to Him. As with proverbs, the collection and study of religious songs is very scanty, and yet this is another rich area where one expects to find repositories of traditional beliefs, ideas, wisdom and feelings. Music, singing and dancing reach deep into the innermost parts of African peoples, and many things come to the surface under musical inspiration which otherwise may not be readily revealed.

These then are some of the ways African peoples worship God. They have no creeds to recite: their creeds are within them, in their blood and in their hearts. Their beliefs about God are expressed through concrete concepts, attitudes and acts of worship. The individual believes what others in his community believe: it is a corporate 'Faith'. And this faith is utilitarian, not purely spiritual, it is practical and not mystical. The people respond to God in and because of particular circumstances, especially in times of need. Then they seek to obtain what He gives, be that material or spiritual; they do not search for Him as the final reward or satisfaction of the human soul or spirit. Augustine's description of man's soul being

[1] Guillebaud in Smith, p. 194 f.
[2] Guillebaud in Smith, p. 194 f.

restless until it finds its rest in God, is something unknown in African traditional religious life.

[d] *Religious intermediaries and specialists*

It is a widespread feeling among many African peoples that man should not, or cannot, approach God alone or directly, but that he must do so through the mediation of special persons or other beings. The reason for this feeling and practice seems to derive mainly from the social and political life of the peoples concerned. For example, it is the custom among some societies for the children to speak to their fathers through their mothers or older brothers and sisters. In others, the subjects approach their chief or king only indirectly through those who are closer to him. This social and political pattern of behaviour is by no means found in all societies, but the concept of intermediaries is found almost everywhere. There are, however, many occasions when individuals or groups approach God directly without the use of intermediaries.

Priests are reported in many societies. As a rule, they are formally trained and commissioned (ordained), they may be male or female, hereditary or otherwise. Their duties include making sacrifices, offerings and prayers, conducting both public and private rites and ceremonies, giving advice, performing judicial or political functions, caring for the temples and shrines where these exist, and above all fulfilling their office as religious inter-mediaries between men and God. We shall return to these personages in a later chapter where a fuller account will be given.

Some societies have seers, 'prophets' and oracles. Little study of these personages has been done. It seems that their main duties are to act as ritual elders, to give advice on religious matters (e.g. when particular ceremonies are to be held), to receive messages from divinities and spirits through possession or dreams and to pass on the information to their communities. Oracles are generally the mouthpieces of divinities and spirits, and tend to be connected with divination. Among the Yoruba, for example, they receive a training of three years, and act also as physicians.

Diviners or medicine-men sometimes have religious functions. For example, the Jie believe that their diviners receive revelations from God. Among the Lugbara it is held that God calls a would-be diviner in her adolescence (mainly women). She wanders about in the woods and after several days, returns with the power to divine. The community then erects a shrine for her, which is referred to as the 'hut of God'; and diviners are called the 'children of God', being regarded as the link between men and God. The Turkana believe that the diviner is God's chief representative, functioning as a doctor, purifier of age-sets, predicting raids and soliciting rain. In time of war, it is the medicine-men who, among the Luo, make sacrifices and prayers to God.

Rainmakers are found in almost every African society, and on the whole they exercise their profession in consultation with God, through prayer, sacrifice and trust. It is generally held that they receive their knowledge and power from God, and some peoples believe that God appears to the rainmakers in dreams. We shall return to these and other specialists later on.

Not all African peoples have or had traditional rulers, but where kings and chiefs existed, their office is usually regarded as having been divinely instituted or maintained. These kings and chiefs are looked upon both as political heads and sacred personages who symbolize the prosperity and welfare of their nations. In some societies, kings lead or take part in religious ceremonies; and in any case, the religious life of their people reflects his person and position. Thus, for example, the Bavenda believe that when God is angry with their chief, He punishes the country with drought, locusts or flood. They also hold that God appears near the chief's house, and makes His will known to the chief in a voice of thunder. The Kaonde headman or chief is the one who prays to God on behalf of the people; just as the Lozi headman conducts the ceremony of blessing the seeds and agricultural implements before planting starts. The Shilluk hold that their national founder, *Nyikang,* who was also their first king, is very close to God, and in their prayers they mention both him and God, believing that he will act as the intermediary between them and God.

Elders also have intermediary functions in a number of societies. In addition to performing religious rituals for their homesteads, they may take part in a regional ceremony, either officiating or helping the priests in making sacrifices, offerings and prayers. This latter is generally the case in societies where there are no formal priests, like among the Akamba, Gikuyu, Ila, Nandi and others. Elders are the people with the longest Sasa, whose Sasa extends deepest into the Zamani period and hence they are ontologically 'nearer' to God than are ordinary, and therefore younger, people.

The living-dead occupy the ontological position between the spirits and men, and between God and men. They in effect speak a bilingual language of human beings whom they recently 'left' through physical death, and of the spirits to whom they are now joined, or of God to Whom they are now nearer than when they were in their physical life. Because of this unique position, the living-dead constitute the largest group of intermediaries in African societies. In effect, since everyone through death passes through the stage of being a living-dead, sooner or later everyone functions, individually or corporately, as an intermediary. It is the highest religious moment for everyone; and when that peak is passed, some become ordinary spirits who may or may not continue to function as intermediaries, and a few are elevated to the status of national heroes or even divinities. It is here that we are to understand and appreciate the respect which African peoples accord their departed. The 'cult' connected with the living-dead is deeply rooted in African life and thought. In many societies, the approach to God is regarded as a corporate act of the whole community of both the living and the departed. Normally the living-dead and other departed convey human requests, needs, prayers, sacrifices and offerings to God, and some-times relay His response back to human beings. Thus, there is a constant and heavy traffic from the Sasa into the Zamani. We may take a few examples to show how this concept of the intermediary function of the living-dead and spirits is put into practice.

When someone among the Basuto wants to approach God, he first starts a chain reaction by asking his brother, whether alive or dead, to relay his request to his father. The father in turn approaches his own father, who is supposed to approach his own father, and so on and on. The process goes on until the message reaches someone among the departed, who is sufficiently worthy to approach God. This 'person' finally relays the human request which has travelled through many 'mouths'. The Ngoni confess that they do not know much about God. They approach Him, therefore, through their living-dead and the departed. This they do by reciting the names of those whom they knew, who in turn are expected to intercede with their more remote forefathers, and these do the same until the message finally reaches God. Both the Shona and Bavenda consider the living-dead of the royal families to be the intermediaries between God and the people. The Luo believe that when the living-dead have been properly buried, they pray to God to bless their human families; and the Lotuko say that their living-dead intercede with God for rain. Examples of these practices and beliefs are found in many other societies, indicating the great importance of the living-dead in African religious life.

As for spirits and divinities, there is little information about their inter-mediary functions. In a few cases, it is held that God specifically created the spirits to act as intermediaries between Him and men. One example of this comes from the Ewe. Otherwise we only hear, but without further details, that spirits act as intermediaries, among the Ashanti, Mende, Nandi, Tonga and a few other peoples. It may be, however, that our sources use 'spirits' here where one would prefer to use 'living-dead'. National heroes or founders of the Barundi, Shilluk and Sonjo are said to act as intermediaries between God and the people.

It is rare that one finds mention of animals being considered as inter-mediaries; and from the available information I have only two or three

such reports. The Sidamo regard the hyaenas and serpents to be intermediaries between God and their chief ritual expert; the Turu consider the
python to be in an intermediary position between God and the departed; and
the Igbira believe that animal spirits, together with human spirits, act as
intermediaries between God and people.

As far as our sources of information are concerned, we find no inanimate
things being regarded as intermediaries. One may conclude therefore, that
neither animals nor inanimate objects are considered by African peoples as
intermediaries between God and men. People have a sufficient number of
other intermediaries in the persons of the priests, rainmakers, elders, diviners,
medicine-men, kings, chiefs and the living-dead. Although life is at times
attributed to non-living objects, or personality given to animals, there is a
clear distinction as to who or what is in the position to communicate
between God and men. This is almost a matter of life and death, and
African peoples are not mistaken about the worth of the intermediaries.
It is not surprising, therefore, that no idols have been reported in African
traditional societies—as far as sources available to me are concerned.
Animals, plants, inanimate things and natural phenomena are in an
ontological category which is inferior to that of man, and cannot, therefore,
have the important role of functioning as intermediaries in the status between
two higher modes of existence. In terms of time, man's ontological category
is in a state of motion. In the rhythm of birth, procreation and death, man
is moving 'backwards' along the Zamani dimension of time, 'approaching'
God in a way that neither animals nor natural objects and phenomena are
drawing 'nearer' to Him. This is man's history in rhythm, and in that
rhythm of passing from the Sasa into the Zamani, man must needs go
through the stage of the intermediary, whether individually or, more often,
corporately. Some persons, however, may occupy this position already
while still in their physical life, such as priests, elders and rainmakers. The
position and function of the intermediaries is central in African religious
life: they do not block the way between man and God, but rather they form
bridges. Man's contact with God through acts of worship may, therefore, be
direct or via the intermediaries. It is not the means but the end that matters
most. Sometimes that end is sought or attained, not by the individual alone,
but corporately with or on behalf of his wider community of which he is a
member or whose religious functions are entrusted to him. In reality, religion
is not, and cannot be, a private affair: it must involve two or more parties.

[e] *Occasion and place of worship*
Evidence shows that African peoples worship God at any time and in
any place, and that there are no rules obliging people to worship at a given

time or place. This is a matter of practice and custom, which varies from one people to another.

In some societies, like the Abaluyia, Azande, Galla, Ila, Nandi and Yoruba, it is the custom to pray to God daily or twice daily, generally in the morning or/and evening. There are others like the Abaluyia, Gikuyu, Gisu and Turkana who make sacrifices and prayers at one or more of the rites of birth, initiation, marriage and death. Some, including the Akamba, Gikuyu, Shilluk, Shona and Sonjo, hold worship ceremonies at the harvest festivals, at which they make sacrifices or offerings and prayers to God. Similarly, there are societies, such as the Akamba, Gikuyu, Lozi, Lunda, Nuba and Tikar, who ask God, at planting time, to bless their seeds and work on the fields. Times of national need, such as war, raid, drought, calamity, distress or other disaster, call for turning to God in prayers, invocations, sacrifices and offerings. Examples of this are found everywhere, and generally the communities concerned have public cere‑ monies involving these acts of worship and sometimes lasting for several days. It is to be noted that these major times of distress come constantly, in one or another part of Africa. By getting together as a group to solicit God's help, the people not only strengthen and encourage one another in the face of distress, but they make the burden of suffering lighter to bear.

There are other times when people turn to God in worship. The Pygmies and the Ngombe pray before or during hunting and food gathering; the Ila and Nuer pray and make offerings when on a journey, and the Lotuko make sacrifices and prayers for success in hunting and fishing. Some societies, like the Jie, hold annual ceremonies to bless the cattle and seek God's favour upon them; the Yoruba blacksmiths make fortnightly sacrifices of dogs; some, like the Banyoro, Bushmen, Katab and Nuer, mark the new moon with religious ceremonies in which they ask for God's prosperity. Before the Luo build new houses, they make offerings to God and ask Him to bless the new home; the Ashanti consider Thursday as a sacred day, and they do no work on that day. Religious ceremonies accompany the coronation of kings or chiefs; and unusual phenomena like the birth of twins or eclipses of the sun and moon also call for acts of worship or other religious rites.

On the individual level there is no limit, and many occasions like meal times, waking up in the morning, during illness and barrenness, searching for lost articles or animals and various undertakings, may call for an act of worship. This may take the form of prayer, invocation, libation, placing food on the ground, or making sacrifices and offerings. The act precipitates, among other things, the feeling of fellowship and sharing, not only of the joys of life's experiences but more often its sorrows and perplexities. As far as 'chronological' or mathematical time is concerned, there are no set hours as such: African peoples turn to God at any time and whenever the need arises. Priests, rainmakers and other 'special persons' who function as intermediaries, no doubt turn to God at many more occasions than the common people; and these, being in the intermediary status, keep mankind in constant liturgical contact with God and the spiritual world.

While people do not feel bound to a particular official spot and occasion, there are, however, shrines, temples, altars, groves and other sacred places used particularly for public sacrifices and prayers. Shrines are reported in many societies and vary considerably in appearance and importance. Trees are found at the centre of Akamba and Gikuyu shrines; these trees may not be cut down, and the shrines are regarded as a sanctuary for animals and humans alike, so that none may be killed there. Barundi shrines are under special trees, and when people go to worship they sit down on the leaves of these trees, and then kneel to pray. The shrine may be entered by other people only in the presence or with the permission of the priest of the shrine concerned. Shrines are found all over the land of the Yoruba; and all the Yoruba 1,700 divinities are said to have shrines in people's houses; and some divinities and spirits have additional shrines in the groves. The Yoruba regard shrines as the 'face' of the divinity concerned.

It is difficult to define what a 'temple' is, and this term is used by various writers. We may regard it as a sizeable house or building used for religious purposes and generally cared for by a priest. Temples are reported among the Akan, Baganda, Basoga, Shona, Sonjo, Yoruba and a few other peoples. To a great extent many have now been forsaken and fallen to ruins, though the Sonjo still maintain their temples in good conditions. The national divinities of the Baganda had temples, some with up to four priests each, in addition to mediums and women servants. Few of these now remain.

Altars are sacred spots where offerings and sacrifices may be placed or made. They are generally to be found inside the shrines or temples, though they may be erected in the open. Akan homesteads are said to have altars of three-forked branches or cement pillars bearing a bowl, where offerings are made to God. Similarly, many Igbo households have altars where family offerings are placed; and villages have their public altars where domestic utensils and hunting trophies are offered. Kipsigis altars which are erected on the right side of the door outside every house, are constructed with sticks and used for making offerings and sacrifices to God.

Some societies like the Bavenda, Shona and Butawa, also used caves as places of worship; many, like the Gikuyu and Shona, have sacred mountains; some like the Indem and Ila use crossroads or threshholds of their houses as sacred places where they make their offerings and prayers. Trees like the wild fig-tree, the baobab, the sycamore or the kapok, are 'converted' into shrines for worshipping God when the need arises. Similarly river banks, water-falls, rocks and the Zimbabwe ruins, may be used as sacred places where worship is offered.

We may conclude that there is no limit as to where and when African peoples perform one or more acts of worship. God is omnipresent, and He is 'reachable' at any time and any place. People worship Him where and whenever the 'need' arises. Set times and places are only the result of regular usage: they are not rules regulating worship as such, and do not impose any limit to man's contact with God and the spiritual world. Similarly, intermediaries are an aid and not an absolute necessity to the establishment and maintenance of that contact. Again we see that to African peoples, this is a deeply religious universe whether it is viewed in terms of time or space, and human life is a religious experience of that universe. So, African peoples find or attribute religious meaning to the whole of existence.

8
SPIRITUAL BEINGS, SPIRITS & THE LIVING-DEAD

The spiritual world of African peoples is very densely populated with spiritual beings, spirits and the living-dead. Their insight of spiritual realities, whether absolute or apparent, is extremely sharp. To understand their religious ethos and philosophical perception it is essential to consider their concepts of the spiritual world in addition to concepts of God. We have repeatedly emphasized that the spiritual universe is a unit with the physical, and that these two intermingle and dovetail into each other so much that it is not easy, or even necessary, at times to draw the distinction or separate them. Although the spiritual world plays such an important role in African life, no serious studies have been made on the subject.[1] This is one of the weakest links in the study of African religions and philosophy.

The spirits in general belong to the ontological mode of existence between God and man. Broadly speaking, we can recognize two categories of spiritual beings: those which were created as such, and those which were once human beings. These can also be subdivided into divinities, associates of God, ordinary spirits and the living-dead. Our time analysis is here very useful in helping us to place the spiritual beings in their proper category, and to grasp the logic behind their recognition by African peoples. We can now take a closer look at these beings that populate the spiritual realm.

[a] *Divinities and God's associates*
I am using the word 'divinity' to cover personifications of God's activities and manifestations, of natural phenomena and objects, the so-called 'nature spirits', deified heroes and mythological figures. Sometimes it is difficult to know where to draw the line, especially since different writers loosely speak of 'gods', 'demigods', 'divinities', 'nature spirits', 'ancestral spirits' and the like.

Divinities are on the whole thought to have been created by God, in the

[1] Reference to spirits is found in many of the books listed in the bibliography at the end of this work, but as a rule the subject is given little space.

ontological category of the spirits. They are associated with Him, and often stand for His activities or manifestations either as personifications or as the spiritual beings in charge of these major objects or phenomena of nature. Some of them are national heroes who have been elevated and deified, but this is rare, and when it does happen the heroes become associated with some function or form of nature. Concrete examples will make these points clearer.

It is reported that the Ashanti have a pantheon of divinities through whom God manifests Himself. They are known as *abosom*; are said to 'come from Him' and to act as His servants and intermediaries between Him and other creatures. They are increasing numerically; and people hold festivals for major tribal divinities. Minor divinities protect individual human beings; and it is believed that God purposely created the *abosom* to guard men.[1] Banyoro divinities are departmentalized according to people's activities, experiences and social-political structure. They include the divinities of war, of smallpox, of harvest, of health and healing, of the weather, of the lake, of cattle and minor ones of different clans. The same pattern of divinities is reported among Basoga, Edo and others.

The Yoruba have one thousand and seven hundred divinities (*orisa*), this being obviously the largest collection of divinities in a single African people. These divinities are associated with natural phenomena and objects, as well as with human activities and experiences. They are said to render to God 'annual tributes of their substance in acknowledgment of His Lordship'. Parallel to the Yoruba social-political structure, these divinities form a hierarchy. *Orisa-nla* is 'the supreme divinity' in the country, and acts as God's earthly deputy in creative and executive functions. *Orunmila* is reputed to be an omnilinguist divinity who understands 'every language spoken on earth', and who represents God's omniscience and knowledge. This divinity shows itself among men through the oracle of divination, and has the fame of being a great doctor. *Ogun* is the owner of all iron and steel, being originally a hunter who paved the way for other divinities to come to earth, for which reason they crowned him as 'Chief among the divinities'. He is ubiquitous, and is the divinity of war, hunting and activities or objects connected with iron. *Sango* represents the manifestation of God's wrath, though legend makes him a historical figure in the region of Oyo near Ibadan. He is the divinity of thunder and lightning, and there is a cult for him. These are but a few of the Yoruba divinities, an interesting study of which can be found in Idowu's book.[2]

There are many societies which have only one or two divinities of any

[1] Busia in Forde, p. 191 f.; Lystad, p. 163 f.
[2] Idowu, pp. 55–106.

major status. The Bambuti recognize *Tore* as the divinity in charge of death, to whom they refer as 'the Gate of the Abyss' and 'the Spirit of the dead'.[1] Although the Dinka have several, three are most prominent. These are *Macardit* who is the final explanation of sufferings and misfortunes; *Garang* who is associated with men, and falling from heaven enters their bodies; and *Abuk* who is in charge of women's occupations.[2] The Vugusu blame their experiences of evil and suffering upon an evil divinity (*Wele gumali*) who is said to have servants.[3] The Walamo have one divinity connected with rain, said to dwell on a mountain where people take gifts in time of drought.

Other examples could be cited but these are enough for our purposes here. It is clear that the weather and natural phenomena are generally associated with divinities, or personified as such. Major objects of nature, like the sun, mountains, seas, lakes, rivers and boulders, are also attributed to have or to be spiritual beings or divinities. Examples of this can be quoted from many parts of Africa. In a pre-scientific environment, this form of logic and mentality certainly satisfies and explains many puzzles of nature and human experience. Through the centuries, it has become an institutionalized part of 'looking at the world', so much that it colours the subconscious corporate and individual thinking and attitude of African peoples. Obviously there are local differences, but the pattern is fairly uniform throughout the traditional environment. Such divinities are in effect 'timeless', they have always 'been' there in the eyes of the peoples concerned. In other respects, they are 'closer' to men, than is God, in the sense that they are constantly experienced in the physical life of man as thunder and lightning, rivers or lakes, sun or moon. Little wonder it is then, that men regard some of them as intermediaries, or even have cults for them. In a sense, these divinities are semi-physical and semi-spiritual: men imagine that there is a spiritual being activating what otherwise is obviously physical. Most, if not all, of these attributive divinities are the creation of man's imagination. This does not, however, cancel their reality: the divinities are *real beings* for the peoples concerned. With increasing scientific knowledge, no doubt most of the divinities will be explained away and the major divinity of science will take over.

There is another class of spiritual beings which are associated with God, and which are chiefly mythological in character. The Ashanti consider the earth to be a female divinity second to God, and observe Thursday as her day; the Igbo regard the earth to be God's daughter who protects

[1] Schebesta, II, p. 174 f.
[2] Lienhardt, p. 81 f.
[3] G. Wagner *The Bantu of North Kavirondo* (Vol. I, Oxford 1949), p. 175 f.

people and helps with the crops. The Zulu are reported to have the so-called 'Queen of heaven' who is said to be of great beauty. The rainbow, mist and rain are emanations of her glory, and she is surrounded by light. She is a virgin, and taught women how to make beer, among other useful arts. A number of societies, including the Baganda, Dinka, Suk, Tiv and others, hold that at one time God had children or sons, some of whom were responsible for the founding of the nations or societies concerned. A few peoples say that God had one or more brothers who played a part in the establishment of human society. Some of these spiritual beings are pictured as messengers or servants of God and we have examples of this concept in several parts of Africa.

The Chagga narrate that God has a minister or servant who carries out His instructions. It was this servant who detected when men broke God's commandment forbidding them to eat a special yam, and who reported the matter to Him. Then God sent him back to punish the people, on this and two other occasions when men acted wickedly. It is thought that the same messenger continues to be sent by God to bring sickness, famines, wars, death and children. The Swazi also speak of God's one-legged messenger. Other peoples personify natural objects and phenomena, or describe them mythologically, as God's agents or servants. For example, the Suk consider rain to be God's servant whose duty is to carry water. When this water spills, men experience or see it as rain. The Didinga do not eat fish, believing that they came down to earth in lightning, as God's messengers.

These mythological figures of a spiritual nature are on the whole men's attempts to historicize what is otherwise 'timeless', and what man experiences in another context as divinities. They explain customs, ideas or institutions whose origin is otherwise lost to historical sight, in the oblivion of the Zamani period. The explanation is an unconscious attempt to bring into the Sasa a phenomenon which is either difficult to grasp or shrouded with the mystery which covers it as it sinks deeper and deeper into the Zamani reality.

[b] *Spirits*

Myriads of spirits are reported from every African people, but they defy description almost as much as they defy the scientist's test tubes in the laboratory. Written sources are equally confusing. We have tried to include under the term 'divinity', those spiritual beings of a relatively high status. If we pursue the hierarchical consideration, we can say that the spirits are the 'common' spiritual beings beneath the status of divinities, and above the status of men. They are the 'common populace' of spiritual beings.

As for the origin of spirits, there is no clear information what African peoples say or think about it. Some spirits are considered to have been created as a 'race' by themselves. These, like other living creatures, have continued to reproduce themselves and add to their numbers. Most peoples, however, seem to believe that the spirits are what remains of human beings when they die physically. This then becomes the ultimate status of men, the point of change or development beyond which men cannot go apart from a few national heroes who might become deified. Spirits are the destiny of man, and beyond them is God. Societies that recognize divinities regard them as a further group in the ontological hierarchy between spirits and God. Man does not, and need not, hope to become a spirit: he is inevitably to become one, just as a child will automatically grow to become an adult, under normal circumstances. A few societies have an additional source of the spirits, believing that animals also have spirits which continue to live in the spirit world together with human and other spirits.

Spirits are invisible, but may make themselves visible to human beings. In reality, however, they have sunk beyond the horizon of the Zamani period, so that human beings do not see them either physically or mentally. Memory of them has slipped off. They are 'seen' in the corporate belief in their existence. Yet, people experience their activities, and many folk stories tell of spirits described in human form, activities and personalities, even if an element of exaggeration is an essential part of that description. Because they are invisible, they are thought to be ubiquitous, so that a person is never sure where they are or are not.

Since the spirits have sunk into the horizon of the Zamani, they are within the state of collective immortality, relative to man's position. They have no family or personal ties with human beings, and are no longer the living-dead. As such, people fear them, although intrinsically the spirits are neither evil nor good. They have lost their human names, as far as men are concerned—i.e. those that once were human beings. To men, therefore, the spirits are strangers, foreigners, outsiders, and in the category of 'things'. They are often referred to as 'ITs'. Viewed anthropocentrically, the onto-logical mode of the spirits is a depersonalization and not a completion or maturation of the individual. Therefore, death is a loss, and the spirit mode of existence means the withering of the individual, so that his personality evaporates, his name disappears and he becomes less and not more of a person: a thing, a spirit and not a man any more.

Spirits as a group have more power than men, just as in a physical sense the lions do. Yet, in some ways men are better off, and the right human specialists can manipulate or control the spirits as they wish. Men paradoxi-cally may fear, or dread, the spirits and yet they can drive the same spirits away or use them to human advantage. In some societies only the major spirits (presumably in the category of divinities) are recognized, and often these are associated with natural phenomena or objects.

Although the spirits are ubiquitous, men designate different regions as their places of abode. Among some societies like the Abaluyia, Banyar, wanda and Igbo, it is thought that the spirits dwell in the underground, netherworld or the subterranean regions. The Banyarwanda say, for example, that this region is ruled by 'the one with whom one is forgotten'; and the Igbo consider it to be ruled by a queen. The idea of the subterranean regions is suggested, obviously, by the fact that the bodies of the dead are buried and the ground points to, or symbolizes, the new homeland of the departed. A few societies like some Ewe, some Bushmen and the Mamvu, Mangutu, situate the land of the spirits above the earth, in the air, the sun, moon or stars.

The majority of peoples hold that the spirits dwell in the woods, bush, forest, rivers, mountains or just around the villages. Thus, the spirits are in the same geographical region as men. This is partly the result of human self-protection and partly because man may not want to imagine himself in an entirely strange environment when he becomes a spirit. There is a sense in which man is too anthropocentric to get away from himself and his natural, social, political and economic surroundings. This then makes the spirits men's contemporaries: they are ever with men, and man would feel uncomfortable if the ontological mode of the spirits were too distant from his own. This would mean upsetting the balance of existence, and if that balance is upset, then men make sacrifices, offerings and prayers, to try and restore it. In effect, men visualize their next ontological stage, in form of spirits, but geographically it is not another stage. The world of the spirits, wherever it might be situated, is very much like the carbon copy of the countries where they lived in this life. It has rivers, valleys, mountains, forests and deserts. The activities of the spirits are similar to those of human life here, in addition to whatever other activities of which men may not know anything.

Yet, in certain aspects, the spirit world differs radically from the human world. It is invisible to the eyes of men: people only know or believe that it is there, but do not actually 'see' it with their physical eyes. But more important, even if the spirits may be the depersonalized residue of individual human beings, they are ontologically 'nearer' to God: not ethically, but in terms of communication with Him. It is believed that whereas men use or require intermediaries, the spirits do not, since they can communicate directly with God. We have already shown that in many African societies the spirits and the living-dead act as intermediaries who convey human sacrifices or prayers to God, and may relay His reply to men. We have also seen that in some societies it is believed that God has servants or agents whom He employs to carry out His intentions in the universe. The spirits fill up the ontological region of the Zamani between God and man's Sasa. The ontological transcendence of God is bridged by the spirit mode of existence. Man is forever a creature, but he does not remain forever man, and these are his two polarities of existence. Individual spirits may or may not remain for ever, but the class of the spirits is an essential and integral part of African ontology.

Becoming spirits is, in a sense, a social elevation. For this reason, African peoples show respect and high regard for their living-dead and for some of the important spirits. Spirits are 'older' than men, when viewed against the Sasa and Zamani periods—they have moved completely into the Zamani period. Their age which is greater than that of human beings compels the latter to give them respect along the same pattern that younger people give respect to older men and women, whether or not they are immediately members of the same family. In relation to the spirits, men are the younger generation, and social etiquette requires that they respect those who have fully entered and settled in the Zamani period.

Spirits do not appear to human beings as often as do the living-dead, and where mention of their appearances is made it is generally in folk stories. They act in malicious ways, as well as in a benevolent manner. People fear them more because of their being 'strangers' than because of what they actually are or do. They are said to have a shadowy form of body, though they may assume different shapes like human, animal, plant forms or inanimate objects. People report that they see the spirits in ponds, caves, groves, mountains or outside their villages, dancing, singing, herding cattle, working in their fields or nursing their children. Some spirits appear in people's dreams, especially to diviners, priests, medicine-men and rain-makers to impart some information. These personages may also consult the spirits as part of their normal training and practice. In many societies it is said and believed that spirits call people by name, but on turning round to see who called them there would be nobody. This sounds like a naughty game on the part of the spirits who probably derive a lot of fun from it. In folk stories it is told that the spirits sleep in the daytime and remain awake at night.

As the spirits are invisible, ubiquitous and unpredictable, the safest thing is to keep away from them. If they, or the living-dead, appear too frequently to human beings people feel disturbed. Then the spirits possess men, and are blamed for forms of illness like madness and epilepsy. Spirit possession occurs in one form or another in practically every African society.

Yet, spirit possession is not always to be feared, and there are times when it is not only desirable but people induce it through special dancing and drumming until the person concerned experiences spirit possession during which he may even collapse. When the person is thus possessed, the spirit may speak through him, so that he now plays the role of a medium, and the messages he relays are received with expectation by those to whom they are addressed. But on the whole, spirit possessions, especially unsolicited ones, result in bad effects. They may cause severe torment on the possessed person; the spirit may drive him away from his home so that he lives in the forests; it may cause him to jump into the fire and get himself burnt, to torture his body with sharp instruments, or even to do harm to other people. During the height of spirit possession, the individual in effect loses his own personality and acts in the context of the 'personality' of the spirit possessing him. The possessed person becomes restless, may fail to sleep properly, and if the possession lasts a long period it results in damage to health. Women are more prone to spirit possession than men. Exorcism is one of the major functions of the traditional doctors and diviners; and when spirits 'endanger' a village, there are usually formal ceremonies to drive away the notorious spirits. In some societies family spirits have to be moved ceremoniously when the villagers move from one place to another. This insures that the family spirits and especially the living-dead, move with members of their human relatives and are not forsaken where there is nobody to 'remember' them in their personal immortality.

Human relationships with the spirits vary from society to society. It is, however, a real, active and powerful relationship, especially with the spirits of those who have recently died—whom we have called the living-dead. Various rites are performed to keep this contact, involving the placing of food and other articles, or the pouring of libation of beer, milk, water and even tea or coffee (for the spirits who have been 'modernized'). In some societies this is done daily, but most African peoples do it less often. Such offerings are given to the oldest member of the departed—who may still be a living-dead, or may be remembered only in genealogies. This is done with the understanding that he will share the food or beverage with the other spirits of the family group. Words may or may not accompany such offerings, in form of prayers, invocations or instructions to the departed. These words are the bridge of communion, and people's witness that they recognize the departed to be still alive. Failure to observe these acts means in effect that human beings have completely broken off their links with the departed, and have therefore forgotten the spirits. This is regarded as extremely dangerous and disturbing to the social and individual conscience. People are then likely to feel that any misfortune that befalls them is the logical result of their neglect of the spirits, if not caused by magic and witchcraft.

For spirits which are not associated with a particular family, offerings may be placed in spirit shrines where these exist. Such shrines belong to the community, and may be cared for by priests. Some of the spirits who are accorded this honour are venerated according to their functions, for example the spirits of the water may receive offerings when people want to fish or sail in the water; and the spirits of the forests may be consulted when people want to cut down the forest and make new fields. Here we merge with the category of the divinities, which we have already described above.

[c] *The living-dead*
The departed of up to five generations are in a different category from that of ordinary spirits which we have been considering. They are still within the Sasa period, they are in the state of personal immortality, and their process of dying is not yet complete. We have called them the living-dead. They are the closest links that men have with the spirit world. Some of the things said about the spirits apply also to the living-dead. But the living-dead are bilingual: they speak the language of men, with whom they lived until 'recently'; and they speak the language of the spirits and of God, to Whom they are drawing nearer ontologically. These are the 'spirits' with which African peoples are most concerned: it is through the living-dead that the spirit world becomes personal to men. They are still part of their human families, and people have personal memories of them. The two groups are bound together by their common Sasa which for the living-dead is, however, fast disappearing into the Zamani. The living-dead are still 'people', and have not yet become 'things', 'spirits' or 'its'. They return to their human families from time to time, and share meals with them, however symbolically. They know and have interest in what is going on in the family. When they appear, which is generally to the oldest members of the household, they are recognized by name as 'so and so'; they enquire about family affairs, and may even warn of impending danger or rebuke those who have failed to follow their special instructions. They are the guardians of family affairs, traditions, ethics and activities. Offence in these matters is ultimately an offence against the forefathers who, in that capacity, act as the invisible police of the families and communities. Because they are still 'people', the living-dead are therefore the best group of intermediaries between men and God: they know the needs of men, they have 'recently' been here with men, and at the same time they have full access to the channels of communicating with God directly or, according to some societies, indirectly through their own forefathers. Therefore men approach

A.R.P.—4

them more often for minor needs of life than they approach God. Even if the living-dead may not do miracles or extraordinary things to remedy the need, men experience a sense of psychological relief when they pour out their hearts' troubles before their seniors who have a foot in both worlds.

All this does not mean that the relationship between men and the living-dead is exclusively paradisal. People know only too well that following physical death, a barrier has been erected between them and the living-dead. When the living-dead return and appear to their relatives, this experience is not received with great enthusiasm by men; and if it becomes too frequent, people resent it. Men do not say to the living-dead: 'Please sit down and wait for food to be prepared!'; nor would they bid farewell with the words: 'Greet so-and-so in the spirit world!' And yet these are two extremely important aspects of social friendliness and hospitality among men in African communities. The food and libation given to the living-dead are paradoxically acts of hospitality and welcome, and yet of informing the living-dead to move away. The living-dead are wanted and yet not wanted. If they have been improperly buried or were offended before they died, it is feared by the relatives or the offenders that the living-dead would take revenge. This would be in the form of misfortune, especially illness, or disturbing frequent appearances of the living-dead. If people neglect to give food and libation where this is otherwise the normal practice, or if they fail to observe instructions that the living-dead may have given before dying, then misfortunes and sufferings would be interpreted as resulting from the anger of the living-dead. People are, therefore, careful to follow the proper practices and customs regarding the burial or other means of disposal of dead bodies, and make libation and food offerings as the case might be. In some societies, special care of the graves is taken, since the living-dead may be considered to dwell in the area of the graves, some of which are in the former houses of the departed. Attention is paid to the living-dead of up to four or five generations, by which time only a few, if any, immediate members of their families would still be alive. When the last person who knew a particular living-dead also dies, then in effect the process of death is now complete as far as that particular living-dead is concerned. He is now no longer remembered by name, no longer a 'human being', but a spirit, a thing, an IT. He has now sunk beyond the visible horizon of the Zamani. It is no more necessary to pay close attention to him in the family obligation of making food offerings and libation, except, in some societies, within the context of genealogical remembrances or in the chain of the intermediaries. By that time also, additional living-dead have come into the picture and deserve or require more attention from the living. Those who have 'moved on' to the stage of full spirits, merge into the company of spirits, and people lose both contact with and interest in them. They are no longer in the human period of the Sasa, even if they may continue to be men's contemporaries. Their plane of existence is other than that of men, they are ontologically spirits and spirits only. In some societies it is believed that some living-dead are 'reborn'. This is, however, only partial re-incarnation since not the entire person is reborn as such, but only certain of his characteristics or physical distinctions.

Since the living-dead are partly 'human' and partly 'spirit', we shall return to a discussion of them when we come to consider concepts pertaining to man's death and the hereafter. They deserve to be considered in the section on spirits and on men. We need now to take concrete examples from different African peoples, to illustrate the points we have been discussing on both the spirits and the living-dead. Our written sources do not distinguish between these two groups, and terms like 'ancestral spirits', 'the ancestors' or 'the spirits' are used to describe both groups. 'Ancestral spirits' or 'ancestors' are misleading terms since they imply only those spirits who were once the ancestors of the living. This is limiting the concept unnecessarily, since there are spirits and living-dead of children, brothers, sisters, barren wives and other members of the family who were not in any way the 'ancestors'. One would strongly advocate the abolition of the two terms 'ancestral spirits' and 'the ancestors', and replace them with 'spirits' or 'the living-dead' whichever is applicable.

The Acholi have three groups of spirits. One comprises the clan spirits said to be 'owned' by the chief, and for which there are shrines on hills and by the rivers. The second group is made up of spirits, presumably the living-dead, of known relatives, some of them being heads of lineages and looked upon as benevolent and protective; and some being of relatives who died with grudges, and are therefore greatly feared. The third group consists of 'spirits of unknown persons and dangerous beasts . . . believed to dwell in streams, rocks, bushes, etc. They are hostile and cause sickness and other misfortunes to an individual'.[1]

According to the Akamba, some spirits were created as such by God, and others were once human beings. God controls them and sometimes sends them as His messengers. Some are friendly and benevolent, others are malevolent, but the majority are 'neutral' or both 'good and evil' like human beings. People say that they see the spirits, especially on hillsides and along the river beds. In such places, their lights are seen at night, their cattle heard mooing or their children crying. It is believed that women have spirit 'husbands' who cause them to become pregnant. In traditional life,

[1] Okot p'Bitek, 'The Concept of Jok among the Acholi and Lango', in *The Uganda Journal*, Vol. XXVII, No. 1, March 1963, pp. 15–29.

families are careful to make libation of beer, milk or water, and to give bits of food to the living-dead. Spirit possession by both the spirits and the living-dead is commonly reported, though less now than in previous years. Around the turn of this century there was a national outbreak of spirit possession in the southern part of the country, when the phenomenon swept through the communities like an epidemic. Some diviners and medicine-men receive instruction through dreams or appearances from the spirits and the living-dead, concerning diagnosis, treatment and prevention of diseases. A considerable number of people report seeing spirits and the living-dead, both alone as individuals and in groups with other men or women. Two pastor friends of mine reported the following experiences with the spirits. One of them was walking home from school with a fellow schoolboy in the evening. They had to cross a stream, on the other side of which was a hill. As they approached this stream, they saw lights on the hill in front of them, where otherwise nobody lived. My friend asked his companion what that was, and he told him not to fear but that it was fire from the spirits. They had to go on the side of the hill, and my friend was getting frightened. His companion told him that he had seen such fires before, and that both of them had only to sing Christian hymns and there would be no danger to them. So they walked on singing, and as they went by the hill, the spirits began tossing stones at them. Some of the stones went rolling up to where the two boys were walking, but did not hit them. As the young men were leaving this hill, they saw a fire round which were shadowy figures which my friend's companion told him were the spirits themselves. Some of the spirits were striking others with whips and asking them, 'Why did you not hit those boys?', 'Why did you not hit them?' The two young men could hear some of the spirits crying from the beating which they received, but did not hear what reason they gave for not hitting the boys with stones.

The other pastor told me that when he was about twenty, he went with several other young men into a forest to collect honey from the bark of a withered tree. The honey was made by small insects which do not sting, and which are found in different parts of the country. The place was far away from the villages. When they reached the tree, he climbed up in order to cut open the barks and the trunk of the tree. While up on the tree, he suddenly heard whistling as if from shepherds and herdsmen. He stopped hitting the tree. The group listened in silence. They heard clearly the whistling and the sound of cattle, sheep and goats, coming from the forest towards where they were collecting honey. The sound and voice grew louder and louder as the spirits drew nearer, and the young men realized that soon the spirits would reach them. Since people do not graze animals in forests but only in plains, and since the place was too far from the villages for men to drive cattle through there, the young men decided that only the spirits could possibly be approaching them. They looked in the direction from which the sound came, but saw nobody, yet whatever made that sound was getting nearer and nearer to them. So the men decided to abandon their honey and flee for their lives. They never returned to that area again.

There are other stories similar to these, and one has no reason to doubt the authenticity of most of them, especially those that are narrated by the people who themselves experienced the things they describe.

The Ankore have guardian spirits (*emandwa*) for their lineage groups, which are benevolent and helpful. Family spirits (*emizimu*) or living-dead, punish bad actions and are thought to be responsible for many misfortunes which are not caused by witchcraft and magic. There is a cult for the guardian spirits. The living-dead are deeply concerned with family affairs. The following story which I have heard from different persons who witnessed the incident or knew the family where it occurred, will illustrate this point further. About 1962 a man died and left instructions that his wife was not to sell the piece of ground which belonged to the family. She decided, however, that she wanted to sell the ground, and in spite of warnings from the brothers of the deceased man she went ahead and sold it. The man who bought it was warned that misfortunes would befall his family if he built and settled on that ground. The man did not outwardly pay attention to this; he went ahead and built a new home. Shortly after-wards mysterious things began to happen in the house. For example, while boiling water the pot would overturn and spill the water over the fire, putting it out; and while sitting inside the house, people would get struck by invisible agents or stones from the outside. The family called the local pastor to come and pray, and when he got into the house he was struck so severely by clubs from the house that he ran away. The family called the police, and two men came. These also were hit by stones and struck with clubs, from invisible agents, and had to run away. It became intolerable to live there, and the man who had bought the piece of ground had to give it up and quit the spot. The woman returned there and peace also returned. People who witnessed these happenings took them to mean that the living-dead who had forbidden the sale of the compound, was disturbing the family which had bought the land.

The Ashanti have spirits that animate trees, rivers, animals, charms and the like; and below these are family spirits thought to be ever present, and to act as guardians. Bambuti spirits are thought to serve God as 'game-keepers'; and are described as small, dark-skinned, bright-eyed, white-haired, bearded, living in tree hollows and stinking. Those of the Ewe are believed to have been created by God to act as intermediaries between Him and human beings. Although they are invisible, people say that they have human form, protect men, live in natural objects and phenomena and are capble of self-propagation. The Fajulu believe that every person has two spirits: one is good and the other evil.

The Baganda recognize spirits which can be considered in three groups. One consists of the living-dead (*mizimu*), who are connected with human families and are thought to dwell around the homesteads. Therefore people 'see' or 'hear' them; and, at least formerly, each home would have a shrine for them where offerings of food and drink would be placed. There are homes today with such shrines still. On the whole the *mizimu* are benevolent, except those that might either have been wicked men or been offended before death. Then there is the group of spirits (*misambwa*) which have no immediate family ties like the living-dead. These are associated with natural objects like rocks, streams, trees and animals. Although they are feared and thought to be ubiquitous, they tend to confine their activities to particular localities or kinship groups. Some are clan 'property', or the 'property' of a given region, and are the object of a spirit cult. The third group concerns those known as *balubaale*, who are mainly leading national heroes and leaders that have been socially and religiously elevated. Among them are what we have already described as divinities, such as those of war (*Kibuka*), of the seas and lakes (*Mukasa*) and of death (*Walumbe*). One writer[1] gives their number as seventy-three, but this is refuted by other Baganda. Formerly there were temples for the major *balubaale,* but only a few of them are left today. The cult of these spirits reached a high degree of development on a national scale, though when occasion demanded it the kings could and did disregard the cult; while at other times they supported and depended on it. In the horizon of the Zamani, it seems as if the *balubaale* are a mixture of historical and mythological figures, together with personifications of major natural phenomena and objects and of human activities. The picture is not clear, even to the Baganda themselves, not only concerning the *balubaale* but concerning the spirit world at large.[2]

To add to this complex situation of the Baganda concepts of the spirits, there is another form of spiritual beings-and-power known as *mayembe* (literally 'horns'). These are objects, chiefly horns of buffaloes and bucks, used by diviners and medicine-men in their practice, which function when spirits are called or summoned by the owners of the *mayembe*. The spirits alone are not the *mayembe*, and yet the horns alone without the spirits cannot

[1] A. Kagwa, *Empisa z'Abaganda* (1905), cited in Welbourn, below.
[2] For further study see F. B. Welbourn, 'Some Aspects of Kiganda Religion', in *The Uganda Journal*, Vol. XXVI, No. 2, September 1962, p. 171 f.

function as *mayembe*. It is the combination of the two that produces the *mayembe*; and the right method of reaching that combination is known only to the experts concerned. A powerful and skilled diviner can create his own *mayembe* which other diviners may borrow or consult even after he has died. Often the *mayembe* are given personal names, and it is these names which are called or sung when the diviners summon the spirits. *Mayembe* are used for all sorts of activities, including divination, diagnosing and healing diseases, 'creating' more love between a man and his wife, finding lost articles, preventing attack by magic or by other *mayembe* from an enemy and so on. Some are more powerful than others, and one group known as *kifaalu* (military tank, tractor or rhino) which came into the picture during or immediately after the Second World War, is particularly feared and considered deadly. These are thought to have come either from Kenya or Rwanda. One diviner assured my students in 1967 that many Baganda possess *kifaalu*, but they are kept secretly since people employ them to haunt, kill or bewitch their enemies and offenders, such as those who take other men's wives or do not pay their debts. The use and purchasing of *kifaalu* seem to be developing into a fat commercial enterprise, and a person may pay up to three hundred shillings (about forty-five U.S. dollars) to a specialist diviner to send the *kifaalu* on a revengeful or harmful mission. Many diviners do not, however, deal with the *kifaalu* type of *mayembe*. It is not clear what kind of spirits combine to make *mayembe*, but certainly not the living-dead, or only very rarely. One would suspect that the spirits are those of the second category mentioned above, but probably from a special type of them.

Similarly the Gikuyu recognize three types of spirits. They have the living-dead who are made up of the departed members of the family, and of whom the parents are the most important. These are known in Gikuyu as the 'spirits of the parents or forebearers' (*ngoma cia aciari*). To these the family gives food and drink offerings, as tokens of fellowship and one-ness. It is insisted by Kenyatta that these are not acts of prayer or worship towards the living-dead in the way that God is worshipped. Individual or family behaviour can please or displease the living-dead, who then would act in the situation the way they would have acted while they lived in the human form. The second group is made up of spirits of the clan, *ngoma cia moherega*, whose immediate and main concern is the welfare of the nation on the level of the clan. They act, or are consulted, in matters pertaining to the behaviour and life of the clan members. Thirdly, there is the category of spirits concerned with age-groups and the nation as a whole, known as *ngoma cia riika*. The Gikuyu see the spirits in the same structure as their own society. This third group of the spirits is not to be thought of as divinities which the

Gikuyu and other peoples do not recognize. It seems that some of the spirits, presumably those whose links with the clan or nation have weakened, turn against people and cause illness. Such spirits are believed to hide around the homesteads, and to be blown by the wind from one homestead to another. For that reason, whirlwinds are thought to be spirits assembling to wage an attack on people. If there is an outbreak of epidemics, the people in the affected area get together to fight against the spirits which, if defeated, take away with them the epidemic and fear to return for another defeat. The best time for this ceremony is in the evening, when the moon comes out. The community appoints a day, and when the time arrives, war horns are sounded. On hearing the sound, everyone rushes out of his house carrying sticks, clubs and wooden weapons. Metal weapons are not used, in case they should shed the blood of the spirits which would defile the ground. The bushes are beaten, people shout and the crowds move towards the river on both banks. On arrival at the river and amidst continued blowing of the war horns, the sticks are thrown into the water. The people beat off dust from their clothes and feet, to remove any traces of the spirits; and then return home, joyfully singing and being careful not to look back. The following day mothers shave off the hair of their children who had not been able to join in the attack against the spirits. The shaving is in the form of the cross, as it is believed that the sight of such children would frighten the malicious spirits. The children are then washed and painted with red ochre.[1] In this battle, the spirits are conceived in human terms, taking the position of the enemy which must be attacked and defeated. The sticks partly symbolize human might, and when they are thrown into the river they symbolize the defeated spirits who are now swept away by the stream of death. Presumably the dust stands for the epidemic, and beating it off the feet and clothes is a dramatization of human victory over the epidemic, just as the spirits who caused it are also defeated. The shaving of the children is a further dramatization of the spirits' defeat, as well as being a sign of 'death and resurrection' from the epidemic. Exactly what the sign or origin of the cross is, I do not know, but it is interesting to recall that the Christians have for many centuries been using it, among other things, for protection against attack by evil spirits. If at one time in the past, Christianity may have reached this part of equatorial Africa, it is significant and remarkable that the 'sign of the cross' in the fight against evil forces, should be the only trace of Christianity which has been incorporated into traditional beliefs and practices. It may be, however, that historians and archaeologists may yet unearth other traces. Until then, the matter must remain no more than speculation.

[1] Kenyatta, p. 260 f.

We must leave the spirits there, although they will continue to crop up now and then, and we will return to the living-dead when we consider man's destiny after death. Parts of this chapter have been no more than broad generalizations, purely because of the scarcity of written information on the spirits. When fuller information is available, obviously some of the statements will be proved wrong, and I shall be only too glad to revise these views in the light of better knowledge. The generalizations cannot be applied to all the different African peoples, as our concrete examples have clearly shown, and readers are warned to be cautious when applying these concepts to individual peoples or regions. Whatever science may do to prove the existence or non-existence of the spirits, one thing is undeniable, namely that for African peoples the spirits are a reality and a reality which must be reckoned with, whether it is a clear, blurred or confused reality. And it demands and deserves more than academic attention.

9
THE CREATION
& ORIGINAL
STATE OF MAN

We have pointed out that African ontology is basically anthropocentric: man is at the very centre of existence, and African peoples see everything else in its relation to this central position of man. God is the explanation of man's origin and sustenance: it is as if God exists for the sake of man. The spirits are ontologically in the mode between God and man: they describe or explain the destiny of man after physical life. Man cannot remain forever in the Sasa period, he moves 'backwards' into the Zamani period, and yet however far he travels in the stream of time, he remains a creature, in the stage between God and physical man. Animals, plants, land, rain and other natural objects and phenomena, describe man's environment, and African peoples incorporate this environment into their deeply religious perception of the universe. We have already seen how some of these objects and phenomena are attributed with life and personality, so that strictly speaking 'nothing is essentially dead or devoid of life (being)' in the sight of African peoples. The remainder of this book will be devoted to a study of the African view of man, in terms of the created man, the corporate man and the changing man.

[a] *The creation and origin of man*
Practically every African society has its own myth or myths concerning the origin of man. H. Baumann's book, *Schöpfung und Urzeit des Menschen im Mythus der afrikanischen Völker* (1936) attempts the colossal task of analysing 2,000 of these myths; and although a second edition has been issued (1964), there are additional myths which have not been included here and which may not yet be in writing. Unfortunately for those who cannot read German this book has not been translated into other languages. Even for readers of the German language, the book is heavy going, particularly because of the many names of African peoples and places. It is, however, a most useful tool for reference purposes with regard to the study of the origin of man, in spite of its prejudices and errors of judgment.

In relation to other things, the majority of African peoples place the creation of man towards or at the end of God's original work of creation. Man also comes into the picture as husband and wife, male and female. It is generally acknowledged that God is the originator of man, even if the exact methods of creating man may differ according to the myths of different peoples.

We can take a few examples to illustrate these points. In the Abaluyia creation story, it is told that God created man so that the sun would have someone for whom to shine. Then He created plants, animals and birds to provide food for him. The husband was made first and then the wife, so that the man would have someone with whom to talk. The Lozi narrate that God was still on the earth when He created man after creating all the other things. He went on to make different peoples, each with its own customs, language and manners. The Lugbara say that God in His transcendent aspect created the first men, husband and wife, long, long ago. These two bore a son and a daughter who mated and produced male and female children, and so mankind increased upon the earth. The Mende also tell that God first made all other things, and then created men, both husband and wife.

As for the actual method of creating man, we can consider the myths under different categories. There are peoples who hold that God used clay to make man, the way that the potter does with pots. For this reason, He is often spoken of as the Potter, Moulder and Maker. The Shilluk believe that God used clay of different colours in making men, which explains the difference in human skin pigmentation. Then He gave man legs with which to walk and run, hands with which to plant grain, and a mouth with which to eat it. Afterwards He gave man a tongue with which to sing and talk, and finally ears so that he may enjoy the sound of music, dance and the talk of great men. Then God sent man out, a complete man.[1] That is clearly a beautiful picture of a skilled Potter's work. The Bambuti Pygmies also have a vivid myth about man's formation from clay. They tell that God made the body of the first man by kneading, and then 'covered him with a skin and poured blood into his lifeless body. Then the first man breathed and lived, and God whispered softly in his ear: "You will beget children who will live in the forest".'[2] Baumann reaches the conclusion that the idea of man's creation from clay is very widespread in Africa.[3]

There are myths from the Akamba, Basuto, Herero, Shona, Nuer and others, which tell that God brought man out of a hole or marsh in the

[1] Young, p. 146.
[2] Schebesta, II, p. 179 f., commented categorically when he heard this story that 'any biblical influence on the Pygmies was out of the question'.
[3] Baumann, p. 203 f.

ground, or from a tree.[1] The Akamba have a rock in the western central part of their country, at Nzaui, which has a hole supposed to be the one through which God brought out the first man and wife. The Herero tell that God caused the first human beings, a man and his wife, to come from the mythical 'tree of life' which is said to be situated in the underworld. Myths that connect man's origin with trees are reported to be widespread from the coast of Angola to the Zambezi region, in addition to other but smaller regions of the Congo, the Sudan and elsewhere. Among the Nuer, it is believed that a tamarind tree which burnt down in 1918, was the one from whose branches men fell off, or under which was a hole from where men first emerged. It was God Who created them, making them different in skin colour, abilities to run and bodily strength.[2]

In a few cases it is said that God brought men out of a vessel. This is in one of Azande stories according to which men and other things were sealed up in a canoe which, of God's several sons (Sun, Moon, Stars, Night and Cold) only the sun was able to open by heating and causing the seal to melt. Then came out men and other things. The Chagga say that God opened up a vessel containing men, and caused them to come out and live. For that reason He is referred to as 'God Who burst (out) men'.

In a related set of myths, it is held among the Ewe, Baluba, Maasai, Nandi, Nupe and others, that men came originally from a leg or knee. This knee or leg belonged to some other being, evidently like men. The leg got swollen until finally it burst, letting out a male person on one side and a female on the other side. These stories sound more like fairy tales, however much they attempt to dramatize or express the origin of mankind.

Among many peoples in scattered parts of Africa, and especially along the upper Nile valley, it is narrated that man came from heaven or another world. The general idea is that God created man elsewhere and then lowered him to this world, or for various reasons man descended and settled here. In another story, the Akamba say that God lowered the first pair or two of mankind from the clouds to the earth. They brought with them cattle, sheep and goats; and the two pairs reproduced so that their children inter- married and formed families of mankind on earth. Similarly the Bachwa narrate how God made everything including the first men whom he lowered from the sky to the earth. These were, naturally, the Pygmies themselves, and for that reason the Bachwa call themselves 'the Children of God'. In another myth, the Chagga hold that the first man descended

[1] Baumann, pp. 186 f., 193 f., 219 f.
[2] Evans-Pritchard, II, p. 6 f.

from heaven on the spider thread, and for this reason the spider is respected among the Chagga. According to the Langi, there is another world beyond this one, which is older, invisible and very far away. It was from that other world that the first husband and wife came, these having been created by God as He had created all things in both worlds. There are stories of this general type among the Ashanti, Azande, Banyoro, Maasai, Mondari, Ovimbundu, Lugbara, Luo, Turkana and other peoples all over Africa. This picture of man's origin places man in a position rather different from that of other earthly created things: he comes from 'above', from 'another' region of the universe, from a position 'nearer' to God than that of other things.

[b] *The original state of man, and God's provision for him*
According to many stories of creation, man was originally put in a state of happiness, childlike ignorance, immortality or ability to rise again after dying. God also provided him with the necessities of life, either directly or through equipping him to develop them, and man lived more or less in a state of paradise. We shall illustrate these general observations with a few stories.

According to the Ashanti, the first man enjoyed a position of great privilege. God made other things for his use and protection, including the spirits. Then 'He ordered animals to eat the plants, and He ordered man to do the same, and to drink from the waters; He also ordered man to use the animals as meat.'[1] In one of the Bambuti myths, it is told that God provided the first people with food, shelter, immortality and the gift of rejuvenating them when they grew old. They lived happily and lacked nothing. Similarly the Tswana say that the primeval state was one of happiness, peace and blessedness, and men neither ate, nor drank nor died. In picturing this state of bliss, the Fajulu tell that there were originally two worlds and the inhabitants of both worlds used to invite one another by the sound of the drum, to go and take part in dance parties. This happy state of affairs ended only when the hyaena cut into two the rope which bridged the two worlds. Similar stories are told among the peoples of the upper White Nile valley.

God made provision for the first men. In the case of the Abaluyia this was in the form of rain which gave them water; and animals, of which they were to eat hoofed ones, and different types of fish. According to the Acholi, God taught the first men all the essentials of living, such as the cultivation of land, the cooking of food and the making of beer. The Azande believe that God provided man with the art of magic and the knowledge of making

[1] Lystad, p. 164.

medicines. So also the Ewe hold that God sent magic power into the world when He had made the first men. The Hottentots, Meru, Akamba, Zulu and many others, say that the first men had the gift of either immortality or rising again after dying; though in some stories this gift never actually reached the first men, for various reasons. There are those like the Nuer, Akamba, Pare and others, who say that God gave the first men domestic animals including cattle, sheep, goats and dogs.

It was not, however, only material provision that God gave to the original man. He Himself was close to man, and some societies picture Him as living among men, or visiting them from time to time. It was like a family relationship in which God was the Parent and men were the children. He provided His presence among them, and all the other things derived from that relationship so long as it lasted. A number of myths speak of this as a state of happiness and blessedness; and some even say that the first men did not need to eat or drink, and therefore there was no necessity to labour for these items of existence. Other myths also indicate that it was a state of ignorance of many things. For example, the Abaluyia say that the first husband and wife did not know how to have sexual intercourse, doing it, unsuccessfully, in the armpit. It was by accident that they discovered the proper method, when the wife climbed to get grain from the granary while the man stayed underneath and looked up. The Kakwa and Tiv narrate that the first men did not know how to cultivate, until God taught them the art of raising crops on the ground. The Zulu, on the other hand, believe that God ordered men to farm from the very beginning saying: 'Let there be men and let them cultivate food and eat!' God also taught men other skills. According to the Acholi He taught them cooking, beer-making and hunting; according to the Bambuti He taught them how to forge metals—something absolutely essential to the Pygmy life of hunting.

From these and other examples, we see that God and His presence provided for the main needs of mankind: food, knowledge of fundamental skills, domestic animals, light and fire, weapons and tools, children, doctors and medicines, on top of immortality, or rejuvenation or rising again after death. Even when man lost or failed to attain the higher gifts of immortality and resurrection, he was nevertheless equipped to survive and live, and God did not leave Him to perish upon the face of the earth. In that family relationship, God gave man certain rules or commandments to observe, and so long as man kept these rules, his relationship with God remained sound and healthy. But this relationship was disrupted, resulting in tragic consequences for man. To this unhappy development we shall now proceed.

[c] *The separation between God and man*

Different peoples tell different myths of how the happy relationship between God and man ended, and how the separation of the two came about. We shall take some examples of these ideas, and then draw some conclusions from them and other stories.

According to the Ashanti, God originally lived in the sky but close to men. The mother of these men constantly went on knocking against Him with her pestle while pounding the traditional food, *fufu*. To get away from this knocking, God moved up higher. The woman instructed her sons to gather all the mortars, pile them and follow God. This they did, but before they could reach to Him, they ran short of construction material. As there was a gap of only one mortar, she advised her children to take the bottom-most mortar in order to fill up the gap. Obediently they did this, only to cause the whole tower to tumble down and kill many of them. The survivors gave up the idea of following God 'up there'.[1]

In the Mende story it is told that God dwelt among the first people. They used to go to Him to ask for things so frequently that He moved off to another place. Before this departure, however, He made an agreement with them concerning their relationship with Him and with one another. He went to His abode in the heavens, for which reason the Mende call Him *Leve*, which means 'Up' or 'High'.[2]

There are a number of peoples, including the Bambuti, Banyarwanda, Barotse, Bushmen, Chagga, Pare, Elgeyo and others, who tell of God giving men a particular rule to observe. When men broke it, then the separation took place. According to these stories, the Bambuti were forbidden to eat of the *tahu* tree; and in another myth they say the first men were forbidden to look at God; the Banyarwanda were forbidden to hide death which God was hunting; the Barotse were forbidden to eat animals which should have been their brothers; the Pare were forbidden to eat eggs and the Chagga forbidden to eat one type of yam (*ula*).

Another set of similar stories comes from peoples of the upper White Nile region, like the Bari, Fajulu, Lugbara, Madi and Toposa. These narrate that originally the heaven or sky and the earth were united by a rope or bridge; and that at times God lived among men on earth. This rope was broken accidentally or by the hyaena, and so the direct link or relationship between God and men was severed.

There are a few peoples who tell that God withdrew from men because of smoke from men's fires. Thus, the Yao narrate that God originally dwelt on earth with men, until they learnt how to make fire by friction. They

[1] Busia in Forde, p. 192.
[2] Harris in Smith, p. 278 f.

then set the grasslands alight, and God withdrew Himself into heaven.

So then, God withdrew from men, partly because of man's disobedience to Him, partly through accident caused by men, and partly through the severing of the link between heaven and earth. However the separation occurred, it brought disadvantageous and tragic consequences to men: man was the main loser. These consequences disrupted the original state of man. According to the Bambuti, God left men alone, death came, and man lost happiness, peace and the free supply of food. The Banyarwanda tell that when a woman decided to hide death, contrary to God's law not to do so, He decided to let men keep death, and so death has ever since remained with men. The Bushmen tell that man lost the gift of the re-surrection and death came among men. According to the Chagga, diseases and old age came to men, they lost the gift of rejuvenation and death came as well. Where the link between heaven and earth was broken, the bliss of the 'heavenly country' also disappeared, and men must die in order to return to the other world (according to some stories).

It would seem that African image of the happy life is one in which God is among the people, His presence supplying them with food, shelter, peace, immortality or gift of the resurrection, and a moral code. For many peoples this is only in the golden age of the Zamani, and others have lost even the mythological sight of it. It is remarkable that out of these many myths concerning the primeval man and the loss of his original state, there is not a single myth, to my knowledge, which even attempts to suggest a solution or reversal of this great loss. Man accepted the separation between him and God; and in some societies God has been 'left' in the distance of the Zamani, coming into the Sasa period only in times of men's crises and needs. In varying degrees the majority of African peoples (if not all) attempt to go after God in the acts of worship such as we have already outlined in chapter seven above. We saw, however, no evidence of man seeking after God for His own sake; or of the spirit of man 'thirsting' after God as the pure and absolute expression of being.

Would it be legitimate to suggest, perhaps, that African acts of worship are basically utilitarian, searching primarily for the lost paradise rather than for God himself? Since in these acts, people are searching for something past, something in the distant Zamani period, it follows that there cannot be myths about the future recovery of the lost paradise or reversal of the *fait accompli*. So long as their concept of time is two dimensional, with a Sasa and a Zamani, African peoples cannot entertain a glorious 'hope' to which mankind may be destined. Relative to the people in the Sasa period, the lost paradise withdraws further into the Zamani until they lose sight of it even mythologically. Indeed this has already happened to many societies whose picture of man's original state is 'forgotten'. When individuals and communities get satisfactory amounts of food, children, rain, health and prosperity, they have approached something of the original state. At such times they do not generally turn to God in the utilitarian acts of worship as much as they do when these items are at stake.

Yet behind these fleeting glimpses of the original state and bliss of man, whether they are rich or shadowy, there lie the tantalizing and unattained gift of the resurrection, the loss of human immortality and the monster of death. Here African religions and philosophy must admit a defeat: they have supplied no solution. This remains the most serious cul-de-sac in the otherwise rich thought and sensitive religious feeling of our peoples. It is perhaps here then, that we find the greatest weakness and poverty of our traditional religions compared to world religions like Christianity, Judaism, Islam, Buddhism or Hinduism. These traditional religions cannot but remain tribal and nationalistic, since they do not offer for mankind at large, a way of 'escape', a message of 'redemption' (however that might be conceived). Is it in this very issue, then, that these other religions have made a universal appeal and won adherents from all mankind? Do religions become universal only when they have been weaned from the cradle of looking towards the Zamani with all its mythological riches, and make a breakthrough towards the future with all the (mythological?) promises of 'redemption'? Such 'redemption' involves rescue from the monster of death, regaining immortality and attaining the gift of the resurrection. It is in this area that world religions may hope to 'conquer' African traditional religions and philosophy, not so much by coercion as by adding this new element to the two-dimensional life and thinking of African peoples. Only a three-dimensional religion can hope to last in modern Africa which is increasingly discovering and adjusting to a third dimension of time. One suspects that it may have been by virtue of having a fairly well defined future dimension of time, that the peoples of the Middle East and India were able to evolve not only 'redemptive' but 'universal' religions. Without the concept of a distant future, these religions would have remained, like African religions, only tribal or national.

10
ETHNIC GROUPS, KINSHIP & THE INDIVIDUAL

Africa has all the main races of the world, and each group can rightly claim to be African. Ethnologists and anthropologists have classified them broadly as follows: The Bushmanoid peoples who are generally short in stature and with light yellowish skins are found in scattered areas of eastern and southern Africa. The Caucasoid peoples are medium to tall in stature, with light to medium brown and pink skins, and are found in the extreme southern, north-eastern and northern Africa. They are a 'recent' arrival in southern Africa where they have driven away the indigenous peoples from the best areas of land, or slaughtered them. The Mongoloid group formerly occupied the island of Madagascar, but in course of centuries the peoples mingled and largely got mixed with Negroid peoples from the continent. The present people of Madagascar are generally short, dark haired and possessing a wide range of skin pigmentation ranging from black, to brown, yellow and pink. The Negroid peoples are found in almost every part of the continent, having occupied it as far north as Egypt and Morocco in former millennia. In stature they range from medium height to very tall; and their skin colour ranges from black to dark brown and brown. The Pygmoid peoples are found in the Congo region, are very short and have light, brown yellowish skins. Obviously there have been and continue to be ethnic mixing both biologically and culturally, and one would not wish to lay great stress on the distinctions which may only have academic value. Unfortunately there are certain quarters, particularly in southern Africa, where racial differences have been blown up beyond imagination, to support a racialism directed towards social and economic suppression of the 'non-white' peoples, the majority of whom are the indigenous inhabitants of the land, to say nothing about their human rights. In other parts of Africa there have been conflicts in recent years, motivated or influenced by ethnic differences or tribal interests.

[a] *The tribes, nations or peoples of Africa*
Most of the indigenous peoples of Africa have lived for hundreds of years,

and continue to live, in units or clusters commonly referred to as tribes. It is difficult to say where 'tribe' ends, since the number of those who make up a single 'tribe' varies considerably. The Yoruba of Nigeria are estimated as twelve million, while the Hadzapi of Tanzania number less than one thousand, and some 'tribes' are dying out completely. Exactly how many 'tribes' there are in Africa, nobody seems to know: they would probably be eight hundred to twelve hundred in all, partly depending on where one draws the line in cases of closely related peoples. A fairly comprehensive list of them, and a summary of their cultural features, are contained in G. P. Murdock's book, *Africa* (1959). In recent years, however, the English use of the word 'tribe' has increasingly acquired semi-bad connotations. For this reason, and the fact that large groups of half a million members and more, are like nations, I have avoided the use of the word 'tribe' in this book and elsewhere, preferring to employ the word 'people' or 'peoples'. What then are the main distinguishing features of different African peoples.

Each people has its own distinct language and not simply a dialect. Naturally, these languages are related to one another, and scholars have classified them into families or stocks. The main linguistic groups are: Bantu, found in eastern, central and southern Africa, and extending westwards up to the Cameroons; Hamitio-Semitic, found in the south-eastern and northern Africa; Khoisan, in southern Africa; Malayo-Polynesian, on the island of Madagascar; Nigritic, in western Africa; and Sudanic, in the Sudan region stretching westwards. In addition there are European languages—English, French, Portuguese, Afrikaans and Spanish —being spoken with local modifications, mainly in areas of former colonial rule. French and English are the main international languages; they are here to stay, and we might as well consider them as 'African' languages, since they are the greatest legacy we have inherited from colonial powers, and this inheritance nobody can take away from us. Arabic is the most widely spoken language in Africa, and where you find it you also find Islam. There are attempts here and there to foster indigenous languages like Swahili and Hausa, but it waits to be seen whether these can have more than a limited impact even on a national level, let alone the international level. One gets the impression that the majority of African youth are more interested in learning and mastering a Euro-African language like English or French, than in spending their energies on national or tribal languages. Whatever feelings and arguments one might privately have concerning the language problem in Africa, we must face facts and the reality. Some of the traditional languages are dying out, partly because the peoples who spoke them may also be dying out, but chiefly because of modern type of education and the drift of population from rural to urban areas. There are as many African languages as there are peoples, so that the curse of Babel seems to have descended mightily upon our continent. This great number of languages is often one of the sources of difficulties in modern nationhood. But even with a possibly high rate of language mortality in the future Africa will, for many generations to come, continue to have enough languages for everyone to learn as many as he can manage.

Geographical region is another factor in determining or describing the limits of one people from another. Each society has, at least traditionally, its own geographical area, its own land and its own country. The size of the land varies from place to place, so that some peoples own vast areas of land while others, who may be more numerical, may own only small areas. Some peoples being chiefly pastoral and not agricultural, would naturally move over a large stretch of land in their nomadic life searching for water and pasture. Where no natural boundaries like rivers or mountain ranges exist, the boundaries between the different peoples have tended to be a source of tension and fighting from time to time, just as we find in the history of other nations of the world. When Europe divided up the con-tinent of Africa at the Berlin Conference of 1885, many African peoples were split by the new and often arbitrary boundaries drawn by colonial powers. This resulted in tragic situations where some members of the same tribal group came under one colonial system while other members came under a different colonial system. The present division of Berlin itself is an ironical, if not tragic, epitomy of the divisions she once imposed on African peoples. Rather than try to do the impossible and extremely explosive job of reversing and revising the colonial boundaries, modern African states have agreed to retain and respect these colonial boundaries however painful they may continue to be. It would be a more positive step forward if the states would unite and thus swallow up or forever abolish these colonial divisions.

A common culture is another characteristic of each people. Members of one people share a common history, which is often traced at least mytho-logically to either the first man created by God, or to national leaders responsible for establishing a particular structure of the society concerned. The names of the first ancestors and other national figures are still re-membered in some societies. Thus, the Gikuyu say that their first ancestors were *Gikuyu* and *Mumbi*; those of the Vugusu were *Umngoma* and *Malava*; those of the Bambuti were *Mupe* and his wife *Uti*; of the Lugbara were *Gborogboro* and *Meme*, and of the Herero they were *Mukuru* and *Kaman-garunga*. The Shilluk mention *Nyikang* as the great national hero; the Baganda have *Kintu*, the Sonjo have *Khambageu* and the Tiv have *Tukuruku* (who is also thought to have been the first man). These figures add to a sense of common origin, unity, oneness and togetherness, and stand for national consciousness. This common culture also expresses itself in the form of common customs, morals, ethics, social behaviour and material objects like musical instruments, household utensils, foods and domestic animals. One finds many cultural similarities which cut across ethnic and linguistic differences, while at the same time some peoples who for generations have existed side by side, exhibit cultural traits that are remarkably different from those of their neighbours.

Each people has its own distinct social and political organization. The family, age groups, special persons in society, marriage customs, traditional forms of government, political personages and the like, are points of distinction, with both similarities and differences from one are to another. Some societies have regional chiefs or headmen who rule or ruled portions of the 'tribe', with hereditary or non-hereditary offices; others have had traditional monarchs or kings, often with absolute authority, ruling over the entire nation but through the help of councils and chiefs; and others delegated their political authority in the hands of age-groups (like the Galla) or elders, both men and women (like the Akamba and Gikuyu).

Religious beliefs and activities are difficult to define since in African societies religion permeates the entire life. Studies of African religious beliefs and practices show that there are probably more similarities than differences, as we are trying to indicate in this book. Each people has its own religious system, and a person cannot be converted from one tribal religion to another: he has to be born in the particular society in order to participate in the entire religious life of the people. As with material culture, religious ideas and activities are exchanged when people come into contact with one another, even though there is no organized missionary work of one group trying to proselytize another. This exchange of ideas is spontaneous, and is probably more noticeable in practical matters like rainmaking, combating magic and witchcraft and dealing with misfortunes. In such cases, expert knowledge may be borrowed and later assimilated from neighbouring peoples. Fundamental concepts like the belief in God, existence of the spirits, continuation of human life after death, magic and witchcraft, seem to have been retained when one people may have split or branched off in course of the centuries, the new groups forming 'tribes' of their own, which now we can recognize under the broad ethnic and linguistic groupings of African peoples. This probably explains the fact of fundamental beliefs being found over wide stretches of Africa. Therefore, names for God, and words for spirits, magic and medicine-men are similar among many peoples, just as are words for man, house, rain and so on which also are of fundamental value.

These then are the main features of an African 'tribe', people, society or nation. A person has to be born a member of it, and he cannot change tribal membership. On rare occasions he can be adopted ritually into another tribal group, but this is seldom done and applies to both Africans and non-Africans. Tribal identity is still a powerful force even in modern African statehood, although that feeling of tribal identity varies like temperature, from time to time, depending on prevailing circumstances.

[b] *Kinship*

The deep sense of kinship, with all it implies, has been one of the strongest forces in traditional African life. Kinship is reckoned through blood and betrothal (engagement and marriage). It is kinship which controls social relationships between people in a given community: it governs marital customs and regulations, it determines the behaviour of one individual towards another. Indeed, this sense of kinship binds together the entire life of the 'tribe', and is even extended to cover animals, plants and non-living objects through the 'totemic' system. Almost all the concepts connected with human relationship can be understood and interpreted through the kinship system. This it is which largely governs the behaviour, thinking and whole life of the individual in the society of which he is a member.

Most of anthropological and sociological studies of African people deal to a certain extent with some aspects of the kinship system of individual peoples. The best study is one edited by A. R. Radcliffe-Brown and D. Forde: *African Systems of Kinship and Marriage.* The topic is too complicated, and beyond the scope of this work, to be dealt with here in detail, except to draw attention to its great importance and make a few observations. The kinship system is like a vast network stretching laterally (horizontally) in every direction, to embrace everybody in an any given local group. This means that each individual is a brother or sister, father or mother, grand-mother or grandfather, or cousin, or brother-in-law, uncle or aunt, or something else, to everybody else. That means that everybody is related to everybody else, and there are many kinship terms to express the precise kind of relationship pertaining between two individuals. When two strangers meet in a village, one of the first duties is to sort out how they may be related to each other, and having discovered how the kinship system applies to them, they behave to each other according to the accepted behaviour set down by society. If they discover, for example, that they are 'brothers', then they will treat each other as equals, or as an older and younger brother; if they are 'uncle' and 'nephew', then the 'nephew' may be expected to give much respect to the 'uncle' where this type of relationship is required by society. It is possible also that from that moment on, the individuals concerned will refer to each other by the kinship term of, for instance, 'brother', 'nephew', 'uncle', 'mother', with or without using their proper names. Such being the case then, a person has literally hundreds of 'fathers', hundreds of 'mothers', hundreds of 'uncles', hundreds of 'wives', hundreds of 'sons and daughters'.

The kinship system also extends vertically to include the departed and those yet to be born. It is part of traditional education for children in many African societies, to learn the genealogies of their descent. The genealogy gives a sense of depth, historical belongingness, a feeling of deep rootedness and a sense of sacred obligation to extend the genealogical line. Through genealogies, individuals in the Sasa period are firmly linked to those who have entered into the Zamani. Genealogies are sacred means of orientation towards the Zamani where the foundations of different peoples lie. Through genealogies, those who are in the Zamani and those who are in the Sasa periods become 'contemporaries' in the timeless rhythm of human life. In some societies people trace their genealogies as far back as the mythological 'first' man, or other national heroes, giving them a sense of pride and satisfaction.

Genealogical ties also serve social purposes, particularly in establishing relationships between individuals. By citing one's genealogical line, it is possible to see how that person is linked to other individuals in a given group. It is also on genealogical basis that organizational divisions have evolved among different peoples, demarcating the larger society into 'clans', 'gates', families, households and finally individuals.

The clan is the major subdivision of the 'tribe'. Some peoples may have up to a hundred clans. Clan systems are by no means uniform in Africa. There are patriarchal clans where descent is traced through the father; but there are also matriarchal clans, especially in parts of central, western and northern Africa, in which descent is traced through the mother. Clans are normally totemic, that is, each has an animal or part of it, a plant, a stone or mineral, which is regarded as its totem. Members of a particular clan observe special care in treating or handling their totem, so that, for example, they would not kill or eat it. The totem is the visible symbol of unity, of kinship, of belongingness, of togetherness and common affinity. Genealogies may be cited as far back as the original founder of the clan, if he has not been forgotten or if the genealogical line has not been broken through loss of memory. Some of the clans were founded by men and others by women, while others seem to have evolved in response to particular historical circumstances.

Another common feature of the clan is that members may not marry fellow members: such are known as exogamous clans. In some societies, however, marriage within the clan is allowed, and these are known to anthropologists and sociologists as endogamous clans. The number of people in a given clan varies considerably, so that some clans may have several thousands while others have only a hundred or so members. An individual has to be born in a clan, and he cannot change his clan, though it is possible that in some societies marriage may lead to a change or weakening of one's original clan membership. In some societies, clans have their separate land areas, while in other societies the clans are intermingled throughout the tribal land. It is possible, in some societies, to tell to which clan a person belongs by means of his name or his locality. In other societies this is possible only by asking the individual concerned to mention his clan.

Apart from localizing the sense of kinship, clan systems provide closer human co-operation, especially in times of need. In case of internal conflicts, clan members joined one another to fight their aggressive neighbours, in former years. If a person finds himself in difficulties, it is not unusual for him to call for help from his clan members and other relatives, e.g. in paying fines caused by an accident (such as accidental wounding or killing of another person or damage to property); in finding enough goods to exchange for a wife; or today in giving financial support to students studying in institutes of higher education both at home and abroad.

There are, in some societies, subdivisions of the clan into sub-clans or 'gates', on the level between the clan and the family. These localize clan matters, and deal with affairs which need not concern the whole clan. It is probably this subdivision which, in the course of time, grows into a full clan of its own. The 'gate' is made up of members from a common ancestor up to six or eight generations back.

[c] *The family, the household and the individual*

For African peoples the family has a much wider circle of members than the word suggests in Europe or North America. In traditional society, the family includes children, parents, grandparents, uncles, aunts, brothers and sisters who may have their own children, and other immediate relatives. In many areas there are what anthropologists call *extended families,* by which it is generally meant that two or more brothers (in the patrilocal societies) or sisters (in the matrilocal societies) establish families in one compound or close to one another. The joint households together are like one large family. In either case, the number of family members may range from ten persons to even a hundred where several wives belonging to one husband may be involved. It is the practice in some societies, to send children to live for some months or years, with relatives, and these children are counted as members of the families where they happen to live.

The family also includes the departed relatives, whom we have designated as the living-dead. These are, as their name implies, 'alive' in the memories of their surviving families, and are thought to be still interested in the affairs of the family to which they once belonged in their physical life. Surviving members must not forget the departed, otherwise misfortune is feared to strike them or their relatives. The older a person was before dying, the greater was his Sasa period and the longer he is remembered and regarded as an integral part of the human family. People give offerings of food and libation to the living-dead because they are still part of the family. The food and libation so offered, are tokens of the fellowship, communion, remembrance, respect and hospitality, being extended to those who are the immediate pillars or roots of the family. The living-dead solidify and mystically bind together the whole family. People say that they see departed members of their family coming and appearing to them. When they do, the living-dead enquire concerning the affairs of the human family, or warn against danger, rebuke the living for not carrying out particular instructions, or ask for food (usually meat) and drink. If the departed have been offended, it is often said that they will take revenge or demand a rectification.

African concept of the family also includes the unborn members who are still in the loins of the living. They are the buds of hope and expectation, and each family makes sure that its own existence is not extinguished. The family provides for its continuation, and prepares for the coming of those not yet born. For that reason, African parents are anxious to see that their children find husbands and wives, otherwise failure to do so means in effect the death of the unborn and a diminishing of the family as a whole.

The household is the smallest unit of the family, consisting of the children, parents and sometimes the grandparents. It is what one might call 'the family at night', for it is generally at night that the household is really itself. At night the parents are with their immediate children in the same house; they discuss private affairs of their household, and the parents educate the children in matters pertaining to domestic relationships. The household in Africa is what in European and American societies would be called 'family'. If a man has two or more wives, he has as many households since each wife would usually have her own house erected within the same compound where other wives and their households live.

The area or compound occupied by one household or joint households, is a village, in the African context of this word. It includes houses, gardens or fields (if these are nearby), the cattle shed, granaries, the courtyard, threshing ground, the men's outdoor fireplace (in some societies), the children's playground and family shrines (where these exist). In some societies the village has a fence round it, marking it as a single village or household, or as a family.

As a rule traditional African houses are round in shape, built around the village compound so that if there are several houses in one compound, they also form a circle or semi-circle. The houses generally face the centre of the compound and towards the main entrance into the village. It is difficult to say dogmatically what this round shape of houses and villages may indicate. Could it be a sign of nature's rhythm, or is it the universe in miniature, or does the circle symbolize security as if the village were like a vast vessel into which both men, animals and crops enter and are kept secure from outside dangers? I do not know, and one can only speculate the symbolic meaning of African villages which so remarkably resemble one another all over tropical and southern Africa.

We have so far spoken about the life and existence of the community. What then is the individual and where is his place in the community? In traditional life, the individual does not and cannot exist alone except corporately. He owes his existence to other people, including those of past generations and his contemporaries. He is simply part of the whole. The community must therefore make, create or produce the individual; for the individual depends on the corporate group. Physical birth is not enough: the child must go through rites of incorporation so that it becomes fully integrated into the entire society. These rites continue throughout the physical life of the person, during which the individual passes from one stage of corporate existence to another. The final stage is reached when he dies and even then he is ritually incorporated into the wider family of both the dead and the living.

Just as God made the first man, as God's man, so now man himself makes the individual who becomes the corporate or social man. It is a deeply religious transaction. Only in terms of other people does the individual become conscious of his own being, his own duties, his privileges and responsibilities towards himself and towards other people. When he suffers, he does not suffer alone but with the corporate group; when he rejoices, he rejoices not alone but with his kinsmen, his neighbours and his relatives whether dead or living. When he gets married, he is not alone, neither does the wife 'belong' to him alone. So also the children belong to the corporate body of kinsmen, even if they bear only their father's name. Whatever happens to the individual happens to the whole group, and whatever happens to the whole group happens to the individual. The individual can only say: 'I am, because we are; and since we are, therefore

I am'. This is a cardinal point in the understanding of the African view of man.

We have travelled a long religious path, from God through the spirits to man as an individual. Some of the ethnic and sociological material in this chapter may seem less 'religious', but it is necessary as the background to what will follow in the remaining chapters of this book. We have arrived at the individual, and now we are going to walk with him from birth to death. He is a deeply religious man living in an intensely religious universe. We must see him in the context of his Sasa period, travelling towards his Zamani.

11

BIRTH & CHILDHOOD

In African societies, the birth of a child is a process which begins long before the child's arrival in this world and continues long thereafter. It is not just a single event which can be recorded on a particular date. Nature brings the child into the world, but society creates the child into a social being, a corporate person. For it is the community which must protect the child, feed it, bring it up, educate it and in many other ways incorporate it into the wider community. Children are the buds of society, and every birth is the arrival of 'spring' when life shoots out and the community thrives. The birth of a child is, therefore, the concern not only of the parents but of many relatives including the living and the departed. Kinship plays an important role here, so that a child cannot be exclusively 'my child' but only 'our child'.

[a] *Pregnancy*
This is the first indication that a new member of society is on the way. The expectant mother becomes, therefore, a special person and receives special treatment from her neighbours and relatives. This special treatment starts before and continues after child-birth. In some African societies, marriage is not fully recognized or consummated until the wife has given birth. First pregnancy becomes, therefore, the final seal of marriage, the sign of complete integration of the woman into her husband's family and kinship circle. Unhappy is the woman who fails to get children for, whatever other qualities she might possess, her failure to bear children is worse than committing genocide: she has become the dead end of human life, not only for the genealogical line but also for herself. When she dies, there will be nobody of her own immediate blood to 'remember' her, to keep her in the state of personal immortality: she will simply be 'forgotten'. The fault may not be her own, but this does not 'excuse' her in the eyes of society. Her husband may remedy the situation a bit, by raising children with another wife; but the childless wife bears a scar which nothing can erase. She will suffer for this, her own relatives will suffer for this; and it

will be an irreparable humiliation for which there is no source of comfort in traditional life.

In many African societies the pregnant woman must observe certain taboos and regulations, partly because pregnancy in effect makes her ritually 'impure', and chiefly in order to protect her and the child. One of the most common regulations concerns sexual intercourse during pregnancy. In some societies as soon as a woman realizes that she is expecting, she and her husband completely stop having sexual intercourse until after childbirth. In other societies this is stopped two or three months before childbirth. This abstinence is observed by the woman after childbirth, for periods ranging from a few days to even two or three years. The husband is not obliged to observe abstinence for such a long time, since he may have other wives. On the average, women abstain until their children are weaned; but the practice varies from society to society.

Another regulation concerns food: expectant mothers are forbidden to eat certain foods, for fear that these foods would interfere with the health and safety of the mother or child, or would cause misfortune to either of them after birth. For example, among the Akamba the expectant mother is forbidden to eat fat, beans and meat of animals killed with poisoned arrows, during the last three months of pregnancy. In addition to other foods, she eats a special kind of earth found on anthills or trees. This earth is first chewed by a certain kind of ant, and then deposited on trees and grass, or piled up to form a mound (anthill). Even for non-pregnant people it is not repugnant to the taste. People believe that such earth 'strengthens' the body of the child. No doubt there is some scientific truth in these beliefs concerning foods, and they have developed as a result of people's experiences. It may be, for example, that eating meat of animals killed with poisoned arrows has in fact caused premature births; and the earth from ants has minerals which do in fact 'strengthen' the child's body in the womb.

Among the Ingassana, the pregnant woman returns to the home of her parents, when the time of giving birth draws near. The same custom is observed by some other peoples. I am not quite sure of the meaning behind it. Perhaps it is a symbolic dramatization of 'fetching' the child from another (the invisible?) world. It may also symbolize the return of life to the homestead where the wife originates. It may also have the social significance of indicating to the relatives that the wife is fertile and productive.

Another taboo commonly observed is in connection with work and the use of tools. Among the Akamba and Gikuyu, for example, all weapons and all iron articles are removed from the house of the expectant mother before the birth takes place. People believe that iron articles attract lightning. Among the Ingassana, both the expectant mother and her husband are forbidden to carry fire, prior to the birth of the child. These and similar prohibitions illustrate the care and protection which both mother and child should and do receive.

There are also social regulations. For example, among the Mao, when the wife is pregnant she does not speak directly with her husband. The couple communicates with each other through an intermediary. Exactly what this means I am not certain. There are several possibilities. It may be that pregnancy makes her ritually unclean, and her husband must therefore be protected from that. It may also be a way of making the husband share the burden of pregnancy. The custom is a means of protecting the expectant mother from any physical, psychological and ritual harm she might otherwise suffer by being in direct contact with her husband.

There are societies where prayers for mother and child are made to God, to ensure their safety. The Nandi pray for the protection of their expectant wives; when a Bambuti woman realizes that she is expecting she cooks food and takes some of it to the forest where she offers it to God with a prayer of thanksgiving. Relevant rituals may also be performed, and some expectant mothers carry protective charms.

[b] *The actual birth*

Practices and ideas connected with the actual birth vary considerably, and we shall take only a few examples as an illustration. Birth generally takes place in the house of the expectant mother, or in the house of her parents where this custom is observed. In a few cases, however, it takes place in a special house constructed for that purpose, either inside or outside the village. For example, the Udhuk custom is that when a woman is about to deliver, she goes alone into the bush to give birth there. She might, however, ask a relative to go with her. After giving birth in the wilderness, she returns home with her child. The custom seems to have arisen from another custom by which a woman who gives birth to twins is killed together with the twins. By giving birth away from other people nobody would know it if she gets twins, in which case she would kill one of the twins and return home with the other. This is an extreme custom and is not reported in other societies.

In many áreas almost any elderly woman can, under normal circumstances, act as a midwife, though this is generally done by specialists. As a rule also, during the giving of birth men are forbidden to be present in the house where delivery is taking place. Among some communities, measures are taken to aid the woman in her final labour pains. For example, Wolof women walk up and down, or pound grain in a mortar. Other societies may use herbs for the same purpose. During delivery, women generally squat. When a Gikuyu woman has given birth, she screams five times if the child is a boy, and four times if it is a girl.

The placenta and umbilical cord are the symbols of the child's attachment to mother, to womanhood, to the state of inactivity. They are therefore the object of special treatment in most African societies. For example, the Gikuyu deposit the placenta in an uncultivated field and cover it with grain and grass, these symbolizing fertility. The uncultivated field is the symbol of fertility, strength and freshness; and using it is like a silent prayer that the mother's womb should remain fertile and strong for the birth of more children. Among the Didinga, the placenta is buried near the house where the birth takes place; among the Ingassana it is put in a calabash which is hung on a special tree (*gammeiza*); and among the Wolof the placenta is buried in the back-yard, but the umbilical cord is sometimes made into a charm which the child is made to wear.

Physically the placenta and umbilical cord symbolize the separation of the child from the mother, but this separation is not final since the two are still near each other. But the child now begins to belong to the wider circle of society. For that reason, the placenta is kept close to the house or placed in a calabash for everyone to see it. The child has, however, begun its journey of being incorporated into the community, so that the separation between the individual mother and child continues to widen as the child's integration into the wider community also increases. These symbols of attachment between mother and child are disposed of by being buried or kept near the house or place of the child's birth. Among some societies, like the Ndebele, the umbilical cord and the placenta are buried right under the floor of the house where the birth takes place. Paradoxically, then, the child is near the mother and yet begins to get away from the individual mother, growing into the status of being 'I am because we are, and since we are therefore I am'.

We find other methods of disposing with the placenta and cord. The Yansi throw them into the river. This also has symbolic meaning: the child is now public property, it belongs to the entire community and is no longer the property of one person, and any ties to one person or one household are symbolically destroyed and dissolved in the act of throwing the placenta and umbilical cord into the river. Such ties are to be remembered no more.

Whatever methods are used for the disposal of the umbilical cord and placenta, the disposal indicates that the child has died to the state of pregnancy and is now alive in another state of existence. It has died to the stage of being alone in the mother's womb: but now it has risen in the new life of being part of the human society.

The details of what follows immediately after childbirth vary widely.

In some societies the baby may not be given its mother's milk until rituals of purification have been performed; in others the mother and child are kept from each other for some days; in others both child and mother may be kept in seclusion from the public for several days or even weeks. As a rule, the whole occasion of birth is marked with feasting and great rejoicing among the relatives and neighbours of the parents concerned.

We shall take a few examples. Among the Akamba, when a child has been born, the parents slaughter a goat or bull on the third day. Many people come to rejoice with the family concerned, and women get together to give a name to the child. This is known as 'the name of *ngima*', the 'ngima' being the main dish prepared for the occasion. Among the Wolof, the woman must first perform the rite of jumping over fire in four directions before she can sit down on her bed. Then the midwife holds the child out to the mother three times, handing over the child on the fourth occasion. This rite is believed to prevent madness. Before suckling, the child is made to drink a charm made from washing off a Koranic verse which has been written on a wooden slate. Then a goat is killed on the day of birth. During the following week, other rites are performed. A fire is kept burning night and day in the house where birth has taken place. Beside this fire stands an iron rod which is used for pressing seeds out of cotton wool, and a pot with pieces of a water plant (*rat*) which have been boiled. The woman drinks the water from this pot. Branches of *rat* and another tree are placed outside the door of the house and at the entrance into the compound. The knife, or other piece of metal, which was used for cutting the umbilical cord is kept under the child's pillow. Both mother and child remain indoors, and if she has to go out, she must carry the knife with her, replacing it with stalks of a plant near the baby's head.[1] When this period is over, then the child is given a name. These rituals are intended to protect mother and child, and are full of symbolic meaning. The everburning fire is a symbol of life's continuation; the knife symbolizes protection and defence against evil powers; and the Koranic verse is meant to keep away malevolent spirits. Seclusion symbolizes death, separation from society; and when it is over then the child and mother are resurrected, they are integrated into the community, and the child receives its name—the symbol of its personality.

Let us consider another example, from the Gikuyu. After the birth of the child, the father cuts four sugar-canes if the child is a girl, or five it it is a boy. The juice from these sugar-canes is given to the mother and child; and the waste scraps from the sugar-cane are placed on the right-hand side of the house if the child is a boy, or left-hand side if it is a girl. Right is the symbol for man, and left for woman. The child is then washed and oiled.

[1] Gamble, p. 62.

If the birth has been difficult, the father sacrifices a goat and a medicine-man is called to purify the house. The mother and child are kept in seclusion for four days if the child is a girl, or five days if it is a boy. During seclusion only close women relatives and attendants may visit the house. When this period is over, the mother is shaved on the head, and the husband sacrifices a sheep of thanksgiving to God and the living-dead. During the period of seclusion no member of the family is allowed to wash himself in the river, no house in the village is cleaned (swept), and no fire may be fetched from one house to another. When seclusion is over, the mother pays a symbolic visit to the fields and gathers sweet potatoes. Thereafter normal life is resumed by everybody in the village.

These Gikuyu rites and observances have their meaning and significance. Seclusion, as we have seen, symbolizes the concept of death and resurrection: death to one state of life, and resurrection to a fuller state of living. It is as if the mother and child 'die' and 'rise again' on behalf of everyone else in the family. The shaving of the mother's hair is another act symbolizing and dramatizing the death of one state and rising again of another. The hair represents her pregnancy, but now that this is over, old hair must be shaved off to give way to new hair, the symbol of new life. She is now a new person, ready for another child to come into her womb, and thus allow the stream of life to continue flowing. The hair also has the symbolic connection between the mother and child, so that shaving it indicates that the child now belongs not only to her but to the entire body of relatives, neighbours and other members of the society. She has no more claims over the child as exclusively her own: the child is now 'scattered' like her shaven hair, so that it has a hundred mothers, a hundred fathers, a hundred brothers and hundreds of other relatives. The forbidden washing, cleaning of houses and moving of fire from one house to another, symbolize the halting of normal life, the death of corporate life in expectation of the new rhythm of life represented in the birth of the child. In the birth of a child, the whole community is born anew; it is renewed, it is revived and revitalized. Life starts again after four or five days, with additional momentum. We have noted that a sheep is sacrificed: this marks one of the key moments in the life of the individual, during which the Gikuyu make special sacrifices and prayers. Not only is God brought into the picture, but also the living-dead since these also participate in the occasion of rejoicing: it is 'their' child as much as it is the child of the human family.

For the Gikuyu this is not, however, the end of the rituals connected with childbirth. While the child is still small, they perform other rites which they consider necessary before the child can be a full member of their society. Four other rites are necessary, and in one of them, the father puts small wristlets of goat skin on the child. After that the child is a full person, and the parents may now resume normal sex relations. Around the age of five or six years, another rite is performed, by means of which the child is now entitled to start looking after goats. The rite of wristlets symbolizes the bond between the child and the entire nation: the wristlet is a link in the long chain of life, linking the child with both the living and the departed. It is the ring of the generations of humanity, linking the Zamani with the Sasa. In effect every generation is a wristlet, a link in the chain of human existence. It is a sacred link which must never be broken.

At a later age, another rite is performed. It is known as 'the second birth' (*kuciaruo keri*, literally 'to be born twice'), or 'to be born again' (*kuciaruo ringi*), or 'to be born of a goat' (*kuciareiruo mbori*). This takes place before the child is initiated; and unless the child has gone through this 'second birth', he cannot participate fully in the life of the community. He is forbidden to assist in the burial of his own father, to be initiated, to get married, to inherit property and to take part in any ritual. This rite is therefore absolutely essential in Gikuyu life. Between the age of six and ten, the child re-enacts its birth. If the mother is dead, then another woman is substituted, and will henceforth be regarded as the child's mother. During the rite, the child is placed between the legs of the mother, and is bound to her by a goat intestine. This intestine is cut through, and the child imitates the cry of a baby. The mother is shaved, her house is swept and she visits the fields to collect food.[1] The rite symbolizes physical birth, but it takes place at an age when the child can remember the occasion. Thus, the child enters into the conscious experience of its birth, the beginning of its Sasa period. But the rite also ends the child's 'babyhood', and brings it to the gate of full participation in the life of the community. Now the child is ready to enter the stage of initiation, ready to be incorporated into the activities and responsibilities of corporate manhood. It now passes from the period of ignorance to one of knowledge, from the state of being a passive member of the community to the new stage of being an active and responsible member of the corporate society. Man has done his part, to 'create', to 'cultivate' and to make 'grow' the child that God has given in a complete physical state to the community.

We have taken much space to examine at some detail the rites of two peoples, the Wolof on the west coast of Africa and the Gikuyu on the east coast, five thousand kilometers apart. There are some symbolic similarities, not only between these two peoples but among other African peoples. There are also differences, especially in the actual rites and their meanings.

[1] Middleton, I, p. 59 f. I have given these rites my own interpretation and understanding of what they mean and signify.

We might cite different examples from the Ndebele and Sonjo rites of putting tribal marks on children. The Ndebele cut holes on the ear lobes of their children when they are aged about ten, and after the operation the hole is plugged with a piece of wood to keep it open. This is a tribal mark of identification and incorporation. All the Sonjo must wear a tribal mark, *ntemi*, on their left shoulder, by means of which they hope to be identified when their national hero, *Khambageu*, returns to 'save' them at the end of the world. These are marks of identification, incorporation, membership and full rights; they are the indelible scars that 'I am because we are, and since we are, therefore I am'. The individual is united with the rest of his community, both the living and the dead, and humanly speaking nothing can separate him from this corporate society.

The birth of twins and triplets is an event out of the ordinary. Therefore, in many African societies twins and triplets are treated with fear or special care. Formerly, some societies used to kill such children; others killed both the mother and the children. This, however, was not the universal practice, for other societies greeted the birth of twins with great joy and satisfaction, as a sign of rich fertility. Children of such births are believed in some societies to have special powers. For example, in central Africa they are known as 'the children of God and heaven' (*Tilo*), and when a village is threatened with calamity, people turn to them to pray on behalf of their communities. This ambivalent treatment of twins and triplets has yet to be carefully studied. On the one hand, people rejoice to see the flow of human life, but paradoxically that rejoicing is turned into sorrows when twins are born. I would suggest that since the birth of twins is something extraordinary, something out of the normal rhythm of things, it gives rise to a feeling of extreme consequences: either consequences of misfortunes, and hence the necessity to kill the children (and their mother if need be), or consequences of unusual powers and hence the need to treat such children with special care or respect. The twins or triplets are not intrinsically evil or extraordinary; it is the unusualness of the event of their birth which makes people attribute extreme associations to them. The same thing happens when there are eclipses or other irregularities of nature. If written records of history and other events were kept, these 'irregularities' would no longer look so irregular when viewed against a large scale time-table. As it is in traditional life, events are kept in people's memories and this is prone to exaggeration or streamlining at the expense of right proportions.

The killing of twins and triplets where and when it occurred, must not be judged purely on emotional reactions, however severely the practice should be condemned on ethical grounds. From the point of view of the corporate community, such births were experienced as heralds of misfortune.

The people concerned experienced them as a threat to their whole existence, as a sign that something wrong had happened to cause the births, and that something worse still would happen to the whole community if the 'evil' were not removed. So they killed the children for the sake of the larger community, to cleanse, to 'save', to protect the rest of the people. If this was not done, then not only would the twins themselves suffer, but the rest of society would be in danger of annihilation. So the killing seems to have been carried out with good intentions, and not in any way as a cruel act against the children. It was a bloody operation done to the corporate group, by the corporate group, for the corporate group. Since this belief was so en-trenched in some societies, I doubt whether the practice of killing twins has been stopped completely by modern governments.

While on this note, we must mention the extremely high rate of infant mortality found in traditional societies. In some cases this was so severe that about half of all the children born alive would die within their first ten years of life. But thanks to the use of modern medicine and better child care this high rate of death among children has been increasingly reduced. This great work was pioneered by Christian missionaries, and has rapidly been taken over or supplemented by African governments. But disease and malnutrition are still the greatest enemies of African infants and children, particularly in the period immediately after weaning. There is hardly a mother in traditional societies who has not tasted the sorrows of losing a child. In her sorrows she is not alone: they are the sorrows of her com-munity, and of African societies at large.

[c] *The naming and nursing of children*
Nearly all African names have a meaning. The naming of children is therefore an important occasion which is often marked by ceremonies in many societies. Some names may mark the occasion of the child's birth. For example, if the birth occurs during rain, the child would be given a name which means 'Rain', or 'Rainy', or 'Water'; if the mother is on a journey at the time, the child might be called 'Traveller', 'Stranger', 'Road' or 'Wanderer'; if there is a locust invasion when the child is born, it might be called 'Locust', or 'Famine', or 'Pain'. Some names describe the person-ality of the individual, or his character, or some key events in his life. There is no stop to the giving of names in many African societies, so that a person can acquire a sizeable collection of names by the time he becomes an old man. Other names given to children may come from the living-dead who might be thought to have been partially 're-incarnated' in the child, especially if the family observes certain traits in common between the child and a particular living-dead. In some societies it is also the custom to give

the names of the grandparents to the children. The name is the person, and many names are often descriptive of the individual, particularly names acquired as the person grows. In view of the African practice of giving names to people, it is confusing and often meaningless to speak of 'family names', since every individual has his own names. Apart from a few societies, there are no single 'family names' shared by everybody in a given family. It is also to be noted that Africans change names without any formalities about it, and a person may be 'registered' (for example in school, university and tax office) under one name today and under another name 'tomorrow'. This practice causes not only confusion but irritation at times.

We return now to methods of giving names to children, and we shall illustrate them by taking concrete examples from different parts of Africa. The Wolof name their children one week after birth. For this occasion friends and relatives of the family concerned are informed beforehand, and if it is the first child a large gathering takes place. The ceremony is performed where the birth occurred, and starts just before noon. On the appointed day, the child's mother extinguishes the fire and sweeps the house, takes a bath and the baby is washed with the medicinal water (which we mentioned in the previous subsection). These are symbolic acts marking the end of one phase of life, and the beginning of a new one. Visitors and guests bring presents: women give their presents to the child's mother, and men to the father. In the centre of the compound a mat is spread where an old woman, usually the midwife, sits with the child on her lap. The child is shaved, starting on the right side. Nearby stands a clay bowl with red and white kola nuts, cotton and millet. The red kola nuts symbolize long life, and the white ones symbolize good luck. An elderly person rubs hands over the child's head, prays and spits in its ears to implant the name in the baby's head. After that the name is then announced loudly to the crowd, and prayers are offered for long life and prosperity. The child and mother are hidden away, if it is the first born, in case someone with an evil eye should see them. The gathering spends the rest of the day dancing and feasting, and a goat or sheep is killed for the occasion. The name of the child is generally according to the day of the week when it was born—a practice found also among Ghana peoples.

The Shona have no special ceremony for naming their children, this being done by the father a few days after birth. Among the Luo, the child's name is sought when the child is crying. During this period, different names of the living-dead are mentioned, and if the child stops crying when a particular name is called out, then the child receives that name. The names have meanings according to the occasion or other significance at the time of birth. The Akamba give names to their children on the third day, the occasion being marked by feasting and rejoicing. On the fourth day, the father hangs an iron necklace on the child's neck, after which it is regarded as a full human being and as having lost contact with the spirit world. Before that, the child is regarded as an 'object' belonging to the spirits (*kiimu*), and if it should die before the naming ceremony, the mother becomes ritually unclean and must be cleansed. When the naming has been performed, the parents perform a ritual sexual intercourse that night. This ritual is the seal of the child's separation from the spirits and the living-dead, and its integration into the company of human beings. Names are chosen by women who have had children, and most of them have meanings.

The period and manner of nursing children vary widely. Some societies take as long as two years or longer for mothers to nurse their children, during which time the wives are not allowed to have sexual relation with their husbands. In other societies any woman suckling a child may be called upon to suckle someone else's child. In others, part of the nursing and weaning process involves sending the child to the home of relatives.

During the nursing period, the child is carried on the back or bosom of the mother or of another female member of the village. This direct contact between mother and child gives the child a deep psychological sense of security. African women, as a rule, suckle their children anywhere taking out their breasts openly and without any feeling of embarrassment or shame. Breasts are the symbols of life, and the bigger they are, the more people appreciate them: they are a sign that the woman has an ample supply of milk for her child. There is nothing 'naked' or 'sexy' about nursing mothers exposing their breasts to suckle their children in market places, church gatherings or buses; and those who judge such mothers as being indecent must revise their understanding of African concept of what constitutes 'nakedness'. Wood carvings that feature mother and child, often 'exaggerate' the breasts: for these are the pride of motherhood, announcing the message that 'I am fertile'. And this is the ideal wish of every African woman.

We see now how both birth and childhood are a religious process, in which the child is constantly flooded with religious activities and attitudes starting long before it is born. A child not only continues the physical line of life, being in some societies thought to be a re-incarnation of the departed, but becomes the intensely religious focus of keeping the parents in their state of personal immortality. The physical aspects of birth and the ceremonies that might accompany pregnancy, birth and childhood, are regarded with religious feeling and experience—that another religious being has been born into a profoundly religious community and religious world.

12

INITIATION
& PUBERTY RITES

We saw in the previous chapter how children are born both physically and religiously. The rites of birth and childhood introduce the child to the corporate community, but this is only the introduction. The child is passive and has still a long way to go. He must grow out of childhood and enter into adulthood both physically, socially and religiously. This is also a change from passive to active membership in the community. Most African peoples have rites and ceremonies to mark this great change, but a few do not observe initiation and puberty rites. The initiation of the young is one of the key moments in the rhythm of individual life, which is also the rhythm of the corporate group of which the individual is a part. What happens to the single youth happens corporately to the parents, the relatives, the neighbours and the living-dead.

Initiation rites have many symbolic meanings, in addition to the physical drama and impact. We can mention some of the religious meanings before we come to concrete examples. The youth are ritually introduced to the art of communal living. This happens when they withdraw from other people to live alone in the forest or in specifically prepared huts away from the villages. They go through a period of withdrawal from society, absence from home, during which time they receive secret instruction before they are allowed to rejoin their relatives at home. This is a symbolic experience of the process of dying, living in the spirit world and being reborn (resurrected). The rebirth, that is the act of rejoining their families, emphasizes and dramatizes that the young people are now new, they have new personalities, they have lost their childhood, and in some societies they even receive completely new names.

Another great significance of the rites is to introduce the candidates to adult life: they are now allowed to share in the full privileges and duties of the community. They enter into the state of responsibility: they inherit new rights, and new obligations are expected of them by society. This incorporation into adult life also introduces them to the life of the living-dead as well as the life of those yet to be born. The initiation rites prepare young people in matters of sexual life, marriage, procreation and family responsibilities. They are henceforth allowed to shed their blood for their country, and to plant their biological seeds so that the next generation can begin to arrive.

Initiation rites have a great educational purpose. The occasion often marks the beginning of acquiring knowledge which is otherwise not accessible to those who have not been initiated. It is a period of awakening to many things, a period of dawn for the young. They learn to endure hardships, they learn to live with one another, they learn to obey, they learn the secrets and mysteries of the man-woman relationship; and in some areas, especially in West Africa, they join secret societies each of which has its own secrets, activities and language.

We shall now consider concrete examples of initiation rites. The details will obviously differ considerably, but the basic meaning and significance are generally similar. For most peoples the initiation rites take place during puberty, but there are places where they are performed either before or after puberty. For this reason it is incorrect to speak of them as 'puberty rites'.

[a] *Akamba initiation rites*
There are three parts to Akamba initiation rites, the first two being the most important. Formerly, everybody had to go through these first two, but only a small number of men went through the third which was performed when the men were over forty years old. Without being initiated, a person is not a full member of the Akamba people. Furthermore, no matter how old or big he is, so long as he is not initiated, he is despised and considered to be still a boy or girl.

Children go through the first stage of initiation rites when they are about four to seven years of age. The ceremony takes place in the months of August to October, when it is dry and relatively cool. Boys undergo circumcision, and girls undergo clitoridectomy. The date for the ceremony is announced in a given region, and when it arrives all the candidates are gathered together by their parents and relatives at the home where the ceremony is to take place. Specialist men circumcise the boys, and specialist women perform the operation on the girls; and a special knife is used in each case. The physical cutting takes place early in the morning. The foreskin of the boys' sexual organ is cut off; and a small portion of the girls' clitoris is similarly removed. Men gather round to watch the boys, and women to watch the girls. The operation is painful, but the children are encouraged to endure it without crying or shouting, and those who manage to go through it bravely are highly praised by the community. Afterwards there is public rejoicing, with dancing, singing, drinking beer and making libation and food offerings to the living-dead. In course of the following few weeks, while the wound is healing, relatives come to visit the initiated boys and girls, bringing them presents of chickens, money, ornaments and even sheep and cattle by those who can afford them.

That is the first stage of the initiation: what does it signify and mean? The cutting of the skin from the sexual organs symbolizes and dramatizes separation from childhood: it is parallel to the cutting of the umbilical cord when the child is born. The sexual organ attaches the child to the state of ignorance, the state of inactivity and the state of potential impotence (asexuality). But once that link is severed, the young person is freed from that state of ignorance and inactivity. He is born into another state, which is the stage of knowledge, of activity, of reproduction. So long as a person is not initiated, he cannot get married and he is not supposed to reproduce or bear children. The shedding of his blood into the ground binds him mystically to the living-dead who are symbolically living in the ground, or are reached at least through the pouring of libation on to the ground. It is the blood of new birth. The physical pain which the children are encouraged to endure, is the beginning of training them for difficulties and sufferings of later life. Endurance of physical and emotional pain is a great virtue among Akamba people, as indeed it is among other Africans, since life in Africa is surrounded by much pain from one source or another. The presents given to the initiates by their relatives, are tokens of welcome into the full community. They also demonstrate and symbolize the fact that now the young people can begin to own and inherit property, they are entitled to new rights and can say, 'This is is my property', even if they own it jointly with the corporate group. Owning property leads eventually to the next important stage, which is the period of marriage.

The dancing and rejoicing strengthen community solidarity, and emphasize the corporateness of the whole group. It is only after this first initiation rite that young people are allowed to join in public dances. Making of offerings and libation to the living-dead emphasizes and renews the link between human beings and the departed, between the visible and invisible worlds. It is to be noted here, however, that children whose parents die before they are initiated, are initiated at a much later age than usual. It is not quite clear why this must be so, perhaps it is in order to allow the children more time to grow since initiation thrusts upon them great responsibilities.

There is no set period between the first and the second initiations, but the latter can take place any time between a few weeks after the first initiation and the age of fifteen or so. The first is primarily physical, the second is mainly educational. The ceremony for the second (known as the 'great' or 'major' initiation) is sponsored by a household from where there are no initiates at the time, and this is a great privilege which the people concerned consider to be granted them by their living-dead. The ceremony lasts from four to ten days, during part of which the candidates are secluded from the public and live in huts built away from the villages. They are accompanied by supervisors and teachers, to whom is delegated the responsibility of introducing the candidates to all matters of manhood and womanhood. The Akamba describe this duty as 'brooding over the initiates', the way that birds brood over their eggs before hatching. On the first day the candidates learn educational songs and encounter symbolic obstacles. On the second day they have to face a frightening monster known as '*mbusya*' (rhinoceros). In some parts of the country only the boys go through this experience, while in other parts both boys and girls do. This is a man-made structure of sticks and trees, from the inside of which someone makes fearful bellows like those of a big monster. The initiates do not know exactly what it is, for that is one of the secrets of the ceremony. Afterwards they are not allowed to divulge the matter to those who have not been initiated. They face this 'rhinoceros' bravely, shooting it with bows and arrows in order to destroy it the way they would destroy a similar enemy. That night, the man and woman who performed the operation at the first ceremony, have a ritual sexual intercourse; and the parents of the candidates have a ritual sexual intercourse on the third and seventh nights.

On the third day, the initiates rehearse adult life: boys go hunting with miniature bows and arrows, and girls cut small twigs (which symbolize firewood for the home). Later the same day the original operators at the first ceremony spit beer over the candidates to bless them, and the children return to their 'home' in the bush. Here they must overcome objects that are placed before them. Each boy is given a special stick, which he must retain; and that evening a dance for the initiates takes place. With their special sticks the boys perform symbolic sexual acts upon the girls; and on the following day, they are examined on the meaning of riddles and puzzles carved on the sticks or drawn on sand. Afterwards the boys fetch sugar-canes, this being a form of permitted 'stealing' acceptable and necessary for that particular purpose; and with the sugar-cane they make beer for their incumbents.

On the fifth day the initiates and their incumbents go to a sacred tree, usually the fig or sycamore tree on the banks of a river. The supervisors take a little amount of sap from the tree and give it to each candidate. The initiates pretend to eat it; and thereafter they may now eat all the foods which otherwise they had been forbidden to eat during the previous day. At this tree the operators make a small cut on the sexual organs of the initiates, and beer is poured on the organs.

The sixth day is spent peacefully. On the seventh day, the boys make a mock cattle raid, while the girls cry out that the enemies have come. The ceremony may end at that point, and the young people now return to their individual homes. The parents have a ritual sexual intercourse that night.[1]

This long description is intended to illustrate at some detail, the significance of the initiation rite. Certain meanings clearly emerge from this ceremony. Corporate living is instilled into the thinking of the young people by making them live together in the special huts in the woods. This experience is like a miniature community. The incumbents play the role of the elders; and it is extremely important that the young respect and obey the older people whether they are their immediate parents or not. Seclusion serves to make the candidates concentrate on what they are experiencing and doing, and becomes like a re-enaction of death. It is a new rhythm for the young people as well as for their wider community. When seclusion is over they emerge as qualified and legally recognized men and women who may establish families, become mothers and fathers and defend their country—hence the mock raid attack and the symbolic sexual act that are part of the ceremony. The frightening ordeal of the 'rhinoceros' is a psychological device partly to emphasize the seriousness of the occasion, and partly to drive out fear from the candidates so that in time of danger they do not flee away but take courage to defend themselves and their families. The riddles carved on the special sticks or drawn on sand are symbols of knowledge, to which the candidates now have full access. The initiates are now entitled to know every secret of tribal life and knowledge, apart from what is known to exclusive groups. The rite at the sacred tree is a reminder of the religious life, and a symbolic visit to the living-dead and the spirits who are thought to live there. The occasion is a renewal of the link with the Zamani period, the link with the spiritual realities and a reminder that the living-dead are 'present' with them. Permission to eat the foods which the initiates were previously forbidden to eat is a symbolic and dramatic way of opening up for them the full participation in all the affairs of the nation. The slight cut on the sex organs at the sacred tree indicates the sacredness of sex, in the sight of God, the spirits, the living-dead and the human community. The return home is like an experience of resurrection: death is over, their seclusion is ended, and now they rejoin their community as new men and women, fully accepted and respected as such. Their parents have a ritual sexual intercourse as the final seal of the ceremony, the symbolic gesture that their own children are fertile, that their children are now initiated and authorized to carry on the

[1] D. N. Kimilu *Mukamba Waw'o* (Nairobi 1962), p. 30 f.; Middleton, I, p. 88 f.

burning flame of life, and that a new generation is now socially and educationally born.

Akamba men have still a third initiation rite, when they are over forty years of age. Only a few of them actually undergo this ceremony, and it is so secret that little is known about it by those who have not participated in it. It is like a ritual mystical experience, and there are grades through which the candidates go after they have finished with the actual rite. Among other things the rite involves very severe tests of endurance and going through great torment. During that stage the men perform acts which are not regarded as their own, since candidates are in a state of having 'lost' them-selves. The ceremony is performed in secret, away from the villages, and the initiated men are under such strong oath of secrecy that even those who later become Christians are unwilling to divulge what actually happens.

[b] *Maasai initiation rites*
Among the Maasai, circumcision rites take place every four to five years, for young people aged between twelve and sixteen. All those who are circumcised together form a life-long age-group, and take on a new special name. As preparation for the ceremony, all the candidates first assemble together, covered with white clay and carrying no weapons. Then they spend about two months moving about the country-side. On the day before the ceremony the boys wash themselves in cold water. When their foreskin is cut off, the blood is collected in an ox hide and put on each boy's head. For four days the boys are kept in seclusion, after which they emerge dressed like women and having their faces painted with white clay and heads adorned with ostrich feathers. A few weeks later, when their sex organs have healed, the heads are shaved and the boys now grow new hair and can become warriors. Girls have their ceremony in which a portion of their sex organ is cut or pierced. They adorn their heads with grass or leaves of a special tree (doom palm). When their wounds have healed, the girls can get married; and in some parts of the country they also have their heads shaved.[1]

In this example we see the same type of meaning as among the Akamba. The underlying emphasis is separation from childhood and incorporation into adulthood. Cutting or piercing the sex organ, and the shaving of the head, symbolize the break from one status and entry into another. The smearing of the face with white clay is the symbol of a new birth, a new person, a new social status. When the ceremony is over, the men begin their career as warriors: they may now defend their country or raid other peoples. The women are ready to get married and often do so immediately.

[1] A. van Gennep *The rites of passage* (E.T. 1960), p. 85 f.

So the rhythm of a new generation is dramatized and played. The young people who have been initiated together become mystically and ritually bound to each other for the rest of their life: they are in effect one body, one group, one community, one people. They help one another in all kinds of ways. The wife of one man is equally the wife of other men in the same age-group; and if one member visits another he is entitled to sleep with the latter's wife, whether or not the husband is at home. This is a deep level of asserting the group solidarity, and one at which the individual really feels that 'I am because we are; and since we are, therefore I am'. This solidarity creates or provides a sense of security, a feeling of oneness and the opportunities of participating in corporate existence.

[c] *Nandi female initiation rites*[1]

For an account of female initiation we shall take the example of the Nandi who have some of the most sophisticated and detailed initiation rites. Nandi female initiation is 'a preparation for adulthood and housewifery', and no woman can get married without it. Long before the initiation, and beginning when the girls are about ten years old, they have to sleep with the boys in places known as *sikiroino*.[2] This is obligatory, and if the girls refuse it, the boys may beat them without the intervention of the parents. It is meant to teach the girls how to behave towards men and how to control their sexual desires. No sexual intercourse is permitted when the boys and girls sleep together in this way. At a later stage the girls would be examined for virginity, and it is great shame and anger to the girls and their parents if any are found to have lost their virginity. In some cases such girls would be speared to death; while virgin ones would receive gifts of cows or sheep.

When the time arrives for the initiation ceremony, several families bring their daughters together to be initiated together. By then the girls are aged about fourteen. The boyfriends make sure that the girls are properly and beautifully dressed for the occasion, and supply each of them with 'a hat of beads and thigh and ankle bells'. Wearing this heavy attire, the girl goes round informing her relatives of the date for the ceremony. The thigh bells, of which there are four on each thigh, are the recognized indicators that a girls' initiation ceremony is about to start. The night before the appointed day, girls sleep with their boyfriends in the *sikiroino*. The girls

---

[1] S. Cherotich 'The Nandi female initiation and marriage and Christian impact upon it', in *Dini na Mila*, Kampala, Vol. 2 No. 2/3, December 1967, pp. 62–77, for a full and very interesting description, from which the substance and quotations of this subsection are derived, with the author's permission.

[2] A *sikiroino* is a house where girls and young men of a given village or group of villages may go and sleep at night.

become very excited, for this is the greatest occasion for them. 'A kind of madness enters them which defies all pain and fear and transforms them into something else. This explains why the girls undergo such hard training and persevere through the painful operation'.

In the morning of the day of ceremony, the girls go with a 'teacher' or 'supervisor' to the forest to cut firewood. The cutting is done ceremoniously: the teacher and each girl cut a piece of firewood, holding the axe jointly. This act is intended to emphasize corporateness among the initiates, who must now feel themselves as one body, one group. This teacher, known as *motiriot* (pl. *motirenik*), is the person who accompanies the initiates right through the ceremony, helping them, teaching them new things and sleeping with them. She is their symbol of unity, their counsellor, their source of strength and comfort.

A dance is held for the girls and their boyfriends, during which time women who conduct the ceremony prepare stinging nettles inside the house where the rite is to take place. The dancing continues until night time. Then the physical side of the operation begins. 'The girls sit down and have their clitorises tied hard with ligament. This will stop any further flow of blood to the clitoris. After this, the girls dance and jump about once more. They dance until they are worn out. They all come together then for a blessing by an elder who prays that the hands of the teachers (*motirenik*) be light to carry their work effectively. Everybody agrees by repeating the word *wisis* (light, not heavy).' The boys begin to vex the girls by calling them cowards and other despising names. This is intended to stimulate bravery and courage in the girls, who long to show this courage when the actual operation is done. The girls sing, blowing whistles and saying that when their boyfriends come they will sleep not on animal skins but on their thighs. They shake the bells vigorously and 'sing themselves to death'.

Later that night, the young men go to sleep for a short while. The girls are taken by their teachers into the operation house, where women sting their clitorises with the stinging nettles. This makes the clitoris both numb and swollen. The nettles are also applied to their breasts. These women sing loudly to counteract any cry of the girls, since the nettles are very painful.

Early the next day, people come to the place of the ceremony and stand about a hundred and fifty metres away. The women participating in the ceremony form a circle, in the middle of which the operator's stool is placed. The operator has a curved knife. By then the women have examined the girls for virginity. Those who are virgins sit on a stool for the operation, and those who are not sit on the bare ground. The initiate sits with her legs naked and wide apart, looking up to the sky. The operator holds the clitoris with the left hand, and with her right hand she quickly snaps away the clitoris. The girl does not feel pain at this stage because the sex organs are numb from the stinging nettles. A small amount of bleeding takes place, except (but rarely) where the blood vessels may not have been properly tied. The girls then put on their thigh bells. The spectators rush away quickly to spread the news of who among the girls have been cowards and who have been virgins, or otherwise. This is the most critical moment for the relatives and families whose girls are initiated. If a girl is reported to be a coward, or not a virgin, the parents and brothers are so ashamed that they threaten to kill themselves or kill the girl concerned. Only the intervention of other people stops them from actually carrying out this threat.

When the physical operation is over, the girls put on skin dresses and vigorously shake their thigh bells. Their boyfriends congratulate them, and take back the ornaments and attire which they had supplied for the occasion. The girls bid farewell to their friends and relatives. The parents of the initiates take home a climbing plant (*sinendet*), which they place at the door of their house to signify that their daughter has been initiated. If their daughter has proved to be a coward the plant is slightly burnt. The girls and their women helpers now go into seclusion for a period of between six months and three years. This is the period of education and introduction into tribal knowledge and wisdom.

In the first four days the girls have much pain, and they are given milk and meat to eat, whether or not they want it. Thereafter they eat with wooden spoons (*seketik*) until their initiation period is over. They are considered religiously impure, and may not touch anything. If one touches her wound she is severely beaten by the incumbents. Men must never see them; and when they go out in the evening or early morning, they must cover their heads and look down. Otherwise they remain indoors the rest of the day.

The incumbents or teachers instruct the girls in matters of housework and marital relations. This includes how to sleep with their husbands, when to refrain from sexual intercourse during pregnancy and up to the time the child begins to walk, how to be attractive wives, and how to bring up children. The girls also learn the 'proper' eating habits. For example, it is forbidden to eat meat and drink milk at the same time; children may not eat honey and meat at the same time otherwise the bees would vacate the beehives. They learn something about the weather, about being industrious, about returning borrowed articles, about being kind and polite and so on. Knowledge about bringing up children is considered the most important part of their education. By custom Nandi men may not touch or have anything to do with their children until they are ten years of age or older. It is therefore the duty of the women to bring up children in every respect.

After childbirth the woman is considered unclean, and may not touch anything or even cook for her husband for about six months or more. Before she can breast feed her child, she must first wash herself in the river and return with her hands lifted up. When she has sat down, someone else brings the child and places it on her lap so that she may suckle it. Failure to observe this regulation strictly can cause great sorrows to her, or even leads to her death.

So, during this educational period of seclusion, 'the girl slowly begins to weave her pattern of life to the women's and gradually becomes a grown up in thought, word and deed. She forgets her old self and looks at her past with contempt. She has found out where she really belongs in life. She is fed well, and in most cases overfed.' By the time the seclusion period is over, 'the girls are changed very much . . . they are huge and well covered with flesh. There is a complete revolution of mind, body and spirit.' They are now confident that they can manage housework, and take up full responsibilities in their community.

On the surface this initiation practice is dying out but very slowly. Attacks on the custom by Christian missionaries have not met with much success. Modern young men who may marry girls that have not been initiated get them 'done' but secretly; and parents who are not brave enough to get their daughters initiated publicly do it secretly. It is believed that if a girl is not initiated, her clitoris will grow long and have branches; and that children of uninitiated women would become abnormal. Women who have not been initiated are considered to be still 'children', and their offspring are known as 'children of children'. Under these circumstances it is easy to understand the psychological importance of the initiation ceremony. Unless a person has been through the ceremony she really is 'nobody', 'incomplete' and still a 'child'. In an atmosphere of corporate existence, it is literally impossible for anyone to miss such a ceremony and get away with it. Sooner or later she would become the laughing stock of her relatives and neighbours, and any misfortune befalling her or her family would be attributed to 'the missing link' in her ritual growth. As soon as the girls have gone through the period of seclusion and the end of the initiation ceremony, they get married. While they are in seclusion, marriage arrangements between their families and those of their boyfriends, are carried out. If one misses this ceremony, one also risks remaining unmarried or bearing abnormal children. Modern life is, however, bringing gradual change in this attitude and practice.

Although in detail the Nandi female initiation may differ from that of other peoples, the basic meaning is fairly the same. It is a rite of maturation, a dramatization of the break with childhood and incorporation into adulthood.

The sex organ is the symbol of life; and cutting it is like unlocking the issues of life, so that thereafter there may be an unblocked flow of life. Seclusion is symbolic of death, the planting of seeds in the ground; and its end is like the resurrection to a new and responsible life, the sprouting of the shoots. Through the initiation ceremony of both girls and boys, the corporate life of the nation is revived, its rhythm is given a new momentum, and its vitality is renewed. Therefore, anyone who refuses to go through the ceremony, or who spoils its harmony (through not being a virgin or showing cowardice), is committing a great offence to the entire Nandi society: she is killing the nation. It is no wonder then, that parents and brothers who are put to shame by their daughters (or sisters), are ready to destroy themselves and the girls for the sake of corporate existence. The ceremony is a deeply sacred one, for in it lies the survival of the nation. It is the solemn religious dramatization of man's conquest over death and disintegration.

[d] *Ndebele puberty rites*

We may yet briefly consider another rite which is different from the initiation ceremonies described above. Instead of a formal initiation rite, the Ndebele have a short, and yet as effective, ceremony to mark the puberty changes. When a boy has his first night emission of sperms, he gets up early the next morning, before other people are up, and goes naked to the river where he washes himself. Then he returns home and stands outside the homestead near the gateway that leads to the cattle shed. When other boys see him there, they come and beat him with sticks. He flees into the woods and remains there for two or three days, being carefully watched by the other boys. During that time he is not allowed to eat food in the daytime, but only at night. When the period is over, he returns home and is given medicated food by the traditional doctor. This is done ceremoniously. The medicine-man puts maize meal at the end of a stick which he thrusts at him and the boy must take hold of it with his mouth. When he succeeds in doing so the medicine-man gives him three or four blows with a stick. People say that this makes the boy hard. His father and relatives give him presents of cattle, sheep and goats. The girls undergo a prolonged washing in cold water after their first menstruation. Some days later, their parents make a big feast, after which the girls begin to wear a full skirt. This now entitles them to get married.[1]

The idea of 'death and resurrection' is represented in the case of boys going to live for a few days in the forest. The break with childhood is dramatized by the act of washing. This ritual washing may also carry with it the deeper religious idea of purification from the state of unproductive life. It also is a

[1] Hughes & van Velsen, p. 96.

dramatization of preparation for adult life: marriage, owning property, bearing responsibility (cf. beating the boys to make them 'hard'). To be considered 'hard' is an approval and qualification that the person may now be fully incorporated into the wider society with all its privileges and responsibilities.

In western Africa there are well-known secret societies for men and women, which are entered as part of the initiation procedure. One reads also about the Igbo that they have special houses for fattening their girls. It is in these houses that girls are kept in seclusion for several months, being well fed and anointed with oil. When they are fully fat, and their cheeks are round, their bosoms big and their waists fully adorned with fat layers, then they are fit for marriage.[1] Women are considered most beautiful when they are very fat. Fat women of Europe and America would have no difficulty in winning crowds of admirers in Africa.

Changes are rapidly taking place in Africa, and the initiation rites are some of the areas of life most affected by modern changes. This is partly because children at that age are going to school; and partly because Christian missionaries and some governments have attacked or discouraged the practices. Yet, where initiation rites were part of the traditional cycle of individual life, the practice still lingers on and often with some modifications or in a simplified form. That these initiation rites are extremely important in traditional life needs no further emphasis. If they are to die out, they will die a long and painful death. They are at the 'middle' of life for the individuals concerned, not only because they coincide often with the puberty changes, but because they close a whole phase of life, childhood in the broad sense of that word, and open up a new and whole phase of life, adulthood with all its implications. Because of this radical change, many African societies mark the occasion with a dramatization and physical-psychological experiences that are hard for the individual to forget.

[1] Parrinder, I, p. 95 f.

13
MARRIAGE
& PROCREATION

Marriage is a complex affair with economic, social and religious aspects which often overlap so firmly that they cannot be separated from one another. We shall deal briefly only with the religious side, but it should be borne in mind that there are these other dimensions which contribute to our fuller understanding of African concepts and practices of marriage.

For African peoples, marriage is the focus of existence. It is the point where all the members of a given community meet: the departed, the living and those yet to be born. All the dimensions of time meet here, and the whole drama of history is repeated, renewed and revitalized. Marriage is a drama in which everyone becomes an actor or actress and not just a spectator. Therefore, marriage is a duty, a requirement from the corporate society, and a rhythm of life in which everyone must participate. Otherwise, he who does not participate in it is a curse to the community, he is a rebel and a law-breaker, he is not only abnormal but 'under-human'. Failure to get married under normal circumstances means that the person concerned has rejected society and society rejects him in return.

We must note also that marriage and procreation in African communities are a unity: without procreation marriage is incomplete. This is a unity which attempts to recapture, at least in part, the lost gift of immortality of which we spoke in chapter nine. It is a religious obligation by means of which the individual contributes the seeds of life towards man's struggle against the loss of original immortality. Biologically both husband and wife are reproduced in their children, thus perpetuating the chain of humanity. In some societies it is believed that the living-dead are reincarnated in part, so that aspects of their personalities or physical characteristics are 're-born' in their descendants. A person who, therefore, has no descendants in effect quenches the fire of life, and becomes forever dead since his line of physical continuation is blocked if he does not get married and bear children. This is a sacred understanding and obligation which must neither be abused nor despised.

The second way in which marriage and procreation as a unity attempt to recapture immortality is in the matter of 'remembering' the living-dead. We have already touched upon the importance of 'personal immortality' in which the living-dead are kept by members of their human families. So long as there are persons in the family who remember someone who has physically died this person is not really dead: he is still alive in the minds of his relatives and neighbours who knew him while he was in human form. His name still means something *personal*, and he can 'appear' to members of his family who knew him and who would recognize him *by name*. These also give him food and drink, the tokens of fellowship and remembrance. This, as we have seen, is extremely important in African societies. It is in one's family that the living-dead are kept in personal memory the longest, after their physical death. I have heard elderly people say to their grandchildren who seem to wait too long before getting married, 'If you don't get married and have children, who will pour out libation to you when you die?' This is a serious philosophical concern among traditional African peoples. Unfortunate, therefore, is the man or woman who has nobody to 'remember' him (her), after physical death. To lack someone close who keeps the departed in their personal immortality is the worst misfortune and punishment that any person could suffer. To die without getting married and without children is to be completely cut off from the human society, to become disconnected, to become an outcast and to lose all links with mankind.

Everybody, therefore, must get married and bear children: that is the greatest hope and expectation of the individual for himself and of the community for the individual. If we bear this in mind, it will throw some light on our understanding of the many customs and ideas connected with African marriages, such as the giving of the bride presents, polygamy, inheriting the wives of the deceased brother, parents arranging marriages for their children, and the like. I plead with people of other cultures and backgrounds, to try and understand the meaning behind African marriage and family life, and to be patient in passing harsh judgments on our traditional marriage customs and ideas.

[a] *Preparation for marriage and procreation*

Preparation for marriage is a long process, the key moments of which may be marked with rituals. When a child has been born physically, it must also be born ritually or religiously in order to make it a social member of the community. At a later age, it goes through a series of initiation rites. These initiation rites are like the birth of the young people into the state of maturity and responsibility. Initiation rites dramatize and effect the incorporation of the young into the full life of their nation. Only after initiation, where this is observed, is a person religiously and socially born into full manhood or womanhood with all its secrets, responsibilities, privileges and expectations. One of the educational purposes of initiation rites, is to introduce young people to matters of sex, marriage, procreation and family life. One could say then that initiation is a ritual sanctification and preparation for marriage, and only when it is over may young people get married. Since the whole community participates in the initiation rites, it is therefore the entire corporate body of society which prepares the young people for marriage and family life.

In addition, and particularly in societies where there are no initiation rites, parents and other relatives gradually educate their children in marital affairs. Girls are taught how to prepare food, how to behave towards men, how to care for children, how to look after the husband and other domestic affairs. The boys are taught what most concerns men, like looking after cattle, behaving properly towards one's in-laws, how to acquire wealth which one would give to the parents of a girl as part of the engagement and marriage contract, and how to be responsible as the 'head' of the family. Sex knowledge is often difficult to impart from parent to child; but girls are probably 'better off' in this respect than boys, since they spend more time with their mothers and older women relatives than boys may spend with their fathers. Much of the sex information is gathered from fellow young people, and it is often a mixture of truth, myth, ignorance, guesswork and jokes. Formal schools and universities in modern Africa are often the centres of even greater ignorance of these matters, so that young people go through them knowing, perhaps, how to dissect a frog but nothing about either their own procreation system and mechanism, or how to establish family life. In this respect, surely traditional methods of preparing young people for marriage and procreation are obviously superior to what schools and universities are doing for our young people.

[b] *Choosing the marriage partner*
Different customs are observed in the matter of finding partners for marriage. In some societies the choice is made by the parents, and this may be done even before the children are born. This means that if in one household there is a young boy, his parents go to another household where there is a young girl or where there is an expectant mother and put in an 'application' for the present girl or for the child to be born in the event that it is a girl. Sometimes these arrangements may be made when two wives know that they are pregnant. The children, however, get married only when they are old enough and *not* immediately after birth or while very young. Examples of this practice are cited in the Sudan region.

A fairly widespread practice is the one in which the parents and relatives of a young man approach the parents of a particular girl and start marriage negotiations. This is done around the initiation period which, as we saw in the previous chapter, often coincides with the puberty period. If either the girl or the young man very strongly and firmly rejects the prospective marriage partner, then the negotiations are broken down; although there are cases where force or pressure is applied to get the reluctant young person marry the partner chosen by the parents and relatives. The normal practice, however, is for the parents to make the choice with the full consent of their son or daughter.

In other societies it is the young people themselves who make their own choice and afterwards inform their parents about it. Then the parents and relatives begin the betrothal and marriage negotiations. Since the individual exists only because the corporate group exists, it is vital that in this most important contract of life, other members of that corporate community must get involved in the marriage of the individual. We shall take some examples to illustrate how these points are carried out in real life.

Among the Udhuk, courtship and marriage take place at an early age. When a boy decides to marry a particular girl, he goes to meet her on the path and openly declares his intentions. The girl pretends to get a shock, and her companions chase the man away. At home she puts her bed against the back wall of the house. At night the boy visits the home when people have gone to sleep, and puts his hand through openings in the wall until he reaches her. She feels the hand and identifies him by the ornaments round his hand. If she still rejects him, she cries aloud and the parents awake. The young man then runs away and probably never returns to persuade her further. If the girl accepts the offer for marriage, she keeps quiet and the two carry on a conversation in whispers. For the next few days and weeks, the young man repeats his visits to the girl. When the relationship is strong, the girl begins to wear beads which immediately make her parents enquire who the suitor is—though already they know all about it! If the parents approve, then the boy and the girl are allowed to meet publicly, and this leads on to marriage.[1]

The parents arrange marriages among the Wolof. When a young man meets a girl whom he intends to marry, he tells his father about the matter. His parents send an intermediary to the girl's parents, to enquire if the suggestion for such a marriage is favourable in their sight. If it is, the boy's parents send kola nuts to the girl's father, together with a formal request for marriage. The girl's father then consults his wife and daughter, and if these agree, he also gives his consent and shares the kola nuts among his

[1] Cerulli, p. 23.

household and family, neighbours and friends. The two young people now begin formal courtship; and every time the boy visits the girl he must take kola nuts to the family and bring her new dresses for the festivals of the year. If the man concerned is already married and wants to take another wife, it is normal for him and his first wife to make the negotiations, and if his parents are still alive they may also help.[1]

The use and help of a marriage intermediary are reported among the Kiga. When parents wish to arrange the marriage of their son and know of a suitable girl, they confide the matter to a close and trustworthy relative. This man acts as an intermediary. He finds out all about the girl and her family, reporting the matter to the boy's family. If they are satisfied, the parents of the boy and the intermediary (*kirima* or *kishabi*) go to the girl's parents and declare their intentions. Should the other parents be unwilling or less enthusiastic, it is the duty of the intermediary to pave the way. The inter-mediary also plays an important role when the time comes for the actual marriage. The girl and boy are not allowed to meet until the wedding has taken place.[2]

In traditional societies marriage is not allowed between close relatives. Since the range of kinship extends very widely, the degree of these pro-hibitions is also very extensive. As a rule, the clans are exogamous, that is, a person marries from another clan. Where marriage may be allowed within the same clan, it is carefully scrutinized to make sure that the couple are not close relatives. Taboos exist to strengthen marriage prohibitions. For example, it is feared that children of close relatives will die, and that the living-dead are displeased with such marriages and would therefore bring misfortune to those concerned. Some individuals, such as lepers, epileptics and those who are mentally deranged, find it difficult if not impossible to get marriage partners; but if they are women it is not rare for them to get children out of wedlock.

[c] *Betrothal and courtship*

Generally there are no rites performed to mark the betrothal occasion or the courtship period. In some societies, however, there are and we shall illustrate this practice with a concrete example from the Batoro. Among these people marriage negotiations are initiated and arranged by the parents. This often starts when two men meet at a beer drinking party. One says to the other: 'I have given you a wife (or husband)'; to which the other replies by falling down and giving thanks. Then a formal introduction of

[1] Gamble, p. 66.
[2] A. V. Byabamazima in a seminar discussion in October 1967 pointed out, however, that this applies to the traditional method only.

the subject is made. The two men go home and inform their children; and a few days later, the boy's parents visit those of the girl, taking with them at least two calabashes of beer. On arrival, the girl's parents give them coffee berries (or formerly something else), and light a pipe which the boy's father puffs four times. The four parents engage in a long conversation about various topics until, finally, the boy's father makes a formal request. He says, 'I have come to be born in this home, to be a son, to be a servant if you like, to take cattle to the river to drink, to make the cattle shed, to buy you clothes, to help alleviate your needs. I am prepared to do all these things and many more, if you give me a wife for my son!' As a rule this request is accepted, and then the two sides fix the amount of presents to be given to the girl's family, which is about three to four cows (or the equivalent in money). Traditional beer is drunk, and the boy's parents are accompanied back to their home. As soon as the agreed present has been given, the date for marriage is fixed.[1]

This is not a dramatic rite, but it is full of meaning. Beer is the symbol of friendship, communion, one-ness and acceptability; and it is used by many African societies in ceremonies, festivals and covenant-making. The beer which the boy's parents take to those of the girl shows their friendly attitude, their willingness to establish fellowship with the other family, and their readiness to form a marriage covenant. Coffee berries are the symbol of fertility, productivity and fruitfulness. The lit pipe symbolizes acceptability; it is a token of sharing something together—breathing in unity the breath of life. The formal words which the boy's father speaks are the means of delivering himself and his services for the sake of his own son. Marriage is an absolute necessity for his son, and the father is willing to be sacrificed, to be humiliated (as a servant), to become a slave so that his son may get a wife. The father is ready to dissolve his own self in the family from where his son gets a wife. The father is here the bridge, the link and the solemn knot in tying the marriage covenant. He is ready to cease to be in order that he may become alive in and through his son. This is a solemn religious act of the father's devotion for the sake of his son and the community.

(d) *The wedding ceremony*

There are as many customs of the wedding procedure as there are African peoples. In some societies the ceremony lasts many days and is full of rituals. In others the bridegroom and his party must fight the bride's people in order to get her. This fight may only be symbolic, but blood is at times shed in course of the struggle. There are other societies in which the boy takes the girl so that they live together until she bears a child, and then

[1] M. Nyakazingo in an essay, February 1965.

the wedding rites are performed. In matrilocal societies the man generally goes to live in the home of the wife and these two establish their own household there. We shall now take a concrete example to illustrate some of the practices, procedures and significance of the wedding and marriage customs.

Let us continue with the Batoro. When the marriage gift has been given, a night is fixed for the wedding to take place. That night the bridegroom sends nine strong men to get the bride. On reaching her home, they must first remove a bundle of leaves (*ekikarabo*) which has been placed on top of the roof of the parents' house. Should the strong men fail to remove this bundle, they have also failed to get the girl and no wedding takes place. If they succeed, then they are allowed to take the bride. But this is not a simple matter, for they must carry the girl on their shoulders up to her new home. On the way back, the men sing to comfort the girl who now is crying, and to warn the people at home that the bride is on her way. On arrival, the party is met by the bridegroom who comes to the doorway of the courtyard and stands there holding a spear. The bride is brought into the house where the bridegroom's parents are sitting against the wall.

A rite is performed by which the bridegroom sits on and off, four times, first on his father's lap and then on his mother's lap. The bride repeats this act, but only three times. She is then taken to another house which has been specially prepared for the occasion. At the door of this house stands someone who has already been married from this same family. The person says to the bride, 'You found me married in this home; you will go away and leave me in here as you have found me!' These words are intended to stop the bride or discourage her from leaving her new home. They are also the signal for dancing and feasting to start.

The following morning the guests who had been invited to the party return to their own homes. The bride and her husband wash themselves in very cold water which has been placed in the courtyard enclosure and which is guarded by the bride's sister. When they come to this water they undress themselves, and each splashes the other with water. This is the ritual of binding themselves to each other, and of cleansing themselves from the former state of unmarried life. Symbolically these ritual ablutions are partly the death of the former life of unproductivity, and partly the resurrection of the new life of procreation. For two days the bride is hidden from the public; and when this period is over relatives from her own home come to bring presents. These relatives are given a very cordial welcome and treated with great respect. They receive a pipe to smoke and coffee berries as well as food and drink. The bride is now brought out and introduced to the public. The things brought from her home are counted, and some are distributed among her husband's relatives who took part in the marriage arrangements. The bride's aunt is given the biggest present, because she is the one who has accompanied the bride from her former home to the new one and remains with her during the period of seclusion. If the girl is found to be a virgin the aunt is given a cow, and another cow is sent to her mother together with the sheets having the stains of the blood of virginity. These stains of virginity are the greatest credit to the mother and family of the bride.[1]

We see a lot of meaning in these marriage procedures. The custom of presenting a gift to the bride's people is practised all over Africa, though in varying degrees. Different names are used to describe it, such as 'bride-wealth', 'bride-gift', 'bride-price', 'dowry'(wrongly in this case) and 'lobola'. Most of these terms are either inadequate or misleading. The gift is in the form of cattle, money, foodstuffs and other articles. In some societies the families concerned may exchange brides. In others, the bridegroom (and his relatives) must in addition contribute labour; and in matrilocal societies the man lives with his parents-in-law working for them for some years in order to 'earn' his wife.

This marriage gift is an important institution in African societies. It is a token of gratitude on the part of the bridegroom's people to those of the bride, for their care over her and for allowing her to become his wife. At her home the gift 'replaces' her, reminding the family that she will leave or has left and yet she is not dead. She is a valuable person not only to her family but to her husband's people. At marriage she is not stolen but is given away under mutual agreement between the two families. The gift elevates the value attached to her both as a person and as a wife. The gift legalizes her value and the marriage contract. The institution of this practice is the most concrete symbol of the marriage covenant and security. Under no circumstances is this custom a form of 'payment', as outsiders have so often mistakenly said. African words for the practice of giving the marriage gift are, in most cases, different from words used in buying or selling something in the market place. Furthermore, it is not only the man and his people who give: the girl's people also give gifts in return, even if these may be materially smaller than those of the man. The two families are involved in a relationship which, among other things, demands an exchange of material and other gifts. This continues even long after the girl is married and has her own children. In some societies if the marriage breaks down completely and there is divorce, the husband may get back some of the gifts he had given to the wife's people; but in other societies, nothing is returned to him.

The Batoro custom of carrying the bride on the shoulders, which is a

[1] Nyakazingo.

very comfortable means of conveyance, is not practised by most other African peoples. It is one way of showing the value of the bride. But its major purpose seems to dramatize the fact that the girl is now being cut off from one family and being joined to another. It is also a symbolic act of breaking her completely from the state of unmarried life. She now becomes a full and mature person: to be unmarried is childhood, to be married is maturity and a blessing. Should an unmarried person die, the Batoro beat up his body with a thorny bush to show that an unmarried person deserves and receives no respect in the eyes of society. So marriage conveys a status which is valid not only in this life but also in the hereafter. The girl celebrates the new status by being carried. Before this rite she is 'nobody', but afterwards she is 'somebody'.

Sitting on and off on the parents' lap is a rite of the 'new birth'. Both the bride and the bridegroom are being born anew, they are made twins, they enter ritually into the stage of maturity. This is also a rite of handing down the torch of life: the parents pass on the drum-beat of life, and a new rhythm starts. It is now up to the couple to reproduce, to have their own children on the lap, to nurture them and keep the stream of human generations flowing. When this rite is over, the couple may now go into their special house and consummate their marriage. The blood of virginity is the symbol that life has been preserved, that the spring of life has not already been flowing wastefully, and that both the girl and her relatives have preserved the sanctity of human reproduction. Only marriage may shed this sacred blood, for in so doing it unlocks the door for members of the family in the loins to come forward and join both the living and the living-dead. Virginity at the wedding is greatly respected in some African societies; while in others it is more or less expected that the couple would have had sexual intercourse before marriage. Virginity symbolizes purity not only of the body but also of moral life; and a virgin bride is the greatest glory and crown to her parents, husband and relatives.

The rite of bathing together is a solemn way of binding the husband and wife into one, just as the marriage gift binds together the two families and their relatives. Water washes away the former state of unmarried life; and it also sanctifies the new state of responsible maturity and intention to procreate. It makes the couple 'ready'. The washing also removes the stains of the blood of virginity.

The seclusion of the couple for a few days symbolizes their departure from unmarried life: it is their death to the life of immaturity, childhood and unproductivity. Their introduction to the public is an act of resurrection to the new life of maturity and procreation.

Marriage customs of other African peoples differ in various respects from those of the Batoro as given here. But from this example we have seen some of the basic concepts of marriage and procreation. It remains now for us to discuss briefly some of the other aspects of marriage in African societies.

[e] 'Polygamy' and inheriting wives or husbands

Technically the term 'polygamy' should mean what its Greek components imply, and that is, marrying 'many' (wives, husbands or times). But in popular usage it is applied to mean the state of marriage in which there is one husband and two or more wives. This should be referred to as 'polygyny'; and where one wife has two or more husbands this is 'polyandry'. I shall use 'polygamy' in the popular sense, even though I realize that linguistically that is only partly correct.

Getting married to two or more wives is a custom found all over Africa, though in some societies it is less common than in others. The custom fits well into the social structure of traditional life, and into the thinking of the people, serving many useful purposes. If the philosophical or theological attitude towards marriage and procreation is that these are an aid towards the partial recapture or attainment of the lost immortality, the more wives a man has the more children he is likely to have, and the more children the stronger the power of 'immortality' in that family. He who has many descendants has the strongest possible manifestation of 'immortality', he is 'reborn' in the multitude of his descendants, and there are many who 'remember' him after he has died physically and entered his 'personal immortality'. Such a man has the attitude that 'the more *we are*, the bigger *I am*'. Children are the glory of marriage, and the more there are of them the greater the glory.

Polygamy also raises the social status of the family concerned. It is instilled in the minds of African peoples that a big family earns its head great respect in the eyes of the community. Often it is the rich families that are made up of polygamous marriages. If the first wife has no children, or only daughters, it follows almost without exception that her husband will add another wife, partly to remedy the immediate concern of childlessness, and partly to remove the shame and anxiety of apparent unproductivity. To be productive, in terms of having children, is one of the essential attributes of being a mature human being. The more productive a person is, the more he contributes to the existence of society at large.

When a family is made up of several wives with their households, it means that in time of need there will always be someone around to help. This is corporate existence. For example, when one wife gives birth, there are other wives to nurse her and care for her other children during the time she is regaining her vitality. If one wife dies, there are others to take over the care of her children. In case of sickness, other wives will fetch water from the river, cut firewood, cook and do other jobs for the family. If one wife is barren, others bear children for the family, so that the torch of life is not extinguished. Where peasant farming is the means of livelihood, the many children in a polygamous family are an economic asset—even if they also must eat plenty of food.

Polygamy helps to prevent or reduce unfaithfulness and prostitution, especially on the part of the husband. This is particularly valuable in modern times when men generally go to live and work in the cities and towns, leaving their wives and children in the rural area. If the husband has several wives, he can afford to take one at a time to live with him in the town while the other wife remains behind to care for the children and family property in the countryside. Later on the wives exchange their positions. In such cases, the husband is unlikely to take and keep concubines or go to female prostitutes. The wives are also given the opportunity to see and enjoy something of their husbands, and to satisfy their marital feelings without waiting for an unbearably long period before they can be with their husbands again. Some of the children also manage to go and be with their father in the town, when their mother goes there. In this way, some family anxieties are removed.

In families as big as many Africans have, there are duties which cannot be adequately performed if the number of people in the family is small. Such duties include looking after cattle in the woods or plains, babysitting, working in the fields, getting firewood from the forest and water from the river, looking for lost sheep or cattle, going to the town to earn some money, cooking, building new houses and granaries, hunting or food gathering (where this is a vital occupation for family sustenance) and the like. Modern life has added to the number of duties, without necessarily making it any easier or quicker to perform them all. These duties are made lighter when there are many people in the family to share them or do them jointly in the spirit of a team.

I am not discussing whether polygamy is right or wrong, good or bad: I am simply presenting the facts and attempting to appreciate the thinking and experience of those involved in polygamous situations. There are problems connected with polygamy and it would be utterly wrong to pretend that everything runs smoothly in polygamous families. Quarrels and fights among the wives and among the children are not infrequent. It is cruel for the husband to neglect some wives because he favours others (especially the latest additions). Where a man has more than six children, unless he is comparatively wealthy, it becomes a great burden for him and his family to educate all these children in modern schools, or even to clothe them properly, or feed them adequately should the crops fail in a given season. Furthermore there are problems of discipline and growing up, which are more difficult to handle in a family larger than average. On the other hand, it needs to be pointed out that the problems of polygamous families are human problems and are not necessarily created by polygamy as such; nor have they been solved or avoided in monogamous families either in Africa or Europe and America. The proportion of polygamous families would not exceed more than twenty-five per cent of the population even in societies where polygamy is most practised. This proportion is slowly diminishing, but it is also giving way to new marital situations and problems.

The custom of inheriting the wife of a deceased brother is fairly common. By brother it should be understood to mean not only the son of one's mother but any other close relative. We pointed out earlier on that a person has literally 'hundreds' of brothers, due to the extensive kinship system found in most African societies. The brother who inherits the wife and children of his deceased relative, performs all the duties of a husband and father. The children born after this inheritance generally belong to the deceased man; though in some societies they are the children of the 'new' father. In some societies, if a son dies before he has been married, the parents arrange for him to get married 'in absentia', so that the dead man is not cut off from the chain of life. It may not matter very much about the biological link: it is the mystical link in the chain of life which is supreme and most important. The deceased sons or brothers are still in the state of the living-dead, and they are not altogether absent since they still belong to their human families. Children may therefore be born long after the person has died physically, but these continue the genealogical line, inherit the property which would have belonged to their deceased 'father', and pour out libation to him even if they may not have known him physically.

Fewer societies have sororate marriages, i.e. when a wife dies, the husband marries one of her sisters. The idea behind this practice is similar to the feeling behind the levirate marriages described in the previous paragraph. The 'sister' in this case must be understood in the wider usage of that term, within the kinship system. If the wife does not bear children, it is occasionally arranged that the husband takes her sister to be his wife whether or not the first is dead. In still fewer societies, two sisters are married to the same man. These are other meanings and practices of sororate marriages.

In both levirate and sororate institutions of marriage we see further at work the philosophical awareness of the individual that 'I am because we are; and since we are, therefore I am'. The existence of the individual is the existence of the corporate; and where the individual may physically die, this does not relinquish his social-legal existence since the '*we*' continues to exist for the '*I*'. This continuity is of great psychological value: it gives a deep sense of security in an otherwise insecure world in which African peoples live. Viewed in this light, the elaborate kinship system acts like an insurance policy covering both the physical and metaphysical dimensions of human life.

[f] *Divorce and separation*

Divorce is a delicate 'accident' in marital relationships. In the African situation what constitutes a divorce must be viewed against the fact that marriage is a 'process'. In many societies that 'process' is complete only when the first child is born, or when all the marriage presents have been paid, or even when one's first children are married. Marriage involves many people, and not just the husband and wife, and the transfer of gifts in form of livestock, money or labour. Once the full contract of marriage has been executed, it is extremely hard to dissolve it. If a dissolution does come about, then it creates a great scar in the community concerned. There are African societies where divorce is reported to be both common and easy. But there are others where, in the traditional set up, divorce is either completely unknown or very rare. Most peoples are between these two positions.

The causes of divorce include sterility or barrenness especially on the part of the wife. This is probably the greatest single cause, since inability to bear children blocks the stream of life. Where the husband is impotent or sterile, his 'brother' can perform the sexual duties and fertilize the wife for him, and thus save the marriage from breaking down. If the wife is barren, the husband may take another wife and keep the barren one which also saves the 'first' marriage. Other causes are continued cruelty from the husband, the practice (and suspicion) of magic and witchcraft on the part of the wife, continued unfaithfulness from either partner and the desertion of one partner by the other. In some societies the marriage breaks down completely if the bride is not a virgin at the time of the wedding. Remarriage after divorce is common especially where the wife has some children whom she retains after divorce. For a barren woman, or one who has passed the childbearing age, finding a husband is more difficult. Since, on the whole, African girls marry before the age of twenty-five, the process of their marriage is complete by the time they pass their childbearing period and it is rare for divorce to take place after that age.

Temporary separations between husband and wife are more common than divorce. These may be caused by a quarrel between the husband and wife, or between the wife and the relatives of the husband; by the failure of the husband to give the full amount of marriage gift as agreed upon between the two families; by jealousies between the 'co-wives'; by the unfaithfulness of one party; or by other tensions in the family. In such cases, the wife goes back to her own people, for any period ranging from a few days to even a few years, until there is reconciliation or the cause of the separation is remedied. These separations may be prolonged with the result that the partners concerned find new partners and the first marriage is broken up and ends in a divorce. Modern life forces husband and wife to live apart for long periods, when he goes to work in a distant city or study in a distant place, leaving her at home in the countryside or away from the place of study. Even such 'inevitable' separations have their detrimental effect on the marriage as a whole, and in serious cases they lead to full divorce.

Where there are children of a divorced or separated couple, these naturally reap a heavy blow. It needs to be pointed out, however, that in the traditional system where kinship plays an important role in the life of the individual, such children are not as severely affected by divorce and separation as would be the case otherwise. In modern family situations divorce and separation pose greater dangers to the children involved than in the traditional set up.

[g] *The place and use of sex in married life*
In African societies sex is not used for biological purposes alone. It has also religious and social uses. For procreation and pleasure, sex plays an important and obvious role in any normal marriage and in any society of the world. There are African peoples among whom rituals are solemnly opened or concluded with actual or symbolic sexual intercourse between husband and wife or other officiating persons. This is like a solemn seal or signature, in which sex is used in and as a sacred action, as a 'sacrament' signifying inward spiritual values. In some societies, like the Nyakyusa, it is believed that sexual fluid is dangerous to children and the wife either keeps away from the husband during the nursing period, or must thoroughly wash herself after intercourse if she has children. Among the Nyakyusa it is also believed that a newly married woman is a great danger to her parents; and a woman should not bear more children when her son has got married. In many societies, it is a great offence on the part of children to look at or talk (joke) about the genitals of their parents. Sexual organs are the gates of life. For many African peoples, the genitals and buttocks are the parts of the body most carefully covered; their lack of covering constitutes 'nakedness' in the eyes traditional Africans.

It is perhaps the religious attitude towards sex which has produced the social uses of sex. In African societies, the kinship system involves, among other things, relationships in which physical avoidance between given individuals is carefully observed. For example, this is the case between a man and his mother-in-law, or a wife and her father-in-law, or teenaged and older brothers and sisters. Physical avoidance protects the individuals concerned from sexual contact. On the other hand, there is the opposite 'joking relationship', in which people are free and obliged not only to mix socially but to be in physical contact which may involve free or easier sexual intercourse outside the immediate husband and wife. There are areas where sex is used as an expression of hospitality. This means that when a man visits another, the custom is for the host to give his wife (or daughter or sister) to the guest so that the two can sleep together. In other societies, brothers have sexual rights to the wives of their brothers (remembering here that a person has hundreds of brothers and their wives are 'potentially' his wives as well). Where the age-group system is taken very seriously, like among the Maasai, members of one group who were initiated in the same batch, are entitled to have sexual relations with the wives of fellow members. In cases where the husband is forced by circumstances to live away from his wife, it may also be arranged by the individuals concerned, and with the passive understanding of the community, that a friend (normally of the 'brother' relationship) may go to his wife and have sexual intercourse with her as may be convenient, partly to satisfy her sexual urge and thus prevent her 'going about' with anybody, and partly to fertilize her and raise children for the absent 'father'. The same arrangements are made where the husband is either too young or impotent or sterile. All these are acceptable uses of sex; but how far they are actually observed in real life one cannot say without a proper study of the subject.

These religious and social uses of sex are held sacred and respectable. If there is a breach of them, this is taken very seriously. Sexual offences of one kind and another are many, and show clearly that Africans consider the proper uses of sex to be sacred and must therefore be safeguarded.

Without going into details we should here mention what constitutes sexual offences in African societies. Ritual offences arise where, on account of taboos and ritual regulations, people (including married couples) are forbidden to have sexual relations at given times. When adultery is discovered it is severely dealt with: in some societies the guilty person (particularly a man) would be whipped, stoned to death, made to pay compensation or have his head or other part of his body mutilated. This severe manner of punishing adultery and other sexual offences has been modified or relaxed in modern times, but not altogether abandoned. Fornication, incest, rape, seduction, homosexual relations, sleeping with a forbidden 'relative' or domestic animals, intimacy between relatives, children watching the genitals of their parents (in the wide usage of the term), all constitute sexual offences in a given community. Society deals variously with these offences, and African peoples are very sensitive to any departure from the accepted norm concerning all aspects of sex. This is a fundamentally religious attitude, since any offence upsets the smooth relationships of the community which includes those who have already departed. For that reason, many of the offences must be followed by a ritual cleansing whether or not the offenders are physically punished, otherwise misfortunes may ensue.

Marriage then, is a religious duty and responsibility for everyone. It forms the focal point where departed, present and coming members of society meet. It is the point of hope and expectation for the unmarried and their relatives; once it has been reached and procreation taken place, the individual may now drift slowly into the Zamani: his (her) solemn duty is performed. The physical sides of choosing the partner, preparation for marriage, actual wedding ceremony and marriage gift, are the outward expression of a religious happening which says: 'We are making a sacred undertaking!' Similarly, the physical aspects like virginity, procreation, polygamy, barrenness, divorce, inheriting a wife or husband, the use of sex, and sexual offences, are all regarded and experienced mainly as religious dimensions of married and social life. Marriage is, therefore, a sacred drama in which everybody is a religious participant, and no normal person may keep away from this dynamic scene of action.

14

DEATH
& THE HEREAFTER

We have seen that birth is the first rhythm of a new generation, and the rites of birth are performed in order to make the child a corporate and social being. Initiation rites continue that process, and make him a mature, responsible and active member of society. Marriage makes him a creative and reproductive being, linking him with both the departed and the generations to come. Finally comes death, that inevitable and, in many societies, most disrupting phenomenon of all. Death stands between the world of human beings and the world of the spirits, between the visible and the invisible.

There are many, and often complicated, ceremonies connected with death, burials, funerals, inheritance, the living-dead, the world of the departed, the visit of the living-dead to their human families, reincarnation and survival of the soul. Death is something that concerns everybody, partly because sooner or later everyone personally faces it and partly because it brings loss and sorrows to every family and community. It is no wonder, therefore, that rituals connected with death are usually elaborate. It would be futile to imagine that we could deal adequately with the subject of death here, but there are interesting studies to which the reader may be referred.[1] We shall take a few specific cases with which to illustrate African concepts of death and the hereafter; and then draw some conclusions from these and other considerations.

[a] *Death among the Ndebele*
When a person falls seriously ill, relatives watch by his bedside. These relatives must include at least one brother and the eldest son of the sick man, because the two are the ones who investigate the cause of the illness, which is generally magic and witchcraft, and take preventive measures against it,

[1] Among the many anthropological accounts available, detailed studies include those of: M. Wilson *Rituals of Kinship among the Nyakyusa* (1957); J. R. Goody *Death, Property and the Ancestors* (1962); and S. Yokoo *Death among the Abaluyia* (dissertation at Makerere University College, Kampala, 1966).

If the sick man lingers on in pain, his relatives kill what is known as 'the beast of the ancestors'. This is generally an ox or a goat (for a poor man), and its killing is believed to hasten death. Attempts, however, may be made to revive the sick through pouring cold water over his body and making him inhale smoke from certain herbs. The presence of the eldest son at the deathbed is a sign that the dying person is nevertheless alive in his children, and this assures him also that there is someone to 'remember' him, to keep him in 'personal immortality', when he has disappeared physically. The slaughter of the so-called 'beast of the ancestors' is also a sign linking both departed and living members of the family, and an assurance that the dying person will not go into a foreign hostile country, but will move into a friendly (even festal) community. The living-dead are present at the death of their human relative, and may be asked, through the slaughter of their animal, to hasten the death of the sick in order to terminate his pain or suffering more quickly.

Immediately after death, the brother starts digging a grave in an un-cultivated ground where other men join and help him. The corpse is wrapped in an animal skin (formerly) or blanket. If the person is the head of the homestead, his body is taken out of the house through a hole in the wall, and through an opening in the fence that surrounds the homestead. It must not be carried through the door of the house or the gate of the homestead. This probably symbolizes the belief that the deceased person has not 'gone' away from, or completely left the homestead: he is in effect still present.

Then follows the funeral procession: the men first, carrying the corpse, with the women coming behind. It is unfortunate for people to encounter such a party on its way, and they must avoid funeral processions. The grave has an east-west shape, presumably capturing the 'movement' of the sun. The oldest son strikes the grave with a spear, and then the body is laid down, facing south: the man is put on his right, the woman on her left. A few personal belongings are put into the grave, and then earth is shovelled over. Thorn branches are piled over and around the grave to keep animals (and possibly witches) from digging up the grave.

The party now returns home where an animal is killed, known as 'the beast to accompany (the deceased)'. This is an ox for a man, or a goat for a woman. The meat is roasted and eaten without salt, and all the bones completely burned. Ashes from the burnt bones are gathered, and with them the medicine-man makes 'medicine' which all the people drink. When drinking this 'medicine', a person swallows the first mouthful and spits out the second. Then all the people go to the river, wash themselves and disperse to their own homes.

The brother and eldest son remain in the homestead for the night. Two or three women relatives or friends also remain there and participate in the formal wailing which takes place the day after the funeral. These women remain there for a week or so. Early the next morning the brother and son visit the grave to see if it has been disturbed. If no disturbance has occurred then it is assumed that the man died from natural causes; but if the grave has been disturbed, then a diviner is called to investigate the causes of death and to take counter-measures.

One to three months later, the burial party is summoned together once more to observe the rite 'to wash the hoes'. For this rite, beer is brewed, all the implements used for the burial are washed with it, and medicine is dispensed to the children in the homestead. A year later another ceremony is performed, which is known as 'the ceremony of calling back the soul of the departed, to his own people'. This is done only for men and women who were married before dying. At the ceremony, all the relatives and friends are gathered for a big festival and dancing. Beer is made from grain grown after the man's death, and from seeds obtained outside the homestead. At this ceremony, all the restrictions hitherto imposed on the normal life of the homestead following the death are lifted and normal life is resumed. Thereafter the widows are free to remarry; the property of the dead man is divided; and a new animal is chosen to be the new 'beast of the ancestors'. This animal is normally a black ox, but never a sheep, and is thereafter cared for by the main heir who is usually the eldest son. The ceremony ritually puts to an end all the interruption of life caused by death.[1]

We see a number of meanings in these funeral procedures. The spear with which the eldest son strikes the grave is a weapon of defence and protection, and when used for this occasion it neutralizes all danger on the way to and in the new country where the dead man is going. Personal belongings are buried with the body to accompany the deceased man, so that he does not find himself poor in the hereafter: these things are part of him, and he must not be robbed by the surviving relatives (or else he will visit them and demand what is his own). The animal killed afterwards serves, as it is called, to 'accompany' the deceased, to provide him with food on the way and livestock in the next world. Drinking 'medicine' made from the ashes of the burnt bones is a rite whereby the departed is mystically united with the members of his family and community who are still alive. Washing in the river is a ritual act of cleansing from the pollution caused by death; and the same applies to the rite performed a month or two later, when the implements are washed with beer. At that ceremony, children are given protective medicine to drink, as a counter-measure against death.

[1] Hughes & van Velsen, p. 100 f.; but the interpretation is my own.

The final ceremony is partly a symbolic way of 'reviving', 'summoning back', 'inviting back' the departed, and thus renewing contact with him in the next world; and partly declaring a formal resumption of life. It is a ritual celebration of man's conquest over death: for death has only disrupted and not destroyed the rhythm of life. It indicates also that the departed is not really dead: he is a living-dead, and can be contacted, invited back and drawn into the human circles. The new 'beast of the ancestors' symbolizes the continuing presence of the living-dead in the family and among his people. These ceremonies also show us the great religious importance of marriage and procreation in African societies: the son plays a leading and continuing role in the ceremonies of his father's funeral, in keeping up his memory and in caring for the ox which mystically links the human world with that of the departed. An unmarried person is not given the final ceremony which in many ways is the most important and most meaningful in man's attempts to symbolize his conquest over death. This would mean that the unmarried is in effect conquered by death, he is not recalled, nor is he ceremoniously invited back into the human family.

[b] *Death among the Abaluyia*

When it seems fairly certain that death is coming, the sick man is placed in front or in the centre of his major wife's house and all the relatives are informed about the impending matter. Everyone must come, otherwise those who do not come will be suspected of having worked magic against the dying man; or the spirit of the man might later on take revenge, as such absence is regarded as showing disrespect for the dying man. The brother or son of the sick man kills a sheep or goat at the family shrine (*lusambwa*) saying, 'All who have already died, come and eat this meat! So and so, so and so . . .' (mentioning the names of the departed). The meat is then eaten by the family, together with the dying man if he can. This animal is the final donation of the man to his living-dead, and the means of requesting them to receive him peacefully. He then bids farewell to the family and apologizes for offences he may have committed unawares against the members of his family and relatives. If the person who used magic against him eats of this meat, it is believed that she would fall sick. The dying man gives instruction concerning the distribution of his property; and all the people sit around him, silently waiting for him to die.

As soon as he dies, the wife bursts out with wailing, and is joined by the sons, daughters and other men and women. The cry for a dead man is: 'Ye, ye, ye——; ye, ye, ye——!'; and for a dead woman: 'Wo-i, wo-i, wo-i ——; wo-i, wo-i, wo-i——!' While wailing, the wife touches and rubs her husband's body. She then goes out, followed by other people, and continues to wail from homestead to homestead, from river to river, from bush to bush, as far as her natal home if it is near. The women put their hands on the back of the head, while the men beat grasses and bushes with sticks and clubs, and old men blow horns.

If the dead person is a young woman with up to two children or none, her body is returned to her parents' home and the marriage gift is given back to her husband. Marriage is not considered complete until she has borne several children. Formerly, the body of a dead person would be kept inside the house for a day, but nowadays it is kept outside the house. The body is laid on an animal skin and covered with it or with banana leaves; and if it is a distinguished man, a leopard skin is used. The body of a clan head is kept for two days, as a sign of respect to him and in order to please his spirit. The body of a child is kept for only a few hours before burial. Since modern conditions send people to work in distant places bodies of the dead are kept for two days, to allow the relatives to come from afar. At night a vigil is kept over the dead, particularly in order to look out for the witch or sorcerer who might come to see the result of her (his) wicked doings. Neighbours and relatives bring beer and food; some play musical instruments, others sing funeral dirges and dance. This is intended partly to please the spirit of the dead person, and partly to comfort the bereaved family. If the widow has been a faithful wife, she dances with spears in her hands, singing the dirges; and if she has passed the childbearing age, she puts on the garment of her dead husband, something which a young widow would not dare to do or else she would never bear more children.

On the day of the burial, the widow is led by an older widow to the river where she is painted with clay; and her children and relatives paint themselves with clay. The procession to the river is accompanied with crying, singing, wailing and dancing; and the clay is the symbol of mourning. On the way home, the party sings, jumps up, dances, brandishes spears and clubs and sticks and shields, and utters shrill cries. The widow praises her husband, saying, for example, 'My husband was very good to me; he gave me many children. He was a very brave warrior and he killed a lot of enemies.'

Meanwhile four brothers or near clansmen dig the grave. No woman or uncircumcised person should dig the grave; and the father cannot dig a grave for his son or daughter, or husband for his wife. If a person has died through unusual causes such as lightning or suicide, then people fear to dig the grave for him as this would infect them with impurities; and his grave diggers must be paid a goat which they kill and wash the impurities with its blood. For the family head the grave is dug inside his first wife's house; for a woman, unmarried son or daughter, or a married man without children or with only up to two children, it is dug on the left-hand side behind the house; for the rainmaker, it is in the centre of his house; for a person who dies from an epidemic, it is dug at the riverside or in the bush so that he does not 'defile' the homestead; and for someone with a humped back or dying from suicide, the grave is in the back of the compound. The grave is rectangular; and grass or banana leaves are placed at the bottom, but for a clan head a cowskin is used instead.

The actual burial takes place in the early afternoon for a woman or ordinary man, but towards sunset for a distinguished man. If the dead is a renowned warrior, a clan or family head, or an elderly man, the burial is preceded by the ceremony of 'breaking the pot'. For this, a cooking or beer pot is ceremoniously broken by the grandson of the dead man, this symbol-izing the loss incurred through death. The body is buried facing west, and completely naked just as the person was when he was born. This 'naked' state symbolizes birth in the hereafter. A deformed person or witch is buried without any ceremony; and if it is a barren woman, all unmarried persons and those who have no children must keep away from the corpse lest they are infested by the same tragedy.

In some parts of the country, the grave now becomes the new shrine for the living-dead of the family. A goat is killed by the grave diggers, and its blood is sprinkled over the new shrine or the grave. The goat and the sprinkled blood are a token of returning thanks to the deceased man for the fame and wealth he has left to the family. For an elderly man or person of distinction, the ceremony of 'cattle drive' (*shilembe*) is performed on the day after burial. This is not, however, done for one who has no son, even if other respects may be accorded him. For this ceremony, cattle are gathered and decorated with weed or grass; people paint their faces with white clay and wear war dresses of cow-skin or leopard skin or of grasses, and bring spears, clubs, shields and sticks. Each clan drives, in turn, its cattle into the homestead, and sings and dances there. The songs include war songs, marriage songs, dirges, praises to the deceased man and appreciation of the contribution he made to his community. The people beat banana trees, bushes or roof of the house; and the 'cattle drive drum' is beaten by two or three brothers of the deceased man. This ceremony is intended to drive away the spirit of the dead man, so that it does not linger around the homestead and cause misfortune.

The day following the cattle drive, the hair-shaving ceremony is per-formed. All those who came into contact with the deceased man, either in his death-bed or during burial, are shaved. It is believed that his breath causes impurity, and makes disease stick to the head of the one in contact with the dead body. The hair is hidden in case a witch gets hold of it, or a bird takes and uses it to build a nest. In the latter case, it is feared that the owner of the hair will thereafter have chronic headaches. The shaving of hair is done starting with the widow, then grave-diggers, sons, daughters and other people. A fowl or goat is killed, and those taking part in the ceremony share in eating the meat. Then people may leave the homestead.[1]

Without going into a detailed interpretation of the coming of death and funeral rites among the Abaluyia, we may point out the underlying paradox that death brings. The dying person is being cut off from human beings, and yet there must be continuing ties between the living and the departed. Relatives and neighbours come to bid farewell to the dying man and to mourn his departure, and yet there is continuity through his children and through the rituals which unite the two worlds. Death causes ritual impurity just as it interrupts normal life; but this is not permanent since it is cleansed and normal life is afterwards resumed. The grave is paradoxically the symbol of separation between the dead and the living, but turning it into the shrine for the living-dead converts it into the point of meeting between the two worlds. In these Abaluyia rites, we see also how the corporate group is involved in the death of the individual; and the whole community, including cattle, joins in 'sending off' the member who leaves for the next world. Even the living-dead are involved, for it is they who will receive the new-comer. Stripping the corpse and burying it completely naked is a concrete externalization of the concept of death as birth into the hereafter.

[c] *The causes and meaning of death*
We saw in an earlier chapter, that most African peoples have mythological explanations of how death first came into the world.[2] Man has since accepted death as part of the natural rhythm of life; and yet, paradoxically, every human death is thought to have external causes, making it both natural and unnatural. People must find and give immediate causes of death. By far the commonest cause is believed to be magic, sorcery and witchcraft. This is found in every African society, though with varying degrees of emphasis; and someone is often blamed for using this method to cause the death of another. We will discuss this subject further in chapter sixteen. The curse is something greatly feared in many societies, and a powerful curse is believed to bring death to the person concerned. The living-dead and spirits are another cause. This applies to those of a given family, particularly the living-dead who may have been offended before

[1] S. Yokoo *Death among the Abaluyia*, pp. 34–39.
[2] See chapter nine above; and H. Abrahamsson *The Origin of Death* (Uppsala 1951), for a fuller account of the myths concerned; and U. Beier *The Origin of Life and Death* (London 1966) which contains a few similar myths.

they died, or may not have been properly buried, or may have a grudge against someone. Although people may fear that the living-dead would cause them to die, there is little evidence of the belief that they actually cause death. This is a point which has been misrepresented in accounts of African concepts of the spirits. If a family feels that its living-dead are dissatisfied, it immediately takes measures to harmonize the situation, and avoid its deterioration to the point of actual death. The fourth cause of certain deaths is God, especially those for which there is no other satisfactory explanation, e.g. through lightning, of very old people (natural death), or where a person may contravene an important custom or prohibition. Even when God may be seen as the ultimate cause of death, other intermediary agents may be brought into the picture to satisfy people's suspicions and provide a scapegoat. One or more of the causes of death must always be given for virtually every death in African villages. This means that, although death is acknowledged as having come into the world and remained there ever since, it is unnatural and preventable on the personal level because it is always caused by another agent. If that agent did not *cause* it, then the individual would not die. Such is the logic and such is the philosophy concerning the immediate functioning of death among human beings.

As for the phenomenon of dying, we need to consider first the terms used to describe the actual act of dying. These terms show the concepts that people have concerning death. Among the Basoga, when a person has died, people say that: 'he has breathed his last', 'he has kept quiet', 'he has gone', 'he has gone down to the grave', 'our friend was told by death to tie up his load and go', 'he is dry as if from yesterday', 'life was snatched into two like a bristle stick'; and if it is an old man from another family, they say, 'it is fair, he has died, he has eaten enough'. Of a murderer's or witch's death, they say, 'let him go, he has finished his job, another mouth has gone away'. Concerning someone who is not liked, people say that death (*walumbe*) 'has beaten him', 'has made him finish food', 'has made him sleep or lie down', 'has made him dry', 'has stiffened him', 'has made him quiet', 'has sneezed him', 'has made him go far away', or 'death has cut him down or forced him down'.[1] Among the Abaluyia death or dying is described as 'sleeping' (for an old man, who dies peacefully), 'falling by oneself' (if it through suicide), 'stepping into the sheet' (since the body is wrapped or covered with a skin or banana leaves before but not for burial), 'wearing a sweater' (if killed by another person), 'going to the place of the dead', 'going home'; and for a hated person, 'looking for an exit' or 'lifting the leg'.[2] The Akamba use the following terms: 'to follow the company of

[1] A. Bulima-Nabwiso, essay on the burial rites of the Basoga, March 1966.
[2] Yokoo, p. 13 f.

one's grandfathers', 'to go home', 'to stop snoring', 'to be fetched or sum/
moned', 'to empty out the soul', 'to sleep for ever and ever', 'to dry up, wither
or evaporate', 'to pass away', 'to be called', 'to reject the people', 'to reject
food', 'to be received or taken away', 'to return or go back', 'to terminate,
be finished or end', 'to have one's breath come to an end', 'to depart or go',
'to go where other people have gone', 'to leave, forsake or abandon', 'to
collapse, come to ruins', 'to become God's property', and 'to have a mis/
carriage' (for a person who dies at an early age).

Similar terms can be quoted from other parts of Africa. From these we
can draw a number of conclusions. Death is conceived of as a departure
and not a complete annihilation of a person. He moves on to join the
company of the departed, and the only major change is the decay of the
physical body, but the spirit moves on to another state of existence. Some
of the words describing death imply that a person goes 'home', which means
that this life is like a pilgrimage: the real 'home' is in the hereafter, since one
does not depart from there. There is a real cessation of part of the person at
death, so that he 'sleeps' but never to wake up again. Death is cruel, it
'stiffens', 'cuts down' or 'evaporates' a person, even if he continues to exist
in the hereafter. This cruelty of death comes out in funeral dirges. A vivid
example of this may be cited from the Acholi who sing:

> *Fire rages at Layima,*
> *It rages in the valley of river Cumu,*
> *Everything is utterly destroyed;*
> *Oh, my daughter,*
> *If I could reach the homestead of Death's mother,*
> *I would make a long grass torch;*
> *If I could reach the homestead of Death's mother*
> *I would utterly destroy everything.*
> *Fire rages at Layima.*

The struggle between man and death is portrayed in another vivid dirge:

> *Behold Oteka fights alone*
> *The Bull dies alone.*
> *O men of the lineage of Awic*
> *What has the son of my mother done to you*
> *That he should be deserted*
> *Behold the warrior fights single handed.*
> *My brother is armed with bows and barbed/headed arrows,*
> *He fights alone, not a single helper beside him;*

> *My brother fights alone,*
> *He struggles with Death.*[1]

This same sense of man's helplessness in the sight of death, can also be seen in an Akan dirge:

> *We are bereft of a leader,*
> *Death has left us without a leader ...*
> *He has died and left us without a leader.*
> *Alas, mother! Alas, father!*
> *Alas, mother! Alas, father! ...*
> *We are being carried away.*
> *Death is carrying us all away ...*[2]

Thus, death is a monster before whom man is utterly helpless. Relatives watch a person die, and they cannot help him escape death. It is an individual affair in which nobody else can interfere or intervene. This is the height of death's agonies and pain, for which there is neither cure nor escape, as far as African concepts and religions are concerned.

From funeral rites and methods of disposing with the dead body, we catch other glimpses of African concepts of death. Burial is the commonest method of dealing with the corpse, and different customs are followed. Some societies bury the body inside the house where the person was living at the time of death; others bury it in the compound where the homestead is situated; others bury the body behind the compound; and some do so at the place where the person was born. The graves differ in shape and size: some are rectangular, others are circular, some have a cave-like shape at the bottom where the body is laid; and in some societies the corpse is buried in a big pot. In many areas it is the custom to bury food, weapons, stools, tobacco, clothing, and formerly one's wife or wives, so that these may 'accompany' the departed into the next world. Yet, in other societies the dead body might be thrown into a river or bush where it is eaten by wild animals and birds of prey. In others, a special burial 'hut' is used, in which the body is kept either indefinitely or for several months or years after which the remains are taken out and buried. In a number of societies the skull or jaw or other part of the dead person is cut off and preserved by the family concerned, with the belief that the departed is 'present' in that skull or jaw; and in any case, this portion of the dead is a concrete reminder to the family that the person lives on in the hereafter. These methods of disposal apply mainly to those who are adults, or die 'normal' deaths. Children,

[1] J. Okot p'Bitek, 'The concept of Jok among the Acholi and Lango', in *The Uganda Journal*, Vol. XXVII, No. 1, 1963, p. 20.
[2] J. H. Nketia *Funeral dirges of the Akan People* (Accra 1955), p. 122 f.

unmarried people, those who die through suicide or through animal attack, and victims of diseases like leprosy, smallpox or epilepsy, may not be given the same or full burial rites, but modern change tends to make burial procedures more even or similar for everybody.

Again it is clear that people view death paradoxically: it is a separation but not annihilation, the dead person is suddenly cut off from the human society and yet the corporate group clings to him. This is shown through the elaborate funeral rites, as well as other methods of keeping in contact with the departed, which we shall discuss below. Death becomes, then, a gradual process which is not completed until some years after the actual physical death. At the moment of physical death the person becomes a living-dead: he is neither alive physically, nor dead relative to the corporate group. His own Sasa period is over, he enters fully into the Zamani period; but, as far as the living who knew him are concerned, he is kept 'back' in the Sasa period, from which he can disappear only gradually. Those who have nobody to keep them in the Sasa period in reality 'die' immediately, which is a great tragedy that must be avoided at all costs.

[d] *The hereafter*

For peoples who think that the hereafter is in another world or a distant place, food and weapons may be buried with the dead body to sustain and protect the person in the journey between the two worlds or places. For the majority of peoples, however, the next world is in fact geographically 'here', being separated from this only by virtue of being invisible to human beings. The Chagga hold that the journey takes nine days from this to the next world, and the soul must travel through a dangerous desert region. On arrival at the other end the soul has to be admitted by older spirits. To make the journey less demanding the corpse is anointed with fat, 'given' milk in the mouth and wrapped with hide, to provide it with food and protect it from the scorching desert sun. A bull is also killed for the grandfather of the deceased, so that he would help the soul when it arrives at the next world. The Lodagaa believe that the land of the departed lies to the west, being separated from this by the river of Death. As soon as the funeral rites are performed, the soul begins its journey. At the river it is ferried across, for a fee of twenty cowries which friends and relatives provide at the funeral. But crossing this river is an ordeal whose hardness depends on the nature of the life that a person has led in this life. Therefore, 'good' people get across easily, but 'bad' people fall through the boat and must swim across the river, which can take up to three years to do. It is debtors, thieves, witches and those who denied something to others, that face the greatest difficulties in either being allowed to cross or in the act of crossing the river.[1] The Ga people also believe that at death the soul must cross a river, and on arrival at the other side, the nose is broken so that the departed speak in nasal tones.

These are a few examples of what the journey to the next world is thought to be or involve. There are many African peoples who do not visualize any geographical separation between the two worlds, and as soon as a person is physically dead he arrives 'there' in his spirit form. This means that a person is thought to be composed of physical and spiritual entities, and among some societies to these is added a 'shadow', 'a breath' or 'a personality'. It is not always easy to divide up a person into more than two parts, and this is an area which requires further research and study.

We have already touched on the spirits and the living-dead in chapter eight above. By some societies, the hereafter is thought to be underground, probably because dead bodies are buried. The ground on which people walk is therefore the most intimate point of contact between the living-dead and their human relatives. It is the ground (grave) which 'buries' them from the sight of their kinsmen, and which in effect erases their physical existence as far as human beings are concerned. Yet paradoxically it is the same ground through which offerings, libation and even divination enable human beings to contact the living-dead. Therefore, family shrines for the living-dead are found generally at or near the spot where the head or oldest member of the homestead is buried; and the cult of the living-dead is carried out within a close proximity to the actual burial place of the family. The land keeps together the Sasa of the living and the Zamani of the departed; and as we saw in the third chapter of this book, the same words are often used for both time and space. For African peoples, the ground has a religious charge, mystically uniting past and present generations, the Zamani and the Sasa.

Many societies locate the home of the departed in the area around people's homesteads. For this reason, they may keep part of the dead body as a symbol of the abiding presence of the departed. Other societies have to remove their living-dead ceremoniously when the village moves to another spot. All this shows how close a mystical affinity the people have towards their departed. It is only in a few societies that the departed of present and recent generations are thought to dwell in the woods or hills rather removed from the homesteads where they once lived. But even then, these living-dead would keep in touch with their surviving relatives through visiting them or receiving libation and offerings from their families.

A number of peoples, including the Basuto, Lozi, Lugbara, Shilluk, Turkana and Yoruba, believe that at death the soul of the person goes to

[1] Goody, p. 371 f., gives a full and interesting account.

the sky or near to God. This does not, however, cut it off from its own human relatives who continue to hold that the living-dead is near to them and can be approached through prayer, libation and offerings. As we have already shown, the living-dead act as intermediaries between men and God, or between men and important, but more distant, forefathers.

The majority of African peoples do not expect any form of judgment or reward in the hereafter. We have only a few exceptions to this statement. The Yoruba believe that after death the person presents himself before God and gives an account of his earthly life. So the people say that

> *All that we do on earth,*
> *We shall account for kneeling in heaven . . .*
> *We shall state our case at the feet of God.*[1]

So also the Lodagaa fear that suffering awaits 'bad' people at the crossing of the river of death; and on arrival in the next world, everyone must endure punishment (a kind of bullying) from older spirits. The Lozi wear tribal marks on the arms and ears so that they may be recognized in the next world and be admitted to live happily 'there'. Similarly the Sonjo believe that wearing a tribal mark on the shoulder will guarantee them recognition when their national hero returns to 'save' them.

The Yoruba are uncertain about the final lot of the departed: some are put in a good place, others in a bad place; the first group meets relatives and lives more or less as the people did in this life, but the second group is thought to suffer without end. Those Lozi members who have no tribal marks are given flies to eat and put on a road which wanders about until it ends in a desert where they die of hunger and thirst.

Apart from these few ideas, we have no concrete evidence of the hereafter being pictured in terms of punishment or reward. For the majority of African peoples, the hereafter is only a continuation of life more or less as it is in its human form. This means that personalities are retained, social and political statuses are maintained, sex distinction is continued, human activities are reproduced in the hereafter, the wealth or poverty of the individual remains unchanged, and in many ways the hereafter is a carbon copy of the present life. Although the soul is separated from the body it is believed to retain most, if not all, of the physical-social characteristics of its human life. Once again we see that although death is a dissolution and separation, man does not accommodate this radical change; and African peoples both acknowledge and deny the disruption of death. A person dies and yet continues to live: he is a living-dead, and no other term can describe him better than that. Whatever happens to the spiritual component

[1] Idowu, pp. 189, 199.

of man at death, surviving relatives do not wish to see him slip immediately out of their Sasa period: they hold on to him, they *remember* him, they retain him in a state of personal immortality. Therefore he survives as a person, as 'so-and-so', as 'my' or 'our' father, mother, brother, son or grandparent. It is the sacred duty of the family then to keep the living-dead within temporal sight of the Sasa period. This is where the cult of the living-dead comes into the picture in practically all African societies. It is a struggle between Zamani and Sasa, and everyone wants to 'be remembered', to be won over to the side of human Sasa, to be kept alive even if the body and spirit have separated. This is for everybody and not for the so-called 'ancestors'.

[e] *The destiny of the soul*
Death proclaims the formal conflict between Zamani and Sasa forces. As soon as a person dies, he becomes a living-dead—he is a 'spirit' in the sense that he is no longer in the body, and yet he retains features which describe him in physical terms. He still retains his personal name, so that when he appears to human members of his family, they recognize him as so-and-so. He is counted part of the family in many ways, even though people know and realize that he has forsaken them. Part of his being survives in the memory of those who knew him while he lived, and in the children who survive him. It is primarily his family which 'keeps him going', so to speak. When the living-dead appears it is to those within his household or family, and rarely if ever, to people not immediately related to him. But, however real the living-dead may seem to those who see him, there is no affectionate warmth such as one witnesses when relatives or friends meet in this life. There is no exchange of greetings, which in African societies is an extremely important social means of contact; and when the living-dead departs, human beings do not give greetings to other living-dead. Socially, therefore, something has happened, something has cooled off, and a real distance between the living-dead and human beings has begun to grow. We have pointed out already that the living-dead may give instructions, or enquire about the family, or make requests to be given something, and may even threaten to punish members of the family for not carrying out particular instructions or for not caring sufficiently for the living-dead. People are keen to do their 'best' for the living-dead, chiefly because these are in a position of need just as little children have to be cared for by adults. The personal immortality of the living-dead is for all practical purposes dependent on his progenies. At the same time, the living-dead are in the intermediary position between man and God, and between man and the spirits. Human beings keep the relationship going between them and their living-dead,

chiefly through libation, offerings of food and other items, prayers and the observation of proper rites towards the departed or instructions from them.

This process continues on a personal level as long as someone who knew the living-dead is still alive. This may be up to four or five generations. By that time, the living-dead has sunk further and further into the Zamani period, with only loose strings of memory still holding him feebly in the human Sasa period. When the last person who knew him dies, the living-dead is entirely removed from the state of personal immortality, and he sinks beyond the horizon of the Sasa period. He is now dead, as far as human beings are concerned, and the process of dying is now completed. The living-dead is now a spirit, which enters the state of collective immortality. It has 'lost' its personal name, as far as human beings are concerned, and with it goes also the human personality. It is now an 'it' and no longer a 'he' or 'she'; it is now one of myriads of spirits who have lost their humanness. This, for all practical purposes, is the final destiny of the human soul. Man is ontologically destined to lose his humanness but gain his full spiritness; and there is no general evolution or devolution beyond that point. God is beyond, and in African concepts there is neither hope nor possibility that the soul would attain a share in the divinity of God.

In a few societies it is held that national heroes or founders have reached very close to God. We can cite examples from the Shilluk concerning Nyikang who founded the nation, from the Nupe concerning Tsoedi their first king, and from the Sonjo concerning Khambageu who helped in the physical and religious life of the people. In such cases, the heroes are sometimes so closely associated with God that prayers, offerings and sacrifices are addressed to both God and the hero as if there was no clear distinction. We have societies who recognize divinities, like the Yoruba, Igbo, Akan, Baganda and others, some of which were once historical figures who have now been elevated to a status higher than that of ordinary spirits. These divinities are the exception in that a person does not hope to become a divinity eventually: this is not within the normal rhythm of the destiny of the human soul. Although final judgment in this matter must await a fuller study of divinities, one suspects that those who have been made divinities were, during their human life, in positions of political or social leadership, and that it is this same status which has been transferred to the hereafter. If this is valid, then these divinities have not 'evolved' from or through the stage of being ordinary spirits. They have only retained the hieararchical position which they held while they were human beings. Some of the divinities are only a personification of natural objects and phenomena, so that the question of human destiny is out of place in this case. Available evidence points us to the conclusion that, as far as traditional

African concepts are concerned, the human soul is destined to the ontological mode of the spirits and not beyond that point, whether or not some
of these spirits hold a higher position than others. Collective immortality
is man's cul-de-sac in the hereafter. Whether this immortality is relative
or absolute I have no clear means of judging, and on this matter African
concepts seem to be vague. Some of the spirits become attached to natural
objects and phenomena, some are feared when encountered by human
beings, some possess people, but the majority seem to 'vanish' out of human
contact and thinking. Zamani has now won the battle, it claims all these
spirits, and man has no clear way of penetrating into what is (to him) lost
from sight.

Genealogies are found in many African societies. These are, beyond
four or five generations, 'empty' names as far as human beings are concerned.
The genealogical names are like the bones of the spinal cord: they are the
lingering remains from what Zamani has swept away, and they do not show
us the full skeleton. Many other names are lost once the living-dead
sink into the state of ordinary spirits.

Belief in reincarnation is reported among many African societies. This
is, however, partial reincarnation in the sense that only some human
features or characteristics of the living-dead are said to be 'reborn' in some
children. This happens chiefly in the circle of one's family and relatives.
The living-dead who has been reincarnated continues, however, to have his
separate existence and does not cease to be. I suspect that this belief is partly
the result of externalizing people's awareness of the nearness of their living-
dead, and partly an attempt to explain what is otherwise a purely biological
phenomenon which applies not only to human beings but also to animals.
Those who hold someone in the state of personal immortality see biological
or character resemblances in a young child, and immediately feel that since
the particular living-dead has not yet sunk into the oblivion of the Zamani
period, he has 'returned' to them. It pains the community, therefore, that
someone should die without getting married, since this dwindles the
chances of his being 'reborn'. Anybody can be reincarnated in this way,
whether married or not, whether young or old, but it is mainly those who
have had children of their own, and in some societies it is definitely said
that a person who is unmarried or has no children cannot be reincarnated.
In practice only a few people are actually 'reborn' in this sense, and some are
reincarnated in several individuals simultaneously and without regard to the
sex of the living-dead. Some societies mark this belief through naming their
children after the particular living-dead who is thought to be 'reborn' in
them. Although the belief in partial reincarnation exists, it is not expected
that everybody will automatically be 'reborn'; and the belief is not reported

at all in some societies. When relatives notice that one of their living-dead has been reincarnated, they rejoice about it and this is another level of keeping warm the relationship between the two parties. Once the living-dead has moved on into the Zamani period and into the state of ordinary spirits reincarnation for him also ceases. This means, therefore, that if and when partial reincarnation does take place, it is a temporary pheno-menon during the intermediate period when the living-dead is still in the state of personal immortality. The soul of man is destined to become an ordinary spirit, and once that stage is reached, there is no more possibility of its returning to the human mode of existence. In some societies the spirit (or the living-dead) is thought to visit human beings in the form of snakes, rats, lizards or other animals, which may not be killed.

According to African religions and philosophy, the grave is the seal of everything, even if a person survives and continues to exist in the next world. There is an accelerated rhythm from death through the state of personal immortality (as the living-dead) to the state of collective immortality (as ordinary spirits). This final 'beat' of the rhythm may or may not have an end. There is, however, nothing to hope for, since this is the destiny for everybody; though older people do not seem to fear, and may even long for, the 'departure' from this to the next world. There is no resurrection for either the individual or mankind at large, nor can such a concept be accommodated where the process of dying sweeps the individual from the Sasa into the Zamani, from the period of intensive personal experience to the ever vanishing period where humanness is completely obliterated. The departed do not grow spiritually towards or like God, though some may act as intermediaries between men and God and may have more power and knowledge than human beings. Such is the anthropocentric view of the destiny of man, and as far as traditional African concepts are concerned, death is death and the beginning of a permanent ontological departure of the individual from mankind to spirithood. Beyond that point, African religions and philosophy are absolutely silent, or at most extremely vague. Nothing can reverse or halt that process, and death is the end of real and complete man.

15

SPECIALISTS

Medicine-men, Rainmakers, Kings & Priests

This is one of the areas in which the question of terminology is extremely difficult, in describing either collectively or individually the people to be discussed here. I shall call these people 'specialists', in virtue of their specialized office, knowledge and skill in religious matters; but other terms are used, such as 'sacred personages', 'special men', 'sacred men' or 'sacred specialists'. As we shall see, there are different terms for each of the specialists and some of these terms overlap just as the nature and role of some specialists also overlap. Written information varies widely from good and thorough studies to unreliable and worthless material. It needs to be pointed out also, that since specialists belong to a 'special' category of their own, they have a language, symbolism, knowledge, skill, practice and what I may call 'office personality' of their own which are not known or easily accessible to the ordinary person whether he is a villager or a scholar in search of know-ledge. As such, there still remains a great deal of inner information to be gathered and made available to the public. Specialists play an important role in the life of African villages and communities, but we shall limit our discussion to their religious significance.

[a] *The medicine-men*
To African societies the medicine-men are the greatest gift, and the most useful source of help. Other names for them are 'herbalists', 'traditional doctors' or '*waganga*' (to use a Swahili word). These are the specialists who have suffered most from European-American writers and speakers who so often and wrongly call them 'witch-doctors'—a term which should be buried and forgotten forever. Every village in Africa has a medicine-man within reach, and he is the friend of the community. He is accessible to everybody and at almost all times, and comes into the picture at many points in individual and community life.

There is no fixed rule governing the 'calling' of someone to become a medicine-man. This may come when he is still young and unmarried, or in his middle or later life. In other cases, a medicine-man passes on the profession to his son or other younger relative. There are medicine-men who believe that spirits or the living-dead have 'called' them, in dreams, visions or in waking, to become medicine-men. There are both women and men in this profession. Their personal qualities vary, but medicine-men are expected to be trustworthy, upright morally, friendly, willing and ready to serve, able to discern people's needs and not be exorbitant in their charges. On the whole they are influential, though in some societies they have no official position outside their professional duties. The skill and success of medicine-men vary, naturally, from person to person. In some societies it is believed that the medicine-men possess special gifts or powers obtained either through birth or eating certain 'medicines'.

In every case, medicine-men must undergo formal or informal training. Among the Azande, for example, their training is long and expensive, even starting the preliminary preparations at the age of five years in some cases. When a young person has made his wishes known that he intends to become a medicine-man he is carefully scrutinized by his would-be teacher, to ascertain that he really 'means business'. Then he is given medicine to eat, which is believed 'to strengthen his soul and give him powers of prophecy; he is initiated into the corporation by public burial; he is given witchcraft phlegm to swallow; and he is taken to a stream-source and shown the various herbs and shrubs and trees from which the medicines are derived'. That is the procedure to becoming a medicine-man among the Azande, but in reality it takes a long time to reach the goal, and it is a complicated affair. Each teacher has his own regulations for his pupils, such as refraining from eating animals like elephants, house-rats and various plants, and from sexual intercourse or bathing for several days when one has eaten certain medicines from one's teacher. Payment for the training also varies, and is made from time to time, as the candidate continues to acquire his knowledge which may occasionally consist of learning one medicine a month or every two months.[1]

This example from the Azande does not by any means apply to all African societies. There are many who have a less formal training. But in either case, part of the training involves some kind of apprenticeship. Candidates acquire knowledge in matters pertaining to: the medicinal value, quality and use of different herbs, leaves, roots, fruits, barks, grasses and of various objects like minerals, dead insects, bones, feathers, powders, smoke from different objects, excreta of animals and insects, shells, eggs and so on; the causes, cures and prevention of diseases and other forms of

---

[1] E. E. Evans-Pritchard *Witchcraft, Oracles and Magic among the Azande* (1937), pp. 202–50, gives a full and detailed account of the training of medicine-men. It gives perhaps the best study of the medicine-men in a given African society.

suffering (such as barrenness, failure in undertakings, misfortunes, poor crop yield in the field); magic, witchcraft and sorcery, and how to combat (or even use) them; the nature and handling of spirits and the living-dead; and various secrets some of which may not be divulged to outsiders. When the training is over, the candidate is, in some societies, formally and publicly initiated into the profession of medicine-men, so that everyone may recognize him and his qualification. Medicine-men form associations or corporations in some societies, such as among the Azande.

The duties of medicine-men are many and varied, and overlap with those of other specialists. We shall take two examples to illustrate this point. Among the Ndebele, the medicine-man supplies medicated pegs for the gates of a new homestead. He combats witchcraft and magic by preventing their action and sometimes by sending them back to their authors. After the burial, it is the medicine-man who performs the ceremony of 'striking the grave', if the person has died from witchcraft. The ceremony is performed at sunset. The son and brother of the dead man visit the grave together with the medicine-man. The medicine-man carries a medicated stick with which he strikes the grave saying, 'So-and-so, wake up! Go and fight!' It is believed that the spirit of the dead person wakes up and goes in the form of a small animal to the home of the witch who killed him. The animal waits there until one of the members of the witch's family sees and kills it. Then members of this family begin to die. If the family of the witch admits guilt then the members pay cattle to the family of the dead man and the 'curse' of the revenge is closed, or a powerful medicine-man is called to remove or stop it.[1]

Among the Azande the medicine-man cures the sick and warns of impending danger. It is he who removes failure from hunting and from farming. 'He can harm or protect, kill or cure.' He attacks witchcraft and magic with his medicines of which he knows and keeps plenty for this and other purposes. Nobles are said to patronize medicine-men 'because their magic is good magic. It causes no one an injury and protects many from harm.' All the people are agreed that 'the medicine-man is harmless, and everyone praises his medicine', even if the medicine-men may fight among themselves which they do without harming other people. They are constantly being summoned to court or to people's homes; and they practise also as diviners. They perform at seances intended to watch over the witches, expose their intentions and frustrate their activities. In all important situations the Azande may summon the medicine-man 'with a general commission to ferret out witch-activities in the neighbourhood and to protect people against them'. Princes also patronize and protect medicine-men, especially

[1] Hughes & van Velsen, p. 108.

in order to get protection against witchcraft and political conspiracy. Every medicine-man is 'a professional indicator of witchcraft'.[1]

We may summarize the duties of medicine-men from these and other accounts as follows. First and foremost, medicine-men are concerned with sickness, disease and misfortune. In African societies these are generally believed to be caused by the ill-will or ill-action of one person against another, normally through the agency of witchcraft and magic. The medicine-man has therefore to discover the cause of the sickness, find out who the criminal is, diagnose the nature of the disease, apply the right treatment and supply a means of preventing the misfortune from occurring again. This is the process that medicine-men follow in dealing with illness and misfortune: it is partly psychological and partly physical. Thus, the medicine-man applies both physical and 'spiritual' (or psychological) treatment, which assures the sufferer that all is and will be well. The medicine-man is in effect both doctor and pastor to the sick person. His medicines are made from plants, herbs, powders, bones, seeds, roots, juices, leaves, liquids, minerals, charcoal and the like; and in dealing with a patient, he may apply massages, needles or thorns, and he may bleed the patient; he may jump over the patient, he may use incantations and ventrilo-quism, and he may ask the patient to perform various things like sacrificing a chicken or goat, observing some taboos or avoiding certain foods and persons—all these are in addition to giving the patient physical medicines. In African villages, disease and misfortune are religious experiences, and it requires a religious approach to deal with them. The medicine-men are aware of this, and make attempts to meet the need in a religious (or quasi-religious) manner—whether or not that turns out to be genuine or false or a mixture of both. Obviously some of the activities involved in dealing with illness may not have any overt value, but they are psychologically vital and no doubt play a great role in healing the sick or helping the sufferer. In this case, the means are less important than the end, and that is how both the medicine-man and his patient see and experience the situation which brings them together.

On the whole, the medicine-man gives much time and personal attention to the patient, which enables him to penetrate deep into the psychological state of the patient. Even if it is explained to a patient that he has malaria because a mosquito carrying malaria parasites has stung him he will still want to know why that mosquito stung him and not another person. The only answer which people find satisfactory to that question is that someone has 'caused' (or 'sent') the mosquito to sting a particular individual, by means of magical manipulations. Suffering, misfortune, disease and

[1] Evans-Pritchard, I, pp. 251-57.

accident, are all 'caused' mystically, as far as African peoples are concerned. To combat the misfortune or ailment the cause must also be found, and either counteracted, uprooted or punished. This is where the value of the traditional medicine-man comes into the picture. So long as people see sickness and misfortunes as 'religious' experiences, the traditional medicine-man will continue to exist and thrive. Modern hospitals may deal with the physical side of diseases, but there is the religious dimension of suffering which they do not handle, and for that purpose a great number of patients will resort to both hospitals and medicine-men, without a feeling of contra-diction, although if they are Christian or 'educated' they might only go secretly to the medicine-man or follow his treatment.

Another important duty of medicine-men is to take preventive measures. We have just pointed out that people experience suffering as being caused by mystical forces applied or used against them by their enemies or by those who hate them. This is often magic, witchcraft, sorcery, 'evil-eye' or bad words. The medicine-men must therefore supply people with counter-measures. These are generally in form of charms, performing rituals at the homes or fields of those in need, or applying medicines that are swallowed or rubbed into the body.

Medicine-men also give aid to increase productivity or give good results. They advise and assist on how a man may win more love from his wife; they give help to impotent men; they 'treat' people in order to prosper in business or succeed in politics; they supply various aids to students to 'enable' them to pass their examinations; they perform various rites to increase the fertility and productivity of the fields or livestock; and barren women (or their husbands and relatives) continually consult them in search of being able to bear children.

It is also the duty of the medicine-men to purge witches, detect sorcery, remove curses and control the spirits and living-dead. They have access to the force of nature and other forms of knowledge unknown or little known by the public. Therefore the public entrusts them with the duty of removing what may harm the community. This is an area which goes deep into the beliefs of people, whether these are objective realities or not.

In short, the medicine-men symbolize the hopes of society: hopes of good health, protection and security from evil forces, prosperity and good fortune, and ritual cleansing when harm or impurities have been contracted. These men and women are not fools: they are on the average intelligent and devoted to their work, and those who are not simply do not prosper or get too far. As in any country or profession, there are those who deliberately cheat their fellow men for the sake of gain and publicity. Some genuine medicine-men are also involved in harmful practices in the course of the performance of their duties. Whatever abuses may be apparent in the activities of medicine-men, it would be extremely unjust to condemn their profession. Medicine-men are the friends, pastors, psychiatrists and doctors of traditional African villages and communities.

Even in modern towns one still finds or hears of medicine-men some of whom are quite prosperous both professionally and economically. The strain of urban life has precipitated new situations of need, and these men are no doubt making a contribution towards the solving of the new problems by means of traditional methods. One gets the impression, however, that urban medicine-men are less trustworthy than those in the country-side. Part of the reason for this is the more impersonal life of urban society, and the other part is the money economy which encourages quick gain by either honest or dishonest means. The medicine-man is one of the specialists whose profession is likely to continue in Africa for several generations, especially since people's needs continue to increase through modern change, and he is moving his practice into the urban centres where these needs are most concentrated. Leading politicians in a number of African countries are known to consult medicine-men, just as do university students, which no doubt gives the medicine-men quite a high status and ensures the continuity of their profession. A number of university graduates are known to have become, or work with, medicine-men; and I have heard that in at least two countries there are medicine-men working side by side with doctors or in hospitals. Undoubtedly careful research into traditional medicine and medical practices may one day yield great benefits for all mankind. My little research among medicine-men has shown me that they need and deserve to be respected both as persons and for their profession. It is only by approaching them with such an attitude and spirit of humility, that the scholar or scientist may hope to have access to their specialized knowledge, though some of that knowledge can be acquired only by the initiated and probably under an oath of secrecy.

[b] *Mediums and diviners*

These specialists belong to the category of the medicine-men both in their training and duties. In their profession they also deal with the living-dead and spirits, whereas medicine-men generally do not. This is, however, chiefly an academic distinction and often the same specialist plays the role of both medicine-man and diviner, and African names for them are often the same.

The main duty of mediums is to link human beings with the living-dead and the spirits. Through them messages are received from the other world, or men are given knowledge of things that would otherwise be difficult or impossible to know. For example, through a medium who gets in touch with the spirit world, a person may be directed to find a lost article or to know who stole his goods. Mediums function in this role only when 'possessed' by a spirit, otherwise they are 'normal' people without specialized abilities. Their distinction is the ability to be 'possessed' or get in touch with the spirit world, but this also depends on the 'willingness' of the departed or other spirits to get 'into' them and communicate through them. I recently witnessed and tape-recorded one such case some twenty kilometres from Kampala. A young man was dressed up in a barkcloth, put on a ring made of a creeping plant, and held another plant half a metre long in his hands. He sat down in the diviner's room where a crowd of twenty-five to thirty people gathered. One of the men started to sing a highly rhythmical song, and the rest of the crowd joined with singing, clapping and rattling small gourds. The medium-to-be sat quietly on the floor without even turning his head. The singing and rattling went on for about thirteen minutes when suddenly the young man's hands began to tremble. Three or four minutes later he started talking in an entirely different voice. The singing stopped and the diviner could then talk with the medium for about fifteen minutes, in the middle of which the medium (or spirit in him) requested another song to be sung. At the end, the medium jumped about like a frog, banged his head hard on the floor and with his fist hit his own chest very hard twice or thrice. Then he was 'normal' once more. When I 'cross-examined' him afterwards, he assured us that he was not aware of what he said or did during the time he was acting as a medium. My colleagues and I got the impression that he was in his right mind and that he told us the truth concerning what he felt and did while he was in that trance. The spirit which entered this young man, who was an apprentice to a diviner, has been kept at the home of the diviner since 1958 (as he told us), living in a buffalo horn (*yembe*, in Luganda).

This is an example of a medium working with a diviner or medicine-man. The medium gives information concerning the cause, nature and treatment of disease (or other form of misfortune), and concerning thefts or loss of articles. It is then the duty of the diviner to follow or interpret the instructions from the medium. In some cases, diviners or medicine-men may be 'possessed' and temporarily become mediums. During the medium-ship the person 'loses' his own being or senses, and becomes simply an instrument of the spirit in him. He can then be led to act and speak according to the wishes of the spirit, seemingly without hurting himself. I have heard from eye-witnesses of cases where the medium would lick with his tongue a red-hot knife or piece of iron until it cools off, without burning either his hand or tongue. The medium I described in the previous paragraph did not seem to sustain any noticeable injury from banging his head on the floor and hitting his chest hard. He, however, breathed very hard and his arm muscles stiffened considerably during the period of mediumship. Spirits that come into mediums are not harmful: they are friendly, are welcomed by people and remain briefly or temporarily in the mediums concerned. Most mediums are women.

There is another type of medium associated with priests and temples or shrines. These mediums are reported in societies like the Ashanti, Baganda, Ewe, Fon, Yoruba and a number of other peoples especially in western Africa. It is reported, for example, that 'many Dahomean priests are never subject to possession themselves, but have mediums attached to their temples who enter into trance at will. Possession . . . generally occurs for the first time when the person is attending a public religious ceremony. At the movement of the dance and the example of some inspired devotees, the new person falls down in a fit or leaps into the ring and dances in an extravagant fashion. The presiding priests interpret this as a divine call, and persuade the inspired one to begin training for the service of a god.' This training may last two or more years, during which the person must observe strict chastity. At the end, a sacrifice is offered, and the trainee says to the divinity concerned: 'Today you have completed marriage with me'; after which the person may marry or resume his marital position and duties if already married.[1]

Among the Ga, mediums are trained by priests, some being officially appointed by the priests or village elders. If already married, they have to leave their families and when their training is over male mediums or medicine-men may remarry. The training lasts two or three years for many, under strict discipline. If after receiving a call to become a medium, a person does not obey it, people say that 'the (divinity or spirit) troubles him so much that he goes mad'. During training the candidate sleeps on hard floor and with insufficient covering even during cool nights, hews firewood, draws water and completely refrains from sexual intercourse. Training also involves dancing while possessed. An account is given of such dances: 'Various people enter the ring two or three at a time, dance and rejoin the crowd. The mediums may do the same, dancing ordinarily in the capacity of ordinary human beings, or they may disdain to do this, and sit still. Suddenly a medium will start to look worried and oppressed, then she will begin to tremble and rock about on her stool, rolling her eyes terribly, and perhaps struggling and fighting the air.' The attendants then 'get her to her feet, steer her behind the scenes, strip her, paint her with white clay . . .

[1] E. G. Parrinder *West African Religion* (revised 1961), p. 78 f.

and deck her with her grass or coloured cotton skirt, her beads, anklets, bells and amulets. Then they bring her out again.' She jiggles and shakes and remains 'on her feet in constant motion for hours. She often performs feats of endurance impossible in ordinary life.' During the possession she may have either one 'personality' or several, depending on how many divinities or spirits enter her at a time. She then behaves in the manner of the divinity or spirit possessing her, e.g. like a warrior, or pregnant woman, or lame man, and sometimes animal spirits 'come into mediums and make them bark, snarl, or go on all fours'. At the end of the fit, the spirit shouts (through her) that it is time for it to depart, and she collapses into the arms of the attendants: 'she looks as though she had just awakened from sleep, and, indeed, a medium always says she has no recollection whatever of the part she took in the dance'. If one is old, her face resumes the looks of old age whereas she 'looked quite young while dancing'. Outstanding mediums hold annual feasts to thank their particular divinity or spirit, attended by people who have been helped through the mediums.[1]

It is reported that the Fon and some Yoruba have 'convents' where mediums are trained: nine months for a boy, and three years for a girl. 'At the beginning the novice is possessed by the god, but when he emerges from the seclusion of the convent he is not simply a changed being, but a new and different personality. He does not recognize his own parents or former companions, he speaks another language as if he were a stranger from a foreign country, and bears a new name. Henceforth it is absolutely for-bidden to call him by his old name, and he will relearn his old language slowly when he re-emerges from the convent to live among his family again.' The trainees are normally aged between ten and sixteen years, though occasionally married people may be among them. The choice of the trainee may come spontaneously during the dances at the annual recruiting ceremonies, or a person may be delivered by his family on request from the principal priest, or it may be that in gratitude for answered prayers the parents already vow to the divinity concerned that they would dedicate their child to it. If the novice is unwilling to go into training, he is taken at night into the convent. The priest concerned interviews the trainee-to-be, confronting him with: 'The god has told me that he wishes to call you today. Do you agree?', for which the answer must be 'Yes!' An initiation dance follows the next day, and other ceremonies are observed during the following seven days at the end of which the novice becomes a 'prisoner of war' to the divinity concerned. After that he goes into complete seclusion until his training is completed, though his family must continue

---

[1] J. M. Field *Religion and Medicine of the Ga People* (1937, reprinted 1961), pp. 100–9.

to provide him with material needs in the convent, yet without actually seeing him.

Training in the convent involves a number of things. The neophytes practise 'the imitation of death and resurrection', take part in sacrifices, have all their hair shaved from time to time (which at the end is gathered and burned), drink from earthen pots, eat communally from one dish according to their sex and with the left hand (which belongs to the divinity concerned), strictly refrain from sexual relations and are severely dealt with when they fall into a serious fault. Since the main aim of the training is to create new personalities, the candidates learn a new language, which they will later use in the transaction of their duties as mediums, and in greeting other mediums. They each receive a new name by which they will henceforth be known. They wear common dress, live in the compound of the convent consisting of up to a dozen houses, one of which is the temple of the divinity. The trainees meet on the day sacred to the divinity concerned, for 'common devotional exercises'. They also learn rules of eating, drinking and dressing as mediums, the songs, prayers and blessings of their cult, dances and exercises to produce the state of possession (or mediumship). They do daily chores of sweeping and cleaning, and learn serious skills like weaving which afterwards become valuable sources of income. In the early part of the training they receive ritual tattoos on the cheeks, neck and shoulders, varying in size and shape according to different divinities; and at least the facial ones become permanent scars. After seven months they are occasionally allowed to leave the convent briefly at night, but must not speak to strangers if they meet any. When the training is over, they are given final instructions by the chief priest concerning their work and conduct, especially 'not to kill, not to steal, not to deceive, not to be proud, to obey parents and elders, to be discreet', and not to quarrel even if provoked to do so. 'A great ceremony is held for the coming out of the new devotees from the convent. Friends and relatives come in crowds to witness this ceremony, to give money and cloths, and to receive blessings. It is a costly affair, and the expenses are paid by the families of the devotees.' For all practical purposes the candidates now resume normal life and the practice of their profession, returning to the convents for further training if they so wish, or for refreshing their memories in springtime.[1]

We have described different types of mediums. What do they signify and how are we to view their roles in African societies? The spirits and divinities that possess mediums belong to the time period of the Zamani. By entering individuals in the Sasa period, they become our contemporaries.

---

[1] Parrinder, II, pp. 81–94, gives a full and interesting account of which these two paragraphs are a summary.

The state of mediumship is one of contemporarizing the past, bringing into human history the 'personality' of beings essentially beyond the horizon of the Sasa period. This phenomenon is, however, temporary, and the two time periods slip apart when the state of possession is ended. The experience seems to generate ultra-human power which gives the medium ability to perform both physical and mental activities that would otherwise be extremely difficult or dangerous under normal circumstances. This possession is not on the whole harmful or resented by society; and except on rare occasions the medium resumes normal life when the state of possession is over. During possession the individual loses temporarily the control or exercise of his personality, and depicts or mirrors the influence or semi-personality of the spirit or divinity in him. Useful information is obtained from the spirit world, so people believe, whether or not that information is genuine. For that reason, mediums are associated with diviners or medicine-men or priests whose duty it is to receive, relay or interpret the messages received via the mediums. As such, mediums are like radio-sets functioning between two termini: the source (spirits or divinities) and recipients (diviners, medicine-men or priests) of the broadcast. They lose, or sometimes pretend to lose, their mental and physical senses so that the spirit world through them can 'pop up' into the human world without causing fear, disturbance or disgust among people. Mediums do the 'donkey work' of establishing the bridge between the two worlds, both willingly and devotedly. They enrich and dramatize the religious perception and activities of their communities. Human beings, however, give little if any information or instruction to the spirits or divinities through the mediums; instead their part is to obey and follow what comes from the spirit world, or to await the blessings from there. I have no information whether God ever functions or comes into the picture in this manner.

We take note also of the concept of 'death and resurrection', enacted particularly in the training and activities of mediums serving divinities, of which the Fon and Yoruba supply our best examples. The idea of renewal is also dominant, especially in the period of training when the candidates shed off their former personalities, at least ritually and symbolically, and acquire new personalities dedicated to the service of their divinities and communities. This is similar to what we have seen in connection with the rites of childhood, initiation and marriage. The trainees are cut off, or killed, from the solidarity of ordinary society, when they enter their convents. During their seclusion, they undergo growth like an embryo in the womb; and it is significant, though probably not meant to be so, that the training lasts nine months for boys (though longer in former years), which corre-sponds to the gestation period of human beings. Then the trainees are 'born anew' when they emerge from seclusion. They have new names, the token of renewal, rebirth, newness and resurrection. They are then able to rejoin their wives or get married and resume normal life. But they have been initiated into the mysteries of their divinities or spirits, and carry both inward and outward marks of dedication and devotion to their task as mediums. Henceforth they are personalities of two worlds: the human world under normal circumstances, and the spirit world when in the state of possession.

Diviners, as their name implies, are concerned primarily with acts of divination. But as a rule, this is done as part of wider functions, especially of a medical or even priestly nature. They are the agents of unveiling mysteries of human life. This is done through the use of mediums, oracles, being possessed, divination objects, common sense, intuitive knowledge and insight, hypnotism and other secret knowledge. They also keep their ears and eyes open to what is happening in their communities so that they have a store of working knowledge which they use in their divination. The nature of their profession creates an unnecessary halo of secrecy about it, which adds to their respect, stature and dignity in the eyes of their communities. Therefore people resort to them freely for both private and public affairs. Like the medicine-men, and many practise as such, the diviners are regarded as friends of their communities. They play the role of counsellors, judges, 'comforters', suppliers of assurance and confidence during people's crises, advisers, pastors and priests, seers, fortune-tellers and solvers of problems, and revealers of secrets like thefts, imminent danger or coming events.

With a few exceptions, African systems of divination have not been carefully studied, though diviners and divination are found in almost every community. Parrinder describes Yoruba divination which is said to be the most highly developed in western Africa, known as the Ifa system.[1] It is connected with *Orunmila* the divinity of divination. Accordingly, the diviner (as among the Fon) is called a 'father of mysteries' and observes each fifth day as the 'day of mysteries' when he consults the oracle. The Ifa system is a series of 256 figures 'each with its own name, and these are worked out either by using sixteen palm nuts or by casting a string or chain of eight half nuts or shells', using a piece of board. Sitting in front of this board, the diviner manipulates the nuts rapidly, marking the results in two columns on the board. This involves complications of numbers, combina- tions, names and different interpretations, and the application that the diviner finally gives to the inquirer. 'The Ifa system of divination is used

[1] Parrinder, II, pp. 137–55, from which the example of Yoruba and Fon divina- tion and diviners is here derived. A fuller study is made by B. Maupoil *La Géomancie à l'ancienne Côte des Esclaves*, Paris 1943.

at all the important occasions of life', among both Yoruba and Fon. A diviner may also advise the consultation of Ifa; and it is normally the men who do it, though occasionally women may also consult it.

Diviners are trained privately by other diviners, and work as apprentices, for periods ranging from three to seven years. Some inherit the profession from their fathers. Training involves learning the names and signs of divination figures, the proverbs and stories connected with them, and the practice, rites and cult of divination. There is a final ceremony attended by other diviners in the area, when the new one is authorized to practise, the initiation being brought to a climax by the new diviner taking 'flames from a lamp into his hands, without his skin being burnt'. After that, he prays alone daily to *Orunmila*, and once a month together with his family for whom he then prays. Parrinder observes that in the Ifa system there is nothing about the stars or mythical astrology; and that the system is used, with variations, in parts of Nigeria, Dahomey, Togo and Ghana.

There are other methods of divination in different parts of Africa, using divination stones, gourds, numbers, palm reading, 'forming' or seeing images in pots of water, interpreting animal marks, listening to and inter´preting sounds, and using seances by means of which the diviner (or another medium) gets in touch with the spirit world. Some, probably many, diviners do not undergo prolonged formal training such as those found among the Yoruba and a few other West African peoples. They learn their trade more through practice than 'formal schooling'; depending on what else they do in addition to divination. There are, no doubt, some who act as diviners for the sake of gain, and manipulate conjuring tricks to get by.

The art of divination presents us with puzzling problems which I make ¯no pretence to solve. A certain amount of communication goes on between diviners and non´human powers (whether living or otherwise or both). It is difficult to know exactly what this is: it might involve the diviner's extra´sensory ability, it may involve spiritual agents, it might be telephathy, it might be sharpened human perception, or a combination of these possi´bilities. Whatever it is, divination is another area which adds to the com´plexity of African concepts and experiences of the universe. Divination links together in its own way, the physical and the spiritual worlds, making it a religious activity. The diviner fulfils an intermediary function between the physical and the psychical, between the human and the spiritual, for the sake of his own community.

As a rule, most diviners are men while most mediums are women. Sometimes these practise as husband and wife.

[c] *Rainmakers*

In African societies rain is regarded as a great blessing, and whenever it rains people rejoice (unless excessive rain damages crops or causes harmful flooding). Whether they are farmers or pastoralists, the entire livelihood of the people depends on rain. Near the Equator there are generally two rainy periods and two dry ones in the year. Further away from the Equator these two sets of seasons tend to merge and produce one long period of rain and one long dry season. In either situation, if the rain is delayed considerably it means that for that season there will either be insufficient harvest or none at all, and this causes a lot of anxiety to everyone. The seasons control the rhythm of community life, and in many societies the change of the seasons is marked or observed with ritual activities. There are rites to mark many occasions like the start of the rain, the planting ceremony, the first-fruits, the harvest of the crops, the beginning of the hunting or fishing season. These communal rites and activities are extremely important in strengthening community consciousness and solidarity, and are educational occasions for the young people concerning both social and spiritual matters. Rainmaking is one such communal rite, and rainmakers are some of the most important individuals in almost all African societies.

The Zulu speak of rainmakers as the 'shepherds of heaven', and people do indeed look upon them as the shepherds of men, cattle and plants all of which depend on rain. The best description of the person and work of a monarchical rainmaker is on the Luvedu.[1] The queen of the Luvedu is also their supreme rainmaker, and in this dual position she serves the country as the political head and the providential head of the kingdom. It is more because of her rainmaking, than her political position, that she is so renowned and respected, though obviously each adds to the elevation of the other. Her moods are believed to affect the weather, and at her death drought is said to be inevitable. She gets her knowledge from the living-dead, and hands it down to her successor. She has assistant rainmakers under her, but she is the ultimate authority over the making and stopping of rain—being able to do the latter as a weapon against her enemies in neighbouring territories.

Among the Koma, rainmakers live in caves and drink milk mixed with water. People go to them in procession, taking gifts. Part of the rainmaking rite involves bringing a skin full of water to the rainmaker, which he drinks publicly. The rainmakers among the Udhuk nearby perform complicated rituals using red, white and blue rainstones.[2] Formerly the Akamba used to bury a child alive, as part of the ceremony or sacrifice for rain when severe

[1] E. J. & J. D. Krige *The Realm of a Rain-Queen* (2nd edition, 1960).
[2] Cerulli, p. 36.

A.R.P.—7

droughts struck the country. Katab rainmakers address their prayers direct to God, but if rain comes they offer thanks to their most remote forefathers. The Lugbara believe that God give special mystical power to the rainmakers and diviners. Therefore people say that 'rainmakers know the words of God', 'that is their work'.[1] In the Sudan region and southern Africa, rainmakers have a special class of their own and enjoy the power and authority above that of any other single individual. In some societies, the knowledge and powers of rainmaking are handed down from one individual to his near relatives.

From these and other examples all over Africa, we can see the importance of rainmaking. Certain conclusions emerge which we may summarize as follows. Though the majority of rainmakers are men, there are also women rainmakers as exemplified by the rain-queen of the Luvedu. Their work is not only to 'make' rain but also to 'stop' it when too much comes in a short time or when it is not particularly welcome at a given moment. One has heard cases both in Uganda and Nigeria where couples request rainmakers to 'stop' rain during their wedding parties—and not without some success. When the rainmaker fails to produce rain, this can lead not only to the loss of his prestige but may even endanger his life. In 1965 I heard of a case among the Luo where, on failing to produce rain during a severe drought, a local rainmaker was put in prison, partly to protect him and partly to quench the fury of his community. In March 1968 five rain-makers were jailed in Tanzania for allegedly causing too much rain which destroyed people's fields. The physical life of the people, as well as their prosperity and wellbeing, depends on rain.

In many societies, rituals or other ceremonies accompany rainmaking, which is a community affair. Sacrifices, offerings and prayers are made, either directly to God or through the intermediary of the living-dead and spiritual agents. From many parts of Africa it is reported that both people and rainmakers know for certain that only God can 'make' or 'produce' rain. Therefore, rainmakers play the role of intermediaries, whatever else they might do to enhance their position and activities. Rainmakers are thus the focal point of communal need and request for rain. In some societies there are no official rainmakers, and any elder can officiate at the rainmaking ceremony provided he fulfils the requirements for such a duty. It is more in the drier parts of Africa that both the office and person of the rainmaker tend to be socially and even politically outstanding; otherwise so long as normal rain is falling, most societies more or less forget about their rainmakers. But, since rainmakers are not fools, their intellectual abilities tend to place them in leading positions in their communities, so that they are 'specialists'

[1] Middleton, II, pp. 31, 207, 258.

in more things than one. Some practise as diviners, medicine-men, mediums and priests. All these are mediatorial positions between men and God or the spiritual realm. The actual practice of the rainmaker involves the use of sacred objects especially 'rain-stones' some of which are rare and others are believed to have fallen from the sky. Burning of rain-leaves or other com-bustibles is another method, whereby the smoke from them is thought to 'capture' the rain from the sky and bring it down. Other rites involve the use of water in various ways, such as ceremonial sprinkling of water on the crowds or at the place of the rainmaking ceremony, drawing water from special or sacred wells, or collecting perspiration and spraying it in the air. Water in these cases symbolizes rain.

Those engaged in the art of rainmaking (and rainstopping) are well versed in weather matters, and may spend long periods acquiring their knowledge. This they obtain from other rainmakers, from observing the sky, from studying the habits of trees, insects and animals, from a study of astronomy and the use of common sense. For example, none would be foolish enough to attempt to make rain during the peak of the dry season. They keep their eyes fixed towards the sky: not only to study the weather conditions, but also to pray to God Who is both Maker and Giver of rain. When they fail to do so, they also fail to make or stop rain.

Rain is regarded by African societies as a sacred phenomenon. We have already indicated that in some it is so intimately associated with God that the same word is used for both, or when it rains people say that 'God is falling'. In others, the name for God means 'Rain Giver'. There are many who personify rain, or regard it as being controlled by a divinity (subject to God). Some observe days of rest to mark the start of the rain season; and many greet the season with ceremonies of thanksgiving and prayers for sufficient rain. For many, rain is the most explicit expression of the goodness and providence of God. Thus rain is seen as the eternal and mystical link between past, present and future generations. It is one of the most concrete and endless rhythms of nature: as it came, it comes and it will come. African peoples know no end to this vital rhythm of creation. As it comes from above, so rain links man with the divine. Rain is a deeply religious rhythm, and those who 'deal' in it, transact business of the highest religious calibre. Rain is the manifestation of the eternal, in the here and now. Rainmakers not only solicit physical rain, but symbolize man's contact with the blessings of time and eternity.

[d] *Kings, queens and rulers*

As this is a big subject with a considerable amount of literature,[1] we shall content ourselves with a few observations. The personages in this category are unlike the other 'specialists' like medicine-men, rainmakers, diviners and priests. It is by virtue of their office that they hold a special place in African life and concepts. It needs to be borne in mind, however, that not all African peoples have had traditional rulers in form of kings, queens or chiefs.

Where these rulers are found, they are not simply political heads: they are the mystical and religious heads, the divine symbol of their people's health and welfare. The individuals as such may not have outstanding talents or abilities, but their office is the link between human rule and spiritual government. They are therefore, divine or sacral rulers, the shadow or reflection of God's rule in the universe. People regard them as God's earthly viceroys. They give them highly elevated positions and titles, such as: 'saviour', 'protector', 'child of God', 'chief of the divinities', 'lord of earth and life'. People think that they can do what they want, have control over rain, and link them with God as divine incarnation or as originally coming from heaven. They regard their office as having been instituted by God in the Zamani period. Myths surround the origin and person of the kings, as do also all kinds of taboos, superstitions, prohibitions and ideas. Rulers are, therefore, not ordinary men and women: they occupy a special office, and symbolize the link between God and man.

This sacred position of African rulers is shown in many ways. Some rulers must not be seen in ordinary life—they wear a veil, take meals alone

[1] See, among other works: K. A. Busia *The position of the chief in the modern political system of the Ashanti* (Oxford 1957); E. L. R. Meyerowitz *The divine kingship in Ghana and ancient Egypt* (London 1960); T. Irstam *The king of Ganda* (Stockholm 1944); M. J. Herskovits *Dahomey: an ancient African kingdom* (2 vols., New York 1938); J. Beattie *Banyoro, an African kingdom* (New York 1960); M. S. M. Kiwanuka *Mutesa of Uganda* (Nairobi 1967); E. E. Evans-Pritchard *The divine kingship of the Shilluk* (Cambridge 1948); M. Fortes & E. E. Evans-Pritchard, eds., *African political systems* (Oxford/London 1940); P. Hadfield *Traits of divine kingship in Africa* (London 1949); E. J. & J. D. Krige *The realm of a rain queen* (Oxford 1943); H. Cory *The ntemi* (London 1951); O. Pettersson *Chiefs and Gods* (Lund 1953); Y. Asfa Haile Sellasie, *Emperor of Ethiopia* (London 1936); W. T. H. Beukes *Der Häuptling in der Gesellschaft der Süd-, Ost- und Zentral-Bantuvölker* (Hamburg 1931); W. Schilde 'Die afrikanischen Hoheits-zeichen' in *Zeitschrifft für Ethnologie*, LXI (1929); L. A. Fallers *The king's men* (Oxford 1964); A. I. Richards *East African chiefs* (London 1960); R. E. S. Tanner 'The installation of Sukuma chiefs' in *African Studies* XVI, 1957; B. A. Pauw *Religion in a Tswana Chiefdom* (Oxford 1960). Many of these have useful bibliographies.

(e.g. Shilluk, Baganda and Shona), their eating and sleeping may not be mentioned; in some societies (like Lunda, Nyamwezi and Baganda) the king must not touch the ground with his feet, and has either to be carried or walk on a special mat; parts of the ruler's body (like saliva, faeces, hair and nails) are buried lest they should be seen by ordinary people or used in malicious ways against them. To protect and strengthen the position and investure of the king, various measures are taken, mainly in form of sacrifices (of animals, subjects and prisoners), the wearing and keeping of amulets, consulting diviners and ritual slaying of the rulers (regicide). In societies like the Baganda, Lunda and Baluba, parts of the dead ruler's body (e.g. jaw, skull or genitals) are preserved and used in ceremonies or for con sultation by the reigning ruler. In many areas the ruler takes part or leads in national ceremonies, and may play the role of the priest, rainmaker, inter mediary, diviner or mediator between men and God (e.g. Luvedu, Shilluk, Shona, Sukuma). In any case almost all the rulers have shrines, temples, sacred groves, personal priests and diviners in or near their palace. The spirit of the departed king may also continue to play an active part in the national affairs of his people (by being re-incarnated, possessing the suc cessor or recognized medium, and being consulted or having sacrifices and offerings given to it). The Zulu, Shilluk, Ashanti, Lunda, Nyamwezi and others make sacrifices and offer prayers at the graves of departed kings. Often the graves are sacred places, with servants, guards and sometimes priests, and in some societies they are a sanctuary for animals and men so that none would be killed there. People consider kings to be holy, mainly in a ritual rather than spiritual sense, and they must therefore speak well of them, respect them, bow or kneel before them, let them have sexual rights over their wives, pay them taxes and dues, obey them, refrain from copying their clothes or coming into direct contact with them, and even render them acts of reverence and obeisance.[1]

The death of a ruler is, naturally, a great event for his nation. Some societies like the Banyoro, Shona, Luvedu, Amhara and others, formerly performed ritual killing of their rulers when these grew old, became sick, were injured, had fulfilled their period of reign or became unsatisfactory. The method of killing was through poisoning, strangling, suffocation or suicide. This practice is reported all over Africa. In some societies (for instance the Baganda, Zulu, Amhara, Ngoni, Gogo, Shilluk), the death of the king is kept secret for any period from a few days to one or more years, or until the new one is chosen and installed, or until after the burial is over or the corpse has been smoked (as in the Congo). Since the king is sacred, his death is not spoken of in the normal manner: e.g. among the

[1] T. Irstam *The king of Ganda* (1944), p. 180 f.

Banyoro the people say, 'The milk is spilt'; the Amhara say, 'The air at this
season is evil towards kings'; or people simply say that he has returned to the
sky, or gone up, or fallen sick. The ruler's death brings the rhythm of life to
a standstill or upsets it for a while: e.g. work stops (among the Tswana,
Baganda, Banyoro), mating among men and animals is stopped (Barundi,
Ankore and Banyarwanda), and a time of complete lawlessness, anarchy
and chaos follows (Shilluk, Lunda, Amhara, Baluba and others). It was
also formerly the custom to provide company and food for the departed
ruler, for which reason his wives, servants, slaves, some subjects, cattle,
prisoners, would be killed and buried with him (for instance among the
Baganda, Shilluk, Kpelle, Nyamwezi).[1] Since the health and prosperity
of the king symbolize the welfare of the nation, it is understandable that his
death would bring a complete disruption to life, and only a new ruler
would both restore order and symbolize normality once more. As life for the
king continues in the hereafter, he must therefore be provided with wives,
servants and food so that he can continue to enjoy his privileged position
in the spirit world. Elaborate funeral rites would be performed, but in some
societies the departed ruler is disposed of secretly or quietly.

Succession procedures differ considerably all over Africa. The ruler's
son, daughter, brother, nephew, mother, uncle or other member of the royal
relatives may succeed him. In some societies the new ruler is chosen by a
council, chief ministers or in consultation with the spirits of the departed
rulers. Many customs and ceremonies are followed at the coronation of the
new ruler. Irstam gives a good summary of these, which include items like
ceremonies symbolizing death and rebirth (e.g. Shilluk), the king wearing
special robes (Baganda, Amhara, Banyoro and many others), giving a new
name to the ruler (Amhara, Galla, Tonga), ritual washing or sprinkling
(Hausa, Shilluk, Bacongo), anointing the king with oil or clay (Amhara,
Banyoro, Ankore and others), seating him on a throne (a very widespread
practice), crowning him (also fairly common), making human sacrifices
(Shilluk, Baganda and others), killing his relatives who might contend the
throne (Galla, Amhara, Banyoro, Barundi and rulers of Benin in Nigeria),
and festivals. Where a sacred fire is kept, it is extinguished at the death of
one ruler and relit at the coronation of another. In some societies, like the
Shilluk and Kpelle, people make fun of the king, jeer at him and cause
him to face difficulties for a while after his coronation, in order to teach him
humility.[2]

Rulers have their insignia which also reflect the way people regard them.
At their coronation, Baganda, Amhara, Shilluk and other kings, are made

[1] Irstam, p. 142 f. See this work for detailed and comparative study.
[2] Irstam, p. 56.

to mount royal hills, a symbol of their cosmic accession: showing that they stand now at the top and as head of their nation. For their sceptre they carry twigs, spears, staff, fork, two-bladed sword, lance or hoe. In most societies their robes are made of or include leopard or lion skins—these animals symbolizing power and strength. Royal drums are reported from all over Africa, and are regarded as sacred so that they are played only on certain occasions or to announce important messages, and are kept in sacred houses. Thrones vary considerably in size, shape and composition: some are covered with gold, beads, ostrich or other feathers, silk, horns, barkcloth, beads; some are portable, and others are highly elevated; some are simple earthen platforms perhaps covered with lion or leopard skins. The keeping of sacred fire is reported in many African societies, and is associated with the king or ruler. At the death of one ruler, this fire is extinguished but relit when the new ruler is installed (e.g. Banyoro, Shilluk, Amhara and others). That fire must be kept burning perpetually during the reign of a given king; and in some societies it is the new ruler who lights the new fire. In many areas, rulers also have sacred cattle (e.g. Lunda, Pare, Gogo, Hausa, Shona, Tswana and others). These are used for meat, milk, sacrifice, and often their hide would be used to wrap the body of the dead ruler.[1] Fire and cattle may not be part of the ruler's insignia as such, but they are closely connected with his welfare and position. Fire symbolizes life, continuity and vitality: its burning is the symbol of the prosperity of the ruler and his people. Cattle are symbols of providence—food, drink, property—and means of keeping in touch with the spirit world (through sacrificing them and wrapping the ruler's corpse in them). The king's blood which is the very essence of his life and therefore that of his nation, must not be shed at all, and many societies all over Africa observe this taboo. The rulers themselves must also observe various taboos, the breaking of which might disqualify them from office.

As the kings, queens, chiefs and other rulers are given this sacred position and regard, those related to them are also treated with special respect. The queen enjoys great esteem (e.g. among the Amhara, Luvedu and others), and can be the wife, sister or mother of the reigning ruler. His mother, who might be the real biological mother, or another woman from among the royal members, or an appointed woman, may also wield great influence as among the Zulu and Amhara. In some societies, the king has to marry an agnatic sister (e.g. the Shilluk, Lunda, Banyarwanda and others). Other important officials include subchiefs, councillors, advisers, governors, instructors and religious personages (like priests and diviners). It is through these that the ruler manages to maintain his authority over the kingdom,

[1] Irstam, pp. 91 f., 131 f.

know what is going on, be reachable by his subjects, keep his position and be in contact with the spiritual world.

Such then is the picture of the person and office of traditional rulers, some of whom are men and others women. Colonial administration generally tended to incorporate traditional rulers into its political structure. Their powers and charismatic image decreased considerably. In some cases the colonial governments did away altogether with traditional rulers, and this not always peacefully. The office of the king has survived in some societies into the modern independent African states, with some rulers taking on leading positions. For example, when Uganda became in, dependent in 1962 the then king of the Baganda became the president of Uganda (until 1966); and Seretse Khama became head of his country Botswana, when it regained independence in 1966. Emperor Haile Selassie of Ethiopia is carrying on perhaps the longest line of rulers in the world. The modern trend, however, is towards the dissolution of traditional monarchs in Africa; and what we have described above in the present tense does not apply in many situations, or only in a modified form. The dis, solution or weakening of the office of traditional rulers must naturally generate tension if not open clash between them with their supporters on the one hand, and African statesmen who think in terms of nationhood rather than local kingdoms on the other.

The office of the traditional monarch is losing its sacredness, and seems to be degenerating to the unenviable point of being a political anachronism and an economic debit. This fate of African rulers is certainly a world, wide fate, and reflects the feeling that perhaps man has had enough of traditional monarchs whose history is not always the brightest part of their image. Few will, therefore, bemoan the end of traditional rulers if their office can be superseded by a new and more relevant, but not necessarily less corrupt, political structure. Sacral rulers are intimately bound up with the Zamani period; and they have become too heavy to be lifted into the orbit of the future dimension of time which African peoples have discovered and begun to extend. Their strength lay, or lies, in the religious myths, traditions and taboos that surround them, all of which are Zamani oriented; and without a myth of the future, these rulers have neither the place nor the respect they have enjoyed throughout the history of their people. Changing concepts of time, perhaps more than those of politics, are the main forces working against sacral rulers. If the office and position of these rulers had messianic elements with a future hope attached to them, then one would expect the sacral rulers to enter into the stream of modern African history. But, since the future dimension of time in African societies was so short, there could have been no messianic hope, and our traditional rulers are rooted only in the Sasa and Zamani periods. The most they can now expect is that with the dissolution or diminution of their office, a strong mythology will almost certainly build around them and their office. In western Africa they will probably last longer than elsewhere.

One element of interest will be to study religious changes of the beliefs and practices which, in traditional life, had evolved around the person and office of the sacral rulers and which must be undermined once the cenral figure of their structure is removed or weakened. Perhaps a revival or creation of kingly cults will evolve in the societies concerned, incorporating dead, deported or demoted kings, and cherishing some myths about them. But the traditional activities associated with royal events and personages will certainly die out or be replaced by modern national events and leaders. Personality cults seem to be ingrained in African attitudes and feel-ings and it is easier to transpose them to new situations than to remove them.

[e] *Priests, Prophets and Religious Founders*

On priests there is a fair amount of literature, although the term is used loosely to include almost every religious leader.[1] Strictly speaking priests are religious servants associated with temples; but in the African situation the word is used to cover everyone who performs religious duties whether in temples, shrines, sacred groves or elsewhere. There are priests reported among many societies including the Ankore, Yoruba, Igbo, Akan, Shona, Baganda, Basoga, Ewe, Sonjo and others. The tradition of priests is stronger in West Africa than in other parts of the continent. Of this Parrinder writes that 'priests and devotees, mediums devoted to the gods, are set apart for divine service and receive some kind of initiation and training for it. There are different methods of training, from very simple to highly elaborate, but the priesthood as a class is distinct and developed. . . . Their training may comprise seclusion from the world, instruction in the laws, and sometimes "possession" by the divinity. The vocation of priest and devotee is highly honoured; it is generally open to both men and women.'[2] Concerning the priest among the Yoruba, Idowu writes that 'the priest has always been an important social figure. He is inevitable in the social

---

[1] Many anthropological and religious writings include accounts of priests, such as: E. B. Idowu *Olodumare: God in Yoruba belief* (London 1962); E. G. Parrinder *African Traditional Religion* (London 1954/1962), and *West African Religion* (London 1961); A. Friedrich *Afrikanische Priestertümer* (Stuttgart 1939), E. O. James *Das Priestertum* (Wiesbaden, Germany n.d.); E. W. Smith, ed., *African Ideas of God* (London 1961); E. E. Evans-Pritchard *Nuer Religion* (Oxford 1956); G. Lienhardt *Divinity and Experience* (Oxford 1961).

[2] Parrinder, II, p. 75 f.

pattern of the Yoruba since the keynote of their national life is their religion. Virtually nothing is done without the ministration of the priest. For, apart from looking after the "soul" of the community, he features prominently in the installation of kings and the making of chiefs.'[1]

We make a few observations here concerning priests, and readers are referred to appropriate literature for detailed or further studies. The priest is the chief intermediary: he stands between God, or divinity, and men. Just as the king is the political symbol of God's presence, so the priest is the religious symbol of God among His people—though we need not stress the religio-political distinction, since both persons are religious 'specialists' and in some societies one and the same person combines both offices. Among the Ewe, for example, the priests are 'called' by God, then trained, initiated and finally cleansed or 'ordained'. Their duties include the performing of daily and weekly rites, making libation, and offering prayers for blessings and for the barren and other needy people. Among the Baganda the king used to play a leading role at the annual national festivals, when he would make an offering and sacrifice of nine men, nine women, nine cattle, nine goats, nine fowls, nine loads of barkcloths and of cowry-shells.[2] The Lozi have a high priest who makes offerings to God on national crises; and under him are other priests appointed by the king in council and put in charge of the royal graves.

The duties of the priest are chiefly religious, but since Africans do not dissociate religion from other departments of life, he has or may have other functions. He is the spiritual and ritual pastor of the community or nation: it is he who officiates at sacrifices, offerings and ceremonies relating to his knowledge. He may also contact the spiritual world by acting as a medium or having other individuals as mediums. Where temples exist, there are often mediums, generally women, who assist in the upkeep of the temple in addition to being oracles of the divinities or spirits concerned. Where lengthy training is part of the preparation for the priesthood, the priests are the depositories of national customs, knowledge, taboos, theology and even oral history. This wide knowledge qualifies them to act as political heads, judges and ritual experts. For example, Rukuba priests are also political heads of their villages. Their duties include making intercession with God on behalf of the people, performing the rainmaking ceremonies and leading their communities in the fertility festivals. Each priest is on probation for seven years or longer. If drought, pestilence or shortage of wives should occur during his probation period, he is disqualified and deposed. Among the Butawa, the high priest is elected and is known as

[1] Idowu, p. 139, see also p. 129 f.
[2] J. Roscoe *The Baganda* (1965, 2nd ed.), p. 298; see further, p. 292 f.

the 'father of the country', while the high priestess is known as the 'mother of the country'. Thus, people regard them as symbols of their country's existence, prosperity and continuity.

Among some societies, priests serve both God and the divinities, or only the latter. This is in societies which recognize divinities in addition to God, such as the Ankore, Baganda, Ashanti, Yoruba and others. When people go to make offerings and intercede with God or the divinities, it is the priests that receive them, take and use the offerings and make intercessions on behalf of the needy. They are the living representatives of their cult.

Priests also occupy themselves in non-spiritual matters like hunting, the work of blacksmiths, and social activities. Rarely do they remain unmarried; and in some societies the office of the priesthood is hereditary. Certain standards of social, moral and ethical behaviour are expected of priests, though this is by no means uniform. On the whole, they are men and women of respectable character: trustworthy, devout, obedient to the traditions of their office and to God or the divinities that they serve, friendly, kind, 'educated' in matters of their profession, and religious. There are regulations governing the moral and spiritual state of priests before, during and immediately after officiating at formal ceremonies; for example, they may not be allowed to have sexual intercourse, to eat certain foods, to mix with people or wear certain clothes. Thus, among the Baganda, if one priest died, surviving priests of *Mukasa* (the divinity of the seas), 'instructed his successor and initiated him into his office. When officiating, these three priests wore the same kind of dress, which consisted of two well-dressed barkcloths, one knotted over each shoulder; in addition to this they tied nine white goat-skins round their waist. They shaved their hair, each of the three adopting a distinct pattern.'[1] When robed for duty, people may neither touch them nor draw near to them. Sonjo priests and their families wear only skin garments, and qualified priests wear metal bracelets on the left wrist.

We must take note of ritual leaders of different kinds in every African community. Households are generally led and represented by the head of the family, whether male or female, in making family offerings, libation and prayers. Each community has elders or other recognized leaders who take charge of communal rites, ceremonies, weddings, settlement of disputes, initiations, festivals, rites of passage, rainmaking ceremonies, cleansing ceremonies, upkeep of shrines and sacred objects and places, and appoint-ments, or various other functions of the community. These are 'priestly' duties, even if the officiating persons may not be called 'priests' in the

[1] Roscoe, p. 296.

narrow sense of the word, they are the 'lay-priests', and are not on 'full-time' employment.

In the strict biblical sense of *prophets* and the prophetic movement, there are no prophets in African traditional societies, as far as I know. I attribute this primarily to the lack of a long dimension of the future in African concepts of time, though there might be other contributing factors. When this dimension is discovered and extended, types of 'prophets' also begin to emerge, as witnessed by the increasing number of 'prophetic' leaders of independent Christian sects in Africa.

Some anthropologists talk about 'prophets', and describe them in some African societies. These 'prophets' belong to the category of diviners, seers and mediums, and may have other religious or political functions in their societies. For example, among the Nuer 'prophets may perform sacrifices on behalf of individuals or of the people of their neighbourhoods in times of sickness, for barrenness, and on other occasions when spiritual aid is required, but the main social function of the leading prophets in the past was to direct cattle-raids on the Dinka and fighting against the various foreigners who troubled the Nuer'. A prophet is a person 'who is possessed by a spirit of the air'. Evans-Pritchard describes Nuer prophets as 'a recent development', and having charismatic powers whose virtue resides in themselves rather than in their office. 'When they speak as prophets it is Spirit which speaks by their lips, theopneustic speech. The prophet in making his declarations says, "I am such-and-such", naming the spirit. . . What the prophet says and what Spirit says are all mixed up together, the two being interspersed in such a manner that they cannot be separated.' The writer points out that whereas the priests deal only with God, 'the prophets deal with particular spirits, "spirits of the air" or "children of God". God does not enter into men and inspire them.'[1]

We may take another example, from the Meru who have a religious leader known as the *Mugwe*. He is described by Bernardi as a prophet. The office and figure of the *Mugwe* have mythological origins and are connected with the birth of the Meru as a nation. The old men say that 'his power came out, originated, from where the Meru came out or took their origin'. He has hereditary power consisting in great moral virtues: he must be free from all blemishes both physical and moral, must follow correctly the ancient customs of the Meru, and must start training at an early age. The training is carefully and closely supervised by the reigning *Mugwe*. He must be sober, kind to all people, and have a happy married life. He acts as judge, prays for the people, blesses them and curses those who deserve it. It is believed that the *Mugwe* is in direct contact with God, and

[1] Evans-Pritchard, II, pp. 45, 303 f.

therefore represents people's needs and requests to God. People describe him as the keeper of tribal medicines; and he also performs as a diviner. He has parental authority supported by sanctions and curses.[1]

From these two and other examples, we may conclude that persons occasionally described as 'prophets', do not fit into the strict meaning of that term, though among other functions they may perform 'prophetic' duties. These persons play the role of political leaders, diviners, ritual leaders, mediums and even legal and moral advisers to individuals or communities. As our study of such 'specialists' is far from being adequate, we are not in a position to make more than these brief and passing observations about them. I do not know of 'prophets' in traditional societies who claim to be the prophetic mouth-piece of the Supreme God, in the manner similar to biblical or koranic prophets.

There are no *religious founders*, as far as I know. Since religion merges into the whole of life, to speak of religious founders is almost meaningless. There are national founders, however, who have a cult and religious mythology built around them, so that they are an essential part of the religious and philosophical life and attitude of their respective peoples. We may cite two examples of this development. For the Shilluk, Nyikang is the founder of the nation, the first king, the culture hero and at the centre of the religious activities. He is thought to have 'disappeared' (rather than died), and to be immortal. He now acts as the great intermediary between the Shilluk and God, and is believed to participate in some way in God. People make their prayers through Nyikang, and have one special prayer believed to have been taught them by Nyikang himself. God and Nyikang are closely linked in the thought and activities of the people, and Nyikarg is assimilated to the universe and the universe to him. It is said that the Shilluk understand the abstract notion of God through their understanding of the less abstract Nyikang. The ancestry of Nyikang is traced back to a man who came down from heaven, or from a special creation of God.[2]

The Sonjo trace their religious and national life to a figure known as Khambageu. According to their myths, Khambageu just appeared among the people, 'without parents', many years ago. He lived among them, performing miracles of healing the sick, opening the eyes of the blind, ensuring good crops and even raising the dead. He also acted as a judge, settling people's disputes; and went from one village to another, living for

[1] B. Bernardi *The Mugwe, a failing Prophet* (1959).
[2] E. E. Evans-Pritchard *The Divine Kingship of the Shilluk of the Nilotic Sudan* (Cambridge 1948), pp. 17, 21; G. Lienhardt 'The Shilluk of the Upper Nile', essay in *African Worlds*, ed. by D. Forde (1954), pp. 146, 149 f.

some years in each place. Where people got tired of him, they mistreated him and even tried to kill him, forcing him to flee to other villages. Eventually he grew old, then went into his house and died there. Before dying he instructed the people to have his body buried in a particular village, or left on a rock to dry in the sun. These people did not, however, bury him where he asked to be buried; they put him in a grave in another village. On hearing about this news, members of the village where he should have been buried went to claim the body. They dug up the grave, but found it empty except for the sandals which Khambageu had been wearing. It was reported that some people saw him rise again from his grave and fly to the sun.

This is the myth which surrounds Khambageu, and he is now closely associated and identified with God. He is said to rule the heavens and to have the stars as his children. Sonjo religious life is centred upon their stories about Khambageu. They have sacred places, trees, temples, traditions and customs associated with his life; and they give him a central position in their national life. While one may immediately see some parallels between the life of Khambageu and that of Jesus, Gray points out emphatically that the story of Khambageu does not originate through Christian influence or contact of modern times.[1] These few similarities should not overshadow the fact that there are obvious and significant differences from the Gospel stories, and neither has Sonjo religious life crystallized into anything like the Christian Church. But as Khambageu is integrated into the religious and national life of the Sonjo, he approximates the title of a 'religious-national founder'.

The myth or story of Khambageu is unique in African societies. But many have outstanding national heroes who are either historical, mythological or both, and some of whom are honoured as divinities and therefore religious figures. Many of these act as intermediaries and symbolize national origin and unity. There are no religious reformers, missionaries or official propagators of traditional religions and philosophy. In some societies there were leaders who, in their time, did introduce innovations, new cultural ideas, changes or moves which had religious implications. But these were primarily national changes rather than purely or purposely religious; and their religious elements were due to the fact that religion permeates into the whole of life. We do not know the history of traditional religions sufficiently well, however, to be able to discern or discover what religious changes have taken place and whether or not there have been reformers.

[1] R. F. Gray *The Sonjo of Tanganyika* (1963) gives a full study; but a shorter account is in his essay, 'Some parallels in Sonjo and Christian mythology' in *African Systems of Thought*, ed. M. Fortes & G. Dieterlen (1965), pp. 49–61.

These then are the religious 'specialists' in African societies. Our list and discussion of them are not exhaustive. For example there are family and ritual elders, operators at initiation rites, persons like twins, hunchbacks and mental patients, who by nature of biological and environmental circumstances are treated and regarded with religious awe and respect. These also play their role as unofficial 'specialists', partly by what they actually do and partly by virtue of the religious attitude towards them which their communities might accord them. They are part of the religious milieu of African societies.

'Specialists' are in effect the repositories in knowledge, practice and, symbolically, of the religious life of their communities. They are the ones who make the history of African traditional societies both sacred and religious. 'Specialists' are the symbolic points of contact between the historical and spiritual worlds. In them are the continuity and essence of African religious thought and life. These are the men, women and children whose sacred presence in society makes their life and that of their communities a profoundly religious experience. Every village is within reach of one or more such 'specialists'. They are the concrete symbols and epitomy of man's participation in and experience of the religious universe. Without them, African societies would lose sight of and contact with this religious phenomenon. African religiosity demands and appreciates their presence in every community, and for that reason one 'specialist' may be expected to function in more than one capacity.

16
MYSTICAL POWER, MAGIC, WITCHCRAFT & SORCERY

On the subject of magic and witchcraft in Africa there is a great deal of literature.[1] And yet, one is struck and disappointed by the large amount of ignorance, prejudice and falsification which keeps coming out in modern books, newspapers and conversation on this subject. Discussion is centred on two camps at opposite ends. The larger camp has those who expose their own ignorance, false ideas, exaggerated prejudices and a derogatory attitude which belittles and despises the whole concept of mystical power. The other is represented by a few scholars who seriously consider African views, fears, uses and manipulation of this power. Most of the distorted ideas have come through European and American popular writers, missionaries and colonial administrators. Every African who has grown up in the traditional environment will, no doubt, know something about this mystical power which often is experienced, or manifests itself, in form of magic, divination, witchcraft and mysterious phenomena that seem to defy even immediate scientific explanations. I shall illustrate this with a few stories and then make some general observations.

When I was a schoolboy a locust invasion came to my home area. An elderly man who was a neighbour and relative of ours, burnt a 'medicine' in his field, to keep away the locusts. Within a few hours the locusts had eaten up virtually everything green including crops, trees and grass, and then flown off in their large swarms. Everybody was grieved and horrified by the great tragedy which had struck us, for locust invasions always mean that all the food is destroyed and people face famine. Word went round our community, however, that the locusts had not touched any crops in the field of our neighbour who had used 'medicine'. I went there to see it for

---

[1] For example: E. E. Evans-Pritchard *Witchcraft, Oracles and Magic among the Azande* (Oxford 1937); E. G. Parrinder *Witchcraft* (Penguin, London 1958); J. Middleton & E. H. Winter, eds., *Witchcraft and Sorcery in East Africa* (London 1963); H. Debrunner *Witchcraft in Ghana* (Kumasi 1959); G. Bloomhill *Witchcraft in Africa* (Cape Town 1962); plus all the various anthropological and sociological works which contain sections on magic and witchcraft.

myself, and sure enough his crops remained intact while those of other people next door were completely devastated. I had heard that a few people possessed anti-locust 'medicines', but this was the first person I knew who had actually used such medicine and with positive results.

In a book, *Ju-Ju in My Life* (1966) by J. H. Neal, the writer gives an account of his experiences with mystical powers in Ghana where for ten years he was the chief Investigations Officer until 1962. Neal, an Englishman, saw, met, tasted and fought against these powers until finally he had to take refuge under the same powers, something that few Europeans ever experience, or believe could happen in Africa. We shall take two accounts from this book.

During the construction of the new modern harbour at Tema near Accra, building materials and equipment began to be stolen mysteriously. Reports reached Neal who went there to investigate. The construction work was under European supervisors, and Neal advised one of them on how to take better security measures against theft. As he was leaving, this supervisor complained to him that one tree was giving them a headache. Neal went over to see the tree which he found standing alone in a large compound where all the other trees and shrubs had been cleared. It was a small tree. The supervisor told Neal that all the mechanical equipment had failed to uproot that tree. The African foreman insisted that it was a 'magic' tree, which could be removed only if and when the spirit living in it agreed to forsake it and go to another tree. A traditional 'priest' (probably a diviner) was summoned, who asked for a sacrifice of three sheep and an offering of three bottles of gin to be given to the spirit, and £100 (about $290 US) as his payment. When the sheep had been killed and their blood poured at the foot of the tree, and the gin poured as libation at the base, the diviner became a medium and conversed with the spirit, persuading it to leave that tree and go to another and even better tree. When the rite was over, the European supervisor ordered tractors and bulldozers to uproot the tree, but the diviner stopped him telling him that a few African labourers could pull out the tree. This they did with the greatest of ease—to the amazement of European spectators and satisfaction of African onlookers.[1]

Further experiences of this mysterious nature convinced Neal that there was something in or behind these forces and the beliefs connected with them. He became an object of attack from the workers of magic, and he had to seek counter measures to protect himself against them. In another chapter he tells how his enemies sent the forces to attack him, but since he was already protected by 'medicine' from African experts, he was not harmed. Instead, the mystical power split two big trees outside his house. All he

[1] J. H. Neal *Ju-Ju in My Life* (London 1966), pp. 19-24.

suffered was an itching of the body which medical treatment in the hospital could not cure, but was cured by a traditional medicine-man. Elsewhere he relates how a magician sent a snake to kill him, arriving at his house while he and two African servants were watching the body of a cobra they had just killed outside the house. The second snake was, however, a 'magic' snake. As it approached the house suddenly it stopped still as if it had met with an invisible wall. Neal writes that this was precisely at the spot where 'medicine' had been dug into the ground around his house to protect him. On seeing the snake, the servants immediately recognized that it was a 'magic' snake so deadly that there was no remedy against its bite. They told him that it would not bleed if killed; but he did not believe them. So they took long knives and chopped off the head of the snake. To his amazement, no blood whatsoever trickled from this 'magic' snake.[1]

At the end of 1967 a friend whom I have known since he was a schoolboy told my wife and me that an elderly man with whom he had had a serious quarrel was sending snakes to kill his family. Mr M. told us that twice within a short time, snakes had entered his house and gone to the children's beds, while the children slept at night. Fortunately they were killed before they had bitten the children. Mr M. decided to do something, which at first he was not very keen to disclose to us for fear that as a pastor I might 'condemn' him. When he went home to the country for Christmas he consulted a specialist medicine-man, who instructed him on what ritual to follow in order to destroy the snakes which were threatening the life of his family. Mr M. killed a cock and followed the instruction of the medicine-man. The next morning seven snakes were gathered at the door of the house where he had poured out the blood from the cock. He was then able to kill them all without danger; and since then his wife and children have had no more snakes coming to the house.

In her book *Witchcraft in Africa* Bloomhill tells the story of a European farmer in Rhodesia who lived next door to another European farmer. Both were unmarried, and seemed to match each other. The man proposed to the woman and was accepted. She unexpectedly visited him one evening and was infuriated to discover that he was having love affairs with his African maid. She burst out in fury, and calling the maid 'a filthy black bitch' broke off the engagement, never wishing to see him again. The next day the woman saw 'a black bitch and a white ram' on her farm; and a few moments later, her dog was dead, as if bitten by a snake. Two days later the same 'black bitch and a white ram' came and entered the cattle kraal; and a few moments later her finest Jersey cow was dying, with the front legs broken off. Disaster after disaster came upon this woman farmer, and every time

[1] Neal, pp. 77–85; see the book for other accounts and incidents.

it occurred after she had seen the 'black bitch and white ram'. Finally she sent for an expert African medicine-man. He prepared the right 'medicine' and, taking her with him, secretly followed the two animals the next afternoon. The animals dived into a river nearby, emerged and went to the home of the European farmer. The woman and the medicine-man followed them there and found them dripping water. But they were no longer animals: they were the farmer himself and his African maid. The medicine-man gave them his 'medicine' from a horn, and cured them from the power to change into animals. This also ended the disasters of the woman farmer.[1]

Every African living in a village can tell an almost endless number of such stories. To an outsider they sound more like fiction than reality. But the whole psychic atmosphere of African village life is filled with belief in this mystical power. African peoples know that the universe has a power, force or whatever else one may call it, in addition to the items in the onto-logical categories which we discussed in chapter three. It is difficult to know exactly what it is or how it functions. Even where allowance is made for conjuring tricks, obvious cheating, superstition, manipulation of hidden means of communication and other skilled use of laws of nature, one is left and confronted with phenomena which as yet cannot be scientifically explained away. The incidents I described above are not very dramatic, and yet they cannot be dismissed as trickery, hypnotism or purely the result of psychological conditions of those who experience them. To my knowledge, there is no African society which does not hold belief in mystical power of one type or another. It shows itself, or it is experienced, in many ways.

There is mystical power in words, especially those of a senior person to a junior one, in terms of age, social status or office position. The words of parents, for example, carry 'power' when spoken to children: they 'cause' good fortune, curse, success, peace, sorrows or blessings, especially when spoken in moments of crisis. The words of the medicine-man work through the medicine he gives, and it is this, perhaps more than the actual herb, which is thought to cause the cure or prevent misfortunes. Therefore, formal 'curses' and 'blessings' are extremely potent; and people may travel long distances to receive formal blessings, and all are extra careful to avoid formal curses. The specialists whom we discussed in the previous chapter have much mystical power both as individuals and by virtue of their professions or offices.

There is mystical power which causes people to walk on fire, to lie on thorns or nails, to send curses or harm, including death, from a distance, to change into animals (lycanthropy), to spit on snakes and cause them to

[1] G. Bloomhill *Witchcraft in Africa* (Cape Town 1962), p. 164 f.

split open and die; power to stupefy thieves so that they can be caught red-handed; power to make inanimate objects turn into biologically living creatures; there is power that enables experts to see into secrets, hidden information or the future, or to detect thieves and other culprits. African peoples know this and try to apply it in these and many other ways. For that reason, they wear charms, eat 'medicines' or get them rubbed into their bodies; they consult experts, especially the diviners and medicine-men to counteract the evil effects of this power or to obtain powerfully 'charged' objects containing the same power. Some may even pay fantastic amounts of wealth to have a reasonable access to it, in one form or another. The majority, if not all, fear it, and many of them have encountered it in their normal life. This mystical power is not fiction: whatever it is, it is a reality, and one with which African peoples have to reckon. Everyone is directly or indirectly affected, for better or for worse, by beliefs and activities connected with this power, particularly in its manifestation as magic, sorcery and witchcraft. Without going into any exhaustive discussion, we may now draw our attention to magic, sorcery and witchcraft.

Magic is generally considered under 'good magic' and 'evil magic'. The use of good magic is accepted and esteemed by society. It is chiefly the specialists, and particularly the medicine-man, diviner and rainmaker, who use their knowledge and manipulation of this mystical power for the welfare of their community. It is used in the treatment of diseases, in counteracting misfortunes, and in warding off or diluting or destroying evil 'power' or witchcraft. The diviner or medicine-man provides amounts of mystical power to people in form of charms, amulets, powder, rags, feathers, figures, special incantations or cuttings on the body. He uses it to protect homesteads, families, fields, cattle and other property. If you go into African homesteads you might see, for example, a forked post standing in the middle of the compound, or a piece of pot on the roof of the house, or a few lines of ashes strewn across the gate as you enter the homestead; and if you go to the fields you might spot a horn sticking out of the ground, or an old gourd hanging on a tree. If you see babies, they probably will have coils round the neck or wrist, their hair might be shaved off except for small locks left standing on the otherwise bare heads, or the locks might be knotted. These and many hundreds of other articles or visibles signs, are pointers to people's belief in the mystical power: some are protective measures, others are intended to bring good health, fortune or prosperity. It is forbidden and feared in many African societies, to 'praise' somebody else's children or property, for to do so may cause the mystical power to harm or destroy the child or property. One needs eyes to see, to 'read' and to understand the meaning of signs, objects and articles that may be found in African homes, fields, possessions and even on their bodies.

No doubt there are people who believe that protection or prosperity comes from these objects which they wear or otherwise use. This would be magic. But others believe and acknowledge that the objects in themselves have no inherent power as such. Instead, these objects represent and symbolize power which comes from God. This power may directly be supplied by God, or it may be through the spirits, the living-dead or as part of the invisible force of nature in the universe. The objects can also lose their effectiveness, and the owner must then get new ones or if possible get old objects recharged like a car battery. At this point religion and magic merge, and there is no clear way of separating them, any more than magic has been separated from Christianity or Islam at certain points.

Some individuals spend a great deal of their wealth and effort to obtain this type of magical protection and means of prosperity. Some dealers are real experts in the business, but there are others who supply cheap, false articles for the sake of gain. The commonest specialist is the medicine-man, of whom we have already spoken. He uses 'good magic', as do also the diviner and rainmaker who function chiefly for the good of society. These specialists tell that the mystical power which they tap and use, comes ultimately from God; and as we have seen, part of their profession involves praying to God, directly or through the intermediary of the living-dead and spirits, to solicit His help. As such, this is 'spiritual' power functioning through physical means; and as we have seen for African peoples the two worlds are one universe. The spirits have more access to this power than do human beings. It is perhaps this which adds to the stature of the departed, even if these died as children, for upon death, the living-dead enter into a higher 'dynamic' hierarchy than that of the living. As a rule also, younger people will rarely attempt to use this power against older members of their community, unless it is in taking counter measures. The older a person is, and the higher his social status is, the more he is thought or expected to have this mystical power, either in himself or through the possession of the necessary objects in which it may be stored.

It is to be noted in passing that some of the independent Church sects, particularly in southern and western Africa, have men and women who specialize in dealing with this power.

Evil magic involves the belief in and practice of tapping and using this power to do harm to human beings or their property. It is here that we find sorcery at work, in addition to other related practices. We must point out, however, that a great deal of belief here is based on, or derives from, fear, suspicion, jealousies, ignorance or false accusations, which go on in

African villages. People fear to leave around their hair, nails, clothes or other articles with which they are normally in direct contact in case their 'enemies' will use them and work evil magic against them. The hair, or nails may be burnt or pricked or otherwise used in a 'harmful' way, and thus cause infliction on the person from whom they come. It is feared that an enemy might put thorns on a person's foot print, and thus cause harm to him. This is what James Frazer distinguishes as 'contagious magic'. His other useful category is 'homoeopathic magic', which in African societies could be illustrated with endless examples. This involves the belief that what happens to an object which looks like another will affect the latter. For example, an enemy might make a doll which represents a particular person, and by burning or pricking that doll it is believed that the person would be harmed accordingly. These two categories of magical beliefs and practices function, however, in both good and evil ways. It is when used maliciously that this mystical power is condemned as 'black magic', 'evil magic' or 'sorcery'.

Technically speaking, however, 'sorcery' involves the use of poisonous ingredients, put into the food or drink of someone. But this is an academic finesse. For African peoples sorcery stands for anti-social employment of mystical power, and sorcerers are the most feared and hated members of their communities. It is feared that they employ all sorts of ways to harm other people or their belongings. For example, they send flies, snakes, lions or other animals to attack their enemies or carry disease to them; they spit and direct the spittle with secret incantations to go and harm someone; they dig up graves to remove human flesh or bones which they use in their practices; they invoke spirits to attack or possess someone. African peoples feel and believe that all the various ills, misfortunes, sicknesses, accidents, tragedies, sorrows, dangers and unhappy mysteries which they encounter or experience, are caused by the use of this mystical power in the hands of a sorcerer, witch or wizard. It is here that we may understand, for example, that a bereaved mother whose child has died from malaria will not be satisfied with the scientific explanation that a mosquito carrying malaria parasites stung the child and caused it to suffer and die from malaria. She will wish to know why the mosquito stung her child and not somebody else's child. The only satisfactory answer is that 'someone' sent the mosquito, or worked other evil magic against her child. This is not a scientific answer, but it is reality for the majority of African peoples. We may easily get rid of mosquitoes and prevent many diseases; but there will always be accidents, cases of barrenness, misfortunes and other unpleasant experiences. For African peoples these are not purely physical experiences: they are 'mystical' experiences of a deeply religious nature. People in the villages will talk freely about them, for they belong to their world of reality, whatever else scientists and theologians might say. Nothing harmful happens 'by chance': everything is 'caused' by someone directly or through the use of mystical power. If you have your ears open, you will hear the names of people being blamed for misfortunes, sickness, accidents and other forms of suffering, in every village. It is mainly women who get blamed for experiences of evil kind; and many a woman has suffered and continues to suffer under such accusations, sooner or later.

Sorcerers, evil magicians, witches and medicine-men or diviners occasionally employed for this purpose, are believed to send flies, bats, birds, animals, spirits and magical objects (like the 'magic snake' which does not bleed) to achieve their ends; they harm with the 'evil eye'; they dig evil medicine in the ground where the victim will pass; they put magic objects in the homes or fields of their victim; or send 'death' from a distance; they might change into animals in order to attack their victims; or they place harmful medicines where the victim would come into contact with it. All this means that in the villages people cannot feel completely 'safe'. It also means that even the smallest experience of misfortune and sorrow is blamed on the misuse of this mystical power. For that reason, people resort to medicine-men and diviners to supply them with protective objects. The principle or logic at work here is that the good use of this power will counteract the evil use, and thus keep the user relatively safe, so long as his 'medicine' is more powerful than that of his enemy. Charms, amulets, medicines drunk or rubbed into the body, articles on the roof or in the fields, cuts, knots, and many other visible and invisible, secret and open precautions, are used in all communities for seriously religious intentions, to secure a feeling of safety, protection and assurance. In this perspective we see the importance of diviners and medicine-men who, in addition to supplying the objects of cure and protection, may also perform rituals to cleanse people or homesteads subjected to attacks from this mystical power. They also give medicines to cure or 'cool', those who are believed to use that power for evil purposes. Formerly the workers of this type of evil were severely punished by their communities, through stoning, beating, paying of fines and death. Even today one fairly often reads in newspapers of people being attacked, and occasionally killed, on accusation or suspicion of practising evil magic.

A modern trend in the use of mystical power is seen in the activities of 'money doublers'. This racket is reported in western Africa, though it may be starting elsewhere as well. Money doublers cheat people by telling them to leave sums of money at agreed places, promising that by 'miraculous' magical ways they will 'double' the money, and the owners can then collect the larger amount after a while. When people return to collect their money, they find the bags or boxes either empty or filled up with sand, leaves, stones or other worthless material. Even educated people, including Church pastors, are reported to fall victim to 'money doublers'.

Anthropologists and sociologists use the term 'witchcraft' in a specialized way. According to them witches, who are mainly women, are people with an inherent power by means of which they can abandon their bodies at night and go to meet with similar people (other witches) or to 'suck' or 'eat away' the life of their victims. Some societies, like the Azande, can even pin-point the spot in the witch's body where 'witchcraft' is located. If we press this usage of the term witch and witchcraft, we would find that actually some African societies do not hold this belief. It would also mean that some witches do not realize that they are witches; and this makes witchcraft an infectious or hereditary tendency. Some women suspect themselves to be witches while in actual fact they are not. They may also find themselves meeting with other 'witches' at night, physically at least, to plan their activities or share their experiences. I confess that this part of the story hinges close to fiction, and it may well turn out to be extremely difficult to substantiate.

Witchcraft is a term used more popularly and broadly, to describe all sorts of evil employment of mystical power, generally in a secret fashion. African societies do not often draw the rather academic distinction between witchcraft, sorcery, evil magic, evil eye and other ways of employing mystical power to do harm to someone or his belongings. Generally the same word is used for all these English terms; and the same person is accused or suspected of employing one or more of these ways of hurting members of his community. In popular usage the term 'witchcraft' is employed to designate the harmful employment of mystical power in all its different manifestations. I am inclined to use the term 'witch' or 'witchcraft' in this broader sense; and here theologians may wish to part company with anthropologists. In any case, it is easier to say 'bewitch' than 'evil magicize' or 'sorcerize' in describing the use of this power to harm another person. Whatever terminology wins in the end one thing is absolutely certain, that African peoples believe that there are individuals who have access to mystical power which they employ for destructive purposes. In a non-scientific environment belief of this type cannot be 'clean' from fear, falsehood, exaggeration, suspicion, fiction and irrationality. Whatever reality there is concerning witchcraft in the broad and popular sense of the term, the belief in it is there in every African village, and that belief affects everyone, for better or for worse. It is part of the religious corpus of beliefs.

We may conclude this chapter by summarizing a few major points. African peoples are aware of a mystical power in the universe. This power is ultimately from God, but in practice it is inherent in, or comes from or through physical objects and spiritual beings. That means that the universe is not static or 'dead': it is a dynamic, 'living' and powerful universe.

Access to this mystical power is hierarchical in the sense that God has the most and absolute control over it; the spirits and the living-dead have portions of it; and some human beings know how to tap, manipulate and use some of it. Each community experiences this force or power as useful and therefore acceptable, neutral or harmful and therefore evil. On the credit side, mystical power is employed for curative, protective, productive and preventive purposes. For this reason, Africans wear, carry or keep charms, amulets and a variety of other objects, on their bodies, in their possessions, homesteads and fields. Medicine-men and diviners are the main dealers in the use, manufacture and distribution of these articles of 'medicine' or power. On the negative side, it is used to 'eat' away the health and souls of victims, to attack people, to cause misfortunes and make life uncom-fortable. The witches, wizards, sorcerers, evil magicians and people with an evil eye, are the ones who employ this power for anti-social and harmful activities. From time to time, each community undertakes to 'smell-out' or hunt the sorcerers and witches, punish them, 'cool' them off, cure them and counteract their activities. Everyone, however, keeps constant guard against the wicked doings of these 'evil workers', whether they are real or imaginary.

A good number of people spend large amounts of their wealth to obtain access to this power. Expert users spend years to acquire their knowledge and skill some of which is obviously secret and unknown to outsiders. Such experts have their own 'science' in dealing with this mystery of the universe. There are reports of fantastic experiences and phenomena attributed to this mystical power; and some of them defy both repetition and explana-tion by means of modern science.

The subject of mystical power, magic, sorcery and witchcraft, with all the beliefs that accompany it, has other dimensions besides the religious. There are social, psychological and economic aspects which add to the complexity of discussing and understanding this subject. It is also related closely to the question of evil, to which we shall now proceed.

17
THE CONCEPTS OF
EVIL, ETHICS
& JUSTICE

[a] *The origin and nature of evil*

From previous considerations we have seen that African peoples are much aware of evil in the world, and in various ways they endeavour to fight it. Several views exist concerning the origin of evil. Many societies say categori-cally that God did not create what is evil, nor does He do them any evil whatsoever. For example, the Ila hold that God is always in the right, and 'cannot be charged with an offence, cannot be accused, cannot be questioned . . . He does good to all at all times'.[1] One of the Ashanti priests is reported as saying that God 'created the possibility of evil in the world . . . God has created the knowledge of good and evil in every person and allowed him to choose his way', without forbidding him or forcing His will on him.[2] From various myths we saw that when God originally created man, there was harmony and family relationship between the two; and the first men enjoyed only what was good.

Some societies see evil as originating from, or associated with, spiritual beings other than God. Part of this concept is a personification of evil itself. For example, the Vugusu say that there is an evil divinity which God created good, but later on turned against Him and began to do evil. This evil divinity is assisted by evil spirits, and all evil now comes from that lot. Thus, a kind of duel exists, between good and evil forces in the world. There are other peoples who regard death, epidemics, locusts and other major calamities, as divinities in themselves, or as caused by divinities.

In nearly all African societies, it is thought that the spirits are either the origin of evil, or agents of evil. We have seen that after four or five genera-tions, the living-dead lose personal links with human families, and become 'its' and strangers. When they become detached from human contact, people experience or fear them as 'evil' or 'harmful'. Much of this is simply the fear of what is strange; but some are believed to possess individuals and to cause various maladies like epilepsy and madness. If the living-dead are

[1] Smith & Dale, pp. 199 f., 207, 211.
[2] R. A. Lystad *The Ashanti* (1958), p. 163 f.

not properly buried, or have a grudge, are neglected or not obeyed when they give instructions, it is thought that they take revenge or punish the offenders. In this case, it is men who provoke the living-dead to act in 'evil' ways.

We saw in the previous chapter that there are people in every community who are suspected of working maliciously against their relatives and neighbours, through the use of magic, sorcery and witchcraft. As we shall shortly point out further, this is the centre of evil, as people experience it. Mystical power is neither good nor evil in itself: but when used maliciously by some individuals it is experienced as evil. This view makes evil an independent and external object which, however, cannot act on its own but must be employed by human or spiritual agents.

As in all societies of the world, social order and peace are recognized by African peoples as essential and sacred. Where the sense of corporate life is so deep, it is inevitable that the solidarity of the community must be maintained, otherwise there is disintegration and destruction. This order is conceived of primarily in terms of kinship relationship, which simul-taneously produces many situations of tension since everybody is related to everybody else and deepens the sense of damage caused by the strain of such tensions. If a person steals a sheep, personal relations are at once involved because the sheep belongs to a member of the corporate body, perhaps to someone who is a father, or brother, or sister or cousin to the thief. As such it is an offence against the community, and its consequences affect not only the thief but also the whole body of his relatives.

There exist, therefore, many laws, customs, set forms of behaviour, regulations, rules, observances and taboos, constituting the moral code and ethics of a given community or society. Some of these are held sacred, and are believed to have been instituted by God or national leaders. They originate in the Zamani where the forefathers are. This gives sanctity to the customs and regulations of the community. Any breach of this code of behaviour is considered evil, wrong or bad, for it is an injury or destruction to the accepted social order and peace. It must be punished by the corporate community of both the living and the departed, and God may also inflict punishment and bring about justice.

In human relationships there is emphasis on the concept of hierarchy based partly on age and partly on status. In practice this amounts to a ladder ranging from God to the youngest child. God is the creator and hence the parent of mankind, and holds the highest position so that He is the final point of reference and appeal. Beneath Him are the divinities and spirits, which are more powerful than man and some of which were founders and forefathers of different societies. Next come the living-dead, the more important ones being those who were full human beings by virtue of going through the initiation rites, getting married and raising children. Among human beings the hieararchy includes kings, rulers, rainmakers, priests, diviners, medicine-men, elders in each household, parents, older brothers and sisters, and finally the youngest members of the community. Authority is recognized as increasing from the youngest child to the highest Being. As for the individual, the highest authority is the community of which he is a corporate member. This authority also has degrees, so that some of it is in the hands of the household-family, some is invested in the elders of a given area, part is in the hands of the clan, and part is in the whole nation which may or may not be invested in central rulers.

According to some societies, individuals or the people as a body or through its chief or king, may offend against God. For example, the Barundi believe that God gets angry with a person who commits adultery. The Bachwa believe that God punishes people who steal, neglect ageing parents, murder or commit adultery. The Bavenda say that if their chief offends against God, He punishes the whole people with locusts, floods or other calamities.

Most African peoples accept or acknowledge God as the final guardian of law and order and of the moral and ethical codes. Therefore the breaking of such order, whether by the individual or by a group, is ultimately an offence by the corporate body of society. For example, before the Gikuyu sacrifice and pray for rain, they first enquire from a diviner or seer why God has allowed such a long drought to come upon them. The animal for sacrifice must be of one colour, and be donated by or bought from a person who is honest, trustworthy and has not committed 'murder, theft, rape, or had any connection with poison (witchcraft) or poisoning'.[1] In this and the previous examples, we see that murder, theft and the like, are considered offences against God. The guilt of one person involves his entire household including his animals and property. The pollution of the individual is corporately the pollution of those related to him whether they are human beings, animals or material goods. We have considered myths concerning the first men, and seen how the disobedience of the original men involved the rest of their descendants in a corporate offence against God, so that the punishment He executed on them (death, separation from Him, withdrawal of free food, loss of immortality and the like), automatically became the punishment for all their descendants.

Let us take another example from the Nuer. It is thought that a person may offend against God by being proud of his cattle or children if they are many. This causes God to take away the cattle or children. Therefore for

[1] Kenyatta, p. 243 f.

the Nuer, 'the worst offence is to praise a baby', and one should refer to it as 'this bad thing'. The people believe that if a person does wrong, God will sooner or later punish him, and the punishment affects not just the individual alone, but the corporate group of which he is only a part. Praising a baby may cause it to die: the offender is not the baby, but the person who is proud before God. The Nuer, like many other African peoples, have different rules of behaviour. Offences arising from the breach of these, whether deliberately or accidentally, bring misfortune both to offenders and other people who are not directly responsible. For them, the evil lies not in the act itself, but in the fact that God punishes the act.[1] By committing a particular offence, a person puts himself and other people in the dangerous situation where God punishes him and other people. Since the con-sequences are bad, therefore the act which invites them must be bad. The outward manifestations only indicate the bad or evil inside, and the outward misfortune may contaminate other people who are closely related to the offender. Such is the logic of the matter in the sight of the Nuer and, it would seem, many other African peoples. Something is evil because it is punished: it is not punished because it is evil.

There are other societies in which people do not feel that they can offend against God. For example, the Ankore recognize God as the final principle of order, but individuals do not offend Him nor feel guilty towards Him.[2] It is held among the Azande, Akan, Swazi, Banyarwanda and others, that God has no influence on people's moral values.

Various types of offences are considered to be against the spirits and the living-dead. We have indicated that the living-dead, and to a less extent the spirits also, act as intermediaries between God and men, and that they are the guardians or police of tribal ethics, morals and customs. Where such spirits were once the founders or forefathers of the nation, it is commonly believed that they delivered many of the laws and customs of their people. Therefore any breach of these customs is an offence not only to the human society but also to the spirits and the living-dead. The offence is most serious when it is against the patriarchs, kings or other noble men. Unless steps are taken to avert it, the offenders and their relatives must be punished. But it is chiefly within the family circles that spirits and the living-dead are likely to be offended. Therefore the pouring out of libation and making offerings of bits of food are done on the family basis so that members of the family may remain on good terms with their departed relatives. This is in addition to strengthening the fellowship and renewing contact between the two groups. When the living-dead make demands or give instructions,

[1] Evans-Pritchard, II, pp. 14 f., 189 f.
[2] F. B. Welbourn conference paper on 'The High God', 1964.

these are generally followed immediately and obediently, unless they become excessive.

We have emphasized the corporate nature of African communities which are knit together by a web of kinship relationships and other social structures. Within this situation, almost every form of evil that a person suffers, whether it is moral or natural evil, is believed to be caused by members of his community. Similarly, any moral offence that he commits is directly or indirectly against members of his society. The principle of hierarchy is most helpful here. As a rule, a person of a lower rank, status or age commits an offence against another person or being of a higher rank or age. One may also offend against a person of the same status. Never or rarely does a person or being of a higher status do what constitutes an offence against a person of a lower status. What is considered evil or offensive functions from a low level to a higher level; and if a witch, for example, bewitches a little child, this act puts her on a lower level than the child. That is the philosophical understanding concerning what constitutes evil in the context of relationships. Something is considered to be evil not because of its intrinsic nature, but by virtue of who does it to whom and from which level of status.

According to this principle, God does not and cannot commit evil against His creation. We have already mentioned societies like the Akamba, Herero and others who firmly hold that since God does them no evil, they have no need to sacrifice to Him. When people feel that a misfortune or calamity has come from God, they interpret this not as an offence, but as punishment caused by their misdoings. So also the spirits on the whole do not offend against men; the living-dead do not offend against men, the king or ruler does not offend against his subjects, the elder in the village does not offend those who are younger or under him, and parents do not offend against their children. If parents do something which hurts their children and which constitutes an offence against the children, it is not the children as such who experience it as offence: rather, it is the community, the clan, the nation or the departed relatives who are the real object of offence, since they are the ones in a higher status than the parents. Consequently it is not the children themselves but the offended community or clan or living-dead who punish the parents.

This is the ideal. There are exceptions to it as to any generalizations. For example, if the king departs from the laws and customs established by the founders of the nation, he would be considered as offending against his subjects because he has departed from the established order. Indeed the offence is also against the patriarchs and heroes of the nation and, therefore, it is in effect an offence against beings of a higher status. But if he takes the cow of somebody among his subjects, this may not be regarded as an offence against the owner of the cow: for it is the king who has taken the cow, and he has the right to take it.

Within this tightly knit corporate society where personal relationships are so intense and so wide, one finds perhaps the most paradoxical areas of African life. This corporate type of life makes every member of the community dangerously naked in the sight of other members. It is paradoxically the centre of love and hatred, of friendship and enmity, of trust and suspicion, of joy and sorrow, of generous tenderness and bitter jealousies. It is paradoxically the heart of security and insecurity, of building and destroying the individual and the community. Everybody knows everybody else: a person cannot be individualistic, but only corporate. Every form of pain, misfortune, sorrow or suffering; every illness and sickness; every death whether of an old man or of the infant child; every failure of the crop in the fields, of hunting in the wilderness or of fishing in the waters; every bad omen or dream: these and all the other manifestations of evil that man experiences are blamed on somebody in the corporate society. Natural explanations may indeed be found, but mystical explanations must also be given. People create scapegoats for their sorrows. The shorter the radius of kinship and family ties, the more scapegoats there are. Frustrations, psychic disturbances, emotional tensions, and other states of the inner person, are readily externalized and incarnated, or made concrete in another human being or in circumstances which lay the blame on an external agent.

Here then we find a vast range of occasions for offences by one or more individuals against others in their corporate community. The environment of intense relationship favours strongly the growth of the belief in magic, sorcery, witchcraft, and all the fears, practices and concepts that go with this belief. I do not for a moment deny that there are spiritual forces outside man which seem sometimes to function within human history and human society. But the belief in the mystical power is greater than the ways in which that power might actually function within the human society. African communities in the villages are deeply affected and permeated by the psychological atmosphere which creates both real and imaginery powers or forces of evil that give rise to more tensions, jealousies, suspicions, slander, accusations and scapegoats. It is a vicious cycle. Let us illustrate this by moving from the academic to the practical.

Within this intensely corporate type of society, there are endless manifestations of evil. These include murders, robberies, rape, adultery, lies, stealing, cruelty especially towards women, quarrels, bad words, disrespect to persons of a higher status, accusations of sorcery, magic and witchcraft, disobedience of children and the like. In this atmosphere, all is neither grim nor bright. It is hard to describe these things: one needs to participate or grow up in village life, to get an idea of the depth of evil and its consequences upon individuals and society. A visitor to the village will immediately be struck by African readiness to externalize the spontaneous feelings of joy, love, friendship and generosity. But this must be balanced by the fact that Africans are men, and there are many occasions when their feelings of hatred, strain, fear, jealousy and suspicion also become readily externalized. This makes them just as brutal, cruel, destructive and unkind as any other human beings in the world. By nature, Africans are neither angels nor demons; they possess and exercise the potentialities of both angels and demons. They can be as kind as the Germans, but they can be as murderous as the Germans; Africans can be as generous as the Americans, but they can be as greedy as the Americans; they can be as friendly as the Russians, but they can be as cruel as the Russians; they can be as honest as the English, but they can also be as equally hypocritical. In their human nature Africans are Germans, Swiss, Chinese, Indians or English—they are men.

Ritual matters are another area where offence might be committed. Every African society has regulations and procedures about ceremonies and rituals. When offence is committed here, it is often necessary to perform ritual purification. We may cite an example from the Gikuyu, who perform the ritual of 'vomiting the sin', to cleanse a person from ritual evil. For this purpose a goat is slaughtered and its stomach contents taken out. An elder presides over minor occasions, but a medicine⁄man is necessary for major offences. The stomach contents are first mingled with medicines. Then the officiating elder takes a brush with which he wipes off some of the mixture on the tongue of the offender, enumerating the offences com⁄ mitted. Each time the offender spits out the mixture on the ground. Afterwards the walls of his house are brushed with the same mixture. If the house is not so cleansed, it must be demolished. This rite is full of symbolism which is not hard to see.

[b] *Restitution and punishment*
The majority of African peoples believe that God punishes in this life. Thus, He is concerned with the moral life of mankind, and therefore upholds the moral law. With a few exceptions, there is no belief that a person is punished in the hereafter for what he does wrong in this life. When punishment comes, it comes in the present life. For that reason, misfortunes may be interpreted as indicating that the sufferer has broken some moral or ritual conduct against God, the spirits, the elders or other members of his society. This does not contradict the belief that misfortunes are the work of some members, especially workers of magic, sorcery and

witchcraft, against their fellow men. This village logic is quite normal in African thinking. I do not understand it, but I accept it. The Banyarwanda and Barundi express God's punitive acts in a proverb that 'God exercises vengeance in silence'.[1] The Nuer link sickness with the fault that lies behind it, and therefore sacrifice in order to stay the punitive consequences. 'In the one case the emphasis is on the actions from which one looks forward to the sickness which, when it comes, is identified with them. In the other case the emphasis is on the sickness and one looks backwards from it to faults which might have brought it about, even if one makes no attempt to discover what they were'.[2] The same might be said about many other African peoples.

Each community or society has its own set form of restitution and punishment for various offences, both legal and moral. These range from death for offences like practising sorcery and witchcraft, committing murder and adultery, to paying fines of cattle, sheep or money for minor cases like accidental injury to one's companion or when sheep escape and eat potato vines in a neighbour's field. It is generally the elders of the area who deal with disputes and breaches arising from various types of moral harm or offences against custom and ritual. Traditional chiefs and rulers, where these exist, have the duty of keeping law and order, and executing justice in their areas. Nowadays there are governmental law courts, some of which make use of the services of the elders, and incorporate something from the traditional customary law.

There is one form of justice administered through the use of the curse. The basic principle here is that if a person is guilty, evil will befall him according to the words used in cursing him. By the use of good magic, it is believed, a person can curse an unknown thief or other offender. But most of the curses are within family circles. The operative principle is that only a person of a higher status can effectively curse one of a lower status, but not vice versa. The most feared curses are those pronounced by parents, uncles, aunts or other close relatives against their 'juniors' in the family. The worst is the curse uttered at the death-bed, for once the pronouncer of the curse has died, it is practically impossible to revoke it. If the guilty person repents and asks for the curse to be lifted, the person who uttered it can revoke it either automatically or ritually if it is a very serious one. There are many stories in African villages, telling about the fulfilment of curses where a person is guilty. If one is not guilty, then the curse does not function. Formal curses are feared much in African societies, and this fear, like that of witchcraft, helps to check bad relationships especially in family circles.

[1] Guillebaud in Smith, p. 200.
[2] Evans-Pritchard, II, p. 194.
A.R.P.—8

Formal oaths are used as another method of establishing and maintaining good human relationships. There are oaths which bind people mystically together, the best known being the one which creates what is rather loosely referred to as 'blood-brotherhood'. By means of this oath, two people who are not immediately related, go through a ritual which often involves exchanging small amounts of their blood by drinking or rubbing it into each other's body. After that they look upon each other as real 'blood' brothers or sisters, and will behave in that capacity towards each other for the rest of their lives. Their families are also involved in this 'brotherly' contract, so that for example, their children would not intermarry. This oath places great moral and mystical obligations upon the parties concerned; and any breach of the covenant is dreaded and feared to bring about misfortunes. There are oaths taken when people join the so-called 'secret societies', when they are initiated in the rites of passage or in professions like divination. Other oaths are taken when secret information is divulged, to guard some knowledge or other secrets. Oaths may also be taken by children before the death of their parents if the latter want very much that their children observe certain instructions or carry out important requests. Oaths range in seriousness: some are meant to bring about death if they are broken, others cause temporary pain or misfortunes of one type or another. The belief behind oaths is that God, or some power higher than the individual man, will punish the person who breaks the requirements of the oath or covenant. Like curses, oaths are feared and many are administered ritually and at great expense.

[c] Summary and conclusion

African notions of morality, ethics and justice have not been fully studied, and many books either do not mention them or do so only in passing. Idowu is one of the few exceptions here, and he devotes a whole chapter to the question of God and moral values among the Yoruba. He argues that for the Yoruba, moral values derive from the nature of God Himself, Whom they consider to be the 'Pure King', 'Perfect King', 'One clothed in white, Who dwells above' and is the 'Essentially white Object, white Material without pattern (entirely white)'. Character (*Iwa*) is the essence of Yoruba ethics, and upon it depends even the life of a person. So the people say, 'Gentle character it is which enables the rope of life to stay unbroken in one's hand'; and again, 'It is good character that is man's guard'. Good character shows itself in the following ways: chastity before marriage and faithfulness during marriage; hospitality; generosity, the opposite of selfishness; kindness; justice; truth and rectitude as essential virtues; avoiding stealing; keeping a covenant and avoiding falsehood; protecting the poor and weak, especially women; giving honour and respect to older people; and avoiding hypocrisy.[1] This can be applied, with additions to the list of what constitutes good character, to many African societies. It pertains to the traditional concept of 'good' and ' bad' or evil, that is, to the morals and ethics of any given society.

We can here make a distinction between 'moral evil' and 'natural evil'. Moral evil pertains to what man does against his fellow man. There are customs, laws, regulations and taboos that govern conduct in society. Any breach of the right conduct amounts to a moral evil. We find endless examples of that in African societies. It is the opposite of cultivating or manifesting the virtues of good character. Indeed, we can say that good character is 'good' because of the conduct it depicts. What lies behind the conception of moral 'good' or 'evil', is ultimately the nature of the relationship between individuals in a given community or society. There is almost no 'secret sin': something or someone is 'bad' or 'good' according to the outward conduct. A person is not inherently 'good' or 'evil', but he acts in ways which are 'good' when they conform to the customs and regulations of his community, or 'bad' (evil) when they do not. To sleep with someone else's wife is not considered 'evil' if these two are not found out by the society which forbids it; and in other societies it is in fact an expression of friendship and hospitality to let a guest spend the night with one's wife or daugher or sister. It is not the act in itself which would be 'wrong' as such, but the relationships involved in the act: if relationships are not hurt or damaged, and if there is no discovery of breach of custom or regulation, then the act is not 'evil' or 'wicked' or 'bad'.

Those who practise witchcraft, evil magic and sorcery are the very incarnation of moral evil. They are, by their very nature, set to destroy relationships, to undermine the moral integrity of society, and to act contrary to what custom demands. Therefore such people are also instruments of natural evil—at least people associate them with it, so that when accidents, illnesses, misfortunes and the like strike, people immediately search for the agents of evil, for witches, for sorcerers and for neighbours or relatives who have used evil magic against them.

Even if, as we have pointed out, God is thought to be the ultimate upholder of the moral order, people do not consider Him to be immediately involved in the keeping of it. Instead, it is the patriarchs, living-dead, elders, priests, or even divinities and spirits who are the daily guardians or police of human morality. Social regulations of a moral nature are directed towards the immediate contact between individuals, between man and the living-

[1] Idowu, pp. 144–68; cf. P. Tempels *Bantu Philosophy*, pp. 75–108, with some odd conclusions.

dead and the spirits. Therefore, these regulations are on the man-to-man level, rather than the God-to-man plane of morality. One could draw up a long list of them: don't kill another man except in war, don't steal, don't show disrespect to people of a higher status, don't have sexual intercourse with a wide variety of persons, such as another man's wife, your sister or other close relative or children, don't use bad words especially to someone of a higher status, don't backbite, don't tell lies, don't despise or laugh at a cripple, don't take away someone else's piece of land; keep the many taboos and regulations concering parts of the body, proper behaviour according to kinship relationships, and activities such as hunting, fishing and eating; observe the correct procedure in ritual matters and so on. In positive language, the list is also long, including items like: be kind, help those who cry to you for help, show hospitality, be faithful in marriage, respect the elders, keep justice, behave in a humble way towards those senior to you, greet people especially those you know, keep your word given under oath, compensate when you hurt someone or damage his property, follow the customs and traditions of your society.

The list of what should and should not be done is so long and detailed that a person is constantly confronted with moral demands throughout his life. This is seriously so in the environment where the individual is conscious of himself in terms of 'I am because we are, and since we are, therefore I am'. And, as we have seen, within the African communities where kinship makes a person intensely 'naked', these moral demands are uncomfortably scrutinized by everybody so that a person who fails to live up to them cannot escape notice. Therefore, the essence of African morality is that it is more 'societary' than 'spiritual'; it is a morality of 'conduct' rather than a morality of 'being'. This is what one might call 'dynamic ethics' rather than 'static ethics', for it defines what a person *does* rather than what he *is*. Conversely, a person is what he is because of what he does, rather than that he does what he does because of what he is. Kindness is not a virtue unless someone is kind; murder is not evil until someone kills another person in his community. Man is not by nature either 'good' or 'bad' ('evil') except in terms of what he does or does not do. This, it seems to me, is a necessary distinction to draw in discussing African concept of morality and ethics. It should also help us to understand something about the belief in witchcraft, magic and sorcery.

This point is connected with the second form of evil, which we have distinguished as 'natural evil'. By this I mean those experiences in human life which involve suffering, misfortunes, diseases, calamity, accidents and various forms of pain. In every African society these are well known. Most of them are explainable through 'natural' causes. But as we saw for

African peoples nothing sorrowful happens by 'accident' or 'chance': it must all be 'caused' by some agent (either human or spiritual). If our analysis in the previous paragraph is valid, we can see also that the logic or philosophy behind 'moral evil' would not permit 'natural evil' to take place purely by means of 'natural causes'. People must find the agent 'causing' such evil. In some societies it is thought that a person suffers because he has contravened some regulation, and God or the spirits, therefore, punish the offender. In that case, the person concerned is actually the cause of his own suffering: he first externalizes the cause, and then inverts it. But in most cases, different forms of suffering are believed to be caused by human agents who are almost exclusively witches, sorcerers and workers of evil magic. We have seen that these are the incarnation of evil viewed socially. They are also 'responsible' for 'causing' what would be 'natural evil', by using incantations, mystical power, medicines, by sending secondary agents like flies and animals, by using their 'evil eye', by wishing evil against their fellow man, by hating or feeling jealous, and by means of other 'secret' methods. The logic here is that 'natural evil' is present because these immoral agents exist; and these are evil because they do evil deeds. Again I confess that I do not understand this logic, but I accept it as valid for our under-standing of African religions and philosophy. To say, in African societies, that a person is 'good' or 'bad' has extremely profound connotations, for it summarizes the whole image or picture of the person in the context of his actions. One does not 'love' in a vacuum: it is the deeds which signify that there is love behind them; one does not 'hate' in a vacuum, it is the deeds that signify what lies behind them. In such experiences, the world of nature is not divorced from that of man. In the experience of evil, African peoples see certain individuals as being intricately involved, but wickedly, in the otherwise smooth running of the natural universe. This is again another point where we observe that African ontology is deeply anthropocentric.

Our discussion has so far been focused upon the traditional setting. We cannot leave the picture there, without saying something about changes that are taking place all over Africa. These changes certainly have a bearing on traditional religions and philosphy: shaping them and being shaped by them. To these we shall devote the three concluding chapters.

18

CHANGING MAN
& HIS PROBLEMS

In the traditional set-up where the African concept of time is mainly two-dimensional human life is relatively stable and almost static. A rhythm of life is the norm, and any radical change is either unknown, resented or so slow that it is hardly noticed. But from the second half of the nineteenth century and swiftly gaining momentum towards the middle of the twentieth century rapid and radical changes have been taking place everywhere in Africa, and no study of African problems or concepts would be complete without some mention of them. Great emphasis has been put on the social aspects of these changes, but the changes are total, involving the whole existence of African peoples, and making their impact upon the religious, economic, political as well as social life. We have pointed out and demon-strated that in their traditional life, African peoples are deeply religious and experience this as a religious universe. This means that modern changes in Africa have come upon religious societies, affecting their religious attitudes and life and being affected by this traditional religiosity.

[a] *The causes of this rapid change*
Africa is caught up in a world revolution which is so dynamic that it has almost got out of human control. It is a revolution of man as a whole, and therefore no people or country can remain unaffected by this new rhythm of human history. In Europe and north America, this revolution goes back three to five generations. But in Africa we are nearly all in the first generation of the change which took only a few decades for its way to be paved. Without warning and without physical or psychological preparation, Africa has been invaded by a world revolution. Now a new and rapid rhythm is beating from the drums of science and technology, modern communications and mass media, schools and universities, cities and towns. Nothing can halt this rhythm or slow down its rapid tempo. The man of Africa must get up and dance, for better or for worse, on the arena of world drama. His image of himself and of the universe is disrupted and must make room for the changing 'universal' and not simply 'tribal' man. This is the

general world-wide revolution affecting African societies, but there are immediate causes for the changes now taking place.

Christianity from western Europe and north America has come to Africa, not simply carrying the Gospel of the New Testament, but as a complex phenomenon made up of western culture, politics, science, technology, medicine, schools and new methods of conquering nature. The Gospel by its very nature is revolutionary; but Christianity in its modern return to Africa is the main carrier of all the elements of this world revolution. It is necessary to draw a distinction between the Gospel and Christianity which are not synonymous at certain points. Missionaries established and pioneered schools everywhere, and these schools became the nurseries for change: they sowed the Gospel, they sowed Christianity and perhaps unawares and unintentionally they sowed also the new revolution. It is the young men and women in these schools who assimilated not only religion but science, politics, technology and so on; and the same young people are the ones who became detached from their tribal roots. Those attending school also became the vehicles of carrying the new changes and introducing them to their villages.

Through missionaries too came European medicine and knowledge of hygiene which, however, had a slow influence at the beginning. In addition to the physical impact, the new medicine prepared people psychologically to become more receptive to western culture and education. Eventually the new form of medical care and knowledge began to reduce infant mortality and put under control diseases like smallpox, malaria and stomach ailments which had always been the main killers of African peoples. Better health and medical care result in increased population, and a larger population brings more problems.

The physical expansion of Europe into Africa exposed African peoples to the change taking place elsewhere. European conquest of Africa reached its formal climax with the Berlin Conference of 1885 at which the major powers of Europe politically shared out the whole of Africa apart from Ethiopia and Liberia. European ownership of Africa meant, among other things, the arrival of European settlers, businessmen, gold and diamond diggers, colonial administration, the founding of new cities, the construction of railways and roads, the introduction of new laws and new economic systems. In short, whether consciously or unconsciously, Europe began to transform Africa and if possible to make it resemble itself in many respects. Even European names were substituted for African and religious names of local places and individuals. Mini Englands and mini Germanies, mini Frances and mini Italies, were being planted everywhere on our continent. Europe had divided up Africa, Europe meant to rule Africa and Europe began to change Africa. This was the new rhythm and no force could stop it. In some parts Africans tried to resist but they were overcome by Europeans who slaughtered them like beasts, who burnt down their villages, who put men and women into prisons, who forced them to quit their lands and become labourers in European farms or 'house-boys' for European masters and mistresses. The new change started and continued in blood and tears, in suppression and humiliation, through honest and dishonest means, by consent and by force, by choice and by subjection. Every radical revolution in human history costs human blood, human sorrows and human suffering. This was no exception in Africa, and Africa has paid heavily for the change which originated outside and was initially being forced upon her. So the revolution came by both peace and force, and Africa could not be the same any more. Some colonial powers remained here for a relatively short time, being forced out by their fellow colonialists; some eventually had to quit under the pressure of African nationalism; and a few still remain in control but their days are clearly numbered. Some of the colonial powers developed their African countries educationally, medically and economically; but others simply coerced Africans to serve them, dug out African gold, diamonds and copper while doing virtually nothing for the human welfare of the people. Europe continues to exercise great control and influence in Africa, even if about forty African countries are legally and ritually independent. European and American control over Africa is mainly economic and ecclesiastical, together with the subtle influence of mass media. Russia, China and Japan are also increasingly moving into Africa. What happens in America, Europe and Asia has its impact upon Africa, so that the peoples of our continent are increasingly involved in the peoples of the world.

[b] *The nature of this change*

It is a total change and one which affects all spheres of life. On the level of the whole society, this change has been described as 'detribalization'. This means that traditional life is deeply undermined, so that tribal identity is fading away since other identities are making claims on the individual and the community.

In traditional life the family is the nucleus of both individual and corporate existence, the area where a person really experiences personal consciousness of himself and of other members of society. Now, the family is the most severely affected part of African life. Within one family or household may be found two totally different worlds coexisting: the children may be attending university studies, while the parents are illiterate and concerned mainly with cultivating their fields with wooden sticks. In such a family, there are two sets of expectations, economic standards, cultural concerns and world view. Some families are obviously more affected than others. The new change shows itself outwardly in many ways such as education, clothing, houses, food and moral behaviour.

But in the final analysis it is the individual who really feels the change, experiences it, accepts or rejects it, and to a great extent hastens or slows it down. Modern change has brought many individuals in Africa into situations entirely unknown in traditional life or for which that life offers no relevant preparation. Some are forced directly or indirectly to go and work in gold mines, industry, Europeans farms and houses, leaving their land and homes and relatives. This sudden detachment from the land to which Africans are mystically bound, and the thrust into situations where corporate existence has no meaning, have produced dehumanized individuals in the mines, industry and cities. The change means that individuals are severed, cut off, pulled out and separated from corporate morality, customs and traditional solidarity. They have no firm roots any more. They are simply uprooted but not necessarily transplanted. They float in life like a cloud. They live as individuals, but they are dead to the corporate humanity of their forefathers.

For the individual the change has come too suddenly, plunging him into a darkness for which he has not been traditionally prepared. It alienates him both from the traditions of his society and from his roots. Paradoxically, the individual is involved in the change and yet alienated from it. So he becomes an alien both to traditional life and to the new life brought about by modern change. He is posed between two positions: the traditional solidarity which supplied for him land, customs, ethics, rites of passage, customary law, religious participation and a historical depth; and a modern way of life which for him has not yet acquired any solidarity. The change at best offers him a hope for the future, an aspiration and an expectation. The traditional life is fast being brushed into the past, and the further back it recedes the more golden it looks. So the individual is the object of a dual process: one recedes into the Zamani, the other hangs in the future; and the tension between these two is neither harmonious nor creative for the majority of Africans.

There are also general aspects of the change. On the political level, the continent of Africa continues to go through a great upheaval. When colonial powers came, they either destroyed, suppressed or modified traditional political institutions. Many peoples who in their history had never been subjected under foreign rule, or only briefly, suddenly found themselves without political power. For many years their political talents were kept impotent. But this humiliation became too deep to be swallowed indefinitely. After the Second World War, African nationalism began to gain a tremendous momentum. It partly expelled colonial rule and partly inherited a colonial structure of government in the new African states. But the power of nationalism is so enormous that it is hard to bridle and harness. The political situation in which African peoples find themselves today is just as dangerous, difficult and foreign as the situation under colonial rule. The spirit which ignited the fires of nationalism during the colonial days has not lost its power; it has ignited more fires since independence returned to the majority of African states; and it will continue to do so until its energy is harnessed and channelled in other directions. The political pot in Africa is still bubbling, and great is the man who can stir it without getting smeared or even scorched.

A primarily money economy has been introduced to Africa. It is making its force felt even in the remotest parts of the continent. People grow cash crops like cocoa, coffee, tea, cotton and tobacco. Others work for money in all sorts of employment. This new economy introduces the concept of time as a commodity to be sold and bought; it involves also earning and spending money with all the dangers, temptations, difficulties and risks that go with it. African states are realizing more and more that their prosperity and progress depend on their economic life. Many, if not all, are increasingly becoming victims of the so-called 'economic aid' from the richer and industrialized countries. This aid always has many strings attached to it; and the amount is so little proportionally that its effect is much smaller than the publicity given to the aid. Everybody knows now that the 'poor' nations are getting poorer, while the rich nations are getting richer. This puts the richer nations at an advantage which they are not prepared to give up or share more evenly; and why should they?

Urbanization is another aspect of modern change in Africa. There were traditionally only a few cities prior to the colonial days, apart from those in northern Africa, Egypt, Ethiopia, the east coast and some in western Africa. Even now, the population which lives permanently in cities is still small, while the majority of people are living, at least part of their time, on the land. But the movement from the country to the cities is so rapid that many towns mushroom in a matter of a few decades. Examples of this process can be quoted from all over the continent. Rapid urbanization creates more problems than anybody could cope with. We shall return to these in the next sub-section.

In the religious realm we also find great changes. Traditional religious concepts and practices cannot accommodate themselves fully to the changing situation. Neither does Christianity, to which most people have been exposed, accommodate itself fully to either the traditional African life or to the complexity of modern change whether in Africa or Europe and America. A new dichotomy has invaded Africa, driving a wedge between religious and secular life, which is something unknown in traditional life. Those who introduced Christianity anew to Africa, also brought with it doubt and unbelief. Some Africans are now trying to live without religion, at least so they imagine and how far they succeed waits to be seen. This is more in the cities and among the educated elite, than among other strata of society.

The change is also cultural. Traditional cultures are or were suited to the traditional background which allowed little if any radical change. Modern change tries to plant a form of culture which is shallow at least on the African soil. It is a culture of the alphabet and comics, of pop music and the transistor radio, of television and magazines with pictures of semi-naked women, of individualism and economic competition, of mass production and ever accelerating speed of life. Men and women are forced to live in two half cultures which do not unite to form a single culture. Those who bring the foreign culture give it to Africans only in part while withholding the other part. Africans also receive part of that culture and reject the other part; and they kick away part of their traditional cultures while retaining the other part.

Modern change has imported into Africa a future dimension of time. This is perhaps the most dynamic and dangerous discovery of African peoples in the twentieth century. Their hopes are stirred up and set on the future. They work for progress, they wait for an immediate realization of their hopes, and they create new myths of the future. It is here that we find the key to understanding African political, economic and ecclesiastical instability. Africa wants desperately to be involved in this future dimension. Emphasis is shifting from the Zamani and Sasa to the Sasa and Future; and we are part of the historical moment when this great change-over is being wrought. But somewhere there lies a deep illusion. The speed of casting off the scales of traditional life is much greater than the speed of wearing the garments of this future dimension of life. The illusion lies in the fact that these two entirely different processes are made or look identical. This lack of distinction between the two types of process remains in all spheres of modern African life, and so long as it remains, the situation will continue to be unstable if not dangerous. Present structures of political, economic, educational and Church life unfortunately favour the continuation, if not the perpetuation, of this illusion. Here, then, lies the dilemma and the tragedy of the rapid change in Africa.

[c] *Problems of the rapid change*

As indicated in the previous sub-section, Africa has suddenly discovered the future dimension of time, and this discovery has produced a dangerously unstable psychological situation which gives a special or unique flavour to the political, economic, social and religious life in the continent. We can only sketch briefly some of the problems precipitated by modern change. Tribal structures of life which for many generations were produced by and oriented to the two-dimensional concept of time, cannot now be profitably applied in the new orientation towards the future. Two of the major forces against these traditional structures are modern nationhood and urbanization.

The immediate historical phase after colonial rule is the birth of African nations. These nations are composed of peoples of many cultures, histories, languages and traditions. Sometimes the points of unity on the national level weigh less heavily than points of disunity. Truly and rightly the cry of *uhuru* (freedom) has been sounded unanimously and with one accord. But isn't a nation something deeper and more serious than just the uhuru chorus? It is certainly possible to evolve a national solidarity which parallels or replaces tribal solidarity, but as yet we are too close to the change-over to see a clear picture or evidence of it. The undermining or destruction of tribal solidarity does not automatically create a fully integrated and mature national solidarity. This is something of an illusion aggravated by the very myopic future dimension of time, and even colonial powers did not altogether escape falling into the same ditch. Yet, the situation presents African peoples with great challenge and worthwhile responsibility, and there is no need for it to degenerate into a hopelessly grim picture.

On the surface tribal solidarity is disrupted but beneath lies the subconscious mind of the traditional Zamani. Nationhood scratches on the surface, it is the conscious mind of modern Africa. But the subconscious of tribal life is only dormant, not dead. These two levels do not always harmonize, and may even clash in an open conflict to the detriment of both sides. 'Tribalism' is a new phenomenon within and endangering 'nationhood'.

In certain circles there is even a revival of tribal rites and customs, the use of magic in cities is on the increase, and there are national efforts to preserve and take pride in tribal cultures. On the material or economic level, the trend is clearly the cultivation of individual and national prosperity. But on the emotional and psychological level, it is towards tribal solidarity and foundations. Modern African nations have no solidarity with a long tradition and firm foundations similar to tribal solidarity which evolved over a long period. Attempts are, rightly, being made by different countries in Africa to evolve a political life suited to their needs in the modern world.

But some of these attempts are no more than experiments. There is, for example, the so-called 'one party system' in which the ruling political party tends or tries to liquidate all the other parties. There is the experiment of the so-called 'African socialism', which attempts, among other things and at least on paper, to adopt traditional economic systems of corporate life to modern nationhood. In Tanzania there is the philosophy of 'self-help', enunciated in the already famous 'Arusha declaration' of 1967. How far these experiments will succeed remains to be seen; but the great enthusiam with which they have been greeted, and the publicity given to them, perhaps ignore certain aspects of human nature which could cripple the experiments before they are translated from paper to practice. On local levels there are active political groups whose energies are often harnessed towards positive goals of constructing schools and roads. But will this energy continue to be directed only towards positive and constructive goals?

On the level of international relationships there are groupings of African states, such as the East African Community created in December 1967, and the Union of Central African States created in April 1968. There are discussions about expanding these groupings and their scope, and creating additional ones. The Organization of African Unity was created in 1963. Among its slogans is the loud cry for African unity which at present looks more of a myth than an immediate possibility. Each nation is being pulled by forces of 'tribalism' or 'regionalism' in the lower ranks, while at the same time the forces of 'pan-Africanism' are pulling in the higher ranks. The economic and personnel resources of Africa seem, at present, to discourage an early continental political unity.

In world politics, African countries talk much about taking a neutral position with regard to the east-west ideological and political conflict. My impression is that nobody can be neutral, and even the dead are not neutral. We receive economic and 'advisory' aid from both capitalist and communist countries. This aid is not given freely, for there is no aid without a bait, and few are the men who see that trap, and fewer still are those who can entirely escape it. There are political and economic ties which enslave us firmly to the countries by which the aid is given. In the long run any continued aid begins to undermine our potentialities. Some of the personnel is made up of secret agents; and foreign embassies are not altogether free from political interference, so that sometimes they engineer, suggest or help in coups which continue to take place in independent African countries. Our economic poverty makes us a great target for political and ideological propaganda from powerful nations, and we must be aware of this helpless situation.

Social problems are many and deep, since all human problems are ultimately social. Traditional societies have been disrupted: we can neither cry over that, nor ignore that this is a *fait accompli*. There is no going back, and the only way open is to go forward for better and for worse. A new sort of society is emerging, partly out of the old society and partly in response to the new change. The emergence of that new society whatever it will be brings with it new problems for itself and sprays other problems over the traditional society. Most of the problems of the emerging society are concentrated on people living in the cities. There are questions of housing, slums, earning and spending money, alcoholism, prostitution, corruption, and thousands of young people roaming about in search of employment. Many people suddenly come from the country into the city where they have no roots or tradition to help them settle down. Others have lived most of their working life in the cities, and when they retire they do not quite know what to do there, and having lost their ties with country life they cannot easily return to it. There are problems of women with children out of wedlock, and of others who only go to the city for a few days or weeks to stay with their husbands and get fertilized. There are poor people who sit about in the streets begging for money and food, some of whom are cripples and others are too lazy to work. There are problems of unwanted children, orphans, criminals, delinquents and prisoners, all of whom need special social care to be brought up or integrated into their communities. Increasingly there is the gap in wealth between the few relatively rich men in top positions of government and commercial employment and the poor masses who barely earn enough on which to live. This great imbalance in wealth can only breed discontent, jealousy, greed, theft and even open uprising.

Ethical and moral problems also arise from the new social problems. Tribal ethics suited or suits tribal solidarity. But it is not easy to apply it in the changing situation where urban society requires its own set of morals suited to its type of life. The ties of kinship have not the same power in the city as they have in the country. The individualism of urban life demands its own code of behaviour. Whereas in rural life the individual is 'naked' to everybody else, in the city he is a locked up universe of his own. The concept of 'neighbour' differs considerably in the two situations. In the city the individual is one in a loose conglomeration of men and women from different peoples and languages, races and nationalities. These are joined or related together not by bonds of blood and betrothal, but by professions, places of work, clubs, factories, associations, hobbies, trade unions, sports, political parties, Church denominations and religious ties. That is where the individual now finds himself, and often his loyalties are spread over many of these affiliations.

The traditional solidarity in which the individual says 'I am because we are, and since we are, therefore I am', is constantly being smashed, undermined and in some respects destroyed. Emphasis is shifting from the 'we' of traditional corporate life to the 'I' of modern individualism. Schools, churches, economic competition and the future dimension of time with all its real and imaginary promises, are the main factors which, jointly or singly, are working to produce an orientation towards individualism and away from corporateness. So then, for example, amidst the many people who live in the cities, the individual discovers that he is alone. When he falls sick, perhaps only one or two other people know about it and come to see him; when he is hungry he finds that begging food from his neighbour is either shameful or unrewarding or both; when he gets bad news from his relatives in the countryside, he cries alone even if hundreds of other people rub shoulders with him in the factory or bus. The masses around the individual are both blind and deaf to him, they are indifferent and do not care about him as a person. Almost at every turn of his life the individual in the city and under modern change discovers constantly that he is alone or even lonely in the midst of large masses of people. He gets a new picture of himself and of other people. It is a painful discovery, especially for the many who are born in the country, grow up there and only in their late teens or early twenties go to work in the cities. This individualism makes a person aware of himself, but his self-consciousness is not founded upon either traditional solidarity which by its very nature and structure allowed little or no room for individualism, or another solidarity since nothing concrete has yet replaced what history is submerging. The individual simply discovers the existence of his individualism but does not know of what it consists. He has no language with which to perceive its nature and its destiny.

The family experiences great strain in this changing situation. The size of the family is shrinking from the traditional 'extended' family concept to one in which the parents and their children constitute the family in the modern sense of the word. The authority and respect which parents enjoyed under traditional morality and customs are being challenged by the younger generations, and in many homes there is rebellion from children against their parents. The fact of children and young people having to live away from home in order to attend schools or universities tends to weaken family solidarity. The education of children is increasingly being passed on from parents and the community to teachers and schools where it becomes more of book learning as an end in itself than an education which prepares the young for mature life and future careers.

Marriage contracts are increasingly becoming individual affairs and the concern of two persons, rather than the concern of families and communities as in tribal solidarity. The change might be for the better, but this transition is painful especially to the parents and other members of the kinship groups who cannot bear to see their son or daughter contract a marriage without consulting them or even telling them about it. Among other things, such contracts make it difficult, and often impossible, for the exchange of marriage gifts between the relatives involved. Another manifestation of this strain is that a number of parents demand costly marriage gifts in view of the fact that they spend their wealth educating their daughters in modern schools. They forget that it also costs the parents and relatives of the bridegroom to educate him.

Marriage and family instability have increased considerably under modern strain, giving rise to a higher rate of divorce and separation than in traditional life. Polygamy (or polygyny, which is the right term) is dying out though not very fast. But concubinage is rapidly increasing in the cities. One reason for this increase is that often married men have to leave their wives at home in the country and go to work in the towns where they remain for several months or even years without going back to their families. This produces emotional strain which leads to the men taking or keeping other women who are not legally married to them. Prostitution is to be found in every African city and town, this being particularly an economic necessity or convenience for women since it helps them to earn some money, find somewhere to live and meet some of the demands of city life.

One of the most serious problems precipitated by city life in Africa is the situation which forces the men to work in towns while their wives and children remain in the country. This is partly because of shortage of housing in the towns, partly because the men cannot afford to keep their whole families there, and partly because there is land and livestock property in the country which must be looked after. This geographical separation of families creates great strains on the emotional, psychological, sexual and marital life of husband and wife. In addition, the children grow up without a father at home, so that their image of the father is simply someone existing in a distant town from where he occasionally sends them money for clothes and school fees, and comes home once a year or every two years. For the wife, the husband is simply a person who descends upon her once a year or less often, to quench his sexual passion, fertilize her and disappear like a frogman. He hardly shares in the daily responsibilities and concerns of raising a family. The wife is both mother and father to the children. It is inevitable that such family life produces a serious strain upon every member. It is to be noted, however, that many wives in these situations really try hard to create a home and meet the problems with courage and rectitude.

Increasing numbers of mixed marriages are another feature of the modern African family. These are 'mixed' in terms of partners coming from different tribes, church denominations, religious backgrounds, races and nationalities. In themselves such marriages are not unique or peculiarly different from other marriages, but the different backgrounds involved in them are sometimes allowed to undermine their health, stability and even existence. Greater marital strain comes from marriages where there is a wide educational gap between husband and wife, especially where, after marriage, the husband receives university or overseas education while his wife has had only primary or junior secondary school education. A number of these marriages seem to succumb under strain and get wrecked.

One serious drawback in modern African family life is the fact that whereas under the traditional set up both boys and girls receive preparatory education concerning marriage, sex and family life, especially during and after their initiation rites, modern schools give little and often no such preparatory education. These schools spend more time teaching young people about dissecting frogs and about colonial history than they ever spend teaching them how to establish happy homes and family lives. Unless this structure and system of education is changed, we are heading for tragic social, moral and family chaos whose harvest is not far away.

Education is perhaps the greatest cry in Africa today. Since regaining their independence African states have endeavoured to double or even treble their number of schools and institutions of higher learning. Some of these schools are poorly staffed, others have mainly expatriate teachers, and some do not have proper or sufficient equipment. Most children receive only six to ten years of formal education which neither prepares them for any careers or jobs nor for adult life. This educational system is sowing seeds for social and economic chaos one day. A number of Africans have increasingly been going overseas to acquire technical and university education. This is expensive, and most of these students face great difficulties like insufficient finance, new languages, adjusting to another life, and racial segregation in their host countries. Furthermore, since they go to practically every country in the world, they are exposed to different systems of education, economics and politics, which are hard to harmonize when the students return to their home lands and start working. Yet this is better than having no advanced education at all.

Modern change also brings cultural problems in Africa. More and more educated Africans are realizing that this change has alienated them from their traditional cultural roots without giving them a satisfactory substitute. This realization has produced an increasing search for African culture from the traditional solidarity, but making attempts to bring it into the picture of the modern world. This attempt to rediscover the cultural Zamani shows itself in various ways such as Négritude, African Personality and a revival of interest in traditional music, dance and folk stories. At the same time, African artists are consciously attempting to create art, drama, poetry, novels and music which are peculiarly African and yet set in the modern world.

It remains now to say something about the religious aspect of modern change in Africa. We shall devote a whole chapter to it, though obviously it deserves more, just as these other dimensions of the changing man of Africa could be treated more comprehensively than space allows us here.[1]

[1] The subject of modern changes in Africa has been given a great deal of attention and there is a vast amount of literature on it. All we can mention here are some of the books: G. Hunter *The New Societies of Tropical Africa* (Oxford 1962); S. & P. Ottenberg, eds., *Cultures and Societies of Africa* (New York 1960); P. C. Lloyd *Africa in Social Change* (London 1967); C. Achebe *Things fall apart* (London 1958); A. W. Southall & P. C. W. Gutkind *Townsmen in the making* (London 1956); M. Banton, ed., *Political systems and the distribution of power* (London 1965); M. J. Herskovits & M. Harwitz, eds., *Economic transition in Africa* (London 1964); R. Dumont *False Start in Africa* (E T London 1966); J. S. Coleman & C. C. Rosberg, eds., *Political parties and national integration in Tropical Africa* (Berkeley & Los Angeles 1964); G. C. Carter, ed., *Politics in Africa* (New York 1966); B. Davidson *Which way Africa?: the search for a new society* (London 1964); K. Nkrumah *Consciencism* (London 1964) and *Africa must unite* (London 1963); L. van den Berghe, ed., *Africa: social problems of change and conflict* (San Francisco 1965); T. Mboya *Freedom and after* (London 1963); A. A. Mazrui *Towards a Pax Africana* (London 1967) and *On heroes and uhuru worship* (London 1967); A. O. Odinga *Not yet uhuru* (London 1967); K. D. Kaunda *Zambia shall be free* (London 1962); J. E. Goldthorpe *An African élite* (Nairobi 1965); J. R. Rees, ed., *Africa: Social change and mental health* (New York 1959); UNESCO *Social implications of industrialisation and urbanisation in Africa south of the Sahara* (Paris 1956); A. Phillips, ed., *Survey of African marriage and family life* (London 1953); A. W. Southall, ed., *Social change in modern Africa* (Oxford/London 1961); W. H. Sangree *Age, Prayer and Politics in Tiriki, Kenya* (Oxford/London 1966); R. E. S. Tanner *Transition in African belief* (Maryknoll, New York 1967). Most of these works contain useful bibliographies.

19

CHRISTIANITY, ISLAM & OTHER RELIGIONS IN AFRICA

So far we have concentrated on a survey of traditional African religious and philosophical concepts and, in the last chapter, the radically changing situation in Africa. Our survey would, however, be incomplete without saying something about Christianity and Islam, both of which are indigenous in Africa and are deeply rooted in the history of our continent. These two faiths are making a claim on African peoples, particularly invading the areas of traditional religions since the nineteenth century. A great deal of literature exists and continues to increase rapidly on Christianity and Islam in Africa, and it is neither the scope nor the intention of this chapter to deal with the many facets of these and the other religions. I shall confine my observations to some of the main characteristics of both Christianity and Islam in their modern expansion in Africa and their encounter with the traditional background which we have presented in this book. In the next and final chapter I shall raise some of the issues precipitated by this religious milieu and modern change in which Africa finds itself at present. Obviously these issues are too complex to be presented adequately in a few pages and deserve a full and separate treatment. But raising them should at least constitute a way of concluding this introduction to African religions and philosophy.

[a] *Christianity in Africa*
Christianity in Africa is so old that it can rightly be described as an indigenous, traditional and African religion. Long before the start of Islam in the seventh century, Christianity was well established all over north Africa, Egypt, parts of the Sudan and Ethiopia. It was a dynamic form of Christianity, producing great scholars and theologians like Tertullian, Origen, Clement of Alexandria and Augustine. African Christianity made a great contribution to Christendom through scholarship, participation in Church councils, defence of the Faith, movements like monasticism, theology, translation and preservation of the Scriptures, martyrdom, the

famous Catechetical School of Alexandria, liturgy and even heresies and controversies.

Islam, paganism and political pressure eventually checked not only the expansion but also the very existence of African Christianity, until the ancient Church in Africa was greatly reduced, surviving only in Ethiopia and Egypt. In these countries Christianity has kept its identity both as a universal Faith and as an indigenous religion. While it is a minority body in Egypt, the Church in Ethiopia has always enjoyed a leading and privileged position. For many centuries the Church in Ethiopia was cut off from constant contact with the rest of Christendom, which partly helped it to acquire a uniquely African expression, but which also reduced its spirituality and left it with a conservatism extremely difficult to overcome in adjusting itself to modern times. Round churches, many saints, frequent fasts and monthly feasts, a big place given to the Blessed Virgin Mary, observance of many Jewish practices, order of deacons, priests and bishops, seven sacraments, a rich liturgy, a powerful but rarely well-educated clergy, and a Monophysite theology are the main characteristics of the Ethiopian Orthodox Church. It is truly 'African' in the sense that these features have evolved over many centuries and reflect a background that has not been imposed from outside. One element which illustrates this point is the fact that the Christians there 'believe in a whole host of evil spirits'. 'For protection against these and other spirits, everybody carries amulets, which are magical prayers and formulae written by priests on scrolls or in little booklets and carried in leather cases around the neck and arms, and Muslims will be found wearing these Christian amulets as well as others obtained from their own holy men'.[1] Exorcism is a major function of the clergy. Christianity in Ethiopia is the state religion, and imperial history and politics are intricately involved in Church history and life there.

Whereas the Church in Ethiopia survived Islamic invasions and retained its position of being the main religious force in the country, in Egypt, as in other parts of northern Africa, it was almost wiped out. What remains of this Coptic Church has a long tradition going back to the apostolic times and strongly believes that it was St Mark who founded it. The Arabs conquered Egypt in the mid-seventh century, and Islam established itself firmly in that land. The Church went through periods of calm and peace as well as persecution and pressure from Islam and Islamic government which reduced the number of Christians to about four per cent of the present population (compared to about fifty-five per cent in Ethiopia). The Coptic Church has many points of similarity with the Orthodox Church in Ethiopia and the two were for many centuries under the same Patriarch

[1] J. S. Trimingham *Islam in Ethiopia* (Oxford/London 1952), p. 28.

of Alexandria. The Christians use Arabic (Coptic having been forgotten though, like Latin, being found in liturgical books but with Arabic parallels), observe many days of fasting and reflect the type of Christianity practised in Ethiopia. Its clergy consists of a hierarchy of deacons, priests, bishops and the Patriarch.

These then are the two main areas in Africa today where Christianity is rightly 'African', indigenous and traditional, with its roots deeply established in the history and traditions of those who profess it there. In Nubia and other parts of the Sudan it lingered on for many centuries until fairly recently when it succumbed to opposing forces. The ancient Church in these two countries lacked a conscious missionary expansion, though there is ample evidence that Christianity extended further than the present-day Ethiopia and Egypt. The Roman Catholic Church through its priests from Portugal established Christian work along the west coast, the east coast and at the Congo estuary starting in the fifteenth century. Most of this work was aimed primarily at European traders, and only in a few places did it penetrate into the interior and reach a sizeable number of Africans. As Denmark, Holland and Britain expanded their maritime, commercial and colonial activities, their clergy also catered for the increasing number of Europeans.

But this presence of European Christianity hardly touched African peoples, though a few communities, especially at the Congo estuary, seem to have been converted. The real modern expansion of Christianity in Africa started with freed Christian slaves who began to return to western Africa towards the end of the eighteenth century. By the middle of the nineteenth century, Christianity had increasingly large followers along the coast from Sierra Leone to Nigeria. This was a spontaneous expansion, sometimes without even the constant help of the clergy. It also began to penetrate into the interior.

The next phase is represented by missionary activities, starting in the nineteenth century. That time, Britain, Europe and the United States increased their interest in Africa, as evidenced by the arrival of empire builders, philanthropists, explorers, missionaries, hunters, traders, journalists and others from these countries. For our purposes here we must note that Christian missionaries from Europe and America penetrated into the interior of Africa either shortly before, or simultaneously with colonial occupation. The image that Africans received, and to a great extent still hold, of Christianity, is very much coloured by colonial rule and all that was involved in it. We are still too close to that period to dissociate one from the other. A Gikuyu proverb summarizes this fact very well: 'There is no Roman Catholic priest and a European—both are the same!'

Another feature characteristic of mission Christianity is that virtually every sect and denomination in Europe, Britain and America, has started its work in Africa. The result is that Africa does not have a single image of Christianity but several. Different Church structures and traditions have been imported from overseas, and African Christians have inherited them without even understanding their meaning or background. These de-nominations endeavour far more to produce 'perfect' Anglicans, Roman Catholics, Lutherans, Baptists, Seventh Day Adventists, Quakers and so on than to make their converts good followers of Jesus Christ. Denomina-tionalism is one of the worst divisive elements in modern Africa; and some of the denominations have engaged in physical fighting, while today they compete for converts and in homiletical propaganda.

Christianity has expanded rapidly in the first half of this century, through the joint efforts of overseas missionaries and African converts. Schools became the nurseries of Christian congregations, and converts earned the name of 'Readers'. The same buildings were used as schools from Monday to Friday, and as churches on Saturday (for catechumen lessons) and Sunday (for worship). As we saw, it is Africans who have been to school that are most deeply affected by modern changes.

Another point is that the missionaries who began this modern phase of Christian expansion in Africa, together with their African helpers, were devout, sincere and dedicated men and women. But they were not theo-logians; some of them had little education, and most of the African evangelists and catechists were either illiterate or had only little formal learning. These workers were more concerned with practical evangelism, education and medical care, than with any academic or theological issues that might arise from the presence of Christianity in Africa. Mission Christianity was not from the start, prepared to face a serious encounter with either the traditional religions and philosophy or the modern changes taking place in Africa. The Church here now finds itself in the situation of trying to exist without a theology.

Perhaps the most serious, though not unique, phenomenon of Christianity in modern Africa is the growth of independent or separatist Churches. These are, on the average, small sects that have broken off from mission Churches and from one another. About five thousand of such sects are reported all over Africa. Nearly all of them originate from Anglican, Lutheran and Protestant Church background, with only two or three from the Roman Catholic Church and probably none from the Orthodox Church. At least one-fifth of the Christians in Africa belong to these independent Churches. Several causes are responsible for their proliferation and continuation. We can only enumerate them without going into further discussion, as there is a vast literature on this subject.[1] Whatever else might be said in general about the independent Church movements in Africa, they are, in their own ways, attempts by African peoples to 'indigenize' Christianity and to interpret and apply it in ways that, perhaps spontaneously, render Christianity both practical and meaningful to them.

The scandal of division in Protestant mission Churches has set an example to African converts. This is made worse by the fact that missionaries who brought and propagate divided Christianity, are (or were) proud of their denominational founders, traditions and brand of Christianity. This gives the impression that Church divisions do not matter. The logic, from the African point of view, is that since missionaries belong to so many denominations, why should Africans not have their own Churches, founded and led by fellow African Christians? After all, home-made produce is often cheaper than imported goods.

One of the things that sparks off separatism from mission Churches is the control that missionaries exercise over their African converts and congregations. This means that Europeans and Americans are seen as ruling Africans both in political and ecclesiastical matters. Where Africans rebelled against European rule, they were fined, imprisoned, deported or put to death. If they rebelled against missionary rule in the Church, at the worst they could only be excommunicated, and if so they could start their own churches free from missionary domination. In their own churches they would become masters. Thus missionary paternalism and over-domination have led many African Christians to seek local independence and sever their organizational ties with missionary-led churches. Furthermore, African nationalism cannot stop at the political stage; and as long as the Church is in foreign hands, although of brethren in Christ, Africans will rebel against that *status quo*, in quest for ecclesiastical freedom. It is generally in or through independent churches that such freedom is realized.

Connected with the last cause is the fact also that clashes of personality and leadership between missionaries and African Christians, as well as between some of the Africans themselves, have precipitated the breakaway of churches.

A fundamental cause which perhaps is not easily evident, is that mission Christianity has not penetrated sufficiently deep into African religiosity. We have shown how religious Africans are, and that in traditional life they do not know how to exist without religion. Mission Christianity has come to mean for many Africans simply a set of rules to be observed, promises to be expected in the next world, rhythmless hymns to be sung, rituals to be followed and a few other outward things. It is a Christianity

[1] See the literature mentioned at the end of this sub-section.

which is locked up six days a week, meeting only for two hours on Sundays and perhaps once during the week. It is a Christianity which is active in a church building. The rest of the week is empty. Africans who traditionally do not know religious vacuum, feel that they don't get enough religion from this type of Christianity, since it does not fill up their whole life and their understanding of the universe. Furthermore, African Christians often feel complete foreigners in mission churches. For example, much of formal Christianity is based on books but there are older Christians who do not read; the hymns are translated from European, English and American versions and are sung to foreign tunes which have little rhythm and without bodily movements like clapping the hands or twisting the loins as a religious expression. Worship in mission churches is simply dull for most Africans. Independent Churches are an attempt to find 'a place to feel at home',[1] not only in worship but in the whole profession and expression of Christian Faith. Beneath the umbrella of independent Churches, African Christians can freely shed their tears, voice their sorrows, present their spiritual and physical needs, respond to the world in which they live and empty their selves before God.

The sense of estrangement has been precipitated not only by mission Christianity but also by modern changes of which we spoke in the previous chapter. These changes have disturbed traditional solidarity, leaving an increasing number of African people with little or no foundation. The independent Church movements are attempts to establish new foundations which may perhaps form a substitute for the disintegrating traditional solidarity. The rather small groups of members of independent Churches provide psychological areas where uprooted men and women find some comfort, a sense of belonging together, a feeling of oneness, and a recognition of being wanted and accepted. It is relevant to note here the observations of Sundkler that in the Republic of South Africa, the policy of apartheid is one of the main causes of the many independent Churches there.[2]

I see also the question of time as a fundamental root cause for independent Churches. It is significant that nearly all of them have sprung from Anglican-Protestant Churchmanship which in Africa has encouraged individual conversions, reading the Bible (which in full or part is translated into many African languages) and a futuristic hope of an immediate arrival of paradise. Since, as we have seen, traditional concepts of time emphasize the two dimensions of Zamani and Sasa, with little or no concern for

[1] The phrase is used by F. B. Welbourn and B. A. Ogot in their study: *A place to feel at home* (Oxford/Nairobi 1966).
[2] B. G. M. Sundkler *Bantu Prophets in South Africa* (London 1948, 2nd edition 1961).

what lies beyond a few years, the hope of an immediate paradise must loom heavily upon African Christians. They need to see it realized 'immediately' for it to have a real meaning. They cannot conceive the possibility that the end of the world is an ultra-historical myth which cannot be fitted into the immediate conceptualization of individual men and women. They wait for this goal to come, but then they see their Christian relatives beginning to die. There is disappointment from the second generation of Christians onwards; and it is precisely at this moment that separatism begins to take place. Those who make up these sects see, perhaps unconsciously, at least a partial realization of their hope of an immediate arrival of heaven or paradise incarnated in their leader and the principles or features which characterize their new sect. It is in their new movement that a future dimension of time is most concretely realized and meangingful.

At this point we might also sketch some of the main characteristics of these African church movements, as depicting one form of Christianity in this continent. Most of them lay great emphasis on independence from missionary control. It is to be noted, however, that while five thousand of these movements have severed themselves from mission Churches, another one thousand are still attached to mission Churches. Independence is chiefly in terms of organization, leadership, decisions, finance and direction. In other matters they copy mission Churches, and some of them want to be linked with historical Churches both in Africa and outside.

Revelation and healing play important roles in the independent Churches. Some of them forbid their followers to use European medicines, teaching their members to depend entirely on God's power through prayer and healing services. Revelation comes through dreams and visions, and through meditation when leaders withdraw to solitary places for varying lengths of time. Emphasis is also laid on the place and work of the Holy Spirit, and during worship services people seek to be posessed by Him. When they become so possessed, they speak in other tongues.

The literal interpretation of the Bible is common among these Churches. It is to be remembered, however, that some of their leaders cannot even read, and the majority are poorly educated, so that none of them have been to theological colleges or seminaries. There is a tendency among some groups to stick almost exclusively to the Old Testament and its precepts. Some of the leaders are women, and these are fully accepted and respected by their followers.

Discipline varies widely. Some independent Churches are very strict, forbidding their members to eat pig meat, drink alcohol, have more than one wife, smoke, dance in European style, tease, beg and so on in addition to urging them to avoid major sins like adultery, murder, theft and laziness.

Others are lenient. Offenders are disciplined according to the seriousness of their offences: some are fined, others put on probation, and some are even excommunicated when they prove to be too notorious.

In their Church services the independent groups tend to follow the pattern of mission Churches from which they originally broke off. But they take more seriously items like singing and preaching, praying for the sick, exorcisms and the giving of money or other goods to support their leaders and programmes. Most of them, if not all, observe the Sacrament of Baptism, with some members being baptized as often as they wish; but the Holy Eucharist is given a relatively minor place, or left out altogether. The celebration of Christian festivals varies widely, and some groups do not observe Christmas as they consider it to be linked with pagan practices in Europe.

It is difficult to assess the effectiveness and standard of the independent Churches in Africa. Some of them have incorporated traditional practices which are clearly not Christian and which drown and reduce their Christianity to a very low level. Others seriously and sincerely maintain a high standard of Christian life, judged by the morality of their followers, their numerical expansions and their provision of an atmosphere in which the human problems of their members are satisfactorily given attention. Some of the groups, or their leaders, are subject to pressure and persecution from mission Churches and governments, both colonial and independent African. This form of persecution often drives the movements underground and encourages them to gain greater momentum. Whatever may be their causes and development, these independent Churches are an important feature of Christianity in Africa. It may, however, be overstating the case to consider them as constituting an 'African Reformation', as some writers tend to judge them.[1]

There is also what one may call *mission Christianity* in Africa, and on this we must say something, since it is these two types of Christianity which concern us most in the contact between Christianity and African traditional background. Some of its features have been alluded to as we considered what caused the independent Churches to form. Perhaps the strongest feature of mission Christianity is its organizational expansion. It bears not only the stigma of colonialism, foreignness, westernism and paternalism, but also the potentialities and strength of organization, institutionalism, links with the historical traditions of Christendom, financial resources, personnel from overseas, an increasing ecumenical concern, and a deliberate

[1] See the fascinating and most comprehensive single study of these African religious movements by D. B. Barrett *Schism and Renewal* (London/Nairobi 1968).

attempt to relate Christianity to modern problems in Africa. Naturally, some of the mission Churches are better off than others in these respects. Mission Christianity retains many anachronisms, some of which even its European and American origins have begun to shed, for instance its liturgy, hymns, articles of faith, doctrines, architecture, visual aids, form of worship, division of the Church and structure of the ministry.

African converts who profess mission Christianity are often eager to embrace as much of it as possible. But it is a Christianity deeply rooted in Euro-American culture. What Williamson has observed in his study of Christianity among the Akan, seems to summarize the situation in other African societies. He writes that missionary effort has been directed towards drawing converts away from traditional life towards what missionaries thought was the proper, civilized and Christian expression of the new Faith. 'The Akan became a Christian by cleaving to the new order introduced by the missionary rather than by working out his salvation within the traditional religious milieu. . . .' The result has been that 'what passes for Christianity, as so many understand it, is disbelief in gods and fetish, membership of the Church, payment of its dues, and obedience to its regulations'. He comes to the conclusion that mission Christianity 'has proved unable to sympathize with or relate its message spiritually to Akan spiritual outlook. Its impact is thereby dulled'. This form of Christianity called the Akan out of their traditional environment: it did not re-deem them within it.[1] These are the disturbing discoveries of one who worked in Ghana for twenty-six years as a missionary and who died there.

From eastern Africa a similar state of affairs is reported. Both Welbourn, himself serving as a 'missionary', chaplain, warden and lecturer in Uganda for nearly twenty years, and Ogot write that the Protestant and Roman Catholic forms of Christianity have meant separating Africans from their society and putting them on the side of Europeans—evidenced by taking European names, joining mission Churches, receiving literary education and hoping for promotion in the mission or government. This form of Christianity made no positive attempt 'to incorporate ancestors and witches, song and dance, into the Christian scheme'. The two writers conclude that 'in terms of the conversion of a people, the Church has failed, and it has failed, partly at least, because it has largely been unable to present to Africa more than a western image of its faith . . . (the Church) can make men at home in a nation, or in the world, only if they have first learnt to be at home

---

[1] S. G. Williamson *Akan Religion and the Christian Faith* (Accra 1965), p. 170 f. Cf., from a sociological approach, the study made on the Sukuma by R. E. S. Tanner *Transition in African belief* (Maryknoll, New York 1967)

in local terms'.[1] In another study, Welbourn argues that even what mission, aries have meant to bring to African converts has been given in part while withholding another part. Similarly Africans have received it in part while rejecting the other part. This is the main characteristic of what he calls 'missionary culture and the African response'.[2]

Another writer summarizing the Nigerian reactions to Christianity reaches the conclusion that 'Christianity has impressed many as being largely a social organization capable of worshipping God and mammon simultaneously, and demanding payment for the symbols of membership, the administration of the sacraments. Many conversions have been for material reasons. . . . Thus for many Christianity is quite superficial, and so has no real answers to life's personal difficulties, nor any real influence on the people's social problems.'[3] In the same study, another writer on the situation in the Cameroons observes that 'a Christian was defined as "one who has abandoned the customs" . . . Many traditions were forgotten and not replaced: the impression was that of a cultural vacuum which could, to a large extent, be attributed to evangelization. A bishop could say at this point: "We manufacture Christians but life takes them away from us." This amounts to saying that the cultural substratum was not converted.'[4]

Examples of this observation can be quoted from many parts of Africa. They clearly paint a picture of mission Christianity as one which has not gone deep into African traditional religiosity. Its greatest impact has been on a cultural level. In the industrial and urban situations, another study reaches a conclusion that 'for many African Christians the function of religion is understood in terms that are largely utilitarian and materialistic . . . Inevitably Christianity is closely associated with the concept of "civilization". . . . To be able to call oneself a church member, even though one's association is extremely tenuous, confers a certain status; and loss of status is often regarded as the greatest disadvantage in being suspended from a church or in changing from one denomination to another.'[5] Thus, in the villages as well as in the towns, one aspect of mission Christianity is that it is superficial,

[1] F. B. Welbourn & B. A. Ogot *A place to feel at home* (Oxford/London/Nairobi 1966), pp. 140, 143 f.

[2] F. B. Welbourn.*East African rebels* (London 1961), especially p. 169 f.

[3] J. B. Schuyler, S.J., 'Conceptions of Christianity in the context of Tropical Africa: Nigerian reactions to its advent', essay in *Christianity in Tropical Africa* ed. C. C. Baëta (London/Oxford 1968), p. 220.

[4] R. Bureau, 'Influence de la Christianisation sur les institutions traditionnelles des ethnies cotières du Cameroun', essay in *Christianity in Tropical Africa*, p. 180 f.

[5] J. V. Taylor & D. A. Lehmann *Christians of the Copperbelt* (London 1961), p. 272 f.

blended with western culture and materialism and still estranged to the depths of African societies.

It has, however, its other aspects which equally cannot be ignored. Already modern Africa has contributed, as did the ancient Church in Africa, its share of Christian martyrs, particularly among the Baganda and Gikuyu, as well as isolated individuals all over Africa who have found a Faith for which they died or are prepared to die if need be. There is also the East African Revival which, starting in Rwanda in the early nineteen thirties, or late twenties according to some writers, has spread over large sections of the Church and community in eastern and central Africa. Its chief contribution to the Church is that members of the Revival have continued within their denominations rather than forming a separate sect, and show a warm sense of Christian fellowship and brotherhood which immediately cuts across and ignores denominational, tribal, racial and other differences.

Mission Christianity is also consciously endeavouring to meet challenges and exercise a ministry aimed at answering at least some of the needs of modern Africa. We have already seen how missionaries pioneered formal education in Africa. They and African Christians have continued to make outstanding contributions to primary and secondary education, even when schools have increasingly been taken over, organizationally and financially, by independent African governments. The Church also makes its contribution in the medical field, again pioneering this service in Africa and continuing to run hospitals and dispensaries, as well as supplying Christian doctors and nurses to work in Church, private or government establishments. In the field of literature there are Christian publications of books, tracts and magazines, as well as religious and educational programmes put on the radio by Church bodies, through arrangement with national radio stations and the two main Church radio stations in Liberia and Ethiopia. There is also, but less overtly, the level of Christian ethics and morality which permeates the lives of many men and women in Africa who have been exposed to Christian teaching. Many of the leaders of independent African nations other than Muslim states are, to a certain degree, the product of Christian education; and nearly all of them have professed the Faith at one time or another. It is not hard to see signs of Christian ideals in their service for Africa; and some of them play an active part in the Church's life as laymen. There is, also, the large number of African catechists, evangelists, laymen, Church elders, nuns, deacons, pastors, ministers, priests, bishops, archbishops and cardinals, who make up the formal contingent of the Church's officials. These at least symbolize the concrete and serious presence of Christianity in Africa, and its acceptance by African peoples.

Many of the Churches in Africa are awakening to the social needs, especially in urban areas and those raised by modern changes. Both study programmes and practical steps are under way in different areas to assess the meaning of Christianity in Africa and how best it can serve, and not only convert, African peoples. The All-Africa Conference of Churches founded in 1963 has many responsibilities under its various organizational divisions. There are Christian Councils in almost twenty African countries. These, together with the All-Africa Conference of Churches, endeavour to deal not only with ecumenical questions but with the family, education, youth work, literature, refugees, urban life and evangelism, in our modern situations. There have been conferences like the one at which the All-Africa Conference of Churches was formed at Kampala, the Christian Youth Assembly at Nairobi (December 1962 to January 1963), the first Consultation of African Theologians at Ibadan (January 1966), and the Vatican Council II at Rome (1962–5) at which seventy African clerics took part. Study seminars are organized from time to time, for instance the Ecumenical Centre at Mindolo (Zambia), the Seventh International African Seminar at the University of Ghana held in April 1965 to study 'Christianity in Tropical Africa', and the Workshop in religious research held at Nairobi (December 1967 to January 1968). In many of these gatherings, representatives come from Roman Catholic, Anglican, Lutheran and other major Church traditions. In addition to these collective attempts to articulate or assess Christianity in Africa, there are local Church communities and individuals engaged in research, discussion, voluntary or paid work, clubs, prison work, social and welfare work, translation of books, pastoral ministry, witness of the Faith and so on. Some of these individuals and communities are expressing their Christian Faith in extremely difficult conditions, like those in the apartheid-stricken southern Africa, those living in colonial territories, those working among refugees and in areas of civil conflicts.[1]

I see mission Christianity, therefore, as making a real contribution and progress in Africa, in spite of criticisms that could rightly be laid against it.

Such then is Christianity in Africa, with its divisions and developments, achievements and challenges, responses and successes, failures and drawbacks, superficiality and foreignness, estrangement and engagement, strength and opportunities, cultural involvement and undermining, without an indigenous theology and yet with a strong team of local and overseas workers. It is a force to be reckoned with, both in the villages and in the towns, in

[1] See an interesting discussion on the response of the Church in Africa, by T. A. Beetham *Christianity and the new Africa* (London 1967) especially, pp. 91–149. Another approach is by A. Hastings *Church and Mission in Modern Africa* (London 1967).

schools and in slums, in government and in business. Its adherents may be branded 'Made in Anglicanism', 'Made in Lutheranism', 'Made in Roman Catholicism', 'Made in Orthodoxy' or 'Made in Zion African Church of the True God' (independent), or any one of the multitudes of mission bodies and independent groups. But all these are the living testimonies of the presence of Christianity in Africa, whether or not they live up to the ideals of their Faith. The independent Church movements seem to get closer to African traditional aspirations and religiosity than does mission Christianity. But the latter seems better equipped and concerned to move with the changing times, despite signs of lagging and conservatism. In any case, the two forms of Christianity need each other, are perhaps necessary for the moment, and a humble co-operation between them would obviously enhance the impact of Christianity in Africa. The ancient Church in Egypt and Ethiopia has its strength and weaknesses, and can both contribute to and learn from the two newer forms of Christianity. In recent years there has been a growing move to establish a closer link between the ancient and the new forms of Christianity, but previously there were frictions from the doctrines and methods used by foreign missionaries. Statistically Lesotho is the most Christian country in Africa, followed by the Republic of South Africa, Gabon, South-West Africa, Ethiopia, Congo Kinshasa, Congo Brazzaville, Uganda and so on. Historically, Egypt and Ethiopia come first. In relating modern Christianity to the local and traditional situation, probably Madagascar, Ghana, Nigeria and Kenya might be on the lead, though this is only an impression. Christianity is a flexible way of life, and in Africa it is being made to fit into almost anything that different groups wish. Supporters of apartheid in southern Africa use Christianity to justify their practice of segregation and oppression against African and coloured peoples; some independent Church groups are simultaneously, if not primarily, political or nationalistic movements; some missionaries have taught us that Africans are the cursed descendants of Noah; many African Christians in southern Africa search for a so-called 'Black Christ'. These and many others are the uses to which Christianity in Africa has been and is being put, whether or not they can be theologically justified. Whatever Christianity means to individuals and communities in Africa, it holds great prospects in this continent, contrary to the view of some writers who see a grim future for it. On the whole Africans are disposed towards accepting and assimilating Christianity, and its three forms may perhaps constitute a genuine search for a breakthrough and stability of Christianity in the total African milieu.[1]

[1] There is a great deal of literature of varying quality on Christianity in Africa, although little that deals with its encounter with traditional religions and

[b] *Islam in Africa*[1]

Like Christianity, Islam in Africa can be described as 'indigenous', 'traditional' and 'African'. Within a century after the death of the prophet Mohammad in A.D. 632, Islam had swept across the whole of northern Africa and engulfed the Horn of Africa stretching southwards along the east coast. Where it encountered Christianity there was a prolonged battle

philosophy. Of general works we could mention, in addition to those cited above, the following: C. G. Baëta *Prophetism in Ghana* (London 1962); E. B. Idowu *Towards an indigenous Church* (Oxford/London 1965); R. Oliver *The missionary factor in East Africa* (London, 2nd edition 1965); J. B. Webster *The African Churches among the Yoruba 1888–1922* (Oxford 1965); V. E. W. Hayward, ed., *African independent Church movements* (London 1963); C. P. Groves *The planting of Christianity in Africa* (London, 4 vols. 1948–58); R. Ledogar, ed., *Katigondo: Presenting the Christian message to Africa* (London 1965); S. Neill, *A history of Christian missions* (London 1964); J. Mullin *The Catholic Church in modern Africa* (London 1965); D. A. Payne, ed., *African independence and Christian freedom* (Oxford/London 1965); H. W. Turner *Profile through preaching* (London 1965) and *History of an African independent Church* (Oxford/London, 2 vols. 1967); J. F. Faupel *African holocaust: the story of the Uganda martyrs* (London 1962); H. Bürkle, ed., *Theologie und Kirche in Afrika* (Stuttgart 1968); B. Gutmann *Afrikaner-Europäer in nächstenschaftlicher Entsprechung* (Stuttgart 1966); E. Benz, ed., *Messianische Kirchen, Sekten und Bewegungen im heutigen Afrika* (Leiden 1965); H. J. Margull *Aufbruch zur Zukunft: Chiliastisch-messianische Bewegungen in Afrika und Südostasien* (Gütersloh 1962); P. Beyerhaus, ed., *Begegnung mit messianischen Bewegungen in Afrika* (Weltmission Heute, Heft 33/34, Stuttgart 1967); J. V. Taylor *The growth of the Church in Buganda* (London 1958) and *The Primal Vision* (London 1963); E. G. Parrinder *Religion in an African city* (London 1953); B. G. M. Sundkler *The Christian ministry in Africa* (London 1960); M. Brandel-Syrier *Black woman in search of God* (London 1962); there are also reports of study seminars and conferences like *Christian Responsibility in an independent Nigeria* (Lagos 1962), *All-Africa seminar on the Christian home and family life* (held at Mindolo, Zambia, 1963, published in Geneva 1963), *The Church in changing Africa* (conference held at Ibadan 1958, published in New York 1958), *Catholic Education in the service of Africa* (conference held at Kinshasa, published at Brazzaville 1966), *Christian education in Africa* (conference held at Salisbury, published in London 1963); reports of African Christian students in Europe who hold annual seminars to discuss various topics; and periodicals like *Africa Theological Journal* (Makumira, Usa River, Tanzania), *Ministry* (Morija, Lesotho), *Flambeau* (Yaoundé, Cameroon), *African ecclesiastical review* (Katigondo, Masaka, Uganda), *Dini na Mila: Revealed religion and custom* (Makerere, Kampala, Uganda), *The Bulletin of the Society for African Church History* (Ibadan, Nigeria/Aberdeen, Scotland), *Ghana Bulletin of Theology* (Legon, Accra, Ghana), *Sierra Leone Bulletin of religion* (Freetown, Sierra Leone), *The international review of missions* (Geneva/London), and a number of local periodicals in English, French and African languages.

[1] I am very grateful to my Islamist colleague, Mr Said Hamdun, for reading this sub-section and making helpful corrections.

until it firmly established itself everywhere except in Ethiopia, though it was not until the late thirteenth or early fourteenth century that the Christians lost effective power in Egypt.[1] But even in Ethiopia, pockets of Muslim communities remained in the lowlands.

Through the trade routes and commercial transactions between west African states and the Muslim north, Islam began to penetrate in a southerly direction into west African societies, especially those on the fringe of the Sahara, from as early as the ninth century. In the Sudan region, Islam moved from the east to the west through Arab traders and conquerors who finally captured the capital of Christian Nubia near Khartoum, opening the way for Islam eventually to replace Christianity. Even then it made little southward penetration, reaching only as far as about ten degrees north.

It is probable that Islam arrived on the east coast of Africa in the seventh century, where already there were well-established Arab settlements and a flourishing trade. But apart from what is now the Somali Republic, Islam was confined to the coast and only began to move inland in the late eighteenth and nineteenth centuries when Arab trade in ivory and slaves also went further into the interior. On the coast Islam has deep roots, especially centred in Zanzibar, Mombasa, Kilwa, Lamu and other towns and islands. The Portuguese who arrived there at the end of the fifteenth century clashed with the Arabs on several occasions in the sixteenth and seventeenth centuries. At the same time African peoples seem also to have made life difficult, with the result that many of these coastal centres of Islamic culture were reduced to ruins. By the time the Arab and Swahili traders revived their position and began to advance into the interior in the nineteenth century, reaching the now Uganda, Malawi, Zambia and Congo, Europe was also beginning its penetration of the continent. The new political, economic and religious competition checked the speed and distance of the penetration of Islam before many African peoples in the interior could become converted to it.

The position as it now stands is that Africa is predominantly Muslim in the areas approximately north of the tenth parallel. These stretch eastwards from Senegal up to but excluding most of Ethiopia, the whole of Somalia and the east coast as far south as Mozambique, with comparatively small clusters of Muslims in the fringing regions, Uganda and Tanzania. Over forty per cent of the population of Senegal, Mauritania, Gambia, Niger, Chad, Northern Nigeria and the Sudan is Muslim, the percentage rising above ninety in the Muslim States of Africa. The total number of Muslims in Africa is estimated at between seventy and one hundred million, compared to an estimated figure of between fifty and seventy million Christians.

[1] Some would date this statement slightly earlier.

A.R.P.—9

Whatever may be the accurate count, Islam has obviously the largest single following of the different religious traditions in Africa.

Muslims have their factions, though the number is nothing like what Christians might boast. Most of these factions originated from outside of Africa, but were soon imported here; and there are also local Muslim sects which originated here and have an 'African' slant to them. For example the dynamic Ahmadiyyah sect was founded in the late nineteenth century by Ghulam Ahmad (born in India in 1835, died in 1908), and has already split within its short history. It is extremely active in western Africa and, more recently, in east Africa, though keeping its headquarters still in India. This sect is making a prodigious growth both numerically and in its spirit of reforming or attacking Islamic orthodoxy. But, as for any deep impact of the Ahmadiyyah Islam upon Africans, one writer observes that in west Africa 'the Movement is sometimes presented by its adherents as a missionary force extending the fold of Islam there. In fact, Ahmadiyyah contributes almost nothing to the conversion of the Pagan world. There are only a few Ahmadis here and there who were born Pagan, and most of these were first converted to Islam, then to Ahmadiyyah. Ahmadiyyah draws almost all its membership from orthodox Islam and from Christianity.'[1]

There is the Shi'a sect, an early division in Islam, being represented in Africa chiefly among immigrant Muslims of Indo-Pakistan origin. They are found chiefly on the eastern seaboard. The Sunni is another but later sect, being the most dominant group of nearly all the indigenous Africa Muslims. The Ismailis constitute the liberal wing of the Shi'a schism. In Africa they are mainly immigrants and their descendants from India and Pakistan, with a few African converts. Though small in number, this sect, under the direction of its earthly and spiritual head, the Aga Khan, is financially well off, very active in social services, especially education and medicine, and politically involved in the countries where its communities are living. The Indian and African members of this sect, however, do not have much or serious contact, though their schools are open to everybody regardless of race or creed.

There are other Islamic sects and movements into which we need not enter, as our immediate concern here is with Islam and its relation with African traditional religions. We shall first take some concrete examples of different regions and societies where Islam has established itself among African peoples. Then we shall draw some conclusions.

Islam came to the Wolof of Senegambia in the eleventh century, though the most widespread conversion took place only in the late nineteenth century.

[1] H. J. Fisher *Ahmadiyyah: a study in contemporary Islam on the West African coast* (Oxford/London 1963), p. 185.

Wolof Muslims adhere to the prescribed tenets of fasting, observing the five daily rites, keeping festivals, giving alms and making a pilgrimage. The last of these is made not to Mecca but to a local mosque at Baol, which is the centre of the Mouridism sect founded by an African Muslim around 1886. From the age of seven, Wolof boys are given Islamic teaching in which they learn prayers, memorize passages from the Koran and write Arabic. But Muslims still retain many concepts and practices from the traditional African background. For example, it is feared that praising a child might cause evil or harm to come upon it; and after giving it a name ceremoniously the child is hidden from the public in order to avoid harm from an evil eye. Divination combines both traditional methods and the use of Islamic almanacs. People greatly fear witchcraft. Their belief in the existence and working of the spirits and the living-dead is strong, incor-porating from Islam 'the devil (seitane) who makes people mad and who may steal a child and substitute a deformed or abnormal infant'. The spirits are divided into good, evil and mischievous ones—a division which obviously derives from Muslim teaching. 'In some areas, while the men are Muslims, the women have retained an earlier cult of spirit possession.'

The Wolof still observe traditional rites though sometimes mixing them with Islamic ideas. For example, during drought the men pray in the mosque for rain, but if it does not come their 'women perform a rain dance, dressed up in rags, or in men's clothes, and wearing ornaments made from rubbish. They then go out of the village in procession, the children gather branches of trees or shrubs, and on their return beat the grave of the founder of the village with their branches.' Marriages follow a mixture of both traditional and Islamic procedures, but funeral ceremonies tend to be more Islamic. The overall situation of Islam among the Wolof is summed up by Gamble that 'in spite of the impact of Islam, there is still a much deeper layer of pagan belief and observance among the Wolof . . . Men and women are loaded with amulets, round the waist, neck, arms, legs, both for pro-tection against all sorts of possible evils, and to help them achieve certain desires. Most frequently these contain a paper on which a religious teacher has written a passage from the Koran, or a diagram from a book on Arabic mysticism, which is then enveloped in paper, glued down and covered with leather, but sometimes they enclose a piece of bone or wood, a powder, or an animal claw.'[1] These are typical African, rather than Islamic, traits which we have encountered in many traditional societies.

Conversion to Islam among the Nupe of northern Nigeria started with their king Jibiri around 1770, though some of his predecessors bear Islamic names. By the end of that century Islam was well entrenched in the country.

[1] D. P. Gamble *The Wolof of Senegambia* (London 1957), pp. 64–72.

Yet, Islam has 'reached only a portion of the population and in that it often remained superficial', providing the people with new ceremonies in addition to, but not in place of, their traditional ones. In the early phase conversion was motivated by prestige, since the ruling class was Muslim, promise of protection from slavery, and patronage of the nobility to the peasants and craftsmen. Nupe Muslims do not follow strict Islamic traditions. For example, they observe only two of the five pillars of Islam, daily prayers and fasting, omitting the giving of alms, making a pilgrimage and confessing faith in God—the last of these is not significant to them since, like all African peoples, in their traditional religion they acknowledge one supreme God. They recite their regular or prescribed prayers in Arabic, but say their special or personal prayers in the Nupe language. They keep three of the seven major Muslim festivals, these being the New Year (Muharram), Id el Fitr (at the end of the fast month, Ramadhan) and Id el Azha or Id el Kibir (the great feast in the pilgrimage month which ends the year). It is reported that the Nupe lack interest in the historical development and expansion of Islam, and are confused on Muslim hagiology and cosmology. Muslim women are never veiled, and while they are not allowed in the mosques, the girls from upper class society learn the Koran. Muslim teachers and religious leaders, of whom there are many, have little or no learning at all, apart from being able to recite a few chapters from the Koran.

Marriage rules, especially concerning marriage gifts and easy divorce, circumcision, divination, kinship rites and prohibition to eat pigs, are points of similarity, and therefore immediate contact, between Nupe and Islamic traditions, so that here Islam fits well into the Nupe traditional thinking and practice. Whereas in some countries Muslims practise sororate marriage, this is completely forbidden among the Nupe who, however, strictly adhere to their traditions concerning levirate marriages. In matters of inheritance, there is a complete divergence so that Nupe practices prevail against Islamic law. This has prevented the fragmentation of the land which would ensue if Islamic rules were followed. Nadel concludes that since Islam came to the Nupe as a religion of conquerors and the ruling class, 'what counts is, first and foremost, the assimilation to upper-class culture, and only secondarily the deliverance from unbelief'. This is 'social' rather than 'religious' conversion, providing a point of reference for a sense of pride and superiority; but not touching the deep levels of what is considered to matter most in life. Mystic and ecstatic observances of Islam are obviously unknown.[1]

In his study of Islam in the Sudan, Trimingham reaches the conclusion

[1] S. F. Nadel *Nupe Religion* (1954), pp. 232–58.

that south of ten degrees, Africans are almost completely uninfluenced by Islam. North of that latitude, 'Islam spreads only through the breakdown of the extreme clan system'. But even then it is not revolutionary, since 'it does not conquer the animist soul because it accommodates itself to the animist spirit-life. The result of this accommodating character of Islam is that it has not helped the higher religious development of the African.' A great deal of interest is shown only in Islamic eschatological hopes of a future life of material bliss. Otherwise Islam 'causes little internal dis-turbance to the natural man and his social life and customs, for Islam takes over the central features of paganism through syncretism. The pagan customs are retained whilst the spirit of the custom is lost.'[1] Another writer describing Islam among the Nuba in this region, reaches a similar con-clusion, that 'Islam has not made very serious inroads into Nuba social structure yet'; and even where it goes back several centuries, 'the clan structure and many traditional elements remain'. On the cultural level, like the naming ceremonies, initiation rites and marriage procedures, traditional 'elements become partially Islamized, or are remodelled, or continue as before but with an Islamic cachet.'[2]

Taking our brief survey further east we look at the situation of Islam in Ethiopia, Eritrea and Somalia. Trimingham sees two strains of Islamic culture: that of the nomads and that of the town-village dwellers. Of the first type he writes that there is 'practically no Islamic influence upon pagans'. Where Islam has been assimilated the process goes through three stages. In the first phase, the people merely adopt 'superficially certain elements of the material culture of Muslims', such as dress, ornaments and food habits. In the second phase, 'actual religious elements of Islamic culture' are assimilated, especially the recognition or awareness of an impersonal power resident in and working through persons or things. This recognition is, as we have seen, found in African traditional societies. As such it is not peculiarly Islamic; but it forms a point of contact. The third phase is 'characterized by a genuine belief in the efficacy of Islamic sanctions, and involves actual change in customs and habitual conduct'. This is the point when adherents use places for public worship, recite their ritual prayers, keep the month of fasting (Ramadhan) and observe a number of Islamic taboos. Yet, as Trimingham goes on to observe, even at this stage 'the old beliefs

---

[1] J. S. Trimingham *Islam in the Sudan* (Oxford/London 1949), p. 248 f. Mr Hamdun points out to me that the line of ten degrees is 'extremely doubtful', as a delineation of the extent of Islam in the Sudan.

[2] R. C. Stevenson ,'Some aspects of the spread of Islam in the Nuba mountains (Kordofan Province, Republic of the Sudan)', essay in I. M. Lewis, ed., *Islam in Tropical Africa* (Oxford/London 1966), p. 226 f.

do not lose their validity to the African Muslim's life; on the contrary, certain beliefs gain a renewed vitality by acquiring an Islamic orientation'. He gives the examples of continued respect for the living-dead, belief about spirits associated with natural objects, the use of charms and fear of witch-craft, all of which acquire a new vitality. Islamic law clashes with traditional customary law.[1]

We might here cite a concrete case from the Boran of northern Kenya who form part of the peoples in this general region. It is observed that among them the main or apparent influence of Islamic culture is chiefly in material objects like ornament and weapons. Beyond that, the herding of livestock, which is their prime occupation, is scarcely affected by Islam. Family institutions are still basically traditional, though the rites of passage and other personal or family rites are a mixture of traditional and Islamic concepts and practices. Divorce is said to be non-existent, contrary to, and in spite of Islamic practice elsewhere; and inheritance rules remain deeply traditional and untouched by Islamic teaching. The conclusion is that only the Boran who have been defeated by the Somalis and isolated, are Islamized, along the lines of the Somali brand of the religion, whereas those who still live in the traditional roots have rejected Islam or hardly taken notice of it.[2]

On the east coast where Islam arrived in the seventh century, it has since made a strong footing. Among the Africans it is chiefly the Swahili who have nearly all embraced it, in addition to other 'African' peoples like the Arabs and Shirazi of this region. Among the traditional societies, the cult of the departed has been embedded within Islamic thought. But it is to be observed that some of the dead include Muslim 'holy men', people make pilgrimages to their shrines and some have mosques erected in their memory. 'Less pious people are also venerated, though in a way more suggestive of ancestor worship.' The living-dead are 'appeased' through a 'special formula'; offerings and sacrifices of white chickens are given to them; and they reveal themselves to their human relatives in dreams. Islamic influence enters in where spirits are thought to live in the nether world until the day of resurrection. Divination and geomancy are basically traditional, but astrology is borrowed from Islamic background. The Muslims make sacrifices and give alms to obtain success or ward off evil. They wear amulets for fishing success, and as protection for cattle and homesteads. Some of their charms contain Koranic verses. Magic, sorcery and witchcraft have their hold upon the people; and in addition to treating human com-

[1] J. S. Trimingham *Islam in Ethiopia* (Oxford/London 1952), p. 270 f.
[2] P. T. W. Baxter, 'Acceptance and rejection of Islam among the Boran of the Northern Frontier District of Kenya', essay in *Islam in Tropical Africa*, p. 248 f.

plaints, the medicine-men perform exorcisms, sometimes using Koranic quotations as magical formulae.[1] These last observations indicate a clear mingling of Islamic ideas with those of traditional religions.

It seems as if further inland on the east of Africa, Islam has not made much, if any, radical religious impact. For example, it is reported that Islam and its culture are incompatible with Gogo religion and social structure.[2] Muslims are still in the minority among the Baganda and Basoga, although Islam came to Uganda before the middle of the nineteenth century. In recent years, however, these Muslims have increasingly asserted their right to exist as a religious community, they hold leading positions as butchers and taxi drivers, and every year more and more of them fly to Mecca for pilgrimage. African Muslim communities in eastern Africa are found chiefly in towns and thinly in the surrounding rural areas. The Ahmadiyyah movement which began its missionary activities in Mombasa in 1934, has spread inland as far as Kampala in Uganda, with headquarters in Nairobi, Kenya (though originally in Tabora, Tanzania). It is winning an African following especially through schools, and the translation of the Koran into Swahili, Luganda, Kikamba and Gikuyu, a local paper (in English, Swahili and Luganda), pamphlets, missionary work and attack on Christianity and other brands of Islam.

These examples of the encounter between Islam and traditional African societies give us a clear indication of what the situation is like. The position is well summarized by Lewis in his introduction to *Islam in Tropical Africa*.[3] We shall refer to his main points and add a few more which arise from a survey of Islam in traditional African societies. On the political scene Lewis observes that African central rulers have been more inclined to receive elements of Islam and Muslim culture and organization which can be applied to reinforce and extend their established authority. They also add Muslim regalia and ritual elements to their royal rituals. The so-called 'holy war' (*jihad*) has been waged from time to time, with religious zeal and conviction. A good example of this is the Mahdi movement in the Sudan which was led by Muhammad Ahmad ibn Abdullah (1844–85).

[1] A. H. J. Prins *The Swahili-speaking peoples of Zanzibar and the East African coast* (London 1961), p. 113 f.; see also J. S. Trimingham *Islam in East Africa* (Oxford 1964); L. P. Harries *Islam in East Africa* (London 1954).
[2] P. J. A. Rigby, 'Sociological factors in the contact of the Gogo of central Tanzania with Islam', essay in *Islam in Tropical Africa*, pp. 268–95, especially p. 288 f.
[3] I. M. Lewis, ed., *Islam in Tropical Africa* (Oxford/London 1966), pp. 20–91. This book contains a collection of studies presented and discussed at the 5th International African Seminar held at Ahmadu Bello University, Zaria (Nigeria), in January 1964.

This Muslim jihad, though a bloody one, had a legal system and fine organization.

When it comes to the contact between Islamic law (*sharia*) and traditional African practice the situation is complex. In matters where the two systems correspond, such as concerning illicit sexual relations, theft and restitution, they uphold and strengthen each other. But in matters of the inheritance of land, livestock, property and family, traditional procedures are followed more often than Islamic policy. Lewis observes, however, that with the changing economic conditions which now favour individual enterprise, those aspects of Islamic law which stress economic independence of the individual, are readily seized upon. For example, there is a wide difference between Somali nomads and their urbanized kin: the latter relinquish the traditional obligations which kinship prescribes, and justify their behaviour in a strict interpretation of the *sharia*. Even the position of women is radically changed in a few cases to suit the Islamic law as, for example, among the Hausa whose women traditionally do the farming but abandon this occupation, leaving it to their husbands when these are converted.

There is also a great diversity between Islamic and traditional patterns of marriage ideas and practices. A major source of conflict is in matrilineal societies when the husband is a Muslim while the wife is not, as this puts their children in an extremely difficult position. If the wife also embraces Islam, they both switch from the traditional to the Islamic rules of inheritance and affiliation of children. The Islamic marriage gift (*mahr* or *ṣadāq*) is easily and usually adopted into the traditional African systems of exchanging marriage gifts. The only slight change here is the tendency to give the larger share to the bride and not so much to her relatives, for example among the Somali, Fulani and Hausa. In situations calling for inheriting the widow, levirate and sororate marriage arrangements which are disapproved by the Islamic law, 'traditional marital replacement rights are retained'. Widows who, however, wish to sever connections with families of their dead husbands, may do so by applying to Muslim courts. In either case, these widows are obliged to keep the Islamic period of continence (*idda*) before remarrying: this being also a point of similarity with some traditional practices.[1]

Concerning purely religious beliefs and rituals, there are elements of both contact and divergence between Islam and traditional religions. As we have seen, the concept of God is universally acknowledged by African peoples. This is the key doctrine of Islam, as taught and recited in its shortest and most fundamental creed: 'There is but one God, Allah, and Muhammad is his prophet'. Here then, there is no need for Islam to stress

[1] Lewis, pp. 45–57.

the oneness of God, as far as traditional religions are concerned. The position of Muhammad, however, seems difficult to relate to traditional concepts, just as Africans find it impossible to relate Jesus Christ to anything from their traditional concepts and histories.

The Koran mentions many spiritual beings, including angels, jinns and devils, which are easily assimilated into the traditional religious milieu, and 'Islam does not ask its new adherents to abandon their accustomed confidence in all their mystical forces'. Traditional heroes and forefathers, some of whom are in positions of intermediaries, fit into the Muslim concept and recognition of saints. Traditional cults of the living-dead are accommodated and 'persist in a Muslim guise', so that the departed forefathers take on the role of intercessors in Islam, between man and God. For example, 'Somali clan and lineage ancestors are in effect canonized Muslim saints and classed among the saints of Islam generally'. Among the Songhay some traditional heroes are assimilated as angels and others as jinns (ordinary spirits). But since orthodox Islam gives little consideration to spirits connected with natural phenomena and objects, African Muslims tend to have a negative attitude towards them, condemning and incorporating them into the world of non-Muslim jinns. Spirit-possession cults tend to survive in local situations, as among the Swahili, Songhay and west African secret-societies. The ideal Muslim attitude disapproves of them, but African Muslims, especially women, revert to these cults to seek relief from afflictions that are not remedied by Islam.

Another area of ready agreement between Islam and traditional concepts and practices is in matters of divination and magic. Islamic practice encourages divination and the use of good magic; it also recognizes the efficacy of sorcery and witchcraft but condemns them. Islam 'approves and sanctions magical procedures which are directed towards such legitimate ends as the cure of disease, the prevention and curtailment of misfortune, and the assurance of prosperity and success', even if in the background the people retain hope in God. Some Muslims use divination to impress and win converts; but they or others justify the use of witchcraft and sorcery only when employed to protect the rights of people and trap wrongdoers.[1]

Islamic rituals and prayers connected with birth, marriage and burial are fairly readily assimilated into existing traditional ideas and practices. In some cases, Islam introduces new innovations as, for example, circumcision among the Baganda and Basoga Muslims whereas by tradition these societies do not circumcise their boys. It is reported also that Islam has introduced or reinforced clitoridectomy and infibulation among peoples of the Sudan, Ethiopia and Somalia. In funeral matters, the Islamic practice

[1] Lewis, pp. 58-65.

of washing the corpse is widespread, as are also the incensing of the body, the use of a bier and the orientation of the grave towards Mecca. Points of similarity emerge in ritual mourning which includes washing, cleansing, seclusion and purification. But Islamic eschatology takes over from traditional beliefs in the continuation of life after death so that paradise, with a predominantly materialistic bliss, now becomes the destiny of the Muslim faithful, while hell is reserved for the infidels. In traditional religions there is no such division regarding the fate of the departed; and apart from a few vague exceptions, the 'good' and 'bad' continue to live in the same next world, without receiving either rewards or punishment.

Concerning the Islamic year, Lewis observes that 'the Muslim lunar calendar is everywhere adopted with Islam; and tends to displace other systems of time-reckoning, except where these are very firmly entrenched in an unchanging seasonal cycle of economic interests'. Arabic names for months are adopted, and usually given vernacular translations 'expressive of the social and religious content of the month in question'. For example, among the Mende Muslims, Ramadhan is known as the 'moon of deprivation'. Of the chief Muslim feasts, Id el Fitr at the end of Ramadhan is celebrated most widely and most jubilantly.

The giving of alms to the poor is said to be regarded as a kind of insurance policy, especially for a blissful reward in the hereafter or as a means of obtaining favour from God. Alms are considered synonymous with sacrifices. Pilgrimage (*haj*) to Mecca is expensive and difficult to fulfil, but nevertheless popular among African Muslims. Each year plane-loads of pilgrims are reported in many countries across tropical-equatorial Africa; and Muslims who cannot afford to get to Mecca make their pilgrimage to local shrines.[1]

Islam in Africa seems to have benefited considerably from the arrival and presence of colonial rule. Lewis tells us that the new powers did not seek to disestablish Islam nor even succeed in restraining its spread except in the Congo. 'The overall effect of colonization was rather generally conducive to a new expansion of the faith', and the colonial rulers even 'helped their Muslim subjects to build mosques and schools, and often directly subsidized pilgrimage to Mecca or facilitated its organization'. In direct ways, colonial rule also created conditions which facilitated the spread of Islam, such as increased trade, new towns and cities, immigration of Muslims from India and Pakistan to Africa, and quick and more peaceful means of travel. The net result of all this was that within half a century, the number of Muslims in tropical Africa doubled. 'The total effect of the pax colonica, as much involuntary as intended, was to promote

[1] Lewis, pp. 67–74.

an unprecedented expansion of Islam', so that 'in half a century of European colonization Islam progressed more widely and more profoundly than in ten centuries of pre-colonial history'.[1] Hamdun, in a personal communication, says, however, that he is 'beginning to doubt more and more the claim that colonial rule helped in the spread of Islam in tropical Africa: if anything the contrary is the case'. Whichever of these two views is more correct, one thing is unquestionable, namely that there is a clear coincidence between colonial rule and the geographical and numerical expansion of Islam in tropical Africa, and African independence has not halted the increase of Islamic influence.

Such then is the picture of Islam in traditional African societies. On the purely religious front, it has done little to add to or alter radically African religiosity, except in the (in any case external) ritual side where Islamic practices have on the whole been introduced anew or to strengthen existing procedures. Deeper issues of great value remain basically traditional, even if they might gain an Islamic guise. In a few exceptions Islam brings about change, such as when matrilineal families are converted and adopt a patrilineal pattern of family life and relationship. Modern change seems, however, to show itself where individual interests are involved, especially when people leave the country and establish homes in the towns. In this case, new economic and educational conditions make individuals claim justification from the Koran in order to protect their personal interests at the expense of traditional practice.

Unlike Christianity, Islam in tropical Africa does not seem to be officially concerned with attempting to meet the social challenges of modern change. There are, obviously, exceptions, and the Ismailis are a clear example of a Muslim group which endeavours in more ways than simply giving alms, to attend to the wider needs of modern society. The Muslim states of Saharan and northern Africa have their social programmes. But Islamic communities in traditional African societies that have come into existence over the last one hundred years or so, rely more on the traditional methods of help from corporate and kinship solidarity, than on anything specifically Islamic. Conservatism and legalism in tropical African Islam seem to pose the greatest danger to the future of Islam there. Hamdun tells me also that secularism is another and serious danger to Islam especially in western Africa.

No doubt conversion to Islam will continue from followers of both traditional religions and Christianity. But deep religious elements of Islam which, as we have seen, have hardly been embraced, are unlikely to find root in African societies that embrace Islam. Points of similarity between

[1] Lewis, pp. 76–82.

Islam and traditional religions in belief and ritual, paradoxically facilitate quick or smooth conversions but hinder the process and manifestation of a deep or radical Islam. It means, then, that traditional religions accommodate Islam and Islam accommodates them: and this is the current trend, according to the few studies made on the subject. This lack of 'radicality' in the encounter between the two religious systems, gives one the impression that in traditional societies of tropical and southern Africa, Islam has a future only as a veneer of religious experience and social concern. In this region, furthermore, Muslim leaders are poorly educated and not always open to either the understanding or assimilation of modern issues. Their knowledge of the Koran and Islamic law is not questioned, but if they are to present and relate their faith to the modern world, that knowledge alone will not get them very far. Unless they make Islam relevant to the issues, problems and situations in which younger generations increasingly find themselves, Islam will become rusty in their hands. Ironically, there are more Christian scholars of Islamics in tropical Africa than there are Muslim ones, although the number of the latter is steadily increasing. If Islam is to survive and contribute seriously towards providing direction and guidance to modern Africa's search for new values, foundations and identities, it surely must not only convert people but be ready itself to be converted by modern man, that is to be 'modernized' and 'updated'. If it fails to be so stretched, or if it is too rigid and legalistic to be bent into the changing shape of our world, then Islam will remain a statistical giant but a religious anachronism in the new Africa.[1]

[c] *Other religious traditions in Africa*

African Judaism is reported in at least two areas. The oldest community is made up of the Falasha Jews who form part of the Agao peoples of Ethiopia. For many centuries these African peoples have observed a combination of Old Testament Judaism and Christian elements. They do not know Hebrew,

[1] There is an enormous literature on Islam in tropical Africa, in Arabic and European languages. Little, however, has been done on the encounter between Islam and traditional religions. In addition to works already cited in this subsection, we may mention a few more: J. N. D. Anderson *Islamic Law in Africa* (London 1954); J. H. Greenberg *The influence of Islam on a Sudanese religion* (New York 1946); A. Gouilly *L'Islam dans l'Afrique Occidentale Français* (Paris 1952); I. M. Lewis *Marriage and the family in northern Somaliland* (Kampala 1962); V. Monteil *L'Islam Noire* (Paris 1964); J. S. Trimingham *Islam in West Africa* (London 1959), and *A history of Islam in West Africa* (Oxford/London 1962); J. C. Froelich *Les Musulmans d'Afrique noire* (Paris 1962); R. Reusch *Der Islam in Ostafrika* (Leipzig 1931), and journals like: *The Muslim World* (Hartford) and *Islamic Culture* (Hyderabad).

but their priests use the Old Testament (Jewish Bible) and the Apocrypha as their scriptures in the Ge'ez language. Adherents of this religious system strictly observe purification laws and the keeping of the Sabbath (Saturday) as prescribed in the Bible. They also circumcise boys and perform clitori-dectomy on the girls. As a community, they are very skilful and industrious. The Falasha number about fifty thousand. It is impressive that they have kept their community and religious solidarity in spite of living in a tradi-tionally Christian country, and can still be identified as an indigenous representative of Judaism in Africa. Evidently they do not proselytize.[1]

Another community of African Judaism is found in eastern Uganda. Members of this congregation speak of themselves as *Bayudaya* (Jews, Of-Judah). This is a unique community in that it came into existence at the start of this century, and is made up of Africans from the local inhabitants around Mbale. It was started by an African, Semei Kakungulu, who was a leading personality in the history of Uganda at the turn of the century. Kakungulu was a Christian in the Anglican Church, took part in the 'religious wars' and later helped the British to set up an administrative footing in eastern Uganda. Disappointed that neither the Church nor the British gave him a high position, he joined an independent Church, the Bamalaki group, founded around 1913, which was spreading extremely rapidly and whose expansion he aided in eastern Uganda. He was a keen reader of the Bible, and it was this that drew him towards Judaism, and away from even the independent Church. In 1919 he was circumcised, together with his first son; and he circumcised later sons on the eighth day after birth, giving them Jewish names. Yet, he kept Christian traditions like taking the Holy Eucharist (Communion), baptizing the children and saying the Lord's Prayer but still calling himself a Jew from 1919 onwards. In 1926 he met a Jewish trader, Yusuf, from whom he learnt Jewish rites and customs and the basic principles of Judaism. This contact with Yusuf brought about the most radical change in Kakungulu's concept and practice of Judaism, so that he stopped acknowledging Jesus Christ and the New Testament or following any more Christian practices, and began to observe Saturday as the holy Sabbath. He adopted Jewish dress like those worn by Yusuf; and with his followers, began to celebrate Jewish festivals and use Hebrew names for the months. Before he died two years later, he met two more Jews who further instructed and encouraged him and his followers (who by then numbered about two thousand) in Judaism.

[1] E. Ullendorf, 'Hebraic-Jewish elements in Abyssinian (Monophysite) Christianity', in the *Journal of Semitic Studies*, I (1956), pp. 216–56; J. S. Trimingham *Islam in Ethiopia* (London|Oxford 1952), p. 19 f.; E. Dammann *Die Religionen Afrikas* (1963), p. 248 f.

The *Abayudaya* (plural) later decreased in numbers, but recently the movement has been gaining momentum both numerically and in its contact with world Judaism. They have a main synagogue at their centre, and a few smaller ones in the surrounding villages. Their children are forced by circumstances to go to Christian schools; and the followers have no strong leadership, nor are they properly instructed in Judaism. They now pray to the north facing Jerusalem, under the leadership of Samson Israeli. Oded who has made a study of this community, describes them as follows: 'Samson Israeli surprised me as being himself a great expert in the Bible. He knew exactly which chapters and verses of the Bible dealt with the different Mizwoth. He knew a great part of the Old Testament in the Luganda language by heart. He also knew much of the details of the ritual laws. All members of the congregation fast on Yom Kippur and celebrate all festivals mentioned in the Old Testament. Nobody eats bread on Pessah. They had heard very little about Israel. However, they were very interested in Jerusalem and asked whether the temple was already built anew. At the end they brought forward some requests. They want to receive from Israel a Sefer Torah, Talliitim and Mezuzoth and, if possible, a book of instruction in English which would enable them to know the main Mizwoth and laws of Judaism. They would translate it into the Luganda language. They also requested that one of their young students, a graduate of a high school, speaking English, should travel to Israel and be instructed in Judaism. On returning to Uganda, he would be their Rabbi and could help them to keep the Jewish Mizwoth according to the Jewish Law.' Through Oded this community of African Judaism has been put in touch with the World Union for the Propagation of Judaism, which has sent in financial assistance. Between his first and last visits among them (in 1962 and 1966 respectively), their numbers increased from three hundred and fifty to five hundred, some of the converts coming from among the Christians and Muslims. That they are missionary oriented is reflected on the heading of their letters which reads: THE PROPAGATION OF JUDAISM IN UGANDA. Evidently they are concerned about keeping up to the standards of Judaism. 'They would like to be as good and genuine Jews as any other orthodox Jews in the world. With the connection thus recently established with the World Union they hope to reach their goal.'[1]

[1] A. Oded, 'A congregation of African Jews in the heart of Uganda', in *Dini na Mila* (Kampala), Vol. III, No. 1, 1968, pp. 7 f. This is the only study of the community, and I am indebted to the article for my information. An abbreviated statement was published by the same writer in the *Jewish Chronicle*. A fuller study is being written by A. Oded and M. Twaddle called *Abayudaya Community of eastern Uganda* (due to be published in 1969 or 1970).

I have no further information on this community, especially concerning the encounter between Judaism and traditional religious beliefs and practices. It is possible that points of contact, similarity and interest, especially of a ritual nature, may be many which, therefore, would encourage the profession of Judaism among these African followers. If, however, the interest tends to orient the followers only towards the Zamani profession of Judaism, without any attempt to come to terms with our modern world, this form of African Judaism might remain no more than a religious relic, perhaps suitable as a tourist curiosity but without a real impact even on the religious aspirations of its members.

It is to be remembered also that Judaism established itself in northern and north-eastern Africa centuries before Christianity was born. Alexandria gained eminence as a leading seat for Judaism and Jewish learning. Further-more, religious and social life of the ancient Jews is similar to that of many African societies whose religious thought we have surveyed here. Some of the obvious differences lie in the fact that Judaism developed a prophetic movement and a messianic expectation, neither of which has any parallels in African traditional background. The ancient Jews were more 'African' than 'Asian' in many respects, and were it not for the Suez Canal they might be less associated with Asia and more with Africa. In modern times we find Jewish congregations in southern Africa, Kenya and other areas, occupying themselves with commercial transactions. Jews of Egypt and north African states have deep historical roots in Africa; and formerly there were conversions among African peoples, like the Saharan Berbers, to Judaism. But the current tension between Jews and Arabs has created an exodus of Jews from these north African countries. The Jews, conscious of their identity as a people, and perhaps also through the persecution that they have endured throughout their wandering and dispersion, tend to keep to themselves, so that they make little or no direct impact upon the cultural life of those around them. This should not overlook the fact that they have produced great men in all fields of culture and learning with no mean impact on the world scene. But on the level of the religious side of Judaism, they could make an even greater impact and win more following from the Gentiles, than has so far happened. Yet, perhaps it is this religious self seclusion which has ensured and encouraged their survival as a people and as a religious solidarity which in turn strengthens their economic prosperity and cultural identity.

Hinduism is the chief religion of India. In Africa it is found almost exclusively among Indian communities who are reported in western, southern and eastern Africa. For several thousands of years India was in commercial contact with the east coast of Africa, but permament settlement of Indian peoples in Africa only started with the period of colonial rule. Hinduism is a complete way of life, with its own religious and philospohical precepts, social and economic structures which govern the life of the Hindus. The caste system has been exported to Africa, though the number of the untouchables is extremely small. Hindu communities observe rites of birth, marriage and death, the corpse being disposed of by means of cremation; and they follow a religious philosophy which accepts and recognizes many divinities and a host of other beliefs. As in all other religious systems, there are orthodox adherents as well as Hindus who know very little about the religious and philosophical elements of Hinduism. There are also sects within the major body of Hinduism, and others which branched off some centuries or millennia ago.

In eastern Africa, at least, Hindu temples 'welcome' all the different divinities; and anybody, regardless of caste, creed or race, may go into them to worship or meditate, provided he takes off his shoes before entering the temples. But much of Hindu worship goes on in the homes, most of which contain shrines where family members may make offerings and say their prayers. At these shrines there are idols, statues and pictures of divinities and holy men, some even include pictures of Jesus Christ. Holy men from India visit Hindu communities in Africa, which helps to renew and strengthen their cults and community life. *Diwali* is the most important Hindu festival observed in Africa, marking the triumph of good over evil, which is symbolized by the use of lights. Some Hindus claim the Nile to be one of their sacred rivers; they also regard as sacred the 'Mountains of the Moon' (in Uganda-Congo) and Mount Meru (in Tanzania). The Nile is a local substitute for the Ganges, though one does not get the impression that in practice this is actually so. In any case, the ancient belief that Hindu divinities should not cross the seas and that temples should not be built in alien lands has been abandoned since these have now crossed the Indian ocean, some never to return to India. Young Hindus are less rigid in following the caste system or avoiding the rules of pollution; most of them eat meat including beef, and keep only a vague belief in the omniscient God, without wanting to get deeply involved in Hindu philosophy. It is on the question of marriage, however, that they must bow to the wishes and traditions of their parents, this involving, among other things, arrange' ment of marriage by the parents and within the same caste.

To my knowledge only about a dozen Africans in eastern Africa have embraced Hinduism. A person has to be born and made a Hindu to fit into the social structure and assimilate the body of Hindu beliefs and practices. This is what makes it virtually impossible for outsiders to be 'converted' to Hinduism. Most of these African 'converts' are women who have married Indians; and information available to me indicates that they have become accepted in the social circles and life of their husbands. I know also of two African men, one in Mbale (Uganda) and the other in Nakuru (Kenya) who have become Hindus, initially through being employees of Indians. They have learnt Gujarati, are accepted in Indian homes, keep shrines and observe Hindu festivals. When I asked one of my informants to which caste these African Hindus belonged, she replied, 'They have no caste; we shall have to create a new caste for them if more Africans become Hindus!' On the question of whether these men would be allowed to marry Indian women, she replied, 'I don't think so, I doubt it!' These statements indicate that African Hindus are not fully integrated into the Hindu communities, even if they may be accepted on certain levels. But there is no study made of African Hindus, and we cannot here present their case adequately.[1]

Among the peoples of Indian origin in Africa there are other but smaller religious communities, including the *Sikhs, Jains* and *Parsees*, in addition to Christians and numerous Muslims. Sikhism and Jainism are distant branches of Hinduism; but the Parsees follow a form of Zoroastrianism from Persia. The Sikhs in east Africa are keen to make permanent homes there and to contribute to the efforts of nation building in the countries of their new homeland.[2] I have heard of only one African who has joined the Sikh community, and has taken their name and adopted their form of dress. I do not know of African Jains or Parsees. These and the Hindu communities are self-contained, shut-up social entities but with a religious philosophy which qualifies them to be spoken of as 'religious communities', whether or not the individuals live up to, or even know, the basic religious precepts and practices of their communities. They have no 'Faith' to proclaim like Christians and Muslims, and so they have no missionary expansion; their life and religion are one, rather like what we have seen concerning African traditional religions. Their main impact and im-

---

[1] I am not aware of any literature on Hinduism in Africa. My information was gathered from personal contacts with Indians in east Africa. Since Indian communities are deeply involved in commercial enterprises in Africa, economic literature covers this aspect of their life. Literature on Hinduism in general is, of course, vast, including works like: A. C. Bouquet *Hinduism* (London 1948); J. N. Farquhar *Crown of Hinduism* (Oxford/Madras 1915), S. Radhakrishnan *A Hindu view of life* (London 1933); *The Bhagavadgita*—various editions and commentaries.

[2] See the Sikh statements in support of new nations of Africa in: N. Singh, ed., *Sikhs of Kenya say Harambee* (Nairobi 1963); *Opening ceremony of new Sikh temple* (Siri Guru Singh Sabha, Nairobi 1963).

pression upon African life is economic rather than religious or even cultural. Africans know these Indian communities in terms of their being made up of shopkeepers, traders, businessmen, builders, craftsmen, clerks, chemists and doctors.[1]

The *Baha'i Faith* is the latest addition to world religions, having been officially proclaimed in 1863 by Baha'u'llah (born 1817 in Persia, died 1892).[2] Its world headquarters are in Haifa (Israel), but for Africa they are in Kampala (Uganda) where there is also the chief House of Worship (Temple) in Africa. The teachings of Baha'u'llah first reached Africa through his son and heir in 1911 when he made a teaching tour of Egypt and western countries. In tropical and southern Africa, however, the Baha'i Faith arrived much later: only in 1951 did it come to Kenya and Uganda. But its adherents claim that there are many followers throughout Africa. Its main attraction lies in the message of unity of all mankind, religions, faiths, prophets and sects. It preaches brotherhood, justice, equal rights and privileges, and harmony with science; condemns prejudice, slavery, asceticism, monasticism and priesthood; and advocates compulsory education, elimination of poverty, monogamy and obedience to one's government. All these are noble aims, but on the African scene one does not see signs of their being put into concrete and practical application. At the main Baha'i temple in Kampala only a few people gather for worship. There is no, or only little, sense of 'Baha'i community' consciousness among the African followers of this Faith. This generous readiness to unite everybody is in itself the undermining factor in the Baha'i Faith: it lacks a genuine mythical goal in which the individual can feel that he matters. Furthermore, such a grand unity does not give sufficient place and attention to immediate personal and individual problems, even if it aims at improving the wider society of mankind. Lack of ceremonies and a formal order of leadership in the Baha'i Faith are an alien element in the African tradition. Altogether it seems as if Africans in the towns may readily pay attention

[1] An interesting general survey of the one-third million Asians of Indo-Pakistani origin in east Africa is: D. P. Ghai, ed., *Portrait of a minority* (Oxford/Nairobi 1965).

[2] In 1863 Baha'u'llah announced to his followers that he was the 'Chosen of God, the Promised One of all the prophets'. A few years later he publicly announced his mission, won more followers—known thereafter as Baha'is; and then began to send out a series of letters (or summons) to the kings and rulers of the world. The Feast of Ridvan commemorates Baha'u'llah's Declaration of 21 April to 3 May 1863; there are other feasts connected with his life and associates. Fasting is kept for nineteen days prior to the spring equinox. I do not know how much fasting and feasting are observed by African Baha'is.

to the teachings and ideals of Baha'ism, and some are accepting them as sensible ideals in life, but I do not get the impression that this Faith goes very deep nor has it yet begun to reach village communities. Followers of the Baha'i Faith are keen missionaries and propagators of their teaching, using literature in African and European languages as their main weapon. In Uganda they even have two schools attended by children from Christian, Muslim and traditional African homes. No doubt this is a good nursery for the Faith, and will help increase its followers.[1]

Such then is the big religious cauldron in Africa. Many of the tropical African universities, like those of Sierra Leone, Legon (Ghana), Ibadan (Nigeria), Louvanium (Congo), Makerere (Uganda), Nairobi (Kenya), Haile Selassie I (Ethiopia) and the University of Lesotho, Botswana and Swaziland (Lesotho), have incorporated the study of religion and philosophy into their body of courses. This recognizes the great importance of religion as the backbone of African life, and the study of which is necessary for the understanding of both traditional and modern Africa. It rightly deserves a place in the university curriculum, where it may and should be scrutinized as an academic discipline. In these university faculties or departments where Christianity, Islam, African traditional religions and other religious systems are studied, no attempt is made to present one to the exclusion or disparagement of the others, or to try to formulate out of the many one single religious system for the whole of Africa. Each is presented and studied on its own academic merits, strength and weakness. In this way, students of religion are learning something from each system; and each religious tradition, in its own way, is shedding new light on the understanding of one or more of the other traditions. But religion in Africa is not the monopoly of academics: it is a reality moving in the stream of current history of African peoples, as much as it is in the traditions which they have inherited, even if they are relinquishing some of those traditions. I maintain that religion, whatever may be or may have been its confessional and external manifestations, has a central place in traditional Africa and a crucial role to play in modern Africa. It is to this question that we shall now devote the concluding chapter in our survey of African religions and philosophy.

[1] Literature on Baha'ism is on the increase though to my knowledge no study of African Baha'is has been done. Here are a few books: J. E. Esslemony *Baha'u'llah and the new era* (Wilmette, Illinois rev. 1950); Baha'i Publishing Trust *Gleanings from the writings of Baha'u'llah* (London 1949), and *The Baha'i revelation* (London 1955); *Prayers and meditations of Baha'u'llah*, compiled and translated by S. Effendi (London 1957); Abdu'l-Baha *Foundations of world unity* (Wilmette 1945).

20
THE SEARCH
FOR NEW VALUES
IDENTITY & SECURITY

[a] *The religious claim*

In our survey we have shown that in their traditional life African peoples are deeply religious. It is religion, more than anything else, which colours their understanding of the universe and their empirical participation in that universe, making life a profoundly religious phenomenon. To be is to be religious in a religious universe. That is the philosophical understanding behind African myths, customs, traditions, beliefs, morals, actions and social relationships. Up to a point in history this traditional religious attitude maintained an almost absolute monopoly over African concepts and experiences of life.

On the religious front, three systems have been and continue to be most dominant in Africa: Christianity, Islam and Traditional Religions. Christianity has been in Africa for two thousand years and, at one time, claimed up to one-half of the continent geographically. By creed and sword, Islam has won the allegiance of one-third of the population of Africa. Judaism, Hinduism, Sikhism and Baha'ism are other, though numerically small, traditions that add to the present religious turbulence in Africa. Societies whose traditional religions we have here studied, have increasingly been exposed to these other religions and new ideologies. Traditional religions must yield more and more their hold in shaping people's values, identities and meaning in life. They have been undermined but not over-thrown. Modern change is clearly evident almost everywhere and at least on the conscious level. But the subconscious depths of African societies still exert a great influence upon individuals and communities, even if they are no longer the only final source of reference and identity. With the undermining of traditional solidarity has come the search for new values, identity and security which, for both the individual and his community, were satisfactorily supplied or assured by the deeply religious background which we have sketched here. This search seems, however, to be con-centrated more in the religious sphere than in the ideological areas. Ideologies are new and can be grasped only by an extremely small minority of African élite. Religion on the other hand reaches everyone from universities to schools, from palaces to villages, from the old to the young. I maintain that African peoples experience modern changes as a religious phenomenon, and respond to it in search of a stability which is fundamentally coloured by a religious yearning or outlook.

Numerically, the main and most influential contestants are African Traditional Religions, Islam and Christianity. The last two are missionary oriented: they aim at winning converts from those who are outside their allegiance. They expand by pushing traditional religions on to the defensive, expecting them to keep silence, listen to their sermons, copy their examples, yield, give up, disappear and be forgotten. Both Christianity and Islam employ all kinds of methods to reduce traditional religions to ashes and historical anachronisms. That is the basic assumption of Muslims and Christians in Africa. But a careful scrutiny of the religious situation shows clearly that in their encounter with traditional religions, Christianity and Islam have made only an astonishingly shallow penetration in converting the whole man of Africa, with all his historical-cultural roots, social dimensions, self-consciousness and expectations. Obviously there are exceptions, but this statement can be documented from many parts of tropical Africa, as our examples in the previous chapter have shown. So then, this leaves us with an extremely complex religious picture in Africa, out of which several current religious experiences can be discerned. All of these are shaping people's awareness of the universe and their participation in life.

[i] *Conversion* is the most overt and dynamic religious event or process. In Africa it is taking place the whole time in the following direction:

from	*to*
African Traditional Religions	Christianity, Islam, Baha'ism
Christianity	Islam, Baha'ism
Islam	Christianity, Baha'ism

But full conversion is never a point in history: it is always a process affecting the inner man and his total environment. It may take several generations to reach maturity in a given community. But even then it requires a continual renewal if the conversion is to become relevant at every given moment in history. Religions at the receiving end of conversion may have to be more patient with African societies.

[ii] *Re-conversion* is a clear sign of Africa's attempt to find a religious

accommodation which fits her and into which she can fit. Most of this experience takes place within the world religions, thus:

from	*to*
Christianity	Islam, Baha'ism, Judaism
Islam	Christianity, Baha'ism, Judaism
Baha'ism	Christianity, Islam
Christian sect	Christian sect
Muslim sect	Muslim sect

The main area of religious activity here is in the change from one Christian or Muslim sect to another, and as we have seen Africa excels in these sects.

(iii) *Apostasy or 'backsliding'* is another dynamic movement on the religious arena in Africa. It begins to function seriously in the second and subsequent generations of Christians and Muslims, and when crises of life or other demands come upon the individual. It is mainly an individual, rather than community, movement, from Christianity and Islam to traditional religions and secularism. Apostasy poses the greatest danger to these two world religions; and Christians constantly complain about it, but Muslims either tolerate it or do not wish to face its reality. Those who withdraw in this manner, are pointing to the fact that they have found neither a meaningful identity nor sufficient security in Christianity or Islam. They therefore 'return' to the foundations of their forefathers, or, in fewer cases, turn to secularism as a cover for their search. In a sense, apostasy is a judgment upon the universal religions which recruit so many followers only to let them desert them dissatisfied and disappointed.

(iv) *A religious concubinage* is taking place involving partners from almost every tradition. But more often it is between Christianity and traditional religions, Christianity and Islam, and Islam and traditional religions. Baha'ism more or less preaches this religious convenience, and a number of African people are adopting it. Increasingly one hears Africans saying 'All religions are the same': but are they? This type of religiosity has no depth or shape, and often it is religious laziness which drives people to it. This position gives a feeling of social security, and provides an escape from facing the full demands of the religions involved in that kind of concubinage.

(v) *Acculturation* is a more serious element in the search for religious accommodation in Africa. We have seen that in their invasion of traditional African societies, Christianity and Islam have come loaded with western and Islamic culture and institutions. But they did not land on empty ground: they found African peoples deeply immersed in their own traditions and cultures. The encounter between the two sides has resulted in the process of acculturation, producing almost what L. S. Senghor calls 'half-caste cultures'. We noted the process of partial giving and partial receiving, partial witholding and partial rejection, at the encounter between western Christianity and African traditional societies. Islamic cultures and institutions have not gone through exactly the same process, but we saw that touching the points of deep values African Muslims have either rejected entirely what in Islam seems to threaten their security, or accepted it only in part and with modifications especially to suit personal interests. The overall picture here is one of unofficial 'baptizing' of African cultural traditions into the Christian or Muslim way of life, as judged and interpreted by Africans themselves. The same process also involves the reverse: bending Christianity and Islam to fit into the cultural setting of African peoples. We saw clear examples of this phenomenon in the African independent Church movements, and in the case studies we cited of the presence of Islam in traditional societies. Schools have been the nurseries of these half-caste cultures; and the educated Africans are the living symbols of material and religious acculturation. Acculturation is the most sweeping phenomenon in Africa and everybody is affected by it. But what may have started initially as a religious phenomenon is moving more and more into the secular realm; yet most people take with them their corpus of religious beliefs, attitudes and activities into that new realm whether it is religious or otherwise. Acculturation seems like a healthy, if inevitable, cross-fertilization not only of culture but of religion which, whether in Africa, Europe or Arabia, gave birth to the cultures that have now come into contact in Africa.

(vi) Finally there is the rather small island of *Dereligionization* characterized by the claims of Secularism, Communism and Capitalism. In their extreme positions, these -isms despise, reject and even oppose religion. They are movements away from religion, and it is this which makes them relevant to any discussion on religion. Africa has not many converts, yet, to these '-ismic irreligions'. But it is not unaware of them. Traditional religions make no formal resistance; Islam is rather indifferent to them; but Christianity, particularly in its mission form, is resistant and even aggressive towards them. I see no immediate communist revolution in Africa, though socialist principles may well be profitably tried in different countries of Africa. Secularism has an undermining effect upon religion, but it may well be to the good of religion if the latter injects religious principles into secular life instead of waging a war against secularism. Need these two be at enmity, or is it not the duty of religion to justify and exert its presence in the secular world? Capitalism is anti-religious when it exploits man to such a degree that he becomes simply a tool or a robot and loses his humanity. If capitalism reduces man to the material level only, then it has contradicted the religious image of man which, in all traditions, depicts man as both physical and spiritual. Here then, African traditional religions challenge the modern world with their successful evolution of a system in which 'secular', 'socialist', 'communist' and 'capitalist' elements were all har-moniously joined together into a religious whole. In their sober moments, Christianity and Islam could each also present a theological case which accommodates all these elements into their views of God, man and the universe. There is no reason why these ʌisms should be allowed to slip out of the hands of the religious man of Africa and become 'enemies' of religion when he has the historical and theological resources to use them as tools. It makes a lot of difference whether he uses them or they use him.

[b] *The ideological claim*

In addition to the religious turbulence in Africa, there are also ideological movements attempting to define and answer the question of 'Who am I?' We have shown that traditional religions and philosophy for many genera-tions have been the ultimate point of reference in one's identity, foundations and security. But in chapter eighteen we briefly sketched the picture of the changing situation in Africa today. The traditional foundations of African peoples have been shaken, and everyone, whether in the village or in the slum, whether in politics or commerce, whether Christian, Muslim or follower of traditional religions, has now been exposed to the demands of the new situation. He must find his identity and security in a forest of dilemmas. Some of these are religious, as we have sketched them above; but others are purely ideological. The latter we can only mention briefly.

[i] *The ecumenical movement* in Christian circles tries, among other things, to heal the tragedy of division and create an understanding among members of the different Christian traditions. In the African context, the ecumenical movement will mean that Christians here, as elsewhere in the world, must shed off their identity as Lutherans, Roman Catholics, Anglicans, Ortho-dox, or members of independent Churches, in order to put on the full image of united Christendom. The ecumenical movement is destructive, not by annihilating the traditions of the many Church denominations, but by surpassing them so that they are no longer the ceiling of ecclesiastical identity but only the tutors in the direction of the full Christian Man. That is the theological goal of the current Christian movement towards unity. African Christians are becoming increasingly aware of the movement, and are probably more ready to plunge into its practical demands than are overseas Churches which have institutionalized their historical differences. At the same time there are Christian groups in Africa that are passionately

opposed to ecumenism; and in any case, the average Christian does not understand what it is all about.

The real danger to the ecumenical movement in Africa is not the ignorance of what it is all about, nor is it the opposition waged by a few sects. The dilemma lies in attaining a Church unity which then becomes a theological stagnation for those who subscribe or belong to it. If unity is to become a point of reference for Christians in Africa, then that unity must be converted to a means of attaining identity with Christ. This is the point which makes nonsense of all other identities in that it claims the whole person and the whole cosmos as the property of Christ. Then, deriving from this Christocentric identity, the person is free to become whatever else he wishes, to be identified as an African, nationalist, neutralist, trade unionist or even beggar. That is the height to which Christianity in Africa must soar. Without this theological vision the ecumenical ideology can only hope to receive and render lip service in Africa, however much we may move in the direction of Christian unity as an identification movement and ideology in the Church.

[ii] *Négritude* is a philosophical and cultural ideology, and foreign in origin. The phrase was first coined by the poet Aimé Césaire from the West Indies. It has since been elevated and given its philosophical content by another great poet, Léopold Sédar Senghor. Positively and negatively Senghor defines in various ways the concept of Négritude. 'Négritude . . . is not the defence of a skin or a colour . . . Négritude is the awareness, defence and development of African cultural values. Négritude is a myth . . . It is the awareness by a particular social group of people of its own situation in the world, and the expression of it by means of the concrete image.' He sees it in relation to political life: 'It is democracy quickened by the sense of communion and brotherhood between men'; and in the cultural context, Négritude 'is more deeply, in works of art, which are a people's most authentic expression of itself, it is sense of image and rhythm, sense of symbol and beauty'. With a rather emotional outburst, Senghor tells us that 'Négritude, then, is a part of Africanity. It is made of human warmth'; and he urges Africans to opt for Négritude and subscribe to it: 'We ought not to be neutral towards Négritude. We must be for Négritude, with lucid passion . . .' Accordingly, only in so doing can African peoples make a contribution to the growth of what he calls Africanity and beyond that point to the construction of 'the civilization of the universal'. For 'Négritude is the sum total of the values of the civilization of the African world. It is not racialism, it is culture.'[1]

[1] L. S. Senghor *Prose and Poetry* (selected and translated by J. Reed & C. Wake, Oxford/London 1965), p. 96 f.

Certainly these declarations by the chief apostle of Négritude have rescued the ideology from its original position of defence, attack and inspiration, to a new one which makes it an instrument of construction not only for Africa but for his visionary 'civilization of the universal'. But one wonders what makes Négritude a uniquely African trait since the things that Senghor says about it can be said about the peoples of other continents. The concept of Négritude with its many forms and definitions, is an ideological point of reference for the few élite particularly from the French-speaking countries of west Africa. Nobody in the villages under-stands or subscribes to its philosophical expressions. It is a myth of the Zamani when it means 'the sum total of the values of the civilization of the African world'. It is also a myth of the future when it aims at contributing to the macro-mythical 'civilization of the universal'. Négritude is, then, a comfortable exercise for the élite who wants, seeks and finds it when he looks at the African Zamani and hopes for an African future. It has neither dogmas nor taboos, neither feast days nor ceremonies. You only need to imagine it and you will be able to identify it; be lucid about it and you will be able to see it. Négritude is because it is said to be. It is identified with Negro Africans; but do Africans identify themselves with Négritude? That is the dilemma of Négritude as an ideology.

[iii] *African Personality* is another current ideology in the search for new values, foundations and identity. Almost every champion of African Personality has his own image and definition of it. The place where it seems to fit best is in the realm of the arts. Of this, Mphahlele tells us that an African artist dealing with 'African themes, rhythms and idiom . . . cannot but express an African personality. There need be no mystique about it.' And yet, 'the artist must keep searching for this African Person-ality. He can't help doing so because, after all, it is really a search for his own personality, for the truth about himself. But if he thinks of the African Personality as a battle-cry, it's bound to throw him into a stance, an attitude, and his art will suffer.' That is Mphahlele's warning to the artist, but he also warns the public that 'we are not going to help our artist by rattling tin-cans of the African Personality about his ears . . . Every artist in the world, African or not, must go through the agony of purging his art of imitations and false notes before he strikes an individual medium. Leave the artist to this evolution; let him sweat it out and be emancipated by his own art.'[1] If the so-called African Personality is depicted at best by the artist, what of the many millions of African people who are not artists? By what means do they, or can they, search 'for the truth about themselves', i.e. attain an identity of themselves and a security for their existence?

[1] E. Mphahlele *The African image* (London 1962), p. 21 f.

There are sections of African intellectuals and politicians who imagine that by conjuring up emotions under the guise of 'African Personality', they are doing Africa a great service. At a conference on the contributions of religions, Christian, Islam and traditional, to African Personality and Culture, in Abidjan (Ivory Coast) in 1961, some of us who attended it and contributed papers participated in utter darkness as to what this mystical phrase actually meant.[1] To this day, I am not aware of anybody who really seems to know what to do with or about 'African Personality'. Are we supposed to assert it, promote it, establish it, cultivate it, invent it, conform to it, kill it, bury it, or just dream about it as a nice myth? And when does 'African Personality' actually become IT? What are its geo-graphical and historical boundaries? These are not idle rhetorical questions.

Whatever is or is done with it African Personality has become one of the fields in which the African diaspora is scattered, searching for a new homeland, identity, security and meaning in life. There are those who pin it down to biological roots, equating it, or Négritude, with 'Black Africa'. It has become a passion to imagine that being 'black' is a mystique, a virtue and a quality of which one must and should be proud. J. K. Aggrey's saying: 'he who is not proud of his colour is not fit to live', falls into this category. It was he who told that if he went to heaven and God asked him what colour he wanted to have if he could return to earth, he would reply: 'Sir, make me as black as you can!' In Ghana one used to see signs reading 'Black Star', and up to now I have never sorted it out how at the same time a star could be black and shine as a star should. It has become commonplace to hear of 'Black Power' in the United States. Respectable writers have put in a lot of effort to prove that 'Black Africa' was the mother of civilizations. Diop, for example, has demonstrated that the ancient Egyptian civilization was the product of 'black' or 'Negro' Africans.[2] But is it enough to project this so-called 'African Personality' in the Zamani direction? The spirit of this ideology is moving in a more creative direction. For example, it brought into being the first 'Negro' African Arts Festival in Dakar in 1966;[3] and the Présence Africaine with its Society of African

---

[1] The report and papers presented at this conference are published: *Colloque sur les religions* (Présence Africaine, Paris 1963).

[2] C. A. Diop *Antériorité des civilisations nègres: mythe ou vérité historique?* (Paris 1967); also *Nations nègres et culture* (Paris 1955), *L'Unité culturelle de l'Afrique Noire* (Paris 1960), and *L'Afrique Noire precoloniale* (Paris 1960). In the same spirit are the books of B. Davidson: *The African awakening* (London 1955), *The African past* (London 1964, editor), *Black Mother* (London 1961), *Old Africa rediscovered* (London 1959), and *The growth of African civilization* (London 1965); and of J. Jahn *Muntu* (E.T. London 1961).

[3] See the report: *Colloque sur l'Art nègre* (Paris 1966).

Culture, both of which are based in Paris, is promoting 'blackness' in the cultural realm. Yet, it must be granted that the awareness of being 'black' becomes almost an obsession as more and more people discover that 'blackness' gives them a point of reference, identity and self-consciousness. But this is no more than a myth which does not even take into consideration the fact that the majority of African peoples are brown and not black, Africa is greater than 'blackness', and not all its peoples and cultures can be reduced to the narrow categories of 'Black Africa'.

[iv] *African Unity and Pan-Africanism*: The political scene is the most dynamic area of ideological activities in Africa. African Unity, Socialism and Pan-Africanism have become commonplace ideals. In his day Kwame Nkrumah was the most outspoken champion of African unity, putting all his weight to see it realized 'here and now'. He not only preached it but also symbolized the search for African unity. His advocacy of African unity reached its climax at the creation of the Organization of African Unity in Addis Ababa in 1963. But the other heads of state, while supporting the goal as great, important and ideal, could not subscribe to its speedy realization.[1] Senghor advocates a gradual approach to this goal: 'I do not think the United States of Africa are something for tomorrow ... We must unify Africa by stages, making it a continent open to other continents.' Preliminary to this unity must be an 'independence of spirit, cultural independence is a necessary preliminary to all other independence'. Even then, Senghor seems to consider African unity as secondary to other values: 'We want to liberate ourselves politically so that we can properly express our Négritude, our real black values'.[2]

Nyerere, another advocate of African unity, is similarly realistic when he says that it 'has to come by agreement, agreement between equals'. But perhaps not so realistic is the notion that such unity is the key to solving African problems: 'Unity is therefore essential for the safety, the integrity and the development of Africa. Its form must secure these things; otherwise it is pointless', if it does not prevent political exploitation, police itself, and defend itself. He is, however, more at home with socialism which he and others like Senghor believe to be 'rooted in our past—in the traditional society which produced us. Modern African socialism can draw from its traditional heritage the recognition of "society" as an extension of the basic family unit.'[3]

---

[1] K. Nkrumah *Africa must unite* (London 1963), *I speak of freedom: a statement of African ideology* (London 1961), and *Consciencism* (London 1964).
[2] Senghor, pp. 65 f., 74; a fuller exposition of his political ideas is in: *On African socialism* (translated M. Cook, London 1964).
[3] J. K. Nyerere, *Freedom and Unity: Uhuru na Umoja* (Oxford/Dar es Salaam

In a penetrating analysis of these and other political ideas, Mazrui points out that in the search for a Pax Africana, 'decolonization might be a necessary condition for it. But it is far from being a sufficient one.' At work is the principle of indivisible Africa versus the fear of factionalism: 'the mystique of a classless Africa, as well as the denigration of "tribalism", are further manifestations of the same principle of "African oneness". So is the choice of "socialism", presumed to be a centralizing ideology suitable for national integration.' He concludes that since the politicians are far from their goal, 'the quest therefore continues for an African tranquillity capable of being protected and maintained by Africa herself'.[1]

This general political uncertainty in Africa shows itself in the talk about 'neutrality' on the one hand and alignment on the other, the attack on 'neo-colonialism', both real and imaginary, and appeal for 'brotherhoods' of one type or another, and the endless gatherings of regional and continental 'summit conferences'. Arising from the same uncertainty but more positive are economic experiments with the creation of economic communities, affiliation with former colonial masters through the British Commonwealth and the French community, association with the European Economic Community, and the receiving of substantial financial and personnel aid from both capitalist and communist countries.

All these political ideologies and economic attempts point to a progress being made in Africa. But it is a progress in search; it lacks concreteness, historical roots, and a clear and practical goal, at least for the individual to be able to find in it a sense of direction worthy of personal identification and dedication.

[c] *Conclusion: Religion in the African dilemma*

We have tried to analyse the dilemma which has come upon African societies that are rooted in traditional solidarity and yet are increasingly being exposed to modern change. In this dilemma their foundations of existence and sense of security are shaken and undermined. Africa must now search for new values, new identities and a new self-consciousness. In the political and cultural spheres, attempts are under way to relate modern ideas to the values of our African Zamani. Democracy is claimed to have already been an African practice, Négritude and African Personality were already 'there', socialism and African civilization are said to have been 'there' as well. The strength of this argument is simply that these ideas are 'good', 'valuable' and 'honourable' because once they were practised in the normal

---

1966), pp. 170, 335. Cf. Kenya Government's *African Socialism and its application to planning in Kenya* (Nairobi 1965).

[1] A. A. Mazrui *Towards a Pax Africana* (London 1967), p. 211 f.

life of our forefathers. They are valid for today, therefore, because once they were part of African traditional life. It is extremely difficult to demonstrate that these ideas can or cannot be traced to the African Zamani; and it is no use being sentimental about this issue.

In conclusion we must raise the question of whether, in this period of dilemmas and challenges, religion has a place and a role to play in Africa. Almost every religious system of the world is represented in our continent, making Africa look like the dumping heap of the religions of mankind. Given the opportunity, every ideology in the world would also establish a footing here as well. The main strength and contribution of African traditional religions lie in the Zamani. It is in that period when each society evolved its own religious system and in turn the religion shaped the evolution of the society in which it was embedded. Traditional religions then became dangerously institutionalized and part of every department of human life. The same fate of institutionalization has crept into the ancient Christianity in Egypt and Ethiopia, and into Islam in areas where it has deep historical roots. Religion in Africa has produced its own society with a distinctly religious set of morals, ethics, culture, governments, traditions, social relationships and ways of looking at the world.

But precisely because religion became so deeply entrenched and institutionalized in all the different forms of African life, it lost its ability to continue exercising supreme control and holding a position of absolute authority once new challenges and radical changes came upon African societies. The disintegration of the old order means also the disintegration of institutionalized religion whether that is traditional, Christian or Islam: 'New wine must be put into fresh wineskins', and if religion does not respond according to this principle, then such religion is doomed to extinction. Ancient Christianity, legalistic and orthodox Islam, and traditional religions have not been sufficiently ready for radical change and to accompany man wherever that change takes him. This is not the inadequacy of religion as such, but simply because its form, its mode of expression, its structure of beliefs and its thought pattern, all belong to the solidarity which evolved in the Zamani in response to historical and environmental circumstances different from those which define the man of today.

Even if institutionalized religion may not have kept pace with rapid changes, yet paradoxically the changing situation cannot get away entirely from a basically religious orientation. The religious claim, with its activities like conversion, counter-conversion, acculturation and apostasy, is aimed at winning the religious allegiance of the otherwise religious man of Africa. The ideological claim of Négritude, African Personality and African socialism, is similarly oriented to the Zamani roots which, as we have shown, are profoundly religious. But, while these two areas of claim function in or make use of the religious Zamani, they also by intention point to the future. This is the point of departure from the traditional religiosity which is rich in Zamani myths but absolutely devoid of future myths. Through the current religious turbulence and ideological movements, future myths have begun to dawn in tropical African societies. The direction and centre of gravity of the myth have now begun to shift from the Zamani to partly the Sasa and partly the future. There is a Sasa and a future in Négritude, African Personality, African socialism, Christian ecumenism, Muslim brotherhoods and nationalism; and there are purely futuristic expectations like Christian and Muslim paradise and messianic hopes, African unity, economic bounty and the collapse of apartheid. So now, religion is deeply involved in the shift of the myth, partly and chiefly because it has its own myths of the 'now and hereafter', and partly because by its very nature the myth is fundamentally a religious creation.

But religion must have a greater role to play in modern Africa than simply supplying new myths or reviving old ones. Whether or not it continues to hold the sole monopoly of man's understanding of the universe and his participation in it, is of little consequence in the face of present challenges and dilemmas in Africa. It should and can provide tools and inspiration to the man of Africa to think afresh the fundamental issues of his life which matter most, and to find both meaning and security in that life. And it is in its occupation with the Sasa, more than with either the Zamani or the future, that religion can hope to make a lasting contribution to modern Africa.

With a few exceptions, Islam, as we saw, has not fully awoken to the demands of the day. Its legalism and slowness to be bent by modern man are almost certainly going to deposit it in the unenviable position of stagnation and irrelevance, unless it changes radically and rapidly. Mission Christianity is officially and consciously attempting to respond and contribute in form of service to human needs in the slums and refugee camps, schools and hospitals, areas of racial, political and religious tensions, family disintegration and urban loneliness, as far as communities are concerned. Perhaps it is not doing or succeeding as much in the area of individual situations and personal problems such as sex, alcoholism, racial prejudices, tribalism, corruption, dishonesty, business transactions, fear, death, the departed, and the like, all of which seem to be the main challenges for those who want to be identified both as African and as Christian today.

Traditional religions do not have scholarly champions to advocate their case, or to modernize their content and expression. Their main contribution, however, lies in the fact that since they permeate into every department of traditional society, any appeal made to traditional values and practices is ultimately a religious appeal. So long as people appreciate and even idolize the traditional present and past, this religiosity whether recognized as such or not will continue to enjoy a comfortable and privileged place in the emotions of African peoples. The ritual and ceremonial form will decrease as more and more people become urbanized, but their content in form of belief will linger on for a considerable number of generations. Belief dies more slowly than practice, even if in the towns there will almost always be pockets of society where seriously or through curiosity both belief and practice of forms of traditional religions will continue to thrive. Beliefs connected with magic, witchcraft, the spirits and the living-dead are areas of traditional religions which are in no danger of an immediate abandon-ment. So also, however vaguely, the belief in God will linger on in towns and villages, even if acts of worship will increasingly become difficult, irregular and cultistic instead of being public, corporate and spontaneous.

Singly, jointly or in competition, the religions in Africa should be able to exert a force and make a contribution in creating new standards, morals and ethics suitable for our changing society. It is also their responsibility to assist in shaping and defining the dignity of man in the face of power, violence, potentialities of devastation, scientific progress, search for peace and the dehumanization of industrialization. Left to itself, secularism would reduce man to a statistical robot, casting votes for politicians, producing more goods in the factory for capitalists, a figure in population census for com-munist revolutionaries, or just a competitor in the classroom, bus or queue for a dish of rice. Only religion is fully sensitive to the dignity of man as an individual, person and creature who has both physical and spiritual dimensions. It is only religion which embraces and grants an equal place for every member of humanity, whether he is an idiot or philosopher, slave or student, beggar or ruler. It provides a common denominator for all in origin, experience and destiny. It is only religion which contains the area and tools for everyone to search for and fathom the depths of his being. These depths involve a redefinition of not only 'who I am', but also who or what is 'my brother', 'my neighbour', 'the universe' and the whole of existence. In practical terms, religion has a role to play in cultivating reconciliation, harmony, peace and security with and within oneself, the community, the nation and the universe; and in setting the standards by which or in reference to which the individual, community, nation and mankind may live. If all the religions of Africa fail to make this contribu-tion, they will have become anachronisms worse than salt without its saltness, and as such they will have neither a place nor role in modern Africa.

But I am optimistic. I see religions in Africa continuing to exert their presence and influence, but on three levels of influence.

[i] *Contact Religion* is the type in which a person feels no contradiction in holding a mixture of belief and practice from two or more religious traditions in Africa. As we have seen, Christianity, Islam and traditional religions overlap in a number of points, and this makes it fairly easy for a person to be a convinced Christian or Muslim and yet incorporate in his life elements from traditional religions. He may have a Christian or Muslim name, may wear a crucifix or a Muslim cap, but beyond these badges he would know little else about the depths of Christianity or Islam even if he may be devoted to either. His unconscious life is deeply traditional, but his waking life is oriented towards one of the world religions. He has established a link and a contact with two or more systems; and it is in the context of that 'contact religion' that he identifies himself and his interests.

[ii] *Instant Religion* is that which shows itself mainly in moments of crisis like sickness, desperation, emergency, death and tragedy; and comes to the surface also at key moments of life like birth, wedding, death, or national events like independence celebrations, state funerals, the deportation or overthrow of one governing class. Such moments call for instant prayer and 'instant God'. People then turn to religion at these occasions, as they do in their traditional background, partly to 'show off' and partly as a genuine means of finding an outlet for their feelings of joy or tension generated by the particular crisis or important event. Both educated and village dwellers in Africa subscribe to this type of religion. Village people resort more to their traditional methods of seeking help in such moments, like magical practices, divination, contact with the living-dead and the performance of appropriate ceremonies and rituals. They may also go to church or the mosque, often in addition to fulfilling traditional requirements. The educated will generally go to church or the mosque; and on national issues they might preach nationalism and promise new and rational remedies. This type might also be called 'convertible religion' since, at an instant, a religious atmosphere is created if and when the occasion so demands. It gives a sense of security to people to be able to feel and know that they have an instant religion constantly at their disposal.

[iii] *Transfused Religion* is the type which promises the greatest amount of influence on African peoples. Here, religion becomes more and more a social uniformity, without theological depth, personal commitment or martyrs. It is just 'there', somewhere in the corpus of one's beliefs, whether one is conscious of being religious or not. It is not institutionalized but may

crop up during moments of crisis or great feasts of the Church or Islam. This type also makes room for those who wish to belong and keep to rather minority groups of fundamentalist, orthodox, puritanical and conservative adherents of a given faith or religious tradition. It is as equally tolerant as it is indifferent. But this is the form of religious life on which Africa must count to make an impress on the morals, ethics, standards and social conditions of its peoples. It is a religion behind the scenes. People may object to its open proselytism, to its being taught in schools and universities; but they are not opposed to it, they do not seriously and honestly doubt that it has noble standards, and they perhaps fear to face its demands. This type of religion is best injected in the homes, and perhaps in schools as well, for these are the background areas which are most influential in shaping the total image of the individual and his participation in the world. Such religion need not be articulated in a uniform creed, nor must its followers gather for a public and practical expression of their faith; it needs no formal advocates, no formal projects, no formal ceremonies, nor even buildings and priests. It is in the ideals, teachings, standards, principles, ethics and experiences of the institutionalized religions, Christianity, Islam, Traditional, Judaism, Hinduism or Baha'ism, that this transfused religion makes an impact on individuals and society. This type does not exclude those who are devoted to these formal systems, and indeed it reckons on having such devout adherents from the Church, Islam, and the rest, who keep the religious fire burning throughout the human history.

This then is the religious transfusion to which I see African peoples moving. Invisible, unnoticed and even unofficially, the religious traditions of Africa contain the only lasting potentialities for a basis, a foundation and a direction of life for African societies. Man cannot live by the bread of science and politics alone; he also needs the vitamins of ethics and morals, faith and hope, love and security, comfort and attention in the face of death or misfortune, a feeling and experience that as a person he matters infinitely, and an assurance that he is not immediately 'forgotten' or even annihilated when he dies. These are the elements that religion tries to offer. If this formless type of 'transfused religion' makes a contribution to these basic elements in man's search for identity and security, whether institution-alized religions survive or not, they will have bequeathed to Africa something of lasting value and inspiration.

In the light of such a great religious heritage, institutional and orthodox religions need not be apprehensive if their inner and professing adherents are few. They should be able to take comfort in that they will have shepherded a portion of humanity from secular to sacred history, from the slavery of formal religiosity to the freedom of self-hood. Obviously this sounds more of a myth than a practical reality, and I for one have no doubt that it is unnecessary to travel this long mythological route to come to the reality. A shorter path is possible and available by means of which mature manhood and self-hood are attainable. In this schema of things, Christianity which is also 'indigenous', 'traditional' and 'African' like the other major religious systems considered here, holds the greatest and the only potentialities of meeting the dilemmas and challenges of modern Africa, and of reaching the full integration and manhood of individuals and communities. It is highly doubtful that, even at their very best, these other religious systems and ideologies current in Africa are saying anything radically new to, and different from, what is already embedded in Christianity. And yet, the strength and uniqueness of Christianity do not lie in the fact that its teaching, practice and history have all the major elements of the other religious traditions. The uniqueness of Christianity is in Jesus Christ. He is the stumbling block of all ideologies and religious systems; and even if some of His teaching may overlap with what they teach and proclaim, His own Person is greater than can be contained in a religion or ideology. He is 'the Man for others' and yet beyond them. It is He, therefore, and only He, Who deserves to be the goal and standard for individuals and mankind, and whether they attain that ultimate goal religiously or ideologically is perhaps irrelevant. Attainment of that full stature and maximum identity demands that reference be made to an external, absolute and timeless denominator. And this is precisely what Christianity should offer beyond, and in spite of, its own anachronisms and divisions in Africa. I consider traditional religions, Islam and the other religious systems to be preparatory and even essential ground in the search for the Ultimate. But only Christianity has the terrible responsibility of pointing the way to that ultimate Identity, Foundation and Source of security.

However, until that goal is attained by the individual and community, Christianity, Islam, African Traditional Religions and the other religions and ideologies must continue to function, for the sake of their own survival and that of mankind as a whole. Until then, there is sufficient room for religious co-existence, co-operation and even competition in Africa. The final test for the continuing existence of these religions in our continent is not which one shall win in the end. The test is whether mankind benefits or loses from having allowed religion to occupy such a privileged and dominating position in human history, in man's search for his origin and nature of being, in the experience of responding to his environment, and in the creation of his expectations and hope for the future.

SELECT BIBLIOGRAPHY

Additional references are given in the footnotes of this book
E.T. means English Translation; n.d. means No Date.

Abraham, R. C., *The Tiv People*, London second edition 1940.

Abrahams, W., *The Mind of Africa*, London/New York 1963.

Abrahamsson, H., *The Origin of Death*, Uppsala 1951.

Ashton, E. H., *Medicine, Magic and Sorcery among the southern Sotho*, Cape Town 1943; *The Basuto*, London second edition 1955.

Baëta, C. G., *Prophetism in Ghana*, London 1962; ed., *Christianity in Tropical Africa*, London/Oxford 1968.

Banton, M., ed., *Anthropological approaches to the study of religion*, London 1966.

Barrett, D. B., *Schism and Renewal*, London/Nairobi 1968.

Baumann, H., *Schöpfung und Urzeit des Menschen im Mythus der afrikanischen Völker*, Berlin second edition 1964.

Baxter, P. T. W., and Butt, A., *The Azande and related Peoples*, London 1953.

Beech, M. W. H., *The Suk*, Oxford 1911.

Beetham, T. A., *Christianity and the new Africa*, London/New York 1967.

Beier, U., *The Origin of Life and Death*, London 1966.

Bernardi, B., *The Mugwe: a failing Prophet*, Oxford 1959.

Bertholet, A., *Der Sinn des kultischen Opfers*, Berlin 1942.

Beth, K., *Religion und Magie bei den Naturvölkern*, Berlin second edition 1928.

Bleek, D. F., *The Naron: a Bushman Tribe of the central Kalahari*, Oxford 1928.

Blohm, W., *Die Nyamwezi*, 3 vols. Hamburg 1931–3.

Bohannan, L. & P., *The Tiv of central Nigeria*, London 1953.

Brauer, E., *Züge aus der Religion der Herero*, Leipzig 1925.

Bullock, C., *The Mashona*, Cape Town 1927.

Cagnolo, C., *The Akikuyu*, Nyeri 1933.

Callaway, H., *The Religious System of the Amazulu*, London 1870.

Campbell, D., *In the Heart of Bantuland*, London 1922.

Carothers, J. C., *The African Mind in Health and Disease*, Geneva 1953.

Cerulli, E., *Peoples of the South-West Ethiopia and its Borderland*, London 1956.

Claridge, G. C., *Wild bush Tribes of Tropical Africa*, London 1922.

Colin, P., *Aspects de l'Âme Malgache*, Paris 1959.

Culwick, A. T. & G. M., *Ubena of the Rivers*, London 1935.

Dammann, E., *Die Religionen Afrikas*, Stuttgart 1963.

Danquah, J. B., *The Akan Doctrine of God*, London 1944.

Debrunner, H., *Witchcraft in Ghana*, Kumasi 1959.

Deschamps, H., *Les Religions de l'Afrique Noire*, Paris 1960.

Dieterlen, G., *Essai sur la Religion Bambara*, Paris 1951; see also under Fortes.

Doke, C. M., *The Lambas of Northern Rhodesia*, London 1931.

Dornan, S. S., *Pygmies and Bushmen of the Kalahari*, London 1925.

Driberg, J. H., *The Lango*, London 1923.

Dundas, C., *Kilimanjaro and its People*, London 1924.

Durkheim, E., *The Elementary forms of the Religious Life,* E.T. London 1915.

Edel, M. M., *The Chiga of western Uganda,* Oxford 1957.

Eliade, M., *Patterns in Comparative Religion,* New York/London 1958.

Encyclopaedia of Religion and Ethics, ed. J. Hastings, Edinburgh 1908 f.

Evans-Pritchard, E. E., I: *Witchcraft, Oracles and Magic among the Azande,* Oxford 1937; II: *Nuer Religion,* Oxford 1956; III: *Theories of Primitive Religion,* Oxford 1965.

Field, M. J., *Religion and Medicine of the Ga People,* Oxford 1937; *Search for Security,* London/New York 1960.

Forde, D., ed., *African Worlds,* Oxford 1954, with contributions from: K. A. Busia, M. Douglas, G. & M. G. Dieterlen, D. Forde, J. D. & E. J. Krige, G. Lienhardt, K. Little, J. J. Maquet, P. Mercier, and G. Wagner, cited here under the contributor's name 'in Forde'.

Fortes, M., *Oedipus and Job in West African Religion,* Oxford 1959; with Dieterlen, G., eds, *African Systems of Thought,* Oxford/London 1965, contributors cited here by their names 'in Fortes & Dieterlen'.

Friedrich, A., *Afrikanische Priestertümer,* Stuttgart 1939.

Fromm, E., *Psychoanalysis and Religion,* London 1951.

Galling, K., ed., *Die Religion in Geschichte und Gegenwart,* Tübingen 1957 f.

Gamble, D. P., *The Wolof of Senegambia,* London 1957.

Gelfand, M., *Medicine and Magic of the Mashona,* Johannesburg 1956; *Shona Ritual,* Johannesburg 1959.

Geluwe, H. van, *Les Mamvu-Mangutu et Balese-Mvuba,* London 1957.

Gennep, A. van, *The Rites of Passage,* E.T. London 1960.

Goody, J. R., *Death, Property and the Ancestors,* London/Stanford 1962.

Gray, R. F., *The Sonjo of Tanganyika,* Oxford 1963.

Gunn, H. D., *Peoples of the Plateau area of Northern Nigeria,* London 1953; *Pagan Peoples of the central area of Northern Nigeria,* London 1956.

Gutmann, B., *Dichten und Denken der Dschagga-Neger,* Leipzig 1909.

Hadfield, P., *Traits of divine Kingship in Africa,* London 1949.

Hambly, W. D., *The Ovimbundu of Angola,* Chicago 1934.

Hastings, A., *Church and Mission in modern Africa,* London 1967.

Hayley, T. T. S., *The Anatomy of Lango Religion,* Cambridge 1947.

Herrmann, F., *Symbolik in den Religionen der Naturvölker,* Stuttgart 1961.

Hinde, H., *The Last of the Masai,* London 1901.

Hobley, C. W., *Ethnology of A-Kamba and other East African Tribes,* Cambridge 1910.

Hughes, A. J. B., van Velsen, J., and Kuper, H., *The Shona and Ndebele of Southern Rhodesia,* London 1954 (cited under Hughes & Velsen).

Hunter, M., *Reaction to Conquest,* London second edition 1960.

Huntingford, G. W. B., *The Nandi of Kenya,* London 1953; *The Galla of Ethiopia,* Oxford 1955.

Idowu, E. B., *Olodumare: God in Yoruba Belief,* London/New York 1962.

Irstam, T., *The King of Ganda,* Stockholm 1944.

Ittmann, J., *Volkskundliche und religiöse Begriffe im nördlichen Waldland von Kamerun,* Berlin 1953.

Jahn, J., *Muntu*, E.T. London/New York 1961.

James, E. O., *The Origin of Religion*, London 1937.

Jensen, A. E., *Mythus und Kult bei Naturvölkern*, Wiesbaden second edition 1960.

Johanssen, E., *Mysterien eines Bantu-Volkes*, Leipzig 1925.

Junod, H. A., *The Life of a South African Tribe*, 2 vols. London second edition 1927.

Junod, H. P., *Bantu Heritage*, Johannesburg 1938 (cited here).

Kagame, A., *La Philosophie Bantu-Rwandaise de l'Être*, Brussels 1956.

Kenyatta, J., *Facing Mount Kenya*, London 1938.

Kidd, D., *Savage Childhood*, London 1906; *The Essential Kaffir*, London 1904.

Kootz-Kretschmer, E., *Die Safwa*, 2 vols. Berlin 1925.

Krige, E. J. & J. D., *The Realm of a Rain-Queen*, London second edition 1960.

Kuper, H., *An African Aristocracy*, Oxford 1947; *The Swazi*, London 1952.

Lewis, I. M., ed., *Islam in Tropical Africa*, Oxford/London 1966, contributors cited by name 'in Lewis'.

Lienhardt, G., *Divinity and Experience, the Religion of the Dinka*, Oxford 1961.

Lindblom, G., *The Akamba in British East Africa*, Uppsala 1920.

Little, K. L., *The Mende of Sierra Leone*, London 1951.

Lloyd, P. C., *Africa in Social Change*, London 1967; revised edition, New York 1969.

Low, D. A., *Religion and Society in Buganda 1875–1900*, Kampala n.d.

Lucas, O., *The Religion of the Yoruba*, Lagos 1948.

Lugira, A. M., *Ganda Art*, Entebbe 1969.

Luttig, H. G., *The Religious System and Social Organization of the Herero*, Utrecht 1933.

Lystad, R. A., *The Ashanti*, New Brunswick 1958.

Mackenzie, D. R., *The Spirit-ridden Konde*, London 1925.

Mair, L. P., *An African People in the Twentieth Century*, London 1934.

Manoukian, M., I: *Akan and Ga-Adangme Peoples of the Gold Coast*, London 1950; II: *The Ewe-Speaking Peoples of Togoland and the Gold Coast*, London 1952.

Mbiti, J. S., *Concepts of God in Africa*, London/New York 1970.

McCulloch, M., I: *The Southern Lunda and Related Peoples*, London 1951; II: *The Ovimbundu of Angola*, London 1952; III: *The Peoples of Sierra Leone Protectorate*, London n.d. (but about 1952).

Meinhof, C., *Afrikanische Religionen*, Berlin 1912; *Die Religionen der Afrikaner in ihrem Zusammenhang mit dem Wirtschaftsleben*, Oslo 1926.

Merwe, W. J. van der, *The Shona Idea of God*, Ft. Victoria 1957.

Meyerowitz, E. L. R., *The Akan of Ghana: their ancient Beliefs*, London 1958.

Middleton, J., I: *The Kikuyu and Kamba of Kenya*, London 1953; II: *Lugbara Religion*, Oxford 1960; with D. Tait, eds., *Tribes without Rulers*, London 1958; with E. H. Winter, eds., *Witchcraft and Sorcery in East Africa*, London/New York 1963.

Murdock, G. P., *Africa: its Peoples and their Culture History*, New York and London 1959.

Nadel, S. F., *Nupe Religion*, London 1954.

Nalder, L. F., ed., *A Tribal Survey of Mongalla Province*, Oxford 1937.

Nketia, J. H., *Funeral Dirges of the Akan People*, Accra 1955.

Norbeck, E., *Religion in Primitive Society*, New York & London 1961.

Parrinder, E. G., I: *African Traditional Religion*, London second edition 1962; II: *West African Religion*, London second edition 1961; III: *Religion in an African City*, London 1953; IV: *Witchcraft*, London 1958; V: *Comparative Religion*, London 1962; *African Religion*, Harmondsworth/New York 1969.

Pauw, B. A., *Religion in a Tswana Chiefdom*, Oxford 1960.

Pettazzoni, R. T., *The All-Knowing God*, London 1956.

Pettersson, O., *Chiefs and Gods*, Lund 1953.

Phillips, A., ed., *Survey of African Marriage and Family Life*, London 1953.

Preusss, K. T., *Die geistige Kultur der Naturvölker*, Leipzig & Berlin 1914.

Radcliffe-Brown, A. R., and Forde, D., eds., *African Systems of Kinship and Marriage*, Oxford 1956.

Radin, P., *Primitive Religion: Its Nature and Origin*, London new edition 1954.

Rattray, R. S., *Religion and Art in Ashanti*, Oxford 1927; *The Tribes of the Ashanti Hinterland*, 2 vols. Oxford 1932.

Raum, O. F., *Chaga Childhood*, Oxford 1940.

Read, M., *The Ngoni of Nyasaland*, London 1956.

Reynolds, B., *Magic, Divination and Witchcraft among the Barotse of Northern Rhodesia*, London 1963.

Roscoe, J., *The Baganda*, London 1912; *The Northern Bantu*, Cambridge 1915; *The Bakitara or Banyoro*, Cambridge 1923; *The Bagesu*, Cambridge 1924.

Rouch, J., *Les Songhay*, Paris 1954.

Routledge, W. S. & K., *With a Prehistoric People: the Akikuyu of British East Africa*, London 1910.

Ruud, J., *Taboo: a study of Malagasy Customs and Beliefs*, London 1960.

Sangree, W. H., *Age, Prayer and Politics in Tiriki, Kenya*, Oxford 1966.

Schapera, I., *The Khoisan Peoples of South Africa*, London third edition 1960; *The Tswana*, London 1953.

Schebesta, P., I: *My Pygmy and Negro Hosts*, E.T. London 1936; II: *Revisiting my Pygmy Hosts*, E.T. London 1936.

Schilde, W., *Orakel und Gottesurteile in Afrika*, Leipzig 1940.

Schmidt, W., *The Origin and Growth of Religion*, E.T. London 1931; *Die Religionen der Urvölker Afrikas*, Münster 1933 (this being Vol. IV of his series: *Der Ursprung der Gottesidee*, 1926 f.).

Seligman, C. G. & B. Z., *Pagan Tribes of the Nilotic Sudan*, London 1932.

Smith, E. W., ed., *African Ideas of God*, London second revised edition 1961 (ed. E. G. Parrinder), contributors cited by name 'in Smith'.

Smith, E. W., and Dale, A. M., *The Ila-Speaking Peoples of Northern Rhodesia*, Vol. I London 1920.

Southall, A. W., *Alur Society*, Cambridge 1953.

Spieth, J., *Die Religion der Eweer*, Leipzig/Göttingen 1911.

Stayt, H. A., *The Bavenda*, London 1931.

Sundkler, B. G. M., *Bantu Prophets of South Africa*, London second edition 1961.

Talbot, P. A., *Tribes of the Niger Delta*, London 1932.

Tanner, R. E. S., *Transition in African Belief*, Maryknoll/New York 1967.

Tauxier, L., *Religion, Moeurs et Coutumes des Agnis de la côte d'Ivoire*, Paris 1932.

Taylor, B. K., *The Western Lacustrine Bantu*, London 1962.

Taylor, J. V., *The Primal Vision*, London 1963.

Tempels, P., *Bantu Philosophy*, E.T. Paris 1959.

Trimingham, J. S., *Islam in the Sudan*, Oxford 1949; *Islam in Ethiopia*, Oxford 1952; *Islam in West Africa*, London 1959; *Islam in East Africa*, London 1964; *The Influence of Islam upon Africa*, London/New York 1969.

Turner, V. W., *The Lozi Peoples of North-Western Rhodesia*, London 1952.

Wach, J., *The Sociology of Religion*, London 1947.

Wagner, G., *The Bantu of North Kavirondo*, Vol. I Oxford 1949.

Weeks, J. H., I: *Among Congo Cannibals*, London 1913; II: *Among the Primitive Bacongo*, London 1914.

Welbourn, F. B., *East African Rebels*, London 1961; *Religion and Politics in Uganda 1952-1962*, Nairobi 1965; *East African Christian*, Oxford/Nairobi 1965.

Welbourn, F. B., and Ogot, B. A., *A Place to feel at Home*, Oxford/London 1966.

Werner, A., *Myths and Legends of the Bantu*, London 1933.

Westermann, D., *The Shilluk People*, Berlin & Philadelphia 1912 *Die Kpelle, ein Negerstamm in Liberia*, Göttingen 1921; *The African Today and Tomorrow*, London 1939.

Wilder, G. A., *Ndau Religion*, Hartford 1907.

Willoughby, W. C., *The Soul of the Bantu*, London 1928.

Wilson, M., *Rituals of Kinship among the Nyakyusa*, Oxford 1956; *Communal Rituals of the Nyakyusa*, Oxford 1959.

Yokoo, S., *Death among the Abaluyia*, dissertation, Kampala 1966.

Young, T. C., *African Ways and Wisdom*, London 1937; *Contemporary Ancestors*, London n.d. (cited here).

Journals and Periodicals

While some of these are not devoted to religion as such, they contain articles of religious aspects in Africa from time to time. There are also local journals and periodicals in different countries of Africa. *Africa*, London; *Africa*, Rome; *Africa Journal of Theology*, Usa River (Tanzania); *African Ecclesiastical Review* (AFER), Masaka (Uganda); *African Studies*, Johannesburg; *Afrika* and *Afrika Heute*, Bonn; *American Anthropologist*, Washington; *American Sociological Review*, Madison (Wisconsin); *Archiv für Religionswissenschaft*, Leipzig; *Bantu Studies*, Johannesburg; *British Journal of Sociology*, London; *Bulletin of the Institute of Islamic Studies*, Calcutta; *Bulletin of the School of Oriental and African Studies*, London; *Cahiers des religions africaines*, Kinshasa; *Dini na Mila: Revealed Religion and Traditional Custom*, Kampala; *Evangalische Missionszeitschrift*, Hamburg/Stuttgart; *Evangelisches Missionsmagazin*, Basel; *Flambeau*, Yaounde (Cameroon); *International Review of Missions*, Geneva/London; *Le Monde non Chrétien*, Paris; *Man*, London; *Ministry*, Morija (Lesotho); *Religious Studies*, Cambridge; *Sierra Leone Bulletin of Theology*, Freetown; *The American Journal of Sociology*, Chicago; *The Ghana Bulletin of Theology*, Accra; *The Journal of Religion*, Tenri (Japan); *The Muslim World*, Hartford; *The Uganda Journal*, Kampala; *Transition*, Kampala; *Zeitschrift für Ethnologie*, Berlin.

INDEX OF AUTHORS

INDEX OF PEOPLES & LANGUAGES

INDEX OF SUBJECTS